D0613141

RACE AND ETHNIC RELATIONS

RACE AND ETHNIC RELATIONS

FOURTH EDITION

Brewton Berry
THE OHIO STATE UNIVERSITY

Henry L. Tischler
FRAMINGHAM STATE COLLEGE

HOUGHTON MIFFLIN COMPANY   Boston
Dallas   Geneva, Illinois   Hopewell, New Jersey   Palo Alto   London

Photo Credits

Page 2, Museum of the City of New York; page 7, Donald Dietz, Dietz/Hamlin; page 13, Museum of the City of New York; page 22, Dennis Stock/Magnum; page 31, United Nations; page 38, Marc Riboud/Magnum; page 44, Inge Morath/Magnum; page 56, United Nations; page 62, Elizabeth Hamlin, Dietz/Hamlin; page 65, Jacob A. Riis Collection/Museum of the City of New York; page 82, Elizabeth Hamlin, Dietz/Hamlin; page 88, Museum of the City of New York; page 96, Museum of the City of New York; page 114, George Malave/Stock Boston; page 135, George Gardner; page 148, Roger Freeman/Photo Researchers; page 172, Marc Riboud/Magnum; page 191, Dennis Stock/Magnum; page 194, Howard Byrne/DPI; page 200, Burk Uzzle/Magnum; page 206, Charles Harbutt/Magnum; page 214, Louis Goldman/Photo Researchers; page 219, Jacob A. Riis Collection/Museum of the City of New York; page 223, Geoffrey Gove/Photo Researchers; page 232, George Gardner; pages 244, 264, 278, and 279, Donald Dietz, Dietz/Hamlin; pages 256, Jacob A. Riis Collection/Museum of the City of New York; page 288, Cornell Capa/Magnum; page 292, George Gardner; page 294, Henri Cartier Bresson/Magnum; page 312, Bruce Anspach from Editorial Photocolor Archives; page 324, Bob Adelman/Magnum; page 334, Wide World Photos; page 354, Courtesy of YIVO Institute for Jewish Research; page 374, George Gardner; page 401, Donald Dietz, Dietz/Hamlin

Copyright © 1978 by Houghton Mifflin Company, © 1965, 1958, 1951 by Brewton Berry. All rights reserved. No part of this work may be reproduced or transmitted in any form or by any means, electronic or mechanical, including photocopying and recording, or by any information storage or retrieval system, without permission in writing from the publisher.

Printed in the U.S.A.

Library of Congress Catalog Card Number: 77-78901

ISBN: 0-395-25508-2

To our wives,
Margaret Berry and Linda Tischler

Contents

Preface

Information about race and ethnic relations accumulates at a rapid pace. Much of what is written in this area is informative and interesting, but little of it is theoretical. Many authors write to express anger as well as to give insights. Some choose to see themselves as social reformers who can avert future wrongs by passing on some of the "right" information. Unfortunately, much of this kind of writing can be shallow and dated and frequently contributes little to a real understanding of the field.

In the first three editions of this widely used text, Brewton Berry avoided these pitfalls. The first edition of this book was published in 1951, when most people were less concerned with racial and ethnic conflict than we are today. The text was immediately recognized as an outstanding book, and it received the Anisfield-Wolf Award for making a distinctive contribution to the study of race problems. By 1958 a second edition was needed to include the major developments of the 1950s. The 1960s witnessed the acceleration of black protest, the recrudescence of racism, historic decisions by the courts, and the passage of far-reaching civil rights legislation. In other parts of the world, the conflicts between racial and ethnic groups were also increasing dramatically. In addition, sociologists were conducting important research and developing significant theories regarding racial and ethnic contact. Therefore, a third edition encompassing these developments appeared in 1965. During the late 1960s and into the 1970s the field of study again expanded tremendously, and many new approaches to the study of race and ethnic relations developed.

The fourth edition of Race and Ethnic Relations has been thoroughly revised and rewritten — without, however, compromising the authors' basic conviction that the primary function of a textbook is not to record current events but to suggest a way of looking at the world around us. A textbook should provide understanding and perspective, rather than the most current factual information. The latter can be obtained more readily from almanacs and yearbooks. Race and ethnic problems are by no means a new phenomenon in the world. One who gains a historical perspective will realize that prejudice is as old as humanity and that the struggle for status has always been with us.

In this volume the authors attempt to describe and analyze the phenomena that arise when groups of people who differ racially or culturally come into contact with one another. The focus is on *relations*, which includes much more than prejudice and discrimination. There is no basis for the assumptions that race problems include only white-black relations, that they are peculiar to the United States, or that they are more acute in the United States than elsewhere. To be sure, much of the discussion in these pages pertains to the United States, and blacks come in for extended treatment. This approach stems partly from the fact that we have more information about race relations in this country than in other regions of the world, and partly from the fact that the book is intended primarily for American college students, who are more concerned with issues near at hand. Even so, we can best appreciate our own situation by avoiding a provincial point of view, an adherence to which has been a fault of more than one area of American sociology, and by adopting instead a comparative point of view of the sort that has proved so valuable in helping us gain an understanding of various social phenomena.

In addition to its goal of providing a worldwide view, as contrasted with a national or sectional view, this book seeks to add other dimensions to the study of race and ethnic relations. The authors do not make major distinctions between the problems that develop between racial groups and those that develop between ethnic groups. Strictly speaking, races are zoological categories, and social relations do not exist between zoological categories. Instead, relations exist between people distinguished by marks of racial descent. Indeed, race relations are not so much the relations that exist between members of different races as between people *conscious* of those differences, which thereby affect the individuals' conception of themselves and their status in society. Our analysis includes the relations between people who differ culturally as well as racially. Sociologists have long called attention to the fact that the problems confronting the immigrant from Europe, or even the rural migrant to the city, are similar to those affecting blacks, Jews, American Indians, or Chicanos. Cultural differences are augmented and sustained by differences in physical traits, which by themselves would be less significant if they were not symbols of differences in culture.

Still another dimension is that of time. The treatment of race and ethnic relations suffers when it focuses too heavily on the present. This does not mean that we should ignore contemporary discussions. Our new chapter on race and intelligence is clearly contemporary; nonetheless, that discussion is also related to the historical development of ideas that led to the present arguments. While sociologists do not ordinarily approach problems historically, they do recognize the fact that social situations have historical roots and that current situations, in turn, function as roots for the problems of the future. This book reflects the authors' conviction that a knowledge of the past is essential to an understanding of the complexities of the present.

Race and Ethnic Relations has been written for college students, most of whom will have had an introductory course in sociology. Accordingly, free use has been made of certain sociological concepts without the inclusion of thorough analysis and definition. At the same time, the technical terminology has been kept to a minimum, since past editions of this book have also reached nonsociology students.

Some will be disappointed at the book's failure to espouse a program of action or to offer solutions to problems. The authors believe that it is important in the study of race and ethnic relations to demonstrate honest and objective thinking and to encourage the habit of gathering and weighing evidence before forming conclusions. It is hoped that this book will neither foster cynicism, despair, or indifference, on the one hand, nor encourage a romantic zeal for quick and easy remedies, on the other.

I wish to thank Brewton Berry for allowing me to become coauthor of the fourth edition of this widely known and respected book. It is not often that a sociologist has such an opportunity, and I hope my additions have made a worthwhile contribution to the continuation of this fine text. I also wish to thank Charles A. Hildebrandt, Keene (N.H.) State College; John W. Martin, University of Illinois–Chicago Circle; and William H. Martineau, College of William and Mary — all of whom provided valuable comments as the book was being written. My wife Linda has been particularly understanding and supportive throughout the entire endeavor and deserves special recognition.

H.L.T.

RACE AND ETHNIC RELATIONS

Part One

PERSPECTIVES
AND DEFINITIONS

Chapter One
The Study of Race and Ethnic Relations

The sociologist is concerned with understanding society.

— *Peter L. Berger* Invitation to Sociology

Often it is said that the main goal of sociology is to bring about an understanding of social situations, rather than a precise ability to predict outcomes. It is assumed that once we know the variables that are involved in a particular set of events, we will be able to draw conclusions and make some logical decisions. Nowhere is this goal of understanding truer than in the study of race and ethnic relations. Confronted with a variety of factors that frequently lead to numerous outcomes, we can perceive the problem as one of bringing some order and understanding to what may well seem to be a haphazard and potentially volatile series of events.

No one can doubt the seriousness of racial and ethnic conflict in the world today, nor the importance of being alerted to its consequences. Daily we read and hear of the conflict between Israelis and Arabs in the Middle East, between the white and brown peoples in Asia, and between Europeans and blacks in Africa. From the Republic of South Africa come disturbing reports of the whites' desperate efforts to maintain dominance over the more numerous blacks, Indians, and mixed bloods known as Cape Coloureds. In the United States we are continually reminded of the racial and ethnic conflict by the demonstrations and boycotts; the discrimination based on ethnicity and color; the plight of the American Indians; the problems of refugees and illegal aliens;

and the activities of such organizations as NAACP, KKK, JDL, and White Citizens' Council.

Racial conflict is by no means limited to one country or continent. Recently South Africa's white government took a step toward the dismantling of its system of racial discrimination. However, the fact that this step is considered as representing progress shows how deeply ingrained the system of apartheid is. In its "good will" gesture, the government restored to the Africans the right to own their own homes (although not the ground on which the houses stand) in the areas outside the African cities, where more than half of the country's 15 million blacks live.

Since 1967 the blacks have been allowed to own property only in the designated tribal "homelands." Their status in urban areas has always been that of temporary sojourners, whether they were born in the homelands area or in the city. Even with this new regulation, the blacks may still not own their houses indefinitely and must sell or bequeath them during thirty-year lease periods.[1]

Clearly, it is going to be a long time before we can expect the government of South Africa to retreat from its separate development blueprint, and it is going to be even longer before whites and blacks have equal status in that country.

Russia has long tried to create the impression of being a champion of the underprivileged peoples of the world in their struggle for freedom and equality. Through propaganda and diplomatic activities, the country has encouraged and exploited the resentment of Africans, Asians, and Latin Americans toward their real or fancied oppressors. However, for all the sneers at democracies and pious statements of tolerance, Russia has anything but a clean record regarding the treatment of minorities. (See the listing of principal ethnic groups in Figure 1.1.) Reports indicate that numerous ethnic and racial groups within the Soviet Union are none too happy over their conditions and prospects. The case of the Jews has been widely publicized. According to Communist doctrine, anti-Semitism is an extremely repulsive social situation and could only really develop in reactionary, capitalistic, and precapitalistic regimes in which the ruling classes exploit hatred of the Jews for their own gain. Lenin and other Russian revolutionaries were sincere and resolute opponents of anti-Semitism and any form of discrimination against the Jews. However, after the Revolution, and with the establishment of the one-man rule of Stalin, a distinctly anti-Jewish policy emerged.[2] This policy is still in effect today. The discrimination against the Jews manifests itself not just in difficulty in obtaining employment and gaining entrance to universities, but also in active attempts to eradicate organized Jewish life.

The problems that arise from the interactions of peoples who differ from each other racially, religiously, or culturally are commonly referred to as *race and ethnic relations*, and are of more than contemporary or historical interest. They may well prove to be of even greater significance in the future. For all their current import, these problems as a world issue may not seem today to be as acute as either communism or nationalism; but communism diligently exploits racial feeling, and nationalism frequently fuses with it. Many Westerners still think of the race problem as one of maintaining white supremacy in

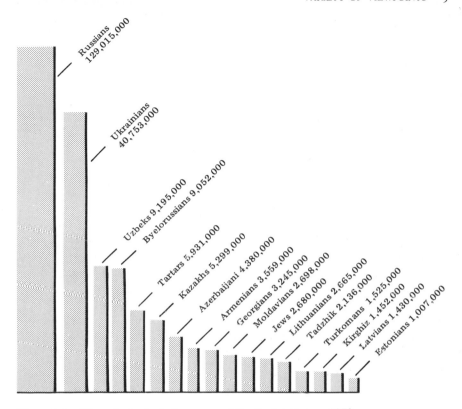

Figure 1.1   The principal ethnic groups of the Soviet Union, 1970.

The Soviet Union has one of the most ethnically diverse populations in the world, with over one hundred different ethnic groups. The major ones are shown above.

Figures from *Encyclopedia Britannica*, 15th ed., vol. 17, 1975, p. 337.

the face of the demands of the Third World for full equality of status. This conception of the problem, however, is already outdated. It is no longer a question of whether or not the red, brown, black, and yellow people will achieve equality. The question is, Will the whites lose it altogether, or will the world move safely toward a system of equality, tolerance, respect, and cooperation? There is no certainty here. The whites are outnumbered, and the disproportion is steadily increasing. A world organized on the basis of antiwhite hatred is by no means inconceivable or impossible.

Variety of Viewpoints

Sociologists, from the earliest days of their science, have been aware of the problems of race and ethnicity, and have given them much thought and study; but the subject, certainly, is not their monopoly. Historians, journalists, clergymen, anthropologists, novelists, biologists, psychologists, poets, politicians, and a host of others have written about them. Race, moreover, presents not a single, clear-cut problem, but a multitude of problems. Consequently, there are many facets to be observed, many areas to be explored, and many angles from which the questions of race and race relations can be approached. How does the sociologist differ from others who venture to write about these things? Before we attempt to answer that question, let us look at some nonsociological points of view as reflected in the recent literature.

The Racist

Individuals with a *racist* point of view are those who have approached the study of race relations from the standpoint of defending, justifying, or rationalizing discrimination and the maintenance of the status quo. The following quotation is a clear example of racist thinking. Before we mention the author, try to imagine who it might have been.

I will say, then, that I am not, nor have ever been, in favor of bringing about in any way the social and political equality of the white and black races; and that I am not, nor ever have been, in favor of making voters or jurors of negroes, nor of qualifying them to hold office, nor to intermarry with white people; and I will say, in addition to this, that there is a physical difference between the white and black races which I believe will forever forbid the two races living together on terms of social and political equality. And inasmuch as they cannot so live, while they do remain together there must be the position of superior and inferior, and I as much as any other man am in favor of having the superior position assigned to the white race.[3]

This passage is from a speech that Abraham Lincoln gave at Charleston, Illinois in September of 1858. Many of us have come to think of Lincoln as "the man who freed the slaves" and as the one who was dedicated to freedom and equality. An examination of racist thinking will provide further evidence that traditionally this school of thought has not been limited exclusively to extremists.

Dr. Henry E. Garrett, former chairman of the Department of Psychology at Columbia University and former president of the American Psychological Association, has recently (1973) written a monograph that supposedly proves that blacks are inferior to whites. Using this premise, Garrett reasons that the attempts at integrated education are doomed to failure. He begins his argument by claiming that the black culture has contributed nothing to the world.

In recent years it has become fashionable to depict in glowing terms the achievements of the Negro over the past 5,000 years, although the truth is that the history of the Black African is largely a blank. Until the arrival of Europeans there was no literate civilization in the continent's black belt. The Negro had no written language, no numerals, no calendar, no system of measurement. He never developed a plow or wheel. He never domesticated any animal. With the rarest exceptions, he built nothing more

Young people imitate the KKK

elaborate than mud huts and thatched stockades. The Negro's external trade was comprised of slaves of his own race, ivory and (on the West Coast) palm oil and mahogany. He carried burdens on his head. All we know of the history and culture of the Negro is from written and oral accounts given by Arab and Portuguese traders.[4]

It is amazing that a knowledgeable individual should believe or write such statements. Clearly, there is no validity in the conclusions that are drawn and one must wonder about what could have motivated such a statement.

If we return to the Republic of South Africa mentioned earlier, we find one of the most notorious examples of racist ideology. This country, with a population of 21,448,169 in 1970, is dominated economically and politically by the 3,750,716 inhabitants of European descent who constitute less than 20 percent of the population. As of 1970 there were in the country 15,057,599 black "natives," 620,422 Asians, and 2,018,533 Coloured, a mixed group formed mainly by interbreeding among early white settlers, the aboriginal Bushmen and Hottentots, and peoples from Madagascar, the East Indies, the eastern coast of Africa, and elsewhere. (Table 1.1 shows the racial structure of the population of the Republic of South Africa.) To deal with the situation, the government has embarked upon a policy known as apartheid (an Afrikaans word, pronounced ə-pärt'hít, and meaning apartness). This policy of *apartheid* calls for the biological, territorial, social, educational, economic, and political separation of the various racial groups that compose the Republic of South Africa.

Table 1.1   The racial structure of the population of the Republic of South Africa

| | European | | Non-European | | | | | |
| | | | Black "natives" | | "Coloured" | | Asians | |
Year	Number	Percentage of total population	Number	Percentage of total population	Number	Percentage of total population	Number	Percentage of total population
1904	1,116,806	21.6	3,491,056	67.4	445,228	8.6	122,734	2.4
1911	1,276,242	21.4	4,019,006	67.3	525,943	8.8	152,203	2.5
1921	1,519,488	21.9	4,697,813	67.8	545,548	7.9	165,731	2.4
1936	2,003,857	20.9	6,596,689	68.8	769,661	8.0	219,691	2.3
1946	2,335,460	20.7	7,735,809	68.7	905,050	8.0	282,539	2.6
1956	2,907,000	20.9	9,306,000	66.9	1,281,000	9.2	421,000	3.0
1960	3,067,638	19.4	10,807,809	68.2	1,488,267	9.4	477,414	3.0
1970	3,750,716	17.5	15,057,599	70.2	2,018,533	9.4	620,422	2.9

Figures from *South Africa 1975: Official Yearbook of the Republic of South Africa*, p. 28.

Dr. John E. Holloway, the Republic's former ambassador to the United States, has written in defense of his government's policy.[5] The racial groups in South Africa, he maintains, are so vastly different in civilization, culture, ways of thinking, and standards of living that apartheid is the only humane, feasible, and reasonable way to resolve the difficulties. The alternative to apartheid is integration; but, he says, "Except in very small fringes the desire for social integration is completely nonexistent." He maintains that integration of peoples of European and African stock in large numbers and on a community basis has nowhere been successfully achieved. He points to the northern states of the United States and insists that even there one finds no "completely integrated white-black community in which people of both races are normally seen living together, eating together, playing together, and intermarrying." And yet, he says, in those northern states the conditions are far more favorable for integration than they are in South Africa, where the Africans are lacking in education, skills, knowledge, and attitudes essential for participation in the European civilization that has been transplanted to South Africa, and upon which the whole population, black and white, is dependent for its survival. Too hasty integration, he maintains, would create more problems than it would solve. Apartheid, on the other hand, would enable each race to develop in its own way, and at a rate suitable to its wishes and capacities.

The policy of separate development has many defenders as can be seen in the following statement by Chief Kaizer Matanzima, the Chief Minister of the Traskei in the Legislative Assembly:

When I delivered my first policy speech in this House in 1964 my position was rather precarious. I had, just a few months previously, been elected as the first Chief Minister of the Traskei by a slender majority of five. In spite of that, however, I had abundant confidence and faith in my political future for I was absolutely convinced that the policy of separate development for which I and my party stood was the only acceptable policy in South Africa, for both black and white. My faith in this policy has been vindicated. Election results have proved that the policy of separate development has become more and more acceptable to the black people of South Africa as it unfolded in its practical implementation and today I command a majority of 61 in this Assembly. People can see with their own eyes how we have steadily forged ahead. . . .

I would like to make it very clear that I and my colleagues on this side of the House openly and unequivocally endorse the policy of separate development; that we regard ourselves as partners in the implementation of this policy and are intent on maintaining cordial relations with white South Africa.[6]

The interesting thing about this statement is that it is made by a black person and not a white member of the ruling power.

The Critic

The viewpoint of the *critic* who writes on the subject of race is that the present situation is undesirable or intolerable, and that something ought to, must, or inevitably will be done about it. Change is the dominant note in such books.

During the late 1960s many books that expressed this view about the condition of blacks in the United States were written by such individuals as Malcolm X, Eldridge Cleaver, Stokely Carmichael, and others. Whether these writings actually brought about any major changes is a matter of opinion; however, no one can deny that they had an effect on the consciousness of blacks and also of whites. In *Soul on Ice* Eldridge Cleaver cites a description of New York's black ghetto, Harlem, written by the noted philosopher, Thomas Merton.

Here in this huge, dark, steaming slum, hundreds of thousands of Negroes are herded together like cattle, most of them with nothing to eat and nothing to do. All the senses and imagination and sensibilities and emotions and sorrows and desires and hopes and ideas of a race with vivid feelings and deep emotional reactions are forced in upon themselves, bound inward by an iron ring of frustration: the prejudice that hems them in with its four insurmountable walls. In this huge cauldron, inestimable natural gifts, wisdom, love, music, science, poetry are stamped down and left to boil with the dregs of an elementary corrupted nature, and thousands upon thousands of souls are destroyed by vice and misery and degredation, obliterated, wiped out, washed from the register of the living, dehumanized.

What has not been devoured, in your dark furnace, Harlem, by marijuana, by gin, in insanity, hysteria, syphilis? [7]

Whenever Cleaver felt himself becoming too relaxed or complacent about the condition of blacks, he would read this passage and would again become infused with indignation and be ready to resume his battle against tyranny and oppression.

Another critic intent on changing his government's policies is author Aleksandr I. Solzhenitsyn. In the *Gulag Archipelago* he wrote of the problems of living in the Soviet Union. The book had been completed and hidden for many years. A women to whom Solzhenitsyn had entrusted a portion of the manuscript for safekeeping revealed its location after 120 sleepless hours of questioning by Soviet Security officers. Realizing what she had done, she then committed suicide. It was this event that the author refers to in the statement that precedes the text: "Now that State Security has seized the book anyway, I have no alternative but to publish it immediately."

In this book Solzhenitsyn reveals the horrifying process of arrest and transport to life in a Soviet prison camp. We see that the most insignificant reasons, and even nonexistent premises, are used for making arrests. Consequently, individuals have become extremely fearful of engaging in any action that can be construed as an act against the state. Even if they themselves escape, actions can always be taken against their families. By publishing this book, Solzhenitsyn hoped to bring worldwide attention to the living situation in the Soviet Union and to create pressures for change.

The Strategist

Those who espouse the *strategist* viewpoint are primarily concerned with the question How? How can changes be brought about? And, in other instances,

How can the status quo be preserved? The question of strategy was always a major concern for black leaders during the civil rights movement of the 1960s. The Urban League followed the road of uplift and persuasion, while the NAACP relied upon the use of political power and winning court decisions. The Southern Christian Leadership Conference led by the Reverend Martin Luther King, Jr. pinned its hopes on a policy of nonviolence, and the use of demonstrations and boycotts. Young blacks became disillusioned by the slow, legalistic approach of their elders and decided on more direct action. First, we saw the formation of the Student Nonviolent Coordinating Committee, which ushered in the era of direct confrontation. The Black Panthers quickly followed, and we witnessed leaders such as Huey Newton, Bobby Seale, and Eldridge Cleaver urging rebellion against the status quo and advocating racial pride and self-help.

The civil rights movements of the 1950s and early 1960s became a militant black revolution. The primary goal of the civil rights movement was to gain integration into the mainstream of American society through nonviolent means. The black revolution, on the other hand, emerged because of the intransigence and unresponsiveness of white America to the needs and interests of blacks. As the desired results were slow in coming, the methods became more drastic.

The Black Muslims have taken a different approach to the problem of racial discrimination. The adherents of this religion strive to separate themselves from white society, as well as from lower-class black society. The assumption is that white dominance is drawing to an end and that blacks must prepare themselves for their rise to power through economic improvement and individual spirituality. The religion provides a basis for identity and self-improvement with a strong emphasis on racial pride. Respectability both within and outside the black community is a primary goal, while at the same time there is a strong sense of responsibility for the welfare of the Muslim community. The basic strategy is one of rejection of white society, rather than of confrontation or assimilation. However, even here there has been a change since the group recently moved to allow whites to join.

The members of the Ku Klux Klan think of their organization as an instrument designed to combat what they consider to be negative changes in the status quo of race and ethnic relations. These individuals believe in white supremacy and have a notorious history of using extreme measures and violence to achieve their goals. As one of their members has stated, "We are training vigilantes and will use them for self-defense if blacks, socialists and communists take over and we lose individual freedom."[8] Contrary to popular opinion, the Klan's activities are not limited to the South, and many chapters can be found in the Northeast and other areas of the United States.

During the late 1960s and early 1970s, the Jewish Defense League made headlines because of its militant approach to the protection of the rights of Jews. In 1970 the JDL placed an ad in the *New York Times* showing a group of boys holding lead pipes and baseball bats. The caption read, "Is this any way for a nice Jewish boy to behave?" The organization believes that discrimination against Jews has arisen because they have held marginal positions in society and have consistently played a middle-man role. This role has caused the Jew to be seen as "a slum lord to blacks, a civil rights worker to Southern whites, a well-heeled business school opportunist to hippies, a student radical to WASP conservatives, an Old Testament witness to Vermont Yankees, an atheist to Midwestern crusaders, a capitalist to leftists, a communist to rednecks."[9]

The JDL has been trying to move Jews away from the attitude of resignation and fatalism that has long determined Jewish tradition. The members have organized themselves into bands that patrol local areas as a reaction against what they perceive as harassment by blacks and Puerto Ricans. In addition, the members strive to regain and take pride in their Jewish identity.

The Assimilationist

It has been widely held that racial and cultural differences are undesirable, and that homogeneity is preferable to heterogeneity. Subscribers to this viewpoint feel that the only solution to the problems of racial and ethnic groups, therefore, lies in the mixing, blending, and combining of the diverse elements. The philosophy of America as the melting pot and the support for programs of assimilation are reflections of this attitude.

The *assimilationist* view assumes that minority problems can be solved by providing the minority-group members with the opportunity to achieve entrance into the mainstream culture. Through a competitive struggle in the marketplace, middle-class status can be achieved. However, some have viewed successful assimilation under this system as the opportunity to discard one's ethnicity in return for financial success.

During periods of massive immigration into the United States, the schools were the main vehicle for the Americanization of the young. In many schools it was strictly forbidden for the children to utter a word of their native language, and the children came to devalue the culture of their parents. Assimilation for these children was a series of conflicts between competing influences, with one environment pressing against another. The influences of the wider American society were often at odds with the values of the immigrant families or ethnic institutions. Parents would often deplore the loss of their authority over their children's behavior, and they bitterly contrasted the American scene with the stable Old World village.

Examples of the assimilationist view are very prevalent in many of the earlier writings in race and ethnic relations. One book written from this point of view deals with the American Indian. The theme is that we must "get away from the sentimental and romantic and think in terms of the realistic." It is unwise to attempt to revive and perpetuate the traditional Indian cultures, to "keep the Indian Indian," to set the Indian apart, to give the Indian special privileges and treatment. The Indian must be "a full participant in our common life," and our policies should be directed to that end. The author quotes the remarks of a young Navajo to illustrate his viewpoint:

Immigrant boy and girl at Ellis Island

Everywhere we Indians go you white boys ask us where our feather headdress, our moccasins, and our "real Indian" costumes are. . . . Don't you know that those are the
ways our great-grandparents dressed a very long time ago? All those things belong back
in the past. Let them stay there. . . . The problems we are facing will never be solved
by feathers.[10]

Israel is another country where the assimilationist pressure has been great.
The problems of mass immigration have been considerable. Immediately
upon becoming an independent nation in 1948, Israel declared that its gates

were open to the immigration of Jews from around the world. In the years that followed, hundreds of thousands of immigrants poured in. Having been developed by pioneers of European background, Israel possessed a culture of the Western type; but more than half of all the immigrants who came after the establishment of the state hailed from the less-developed areas of Asia or Africa (Yemen, Iraq, Kurdistan, North Africa), and brought with them an Oriental type of culture. This situation has produced some tensions, which have been further aggravated by the fact that the old timers are usually better off economically than the immigrants who have arrived more recently.

There has also been conflict between religious Israelis and secular Israelis over the separation of synagogue and state. It has not even been possible to reach agreement on the most basic question, Who is a Jew?

However, even with these problems and immense cultural diversity, the assimilationist process has been moving forward and a larger Israeli culture drawn from European, Asian, and North African influences is now prevalent.

The Pluralist

On the other hand, there are those with a *pluralist* viewpoint who regard cultural diversity as highly desirable, as a source of strength to a nation, as a stimulus to cultural growth, as giving color and interest to a society. They dislike seeing a group lose its identity and uniqueness, discard its traditions, and permit its values, its folk dances, and its arts to perish from want of nourishment. They refer to "the melting pot mistake" and the "failure of the Americanization program."

Michael Novak, a liberal Catholic intellectual of Slovak origin, for whom diverse ethnicity has assumed great importance, has written a book called *The Rise of the Unmeltable Ethnics*. He claims that he was born of "PIGS—those Poles, Italians, Greeks, and Slavs, non-English-speaking immigrants who numbered so heavily among the workingmen of this nation. Not particularly liberal, nor radical . . . born outside what in America is considered the intellectual mainstream." Novak is reacting to American society's condescending attitude toward these groups and wishes to regain pride and identification with his ancestors.

The American Indian has long resisted the pressures to assimilate. Generalizing about Indian tribes is precarious, since the tribes differ so greatly. At the time of discovery of America, the differences in languages and customs from tribe to tribe were as great as those between, for example, the English and the Chinese. It is no less true today. Some groups such as the Zuni and the Hopi have retained a great deal of their old culture, while others (Narragansetts, Nanticokes, Chickahominy, and Lumbees) have preserved very little except their conviction that they are Indians. It is even hazardous to generalize about a particular community, since there are cleavages and differences between the old and the young, and between the ever-present conservative and the progressive.

Even more than twenty-five years ago, before pluralism became a "desirable" trait, a group of social scientists and administrators, all of whom were experienced in Indian affairs, met in Chicago to discuss the basic issues of Indian survival. They concuded that:

Most Indian groups in the United States . . . in spite of strong external pressures . . . have not yet become assimilated . . . and will continue indefinitely as distinct social units, preserving their basic values, personality, and Indian way of life, while making continual adjustments, often superficial in nature, to the economic and political demands of the larger society.[11]

There are other indications that the melting pot philosophy has been rejected. A knowledge of English is still required for American citizenship, but in New York State it is now possible to vote without demonstrating fluency in English. Bilingual education receives federal support, and education for Spanish-speaking students no longer requires the same sort of tribulations and sacrifices on the part of the student as did the education of immigrant children just a short while back.

In colleges we have seen the emergence of black studies, Chinese studies, Puerto Rican studies, Chicano studies, and Jewish studies programs. All of this points to the fact we are now in an era of ethnicity and pluralism rather than the era of assimilationism that dominated our history for so long.

Other Approaches

There are many other points of view that have been adopted by writers on problems of race and ethnicity. Included among these viewpoints is the *theological* approach to the problem. Religious thinkers and writers have also been aware of the differences and conflicts between racial and ethnic groups, and have regarded these problems from their own particular viewpoints. One may even say that the Old Testament itself is such a book, for running through it is the theory that God had a purpose in creating the world, and that He selected one group for the execution of that purpose which, by the way, involves all the others. Other religions, or sects, would have quite different opinions with regard to the outgroup, depending on their doctrines and the degree of their exclusiveness.

Others have approached race and ethnic relations from a *pragmatic* perspective. Here we would include those who ask the question, What must be done in this particular situation to reduce the conflict or to preserve the peace? This individual is not primarily concerned with the justice or injustice of the situation, with the ethical issues, or with the problem of whether the groups change their cultures or retain their individuality. Nor is this person interested in broad, universal principles of race relations, and most assuredly not in determining what the divine plan is for the world. Many books and articles dealing with problems of race relations have been written from this point of view.

Their authors have included colonial administrators responsible for keeping the peace, superintendents and principals of schools located in mixed neighborhoods, and statesmen whose constituents include persons of diverse races and cultures.

There are others who "view with alarm" the course of events but whose writings throw little light on the causes of the trends, and offer slight hope of correcting them; and there are those who adopt an "ain't-it-awful" approach, deploring the situation and documenting beyond any doubt the sad state of affairs. On the more serious side, we find that historians, biologists, physical anthropologists, and psychologists have all manifested an interest in one phase or another of the problem of race, asking the type of questions with which their science is concerned and seeking answers by using the techniques that they have found to be efficacious. Psychologists, for example, have long been interested in the intellectual, mental, and temperamental differences and characteristics of the various races, and the physical anthropologists have been interested in the racial criteria and classification of mankind.

This does not exhaust all of the possible approaches, nor is it presented as a logical classification. Most books, as a matter of fact, combine several. Anyone who speaks or writes about problems of race and ethnicity makes certain assumptions, holds to certain values, and adopts some point of view, whether or not it is explicitly stated or even realized.

We will make no attempt to evaluate these approaches at this time, and will not insist that one is better than the other. We will not even defend the sociological point of view as the best, and certainly not as the only legitimate one. A discussion so complex and so vital as race and ethnic relations permits, even demands, a variety of approaches.

The Approach of This Book

Race has always been one of the major concerns of sociologists. The first two sociological books published in the United States, more than a century ago, dealt with the problem.[12] Both writers sought to justify the prevailing institution of slavery. Fitzhugh undertook to prove that morality and discipline could be maintained only in a society founded upon slavery and Christianity, while Hughes ingeniously denied that slavery existed in the South! Slaves, he said, were people who had no rights at all; but in the South, he insisted, the so-called slaves did possess rights. Therefore, American society was not built upon a system of slavery, as everyone supposed, but instead was a *warranty commonwealth*, a type of social organization having numerous advantages over other types.

Sociologists have not been in agreement as to the nature and scope of their study of race, nor as to their conclusions. The sociological approach has gone through several changes since the issue was first studied. E. B. Reuter, who himself played no small part in developing the field, thinks that there have been three stages through which sociologists have moved.[13] The first period was marked by an emphasis on biological problems. Sociologists were fascinated by the task of classifying mankind, of studying the physical and mental characteristics of races, and of measuring these differences. They spent their efforts in the futile attempt to explain social phenomena in biological terms. The second period witnessed a shift to a cultural frame of reference. The realization dawned that the significant differences among people were not their hereditary, physical features, but their languages, customs, beliefs, technologies, and institutions. These differences, all of which are learned, are the ones that arouse prejudice and lead to conflict. The belief prevailed, therefore, that the key to understanding racial problems lay in the study of social heritages. The third period is marked by an emphasis on relationships among the races, rather than on either their physical or cultural characteristics. The contact and interaction among groups came to be the focus of interest. In this book, accordingly, we attempt to reach an understanding of the phenomena that arise when so-called racial groups enter into relations with one another. Our point of view has seven important features that require some further explanation.

Understanding

It is our purpose to understand race relations rather than to espouse causes or to propose solutions. Most assuredly do we insist that we have no panacea for racial problems. We even doubt that one exists. The problems are too complex to admit of easy, simple, and universal solutions. Take, for instance, the American Indian. The situation on one reservation is quite different from that on another, and programs that would be quite feasible on the one would be disastrous elsewhere.

There are those, to be sure, who will have little sympathy for such a point of view, insisting that what is needed now is action, not investigation. Some will maintain that "everybody knows the answer; it is only a question of applying it." Others will say that "while you fiddle about leisurely," studying the problem, "the whole thing may blow up in your face." We fully appreciate the seriousness and urgency of the situation, but we believe that knowledge and understanding are prerequisites for wise and effective action. We are sympathetic, for instance, with the medical research scientists who work away in their laboratories while an epidemic rages in the community. Why, some will say, do they not do something immediately useful? Why not put into practical use the knowledge and skill that they have, imperfect though it may be? Why waste effort on research when the times demand action? It is our opinion that, in the long run, the research scientists will relieve more suffering by their investigations than by abandoning their study and devoting themselves to therapy.

Objectivity

The sociologist, unlike the reformer, the racist, or the moralist, tries to examine the relationships among the so-called racial groups as objectively as possible. Thus we will endeavor to take a neutral position and to refrain from making judgments as to the justice or injustice, the right or wrong, and the good or bad in a situation as much as possible.

Now there are those who insist that social scientists cannot adopt a position of neutrality on matters in which they are so vitally involved, and that the only alternative is for them to state their biases frankly. The point is well taken. The mere fact that we choose to investigate race relations is indicative of our interest and concern; and our decision to study relationships rather than biological traits betrays our belief that the former are more significant than the latter. The writers, like most persons reared in the American culture, have had inculcated in them the values of the American Creed (democracy, human dignity, humanitarianism, and the like), and find it extremely difficult to look with complete impartiality on a contest between democracy and authoritarianism, or between freedom of speech and its suppression, or between science and superstition. On the other hand, one sometimes feels that objectivity is regarded in some quarters as the supreme virtue, an end in itself. We look upon it, instead, as a means to an end, as an indispensable part of the equipment of the scientist and the scholar. And even though we may agree that a completely disinterested social science is impossible to achieve, we maintain that the sociologist must be disciplined enough to develop an open mind and to look as objectively as possible on the problem under investigation.

Relationships

Sociologists are primarily concerned with the phenomena that arise when people and groups enter into relationships with one another. The contacts among racial groups frequently result in conflict, and sociologists have sought to understand the riots, insurrections, strikes, boycotts, and the other forms that such conflict has assumed. The interactions of racial groups, however, are not limited to antagonism; groups learn to cooperate, they adjust their differences, one group dominates the other, members intermarry, they adopt each other's ideas and customs, they develop myths and creeds regarding themselves and those with whom they come into contact, they become prejudiced, and they organize movements either to defend or to change the social patterns. It is these phenomena, more than the physical and cultural traits of racial groups, that primarily interest the sociologist. This is not to say that racial features (skin color, type of hair, and so on) are ignored, or that the history and the social heritage of a group are of no concern. When groups come in contact, these traits take on meaning and assume importance. The physical characteristics and cultural heritages of groups are studied by anthropologists, historians, and human geographers; but sociologists are not greatly interested in such matters per se.

Groups

The main concern of sociology is with the interrelations among groups of people who are different. Sociologists are vitally interested in groups of people who are conscious of the physical features that distinguish them from others, and who allow that consciousness to influence their behavior. They are interested in the relationships between Americans and Mexicans, between whites and blacks, between Gentiles and Jews, between Europeans and Asians, between Boers and Hottentots. These are groups, but not races in the strict sense. The subject matter of sociology, might better be described as the interactions among racial and ethnic groups, rather than the interactions among races. These terms will be defined at a later point.

Cross-Cultural Perspective

The race problem is synonymous in the minds of most Americans with blacks, and, even more specifically, with blacks in the United States. College courses in sociology bearing such titles as "Race Relations" have often so restricted the field, and popular textbooks have reflected this common tendency. The fact is, however, that racial and ethnic groups have come into contact the world over and for untold centuries, and the phenomena we seek to understand are worldwide in their scope. Sociology is concerned with the interactions of people wherever and whenever they occur, and, accordingly, we will not limit ourselves to the American scene. Unfortunately, our data on race relations in other lands are sketchy. We are in great need of comparative studies of intergroup relations in the various biracial and multiracial areas of the world. Only when such materials are available will it be possible to develop a science of race relations. In the meantime we must enlarge our perspective with the best available information from other lands, and generalize with caution and reservation.

Theoretical Relevancy

In the past there has been an obvious lack of theoretical analysis in the race and ethnic relations area. Weber may have discussed pariah peoples; Marx may have looked upon racism as an outgrowth of the capitalistic system; and Pareto may have provided others with a justification for elitist thinking. However, none of the major sociological theorists including Comte, Marx, Spencer, Durkheim, Weber, Simmel, or Pareto dealt with the issue in any great detail. Consequently, race relations has been out of the intellectual mainstream of sociological writing.

We would need to emphasize the historical dimension to correct this problem. A theoretically guided perspective would locate and define the groups in question in terms of their relationship to the social structure and the historical development of this relationship. With this historical dimension, we begin to see that present group relations have a history, and many aspects of present relationships can be better understood by relating them to that history. In this way, modern race relations can be juxtaposed with historical examples to gain a fuller understanding.

Dynamics of Race Relations

Human society is undergoing a continuous process of change, and race relations are no exception to this rule. What we are attempting to understand, therefore, is not some fixed and static phenomenon, but a dynamic, ever-changing pattern of relationships. Consider, for example, the story of the contacts between Indians and whites in the area of the present United States. For a long time each racial group was bent upon the extermination of the other, and the attitudes and policies of our government were based upon the assumption that the Indian was a vanishing race. Later on there was a shift to a policy of isolation and segregation, and the Indians were confined to reservations and subjected to a paternalistic relationship. Somewhat later the emphasis changed from segregation to forced assimilation, and steps were taken to civilize the Indians and to integrate them into American society. More recently there have arisen doubts concerning the justice, desirability, and practicability of a policy of rapid and compulsory assimilation. The fact is that, from the moment the Europeans arrived in the New World, the nature, forms, and patterns of the interactions and adjustments between the whites and Indians have undergone tremendous changes, and they continue to do so.

The same is true of blacks. American whites have always been convinced that blacks had a place in our society, but that so-called place has continually changed. For two and a half centuries slavery was that "place," but slavery itself was never a permanent, unchanging relationship. Instead, throughout American history before the Civil War, slave status never ceased undergoing a process of redefinition in both the laws and the folkways. Consequently, the slavery of 1850 was quite a different thing from the slavery of 1650. Since the abolition of slavery, the pattern of black-white relationships has continued to change, and these relationships have never changed more rapidly than in the past decade.

Race relations, then, are a worldwide problem, not peculiar to the United States. So serious is the problem that thoughtful people in all walks of life have directed their attention to it, each in their own way and from their own point of view proposing some solution, espousing some cause, or contributing something to our understanding of it. The sociologist, without claiming to hold the complete answer, does insist that the specific discipline has something worthwhile to say about the matter. The sociologist believes that by adopting an objective point of view, not an emotional one, we may hope to gain an understanding of the dynamic phenomena that emerge when groups of people who differ racially and culturally enter into relationships. In the following chapters we will present and analyze what sociologists have learned up to this point.

Notes

1. *New York Times*, 9 May 1975, p. 32M.

2. Keter Publishers, *Anti-Semitism*, p. 57.

3. A. B. Lapsley, ed., *The Writings of Abraham Lincoln*, vol. 4, pp. 1–3; A. P. Blaustein and R. L. Zangrando, eds., *Civil Rights and the Black American*, p. 171.

4. H. E. Garrett, *IQ and Racial Differences*, p. 2.

5. J. E. Holloway, "Apartheid," in *The Annals of the American Academy of Political and Science* 306 (July 1956): 26ff. See also Hilgard Muller, "The Official Case for Apartheid," *New York Times Magazine*, 7 June 1964.

6. Government of South Africa, *Progress Through Separate Development*, 4th ed., p. 57.

7. T. Merton, *The Seven Storey Mountain*, cited in E. Cleaver, *Soul on Ice*, p. 44.

8. *The South Middlesex News*, 10 Dec. 1972, p. 2E.

9. J. Sleeper in J. N. Porter and P. Dreier, eds., *Jewish Radicalism*, pp. xlvii–xlviii.

10. G. E. E. Lindquist, *The Indians in American Life*, p. vi.

11. J. Provinse in B. Berry, *The Education of the American Indians*, p. 71.

12. H. Hughes, *Treatise on Sociology, Theoretical and Practical*: C. Fitzhugh, *Sociology for the South: or the Failure of Free Society*.

13. "Racial Theory," *American Journal of Sociology* 50, no. 6 (May 1945): 452–461.

Chapter Two
The Concept of Race

The term "race" is one of the most frequently
misused and misunderstood words in the
American vernacular.

— *Peter I. Rose They and We*

Strictly speaking this book is not concerned with problems of race. Only incidentally does it raise such questions as: What is a race? How many races are there? How are races classified, and by what criteria? Are some races more intelligent, more artistic, or more warlike than others? Psychologists and anthropologists may address themselves to such questions, but these questions are not the focus of this book. Rather, we are concerned with the problems that arise when groups of people who are different are brought together in face-to-face contact and are confronted with the task of having to live together — groups such as Jews and Arabs, Indians and Englishmen, Mexicans and Texans, blacks and whites, Japanese and Irish, Puerto Ricans and Yankees. These are groups that are loosely held together, but they are not races. However, they often *think* of themselves as races, and they are often so regarded by others. The problems that arise from their association are usually called race problems; the attitudes engendered are called race prejudice; and the interactions that take place are called race relations. We might choose not to designate such groups as races, but it is important that we come to some understanding of the term in any event.

Race is an explosive term. Our language does have its full quota of "loaded" words (*communist, tory, scab,* plus many others that we will refrain from enumerating); but when it comes to arousing people's prejudices, loyalties, animosities, and fears, none is the equal of race, and of the innumerable synonyms, slurs, and epithets related thereto. Race is a subject that few can discuss dispassionately.

Sociologists and anthropologists have found that people everywhere seem to feel that the groups to which they belong are the best, that their ways are the right ways, that their morals are superior, that their religion is the true one. Years ago a pioneer sociologist, William Graham Sumner, observing this well-nigh universal characteristic, coined a term for the phenomenon. He called it *ethnocentrism*, and defined it as the emotional attitude that "one's own group is the center of everything, and all others are scaled with reference to it. . . ."[1] Sumner insisted that each group nourishes its own pride and vanity, regards itself as superior, and looks with contempt on outsiders. This attitude applies not only to the nation or tribe of which one is a member, but to one's other groups as well — church, political party, race, fraternity, college, social class, and community. Sumner found that even primitive, backward peoples, who would seem to have no basis whatsoever for such conceit, were no less immune than the rich and powerful. The simple Lapps, for instance, call themselves (as distinct from outside groups) "human beings," the Kiowa Indians' name for their tribe is "real or principal people," the Tungus refer to themselves as "men," and so on around the world. Outsiders are dubbed in various unflattering ways — infidels, barbarians, idolaters, pig-eaters, the uncircumcised, or "the great unwashed." When it comes to racial and ethnic groups, we in the United States are guilty of displaying our ethnocentrism by the use of many labels that are never appreciated by the people to whom we apply them: bohunk, chink, dago, frog, limey, greaser, nigger, sheeny, and wop are only a few of them.

Many believe that ethnocentrism serves a useful purpose, and this fact accounts for its widespread occurrence. It promotes the loyalty and esprit de corps without which no group would long endure. It performs the functions of discipline and social control essential to all group life. At the same time, it can be very irritating and disruptive; and when it gets out of hand, it may be dangerous and even fatal.

Race as an Ambiguous Term

Race is also a vague and ambiguous term. All sorts of groups of people are referred to as races, and various and sundry criteria are used to assign people to racial categories.

It has been estimated that there are over 1 million different species of animals and plants. These organisms are incapable of interbreeding, and it is not possible to belong to more than one species at the same time. For example, the animal we might be looking at can be a horse (*Equus caballus*), an ass

(*Equus asinus*), or a sterile species hybrid (mule). When it comes to race, there is no agreement among anthropologists or biologists on how many races there are in the human species. At first anthropologists and biologists tried to describe and classify races of humans in the same way as they had done with species of animals. Each was isolated, described, and given a name. However, this approach became problematical since opinions on the number of races varied greatly. In fact, the more the scientists studied human populations, the less clear-cut the differences among races became.

Dobzhansky has made the point that the difficulty arises from the fact that biological species are genetically closed systems, while races are genetically open ones. In other words, species do not generally interbreed and exchange genes. We could say that such systems are reproductively isolated. For examples, interchanges between the gene pools of the species man, chimpanzee, and gorilla cannot take place. Two species may have had a common ancestor, but each species progressed along a separate evolutionary course when it became independent.

This is not the case with humans. All humans belong to one species, and there has been a considerable amount of gene interchange even with the barriers of segregation, apartheid, and slavery. Races are not, and have never been, clearly defined biological groups. The gene interchange between human populations has caused racial boundaries to become more or less blurred.[2]

(For a listing of the principal racial and ethnic minorities in the United States, see Figure 2.1.)

Blacks as a Racial Group

There is a great deal of uncertainty in the definition of who is black. Most people carry in their minds a picture of the physical features of blacks that includes dark skin color, coarse and wiry hair, broad nose, and prominant lips, among others. In the past some states even devised legal definitions during periods when it was important to ascertain racial status. The legal definitions of these states were not in agreement with each other. Missouri, for instance, made "one-eighth or more Negro blood" the criterion, while Georgia and a number of other states classified as "colored" all persons with "any ascertainable trace of Negro blood in their veins." Virginia did likewise, but made an exception for individuals having one-fourth or more Indian "blood" and less than one-sixteenth black "blood." These Virginians were regarded as Indians so long as they remained on a reservation. If they moved, however, they were to be regarded as "colored."

There is also a *social* definition that takes precedence over both the biological and the legal criteria. According to this definition, which holds throughout the United States, anyone is black who has any *known* black ancestry, regardless of how far back one must go to find it. "One drop of Negro blood makes one a Negro" was the common way of expressing the idea. The Bureau of the Census used to instruct its enumerators to report as a Negro any person who

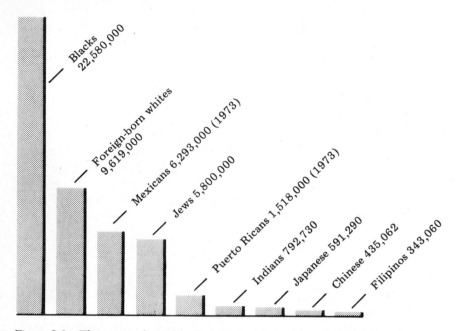

Figure **2.1**   The principal racial and ethnic minorities in the United States, 1970.

Figures from U.S. Bureau of the Census, *Statistical Abstract of the United States*, 1976.

had a mixture of black and white "blood," no matter how small the percentage of black "blood."

The social definition, which is the decisive one in most interactions, pays little heed to the hereditary physical features of the individual or to whether the percentage of black "blood" is one-fourth, one-eighth, or one-sixteenth.   If an individual is defined as black according to the social definition, then the social relationships for that person are based merely on that fact, without consideration of any other physical characteristics.   One professor in a race relations class used to ask students to go into bars and other public places and casually let it be known that they were black.   Hardly any of the students had difficulty convincing individuals of their blackness even if they had no features that would suggest black ancestry.

In Latin American countries the possession of black ancestry or black features does not automatically define an individual as black. For example, in Brazil many individuals are listed in the census as white, and are considered to be white by their friends and associates even if they had a grandmother who was of pure African descent.   It is much the same in Puerto Rico where anyone who is not obviously black is classified as cither mulatto or white.   In the Republic of South Africa a sharp distinction is drawn between the natives and the Capc Coloured, who are black-white hybrids.   The latter, at least until recently, were accorded privileges denied to blacks, and they enjoyed a social position intermediate between that of the dominant whites and the subordinate blacks.

Thus we see that racial definition is subject to considerable variation from country to country, and from time to time.

Who Is an Indian?

The ambiguity so characteristic of the general term race is also true for the American Indian. Who is an Indian? There comes to mind the image of an individual with black, coarse hair, yellow-brown or red-brown skin, wide cheek bones, and a high-bridged, convex nose. Many Indians, however, would not fit this description and, as a matter of fact, there are Indians who have blue eyes, fair skin, and blond hair.

Estimates of the number of Indians in America in 1492 range from seven hundred thousand to 1 million. By 1871 their population was less than half a million. Under the early reservation system the population decreased further and reached a low around 1900. The official census figures show the following:

1890	248,253
1920	244,437
1940	333,369
1950	357,499
1960	523,591
1970	792,730

Many have considered the census figures to be an underestimate. Therefore, the over 100 percent increase in the Indian population between 1950 and 1970 may merely reflect a more accurate count.

The United States Census Bureau has had a difficult time defining the Indian, has allowed the census taker to exercise considerable leeway, and lately has relied on self-reporting. Many negative factors have been associated with being classified as an Indian and many Indians have tried to "pass" and become non-Indians as a result. Now that there is a re-emerging Indian identity, the census statistics may rise as more Indians actually report themselves as being Indians.

Who Are Mestizos?

Mestizo is a word commonly used in Latin America to refer to the offspring of Indians and Europeans, but it is sometimes used to describe other mixtures. The term has also been used in the United States with varying connotations.

Throughout the Eastern states there are numerous "islands" of people whose blood is mixed, but the nature of the mixture is a matter of dispute. Most of their ancestry is white, and their physical features are predominantly those of white people. There is probably some Indian "blood" in them as well that traces back to colonial times. The crucial question revolves around the presence of black ancestry. The whites almost invariably suspect that there is some element of black ancestry in the mixture, and occasionally racial features such as skin color or hair form provide a basis for these suspicions. The members of the isolated groups, however, vehemently deny any black ancestry.

Groups of such people are numerous and widespread. In South Carolina the groups exist in many communities, where they are known as Brass Ankles, Red Bones, Red Legs, Turks, or Yellow-hammers; in Alabama and Mississippi they are called Creoles or Cajuns; in North Carolina, where there are forty-five thousand of them, they are called Croatans; in West Virginia and Maryland, Guineas; in Virginia, Issues; in New Jersey and New York, Jackson Whites; in the Southern Appalachians, where Virginia, Kentucky and Tennessee meet, they are known as Melungeons; in Delaware they are Moors and Nanticokes; in Louisiana, Red Bones; in Southern Maryland, Wesorts; in Ohio, Carmel Indians.[3]

Most of these groups have a long history, generously interspersed with legend and myth. Their origins are generally unknown, but most of them have some story to account for their presence. Those in North Carolina, for instance, profess to be the descendants of Sir Walter Raleigh's Lost Colony; others think they are derived from the Acadians immortalized in Longfellow's *Evangeline*. Although these stories are doubtless fiction, there is evidence to prove the existence of these groups of free, hybrid peoples as far back as colonial times.

The status of these people is ill-defined. The whites, in accordance with their theory that a trace of black ancestry makes one black are disposed to regard them as blacks and to subject them to the customary forms of segregation and discrimination. The mestizos, however, deny any black ancestry, and rebel against being forced into the black caste. They strive, therefore, to achieve the status of whites — or, at least, to avoid being classified as blacks.

For generations the mestizos met their problem by isolating themselves, by forming compact rural communities removed from the whites and blacks alike. Recently, with the shrinking of distances, their isolation has been breaking down; and they have been forced to seek other adjustments. Some of them fight their way into the white race; they migrate to nearby cities or to other parts of the country, where they are not known and where they have little or no trouble being accepted. Others have sought to win for themselves recognition as Indians, deeming such classification preferable to black status. Those in North Carolina and Delaware, especially, have followed such a policy, and with some success, although most whites say they are not "real Indians." Some have followed the line of least resistance and have been absorbed into the black community; but many still continue, in spite of the mounting obstacles, to solve their dilemma by segregation and isolation.

Who Is a Jew?

There are approximately 15 million Jews in the world, 6 million of whom reside in the United States. (See Table 2.1 for a breakdown of population by

Table **2.1**   Estimated Jewish population by countries, 1962 and 1974

Country	1962	1974
United States	5,586,500	5,731,685
Soviet Union	2,385,000	2,680,000
Israel	2,035,000	2,888,000
France	500,000	550,000
England	450,000	410,000
Argentina	450,000	475,000
Canada	254,000	305,000
Rumania	180,000	80,000
Morocco	130,000	31,000
Brazil	125,000	155,000
Republic of South Africa	110,000	118,000
Hungary	90,000	80,000
Iran	80,000	80,000
Australia	66,000	72,000
All other countries	558,500	1,069,785
Total	13,000,000	14,230,470

SOURCE: *The American Jewish Year Book*, vol. 64, 1963, and vol. 76, 1976.

countries.) We have to say "approximately," for it is no easy matter to determine just who is a Jew or to know exactly what kind of group the Jews constitute. There is the popular belief, of course, that there are certain physical features that characterize this group. Of one thing we may be certain, however; there is no Jewish race, if we restrict the word *race* to its biological meaning. There are many Jewish people who do not have the type of nose, for instance, that is a criterion of the group in the popular imagination, and there are many non-Jews who do have that particular nasal form. As a matter of fact, in the Jewish group one will find all kinds of noses, all shapes of heads, a wide range of pigmentation, various sorts of stature, blond and brunette hair colors, a diversity of hair types, and blue and brown eye color. There are even synagogues of black Jews.

If they are not a race then, are the Jews a religious group? Are they not a group such as Methodists, Christian Scientists, or Hindus? Not entirely, for there are among the Jews atheists and agnostics as well as converts to Roman Catholicism and to the various Protestant denominations. Religion has been the identifiable bond that has held the Jewish group together through the centuries, and continues to be a cohesive force today. Nonetheless, many who are not religiously devout still possess a strong feeling of identification.

Nor is it correct to regard the Jews as a nation. They were a nation at one time in the past; and more recently there has been the re-establishment of the state of Israel. However, this nation also has Arab, Moslem, and Christian inhabitants and does not include the millions in other lands who regard themselves as Jews.

Therefore, we see that it is difficult to define the Jews, or to determine exactly what the essential criteria are for inclusion in that group. Perhaps it is *the consciousness of being a Jew* that is crucial. However unsatisfactory this concept may be as a definition, it approaches the reality of the situation to say that Jews are people who think of themselves as Jews and are treated by others as being Jewish, regardless of their physical features, language, or nationality.

Even in Israel the question is a perennial one. According to Jewish religion, a Jew is one whose mother is Jewish or who has converted to Judaism. Members of the Israeli cabinet have repeatedly disputed this definition, and one-time Prime Minister Ben Gurion has even suggested that "being a Jew is so difficult that anyone professing to be one should be believed."

The matter became a major issue in Israel when a certain Oswald Rufeisen, who had been born and raised a Jew in Europe, but who had joined the Roman Catholic Church and become a Carmelite monk, sought to enter Israel as an immigrant. Brother Daniel, as he had come to be known, was extended the privilege of seeking naturalization, but he rejected that offer on the grounds that he was a Jew, and that the law states: "Every Jew has the right to Israeli citizenship." The case was taken to the Supreme Court, where it was debated at great length, and a decision was finally reached after several years. The majority of the justices rejected Brother Daniel's claim, declaring in substance that one cannot be both Jewish and Christian at the same time. The highest court upheld a decision of the cabinet to the effect that "A person who in good faith declares himself to be a Jew and does not belong to another religion shall be registered as a Jew." [4]

Current Use of the Term "Race"

A wide variety of human groups are commonly referred to as races, including the English, French, Arabs, Jews, Gypsies, Irish, Scots, Welsh, Basques, Indians, Nordics, Eskimos, blacks, Hindus, Latins, and Celts. Obviously, these groups are not comparable or similar, and yet they are all frequently spoken of as races. In current use, then, we find that the term *race* is applied in the most general sense to the following kinds of groups and categories:

1. The citizens or subjects of a particular nation, state, or country. Thus the British and the Japanese are often designated as races. Nation or state would doubtless be more appropriate terms.

2. Those who speak a certain language or type of language. The Latins, Irish, and English are examples of this use of the word *race*.

A Sikh preacher addressing an audience in the Golden Temple, the most sacred shrine of the Sikhs, in Amritsar, India

3. A religious group. The Hindus, Sikhs, and, to some extent, Jews are illustrations of this use, or misuse, of the term.

4. A caste. One often hears the expression "the Gypsy race." The Gypsies are, admittedly, a strange group; neither a nation nor a religion, they are certainly not a race. The term *caste* would better describe them.

5. A local population, which has become fairly uniform by reason of its isolation, for example, the Cornish people or the Basques.

6. A hypothetical "pure" type that is assumed to have existed in the distant past, such as the Nordic or the Germanic.

7. A recognizable type, such as the Arab, the American Indian, or the Eskimo. The Arabs, for example, are not a nation, for there are several Arab nations. Nor are they a religion, for even though most of them are Moslem, there are also Christian Arabs, and there are Moslems who are not Arabs.

8. One of the major biological divisions of mankind, such as the Mongoloid, the Caucasoid, or the Negroid.

9. A race-conscious group or what Dr. Robert Redfield has aptly called "the socially supposed races." Examples are the American blacks, the Mexicans, and the Japanese-Americans. Such groups do possess certain visible, physical marks, which set them apart and which tend to enhance their feeling of group solidarity and uniqueness.

10. A group having a common culture and traditions. Some of these groups have, in the past, been nations, such as the Scots; others aspire to become nations.

This list does not by any means exhaust all the current uses of the word *race*. It is apparent, however, that race is a vague, ambiguous term. All kinds of groups and categories of people are designated as races, whether the bond that holds them together be biological or cultural, hereditary or acquired.

Such vagueness offends the sensibilities of scholars and scientists, who try to give definite and precise meanings to the words they use. Accordingly, many of them have proposed that we discontinue altogether the use of the word *race*. Many sociologists, feeling that the word *race* is too vague and misleading have chosen to employ such terms as *minorities, nationalities,* and *ethnic groups*.

The Biological Concept

Making the word *race* a strictly biological concept is easier said than done. To be sure, people have always shown a disposition to classify themselves and others. The most primitive tribes recognize the difference between *we* and *they*; even lower animals, including insects, make a distinction between those who belong and those who do not. The earliest people of whom we have records seem to have classified mankind into such categories as infidels and faithful, lost souls and saved, bond and free, civilized and savage, Greeks and barbarians.

The idea of classifying human beings on the basis of skin color, hair form, and other biological features that we call "racial" seems, however, to be a rather modern practice. The origin of the word *race* is not known. Many authorities suspect that it is of Semitic origin, coming from a word that some translations of the Bible render as "race," as in the "race of Abraham," but that the Authorized Version translates as "seed" or "generation." Other scholars trace the origin to the Czech word *raz*, meaning artery or blood; others to the Latin *generatio*, or the Old French *generace*, or the Basque *arraca* or *arraze*, referring to a male stud animal. Some trace it to the Spanish *ras*, itself of Arabic derivation, meaning head or origin. In all these possible sources the word has a biological significance that implies descent, blood, or relationship.

Whatever its origin, we do know that the word entered the European languages at a relatively recent date. *Razza* makes its appearance in Italian literature in the fourteenth century. It occurs first in the French language in 1684, where there is a reference to "especs ou races d'homme," meaning stem or family. In 1696 Leibnitz used the word for the first time in the German language. Its first appearance in English dates from 1570, where we find "the race of Abraham" mentioned in Fox's *Book of Martyrs*. In 1667 Milton refers to the "race of Satan" in his *Paradise Lost*.

Why did Europeans begin to become so conscious of race in the sixteenth and seventeenth centuries? Why did they begin then to pay so much more attention to hair and skin color, and to attach so much more significance to these physical attributes than they had ever done before? Why did the racial features of individuals take on so much importance that a new word was needed in the European languages? It has been suggested that the introduction of the word *race*, and the thought-content it conveys, is bound up with the rise of nationalism. When people began to think of themselves as belonging to groups known as nations, something other than a mere political bond was necessary to hold them together. It has always been one of the main preoccupations of statecraft to establish, develop, and regulate group sentiment among the multitudes composing the nation or state. Now the blood relationship bond is one of the oldest in human history. Huxley and Haddon believe, therefore, that the concept of race served to transfer to the new aggregate of the nation some of the age-old sentiment and loyalty that had hitherto been devoted to family, clan, and other blood groups. Not only nations, but various human associations such as religious bodies and fraternities, also attempt to appropriate some of this age-old family sentiment and feeling of solidarity by employing such terms as brother, father, mother, and sister. Others think that the concept of race helped the white Europeans justify to their own satisfaction their exploitation of strange peoples whom they encountered when Europe began to expand to all the corners of the earth.

Whatever the reason for the popularity of the race idea, the fact is that Europeans began to give thought to the subject and began to classify the peoples of the earth on a racial basis. Perhaps the first to do so systematically was the French traveler Bernier (1625–1688). Human beings, he decided, fell into the following categories:

1. Inhabitants of Europe, North Africa, and parts of Asia. (Bernier noted that Egyptians and Indians were somewhat dark, but he attributed this fact to the climate.)
2. Africans: "thick lips, flat nose, black skin, scanty beard, woolly hair."
3. Asiatics: "broad shoulders, flat face, small squab nose, little pig's eyes deep set, and three hairs of beard."
4. Lapps: "little stunted creatures, with thick legs, large shoulders, short neck, face elongated immensely, very ugly, and partaking very much of the bear."

He was undecided about American Indians and South Africans.

In 1745 Swedish botanist Carl Linnaeus began the system of racial classification by proposing that there were four races in the world. He based this classification on pigmentation and what he thought were each group's behavioral characteristics. He proposed the following:

1. *Europaeus albus:* "lively, light, inventive, and ruled by rites."
2. *Americanus rubesceus:* "tenacious, contented, free, and ruled by custom."
3. *Asiaticus luridus:* "stern, haughty, stingy, ruled by opinion."
4. *Afer niger:* "cunning, slow, negligent, and ruled by caprice."

The first use of comparative anatomy in an attempt to delineate various races was used by German physiologist Johann Friedrich Blumenbach in 1781. His classification was based on head shape and he divided humans into five races (Caucasian, Negro, Mongol, Malayan, and American Indian). Modifications of this classification and new ones proposing different races on other criteria followed.

Blumenbach's scheme became very popular, and has survived to this day, inasmuch as one occasionally hears of the five races—white, black, brown, yellow, and red.

Innumerable others have followed these pioneers. There was the French scientist Cuvier, who derived mankind from the three sons of Noah, Japhet being regarded as the progenitor of the Caucasian, Shem of the Mongolian, and Ham of the African. The divergence of these types is not explained, except that Ham's blackness was attributed to Noah's curse. Then there was Bory de St. Vincent, who, in 1827, chose the type of hair as the chief criterion, and produced a two-fold division of human beings (1) Leiotrichi, or straight-haired, and (2) Ulotrichi, or woolly-haired.

These, and the host of others who tackled the same problem, seem to have arrived at no satisfactory answer. Nonetheless, two principles of classification have emerged from their efforts. First, certain human differences have proved to be of no value in making biological classifications of human beings. Among these are hair form, nasal index, and the others. This means that dividing *Homo sapiens* into racial categories is a somewhat arbitrary affair. Some scientists will make a twofold division, some a threefold, some a fivefold, or more. The problem is more complicated than that of the teacher who, at the end of the year, is required to divide his students into categories designated A, B, C, D, and F, the arbitrary nature of such divisions being obvious to every teacher and to most students. The customs of the institution determine for the teacher how many categories will exist, but this is not the case with the scientist constructing racial categories.

Another difficulty arises from the fact that the various racial criteria are independent of one another. In other words, any form of hair may occur with any skin color; a narrow nose gives no clue as to the amount of pigment or the texture of the hair of the individual. Thus the Australian aborigines have dark skins, and broad noses, but an abundance of curly to wavy hair; and the Asiatic Indians have much pigment in their skins, but have narrow noses and straight hair. This gives no end of trouble to the classifier. If people are assorted on the basis of color, all kinds of noses, hair, and head forms will appear in the category; and if head form is selected as the major criterion, an equally diverse, but different, aggregation of physical types is incorporated within the pigeon-hole.

It must also be pointed out that the racial traits that scientists use are not biologically important, but are secondary and incidental human characteristics. A narrow head is not one whit inferior to a round head; a Mongoloid eyefold does not make for a less efficient eye; woolly hair is no handicap in the biological struggle for existence. As a matter of fact, human beings, along with several other mammals, have lost most of their hairy covering, and it would not be fatal, or even serious, if they were to lose the rest of it.

There are still other difficulties in handling the racial criteria on which the classification of human beings is based. There is the disturbing fact that these physical features, while hereditary, are not immutable, but are plastic and changing; moreover, they are not immune to environmental influences and human manipulation.

More recently, F. B. Livingston has voiced the view that there are no races, only what he calls *clines*. The clines are simply various combinations of adaptive features that are geographically distributed. For example, skin color gets darker as we move from north to south; hair gets less woolly as we go from Africa across India to northeast Asia; faces become less flat and noses more pointed as we go from northern Asia to Europe. This classification is mainly a denial that races are distinct, discrete units.[5]

We should also point out that there is great genetic variation within each population. For many traits, the variation may overlap widely between groups that could be called separate races. Consequently, we find very light-skinned blacks and dark-skinned Caucasians or flat-nosed Europeans and pointed-nosed Asians.

Let us summarize this discussion of the biological concept of race by venturing the following propositions:

1. The term *race*, as used by most biological scientists, refers to a set of categories rather than to discrete, invariable entities. Races are not so much real things that have been discovered as they are pigeonholes that have been constructed. These categories, to be sure, are based on clusters of hereditary, physical characteristics.

2. No classification yet proposed has won universal acceptance by scientists. Whatever the system of classification, there are many groups that will not fit into the proposed categories.

3. The criteria on which racial classifications are based are nonadaptive, physical, secondary, and have little survival value. Certain societies, however, have come to attach great social significance to these biological trivia.

4. Most of these racial criteria are phenotypically continuous rather than discrete; they overlap; they are dynamic, not static; and most of them can be transmitted independently of one another. These facts make racial classification an appalling and difficult, if not an impossible task.

Race and Culture

Some of the difficulty with the term *race* arises from the fact that people do not make the proper distinction between that which is biological and hereditary, on the one hand, and that which is learned and acquired, on the other. No one denies that we come into the world devoid of political convictions, religious affiliations, recreational interests, and literary tastes. We *learn* all of these things, and we learn them from those with whom we associate. If it be the American society into which we are born, the probability is that we will acquire an interest in football rather than bull fighting, baseball rather than cricket, bridge and poker rather than mahjong. It is a safe bet, too, that we will learn to speak English rather than Romansch, that we will affiliate with a Christian church rather than a Buddhist, Shinto, or Hindu temple, and that our political activities will follow those of the American pattern rather than those of Brazil, Bulgaria, or Thailand. In short, we are born, ignorant and helpless, into a group that possesses a great body of knowledge, beliefs, attitudes, laws, customs, traditions, and skills. We proceed immediately to imitate and acquire these group habits of thought, feeling, and behavior; and the members of the group, at the same time, set about to indoctrinate us with those behavioral patterns that they regard as being right, proper, and natural. The term *culture* is used by social scientists to designate the complex of learned behavioral patterns that are characteristic of the members of a group.

Much of what a person becomes is a result of the culture into which he or she happens to be born. Individuals, however, are not simply carbon copies of their cultures, for if that were true, then all the members of a society would be identical. A culture is a rich and complex phenomenon, and no individual acquires all of any group's culture. Even the simplest societies known to anthropologists possess an amazingly complicated pattern of behavior. Our culture, of course, is far beyond the powers of any single person to encompass. With this in mind, we should have no difficulty realizing that a culture is something that can be carried and perpetuated only by a group of people, some members of which are privileged to carry more of it than others.

Certain parts of a culture are acquired and followed by nearly all members of a society. We have our prohibitions against incest, our dislike for cannibalism, our habit of driving on the right, using the English language, and wearing clothing. Folkways and mores of this type, which apply to all members of a society, Linton has called cultural *universals*. [6] There are other customs, however, that afford us some range of choice; these are known as *alternatives*. Most of us usually eat our meat cooked rather than raw; but we may broil, roast, or bake it, and prefer it rare, medium, or well done, and still remain within the bounds of convention. Finally, there are the *specialties*, or those patterns of behavior that are restricted to certain persons in the society. Thus the Boy Scouts acquire knowledge, skills, and customs that others do not bother to learn; Masons and Elks have traditions known only to themselves; and lawyers, doctors, and soldiers have their own peculiar vocabulary, ethics, and techniques that are strange and incomprehensible to engineers and priests — and sometimes to each other. Here, then, is another reason the members of a society are not "a mob of unnecessary duplicates," as Herman Melville once cynically remarked.

Finally, we come into the world with certain characteristics that we have inherited, and that we do not have to learn. We have a certain type of blood, about which we have no choice whatever. We do not have to be taught to sneeze, to blink our eyes, or to make our hearts beat. Nor do we have control over our skin pigment, type of hair, nose width, or eye color. These are all the products of the genes we inherit from our parents. The genetic make-up of an individual, then, is fixed at the time of conception; while this make-up is somewhat variable, depending on the internal and external environment experienced by the individual, the degree and extent of this variability are definitely limited. Hence a person retains throughout life those features acquired through heredity.

It is not so with cultural characteristics. These may be changed a number of times during a lifetime. It is no easy matter for individuals to change the culture they have acquired, but it can be done. Thus they may learn a new language and forget the language of their childhood; they may forsake their religion and become converted to another; and they may change their nationality any number of times.

Personality, therefore, is a product of several interacting factors — the physical environment in which individuals develop, the biological characteristics they bring into the world, the culture into which they are born and in which they live, and the unique experiences to which they are subjected. These factors make it possible for an infinite variety of personalities to develop, with the result that no two individuals are identical.

We may recognize the fact, then, that each individual has a unique personality, and we may insist that it is unwise and unfair to lump people together and to "think of them in bunches." Despite their differences, however, people do form themselves into groups on the basis of a wide range of interests. Also, we make classifications of categories of people, since it is obviously impossible always to think of the 3 billion human inhabitants of this earth as unique individuals.

Human beings possess so many qualities and traits that there is no limit to the possible classifications to which they are susceptible. We may group them according to their religious affiliations, their political beliefs, their economic status, the language they speak, or the occupations they follow. We may classify them, too, as freshmen, sophomores, or juniors, depending upon the academic credit they have accumulated, by fair means or foul. A university will use certain criteria for classifying the people with whom it deals; the army will use still other criteria; and psychiatrists, merchants, physicians, and politicians will select those traits and make those classifications that suit their respective purposes.

The general feeling among scientists is that, for all its ambiguity, the word

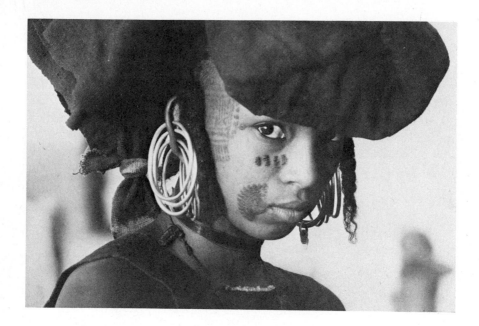

race — like sex — is here to stay. They consider the solution of the problem to lie not in discarding the word as Barzun and others propose, but in divorcing it entirely from all associations with cultural, political, linguistic, and religious characteristics, and rigidly restricting it to a biological meaning. To that end, numerous definitions of the word race have been made. One of the best is the following, formulated by Krogman:

A race is a sub-group of peoples possessing a definite combination of physical characters, of genetic origin; this combination serves, in varying degree, to distinguish the sub-group from other sub-groups of mankind, and the combination is transmitted in descent, providing all conditions which originally gave rise to the definite combination remain relatively unaltered; as a rule the sub-group inhabits, or did inhabit, a more or less restricted geographical region. [7]

When we use the word race, most of us are not thinking of the biological categories constructed by the anthropologists, although it would perhaps be helpful if we would all fall into that habit. Instead, however, we probably have in mind one or more of the other kinds of groups mentioned earlier in this chapter. We are thinking of the British, Japanese, Jews, Gypsies, or Arabs. To refer to some of these groups as races is unpardonable. No informed person would designate as a race a group that more properly should be called a state, a religion, or a linguistic family. Only the unenlightened, for example, will believe that there is an Aryan or a Latin race. There is no justification for our speaking of the Russians or the British as a race. Whatever they are, Jews, Gypsies, and Chinese are certainly *not* races. But what about American blacks, Indians, Mexicans, and Japanese-Americans? Are not these races, and are not their problems racial problems? Certainly these groups are not identical with the categories devised by the biological scientists. They have occasionally been described as the "so-called races" or the "socially supposed races."

To avoid the confusion, some sociologists have proposed that the word *race* be restricted to the biological concept discussed previously, and that other terms be used for the so-called races. Some will enclose the word *race* in quotation marks — "race" — when they are forced to use it, thereby somehow absolving themselves of the guilt of using so ambiguous an expression. The literature abounds in new concepts and phrases, adopted in the hope that thereby the phenomena with which the sociologist is concerned will be set apart from those encountered in the biological fields. Let us examine a few of these terms.

Intergroup Relations

In some quarters the expression *intergroup relations* has supplanted the older and more familiar expression *race relations*. It *is* important that we distinguish between a category and a group. *Category* simply denotes that several objects are *thought of* together, are classified together because of some point of similarity. There need be no contact or even proximity between the objects themselves. Thus fiction is a category under which we think of a great variety of books; but the books may be organized into an infinite number of categories — according to size, color, language, content, and so on. People, too, are continually being thought of in categories, based on health, age, sex, marital status, income, size of family, and cause of death. *Group*, on the other hand, denotes interactivity, interstimulation, interaction. It consists of any number of people who are bound together by the fact that they hold in common at least one *interest*. The members composing a group need not be in close contact; their relations may be indirect and transferred over a long range. Gypsies, Arabs, Hindus, Jews, American blacks, then, are indeed groups. So are the Scots, the British, the Canadians, and the Portuguese. So, too, are the Elks, Floridians, Californians, Bostonians, and the American Medical Association. The members of these groups all think of themselves as *we*, and speak of outsiders as *they*. They regard themselves as a group, however tight or tenuous the bonds may be, and they are considered to be a group by those on the outside.

The colorless term *group*, therefore, avoids some of the pitfalls inherent in the word "race." However, the difficulty with group, is that it is *too* broad a term. Sociologists who study so-called race relations are not concerned with the relations of *all* kinds of groups. They are not investigating the relations among nations (although these are groups), nor the relations among college football teams, between Catholics and Protestants, or between the Smiths and the Joneses. Only the relations among *certain kinds* of groups concern us here.

Minority

Another term that sociologists have adopted, in preference to race, is *minority*. Literally, of course, minority means simply the smaller number. Accordingly, the number of minority groups is infinite (the Prohibition Party, chess players, and the admirers of Picasso's art), and all of us belong to many minorities. Sociologists, however, have restricted the term to certain kinds of groups, have divested it of all statistical meaning, and have selected discrimination and exclusion from full social participation as the essential characteristics. Thus Wirth defines a minority as "a group of people who, because of physical or cultural characteristics, are singled out from the others in the society in which they live for differential and unequal treatment, and who therefore regard themselves as objects of collective discrimination."[8]

Some sociologists have objected to this definition because the word *minority* has a clear-cut numerical connotation. Bierstadt believes that majority-minority relationships are indeed relevant for understanding prejudice. However, it is wrong to conclude that the victims of prejudice are always members of minority groups. There are many minority groups that are not discriminated against, and some majority groups have attracted vicious persecution. For example, sociologists, millionaires, and horse-racing enthusiasts are all minorities in the American population, but they hardly suffer discrimination on that account.[9]

Wirth in his definition, speaks of "physical and cultural characteristics" and not of gender, age, disability, or undesirable behavioral patterns. It is obvious that he is referring to racial and ethnic groups in his definition of minorities. However, some writers have suggested that many other groups are also in the same position as the more commonly thought of minorities and endure the same sociological and psychological problems as the more traditional examples. In this light women, homosexuals, adolescents, the aged, the deformed, the radical right, and intellectuals have been written about as minority groups.

One interesting example of this type of approach is found in Jerry Farber's book, *The Student as Nigger*. Farber's assumption is that: "Students are niggers. When you get that straight, our schools begin to make sense." Farber reaches this conclusion after looking at the organization of the college environment. Students usually have separate and inferior dining facilities, they are politically powerless, but are given a toy government, "run for the most part by Uncle Toms and concerned principally with trivia." The students are expected to know their place, call the faculty member "Sir" or "Professor," and smile and shuffle as they stand outside the professor's office waiting for permission to enter. Farber sees school as a twelve-year course in how to be a slave.

Thus the term minority also has a number of problems and may be no better than the original concept of race.

Ethnic Group

An ethnic group is a human group bound together by ties of cultural homogeneity. Complete uniformity, of course, is not essential; but there does prevail in an ethnic group a high degree of loyalty and adherence to certain basic institutions such as family patterns, religion, and language. The ethnic group often possesses distinctive folkways and mores; customs of dress, art and ornamentation; moral codes and value systems; and patterns of recreation. There is usually some sort of object to which the group manifests allegiance, such as a monarch, a religion, a language, or a territory. Above all, there is a consciousness of kind, feeling of association. An ethnic group may even regard itself as a race, a people with a common ancestry; but the fact of such common descent is of much less significance than the *assumption* that there is a blood relationship, and the *myths* that the group develops to substantiate such an assumption. Ethnic groups, of course, are not all alike, and none would embody all the features we have enumerated. Some will emphasize certain of these characteristics to the exclusion of others. Religion may serve as an important object of allegiance to one and be of little import to another. Furthermore, ethnic groups are dynamic. The folkways may change, the institutions become radically altered, and the object of allegiance shift from one trait to another, but the sentiment of loyalty to the group and the consciousness of belonging remain as long as the group exists. An ethnic group may or may not have its own political unit; it may have had one in the past, it may aspire to have one in the future, or its members may be scattered through existing states. Political unification is not an essential feature of the group. The term, accordingly, would include such groups as Arabs, French Canadians, British Canadians, Welsh, English, Flemish, Walloons, Scots, Jews, and Pennsylvania Dutch. The Soviet Union itself is composed of more than a hundred ethnic groups, including, for example, Polish, Kazak, German, Armenian, Georgian, Tartar, and Ukrainian.

Those who feel that the term *ethnic group* should be substituted for race can support their position with a number of reasons. One advantage to making the substitution is that it would leave all questions of definition open. Ashley Montagu claims that the term "refers specifically to human populations which are believed to exhibit a certain degree, amount, or frequency of undetermined physical likeness or homogeneity. It is a vague term which can be used to avoid some of the difficulties of race."

Another advantage is that this term avoids the belief that humans are merely the result of their biological heredity. The term implies that humans are cultural beings as well as biological organisms and leads us to conclude that it would be wrong to think only in physical terms. As human populations have developed, there have been a wide variety of prescriptive and prohibitive regulations concerning marriage and breeding. Certain groups have been forced to marry each other while others have been forbidden from doing so. This situation has had a significant effect on the evolution of ethnic differences and Montagu believes that these are exactly the kinds of factors that are neglected by those who insist on biological definitions.[10]

We cannot hope, in one chapter, to rescue the word *race* from the slough of confusion into which it has fallen with centuries of misuse. Nor do we feel that the word can be discarded, for the literature of sociology, anthropology, psychology, to say nothing of the language of the layman, abounds in an infinite number of such expressions as *race differences, race relations, race problems, race riot,* and *race prejudice.* To substitute another term appears to be impossible. However, we can bear in mind that race has both a biological and a social meaning, and that it is the latter that takes precedence in the affairs and thinking of most of us. When sociologists speak of race relations, the reference is not to the biological categories of the anthropologists, but to those human groups that may perhaps be more accurately designated as racial and ethnic *groups.* When sociologists do use the word *race* (as we must in the following chapter) we would prefer to insert "so-called" before it, if that were not so clumsy a device.

Notes

1. W. G. Sumner, *Folkways*, p. 13.

2. R. H. Osborne, *The Biological and Social Meaning of Race*, pp. 15–16.

3. See B. Berry, *Almost White*.

4. *The Israel Digest* 5, no. 26 (21 Dec. 1962): 4–5.

5. Osborne, *Meaning of Race*, p. 6.

6. R. Linton, *The Study of Man*, pp. 272–275.

7. W. M. Krogman, "The Concept of Race," in R. Linton, ed., *The Science of Man in the World Crisis*, p. 49.

8. L. Wirth, "The Problem of Minority Groups," in Linton, *The Science of Man*, p. 347.

9. R. Bierstedt, *The Social Order*, p. 479.

10. A. Montagu, *Man's Most Dangerous Myth: The Fallacy of Race*, pp. 441–444.

Chapter Three
Race Differences

I went to the University of Chicago for a
while after the Second World War. I was a
student in the Department of Anthropology.
At that time, they were teaching that there
was absolutely no difference between anybody. They may be teaching that still.

— *Kurt Vonnegut, Jr.* Slaughterhouse Five

It is all very well to say that human beings are the same everywhere, that we are
"brothers under the skin," that we are members alike of one species, that "there
is only one race, the human race." Moreover, these statements are basically
true and do not represent mere sentiment and wishful thinking. Our likenesses
are infinitely more numerous than our differences. Hence a medical student
may learn about anatomy from a black corpse, and then go out to practice on
Caucasians, Mongolians.

There is no denying, however, that racial and ethnic groups are different.
Some peoples are very tall, some short, and some are pygmies. Some are
famed for their production and appreciation of music, while others are barely
interested in it. Some are warlike and show great esteem for martial achievement, while others are unfamiliar with warfare altogether and take pride in
their peaceful pursuits. With some, religion and other spiritual values are paramount, while with others these concerns are of little consequence. Crime
rates are by no means identical for all groups, and in the United States the Japanese, Chinese, and Jews can boast of their good records in this regard. Certain groups have earned a reputation for the sensitivity and acuity of their visual and auditory powers, others for their musical or athletic prowess, and
still others for their scientific and intellectual achievements. It is commonly

believed, that some groups are lazy and improvident; some, aggressive and ambitious; some, emotional and impulsive; some, reserved and stoical. Races are generally thought to have their distinctive odors, to differ in their moral laxity or rectitude, and to be far apart temperamentally, physically, and intellectually.

The crucial problem, however, is this: To what extent are these differences the result of hereditary, biological factors and to what extent are they learned, acquired, and cultural? Popular opinion has always insisted that such common characteristics are "in the blood." Thus Jews are inherently aggressive and mercenary; Indians, naturally stoical and furtive; blacks, cheerful and improvident; British, humorless; and Italians, volatile. Others, without denying that groups are different, have maintained that blood and heredity do not provide the proper key to understanding those differences. John Stuart Mill said, "Of all vulgar modes of escaping from the consideration of the effect of social and moral influences on the human mind, the most vulgar is that of attributing the diversities of conduct and character to inherent natural differences."[1] The distinguished sociologist, E. A. Ross, put it this way: " 'Race' is the cheap explanation tyros offer for any collective trait that they are too stupid or too lazy to trace to its origin in the physical environment, the social environment, or historical conditions."[2]

The differences among racial and ethnic groups have always fascinated people, and the factors causing these differences have long been a subject of debate and speculation. Herodotus, the "Father of History," wrote about the problem in the fifth century B.C., no doubt to the great delight of his fellow Greeks. The following is taken from one of his books:

On the field where a battle was fought I saw a very wonderful thing which the natives pointed out to me. The bones of the slain lie scattered upon the field. . . . If you strike the Persian skulls, even with a pebble, they are so weak that you break a hole in them; but the Egyptian skulls are so strong, that you may smite them with a stone and you will scarcely break them in. They gave me the following reason for this difference, which seemed to me likely enough: The Egyptians from early childhood have the head shaven, and so by the action of the sun the skull becomes thick and hard. The same cause prevents baldness in Egypt, where you see fewer bald men than in any other lands. . . . The Persians, on the other hand, have feeble skulls, because they keep themselves shaded from the first, wearing turbans upon their heads.[3]

Aristotle, a century later than Herodotus, was convinced that some races are born to be masters, and others, slaves; he reasoned that it was entirely proper and natural that the superior Greeks should govern the barbarians. Aristotle believed that the physical and temperamental differences among races could be traced back to climate:

This is a subject which can be easily understood by anyone who casts his eye on the more celebrated state of Hellas, and generally on the distribution of races in the habitable world. Those who live in a cold climate and in Europe are full of spirit, but wanting in intelligence and skill; and there they retain comparative freedom, but have no political organization, and are incapable of ruling over others. Whereas, the natives of

Asia are intelligent and inventive, but they are wanting in spirit, and therefore they are always in a state of subjection and slavery. But the Hellenic race, which is situated between them, is likewise intermediate in character, being high-spirited and also intelligent. Hence it continues free, and is the best-governed of any nation, and if it could be formed into one state, would be able to rule the world.[4]

The Greeks also speculated about the origins of races in the legend of Phaethon, the son of Helios. According to this legend, Phaethon persuaded his father to let him drive the sun chariot. Being inexperienced, Phaethon drove the chariot too close to the earth in some regions, burning the people there black, and drove it too far from the earth in other regions, causing the inhabitants there to turn white from the cold.[5]

Leonardo da Vinci had a similar theory on the origin of races. He believed that all humans are similar and that racial differences are due to environmental differences. People born in hot climates are black because they find the cool nights refreshing and work then, while people in the northern climates are light because they work during the day.[6]

In early Chinese thought there are ideas that are explicitly racist. In the writings of the Han dynasty of the third century we see a discussion of a yellow-haired and green-eyed barbarian people in a distant province "who greatly resemble monkeys from whom they are descended."[7]

Christianity has been notoriously responsible for the persecution of the Jews. The prejudice spread by Christian societies was very similar to modern racism and portrayed the Jews as a group that had physical and moral defects that were passed on from one generation to the next. It was believed that Jews suffered from diseases of the blood that did not affect Christians. The Jews could only cure themselves of these diseases through the use of Christian blood — the basis for the charge of ritual murder. Jewish men were thought to menstruate. Jewish children were thought to be born with their right hands attached to their heads, a condition that required surgery at birth. Consequently, their right hands were blood stained from birth.[8] Ironically all of these genetic defects were cured should a Jew convert to Christianity.

Science and Race Differences

It has only been somewhat more recently that scientists have turned their attention to this perennial problem of race differences. And the task has proved to be a most difficult one, far more complicated than the philosophers, militarists, and even ordinary people ever supposed it to be. The obstacles that scientists must overcome to answer the question are numerous and baffling. First of all, they need to know what a race is and that, as we saw in the preceding chapter, is itself a major problem. How can we generalize about blacks until we decide who belongs to the race? Should the Australian aborigines be included, as some insist? Or do they belong with the Caucasians, as others maintain? Or do they constitute a separate race of their own? Again, it is manifestly wrong to draw conclusions about the black race on the basis of studies made of American blacks, a group that includes people who are very light skinned, and millions of others with varying admixtures of Indian and European blood.

Yet that problem, so far insurmountable in itself, is only one of many. Suppose that we could agree on our races and that we could establish the high prevalence of some particular characteristic in one of those races. Would we then be able to prove a causal relationship? Blacks suffer from tuberculosis more than the whites do, but the authorities know that social conditions are primarily responsible for the prevalence of the disease although they are not prepared to rule out the racial factor entirely. Syphilis, too, has not the same frequency for all races, but here again genetic differences may be of no significance whatsoever. On the other hand, sickle-cell anemia is virtually confined to blacks, a fact that can hardly be explained by environmental conditions. The American Indian's susceptibility to trachoma, and the black's high resistance to it, may well be partly due to their racial affiliations. Cancer is far more serious for whites in all parts of the world than it is for blacks, Chinese, Indians, and others. It is known, however, that mortality from cancer is related to occupation, climate, the proportion of aged people in the population, and so on. This is not to say that race is *not* a factor, but that the extent of its influence is difficult to define and has not yet been reliably determined.

A great deal of evidence, although not enough, has been collected on group differences with respect to blood pressure, pulse, basal metabolism, reaction time, glandular functioning, odors, smell, hearing, vision, and the like. The results invariably show that the groups tested are not identical, but the interpretation of the results is no simple matter. Blood pressure, for instance, reflects wide variation, on the average, from Europeans and Americans at one extreme, to Hindus, Filipinos, Japanese, and Chinese at the other. Some have supposed, therefore, that race is a factor in systolic blood pressure. However, we know that there are other influences, including diet, climate, exercise, and emotional disturbances. There is abundant evidence, too, that the total pattern of the culture, and its tempo, are significant. Studies have shown that Americans who have moved to the Orient and have lived there long enough to acquire some of its spirit have experienced a lowering of blood pressure. The same is true for sense perception, visual and auditory sensitivity, the sense of smell, and other matters. The differences, such as they are, are more likely the result of cultural conditioning and training.

The Question of Racial Superiority

The problem of the physiological and pathological differences among racial groups has been greatly overshadowed by the debate on the question of superiority and inferiority. This problem has existed at least since the time of Aristotle. Each group, if it thinks about the matter at all, invariably reaches the conclusion that it is superior, and finds evidence of a sort to support its claim. Some writers have attributed the superiority of their people to favorable geographical influences, but others incline to a biological explanation. The Roman Vitruvius maintained that those who live in southern climates have a keener intelligence, due to the rarity of the atmosphere, whereas "northern nations, being enveloped in a dense atmosphere, and chilled by moisture from the obstructing air, have but a sluggish intelligence." A certain Ibn Khaldun argued that the Arabians were the superior people, because their country, although in a warm zone, was surrounded by water, which exerted a cooling effect. Bodin, in the sixteenth century, found an astrological explanation for ethnic group differences. The planets, he thought, exerted their combined and best influence on that section of the globe occupied by France; the French, accordingly, were destined by nature to be the masters of the world. Needless to say, Ibn Khaldun was an Arab and Bodin, a Frenchman. The Italian, Sergi, regarded the Mediterranean peoples as the true bearers of civilization and insisted that Germans and Asiatics only destroy what the Mediterraneans create. In like manner, the superiority of Nordics, Alpines, Teutons, Aryans, and others has been asserted by those who were members of each of these groups, or thought they were.

The question of the native endowment of the races (or racial and ethnic groups) has been approached from many angles, but principally the anatomical and the historical.

The Anatomical Approach

It has been argued that the various races are not equally advanced in the evolutionary scale, some being much closer to the brute ancestors of human beings than others. Some claim that whites are the most human, while blacks are the most simian. Proponents of this theory will point to the receding forehead of blacks and to their prognathous jaw and broad, flat nose to prove that there is a close relationship to the ape. However, the physical traits that reverse this order of kinship are conveniently overlooked. Consider the texture of hair. Blacks, with woolly or frizzy hair are farthest removed from the apes, who have straight, coarse hair. The same is true for the quantity of hair; the relative hairlessness of blacks makes them most unlike the other primates, and places hairy Caucasoids closest of all. The black's thick, outrolled lips, too, are in sharp contrast to the thin, grayish, mobile lips of the apes. As to the shape of the head, the apes are inclined to be brachycephalic, the blacks, dolichocephalic. It is obviously impossible, then, to arrange the races in any evolutionary order, for none proves, on close examination, to be consistently more simian than the others. (See Table 3.1.)

The size of the brain, too, has been offered as evidence of the superiority of certain races. Many measurements of cranial capacity have been taken, and some racial or ethnic groups average higher than others. The Scots, for instance, average 1478 cc; the Dutch, 1530; the Swiss, 1546; and the Parisians,

Table 3.1   Human racial types ranked according to subhuman primate characteristics

	Most simianlike	Less simianlike	Least simianlike
Cephalic index	Asian	European	African
Cranial capacity	African	. . . .	Asian
			European
Eye color	African, Asian	. . . .	European
Nasal index	African	Asian	European
Hair form	Asian	European	African
Hair length	European	. . . .	African
	Asian		
Body hair	European	. . . .	African
			Asian
Lip form	Asian	European	African
Lip color	Asian	European	African
Facial prognathism	African	European	Asian
Eye form	European	. . . .	Asian
	African		

From E. A. Hoebel, *Anthropology: The Study of Man*, 3rd ed. (New York: McGraw-Hill Book Co. 1966), p. 225.

1559.   At the other end of the scale, the primitive Hottentots average only 1317 cc; the Australian aborigines, 1347; and the Tasmanians, 1406. Caucasians generally are found to have larger brains than blacks — a fact that racists have seized upon and taken to indicate that whites have superior intellectual powers.

There are many objections, however, to drawing such a conclusion. For one thing, the averages we have just noted fail to reveal the wide range that prevails in each of the groups measured. The Scots, for example, range from 1230 to 1855; the Swiss, from 1250 to 1930; and the Hottentots, from 1183 to 1620. Moreover, the preliterate Eskimos have an average of 1535, and a range of 1418 to 1624; and other peoples of simple culture, such as the Polynesians, Chukchee, Kaffirs, and Javanese can boast of a large cranial capacity. If we followed the reasoning of the racists, we should have to acknowledge the Eskimos as our intellectual superiors, and even the extinct and primitive Neanderthal man would rate as our equal, perhaps even our superior. In short, the mere size of the brain appears to give no indication of the capacities or achievements of ethnic groups, any more than it does for individuals within any particular group.

The Historical Approach

A common-sense, pragmatic approach to the problem of racial quality would seem to lie in a consideration of the achievements of the various races. Certainly, not all of them have produced great civilizations, developed vast empires, made important contributions to the world's culture, and given birth to geniuses, artists, inventors, explorers, and conquerors. "Look at the record," say the racists, and it will be obvious that not all groups are equally gifted. "By their fruits ye shall know them," they repeat with pride and satisfaction. The Australian aboriginal, hugging a campfire trying to keep warm, is ignorant of agriculture, architecture, metals, domesticated animals, writing, and arithmetic and can hardly be considered as the equal of a member of the races that have produced skyscrapers, machinery, television, jet planes, symphonies, and penicillin.

This habit of reasoning from performance to potentiality betrays an ignorance of the history of culture, a lack of perspective, and a misunderstanding of the dynamics of civilization. In the first place, we have no good standard by which to measure achievement. We insist, of course, that all people be judged by those things in which *we* excel. We are proud of our machines, our science, and our power, but we fail to see that not all peoples envy us, nor would they agree to use these as criteria of excellence. We would not come out so well in proving our superiority if our opponents insisted on using as criteria, not science and machines, but ability at sand painting, physical endurance, complexity of grammar, multiplicity of taboos, respect for the aged, ability in hunting, closeness to nature, fear of the deity, reverence for the soil, freedom from authority, disregard for material goods, absence of neuroses, or peace of mind. The fact is that no racial or ethnic group excels in all things, but each has its own interests and values, goals toward which it strives, and channels into which its efforts are directed.

In the second place, the very civilization in which we take pride and to which we point as proof of our superiority is not entirely the product of our genius. Most of it, in fact, we have taken over from others. We are not alone, to be sure, in our readiness to appropriate the inventions and discoveries of others, for every culture is largely a medley of borrowed elements. The students of the history of culture have dealt a blow to our ethnocentrism by proving a foreign origin for many of our most cherished possessions. Thus it can be shown that we Americans owe much to the Chinese, from whom we have learned about silk, paper, porcelain, tea, lacquerware, kites, umbrellas, screens, fans, goldfish, azaleas, chrysanthemums, camellias, papier mâché, grapefruit, soybeans, ephedrine, and many other articles that have become integral parts of our civilization.

In the third place, a reasonable regard for the perspective of time will deflate the claims of the racists. The Sumerians might well, at one time, have pointed to their civilization as proof of their superior blood, and asked why the peoples of Europe had never risen above their barbarism. Three millenia ago the Egyptians might have used the same argument to prove their superiority to the primitive Greeks; and the Romans, a thousand years later, might have invoked precisely the same argument to prove their superiority to the northern Europeans. As a matter of fact, they did exactly that, for in a letter to Atticus, Cicero said; "Do not obtain your slaves from Britain because they are so stupid and so utterly incapable of being taught that they are not fit to form a part of the household of Athens."

The civilization of a people, accordingly, is hardly a trustworthy clue to their intellectual quality. It is a product of many factors — historical, environmental, accidental — and the sheer size and density of the population would have something to do with it. Race, however, on close inspection appears to be of little or no consequence.

Racial Theories in Europe

A well-formulated theory of racial differences did not develop in Europe until modern times, which is not to say that racial myths and race prejudices were unknown to Europeans. They just needed someone to come along and provide them with an eloquent theoretical justification for their prejudices. Count de Gobineau, who has been labeled as the "father of modern racism," was this individual. Gobineau rejected the principles of the French Revolution and was strongly opposed to the democratic philosophy of the Revolution. To him the idea of a brotherhood of man was a vain and empty dream based on a fallacious belief in the equality of man. Gobineau's theory can be broken down into a few main ideas.

Special Race Characteristics

For Gobineau there were three races: the white, the black, and the yellow. The qualities ascribed to the white race included an energetic intelligence, perseverance in the face of great obstacles, great physical strength, and a natural tendency for political organization and stability. The Aryan branch of this race was the highest form of human being and was supposedly found in greatest abundance among the Germans.

While whites were the highest on Gobineau's racial hierarchy, the black people were the lowest. They were supposedly marked by an animal nature and a severely limited intellect. They possessed great energy, will power, sensuality, and instability of mood. He claimed that blacks were immoral, with little concern for their own life and the lives of others.

The yellow race was superior to the blacks, but was apathetic, lacked physical strength, and was uncreative but law abiding.

Race Mixing and Decadence

Gobineau was not totally against race mixing as one might expect from a superficial knowledge of his ideas. In fact, he felt that civilization only occurs when two races mix. Art and government were aspects of civilization that no one race could produce by itself. In terms of physical beauty, the best combination was created by a mixing of blacks and whites. The problem was that civilization led to more and more mixing of "inferior blood" with the "great race" and it inevitably would become more bastardized and decadence would follow. One of the chief weaknesses of the white race was its susceptibility to miscegenation.[9]

What Gobineau was trying to do was offer an explanation for why civilizations rise and fall. If race mixing is seen as the only variable, then steps must be taken to stop it. Certainly the belief in democracy would have to be stopped since it would lead to massive race mixing, the elimination and degeneration of the white race, and the ultimate destruction of civilization. As part of the inevitable destruction, Gobineau foresaw a lowering in human intelligence, and he once remarked to de Tocqueville "I am convinced that the present enfeeblement of mind is not only universal but also incurable."[10]

While Gobineau was against egalitarianism and democracy, he presented no analysis of possible societal improvements that would help in warding off the destruction. He was basically a pessimist and saw no real remedy for what he believed to be the inevitable destruction brought about by race mixing. For example, he looked upon the immigration to North America as an extreme case of the degeneration of the human race and wrote the following in his *Essai*:

They are a very mixed assortment of the most degenerate races of olden-day Europe. They are the human flotsam of all ages: Irish, cross-bred Germans and French, and Italians of even more doubtful stock. The intermixture of all these decadent ethnic varieties will inevitably give birth to further ethnic chaos. This chaos is in no way unexpected or new; it will produce no ethnic mixture which has not already been, or cannot be realized on our continent. Absolutely nothing productive will result from it, and even with the ethnic combinations resulting from infinite unions between Germans, Irish, Italians, French and Anglo-Saxons join in the south with the racial elements composed of Indian, Negro, Spanish and Portuguese essence, it is quite unimaginable that anything could result from such horrible confusion but an incoherent juxtaposition of the most decadent kinds of people.[11]

Those currently reading this book in the United States are the future generation of "the most decadent kinds of people" that Gobineau was writing about.

The Englishman Housten Chamberlain expanded on Gobineau's theory.

He concluded that: "Physically and mentally the Aryans surpass all other men; therefore they are by right the masters of the world. While some men are markedly superior to others, others are somewhat less than human."[12]   Chamberlain's father was an admiral in the British navy and he had three uncles who were high-ranking officers in the army. However, he came to detest everything British and renounced his citizenship to become a citizen of Germany. They alone had "the uncompromising character, the sense of absolute justice, the impelling will to triumph over all circumstances."[13]   Chamberlain's main contribution to racist thinking was the view that the Germans represented the supreme human race that had contributed practically everything of significance to human progress. Consequently, Germans had a right not only to dominate the universe, but also to maintain racial purity.

By this time Gobineau, who was Chamberlain's predecessor in racist thinking, had societies established in his honor all over Germany. Chamberlain, meanwhile, arranged for a personal meeting with Hitler in 1925, which resulted in both men being greatly impressed with each other. Hitler expanded on Chamberlain's and Gobineau's ideas, and published them in his book, *Mein Kampf*. The culmination of this line of thought was the destruction of millions of people. We will refer to this tragic event in human history again in a later chapter.

Racial Theories in the United States

The racial theories of Europe clearly influenced the thinking in the United States. However, if we backtrack a bit and return to the period of the American Revolution, we will see how deeply entrenched racist thinking was before Gobineau's or Chamberlain's writings reached this country. Thomas Jefferson is recognized as an individual who strongly disapproved of slavery and is well known for writing in the Declaration of Independence that "all men are created equal." Yet in his "Notes on Virginia" (1786) he states his reasons for believing that the "Negro" is condemned by nature to an inferior status. He began by noting that blacks were ugly and had "a very strong and disagreeable odor." Then he went on to comment on the inferior moral and mental characteristics of blacks: "in memory they are equal to whites; in reason much inferior," and "in imagination they are dull, tasteless, and anomalous." He concluded "that the blacks, whether originally a distinct race, or made distinct by time and circumstance, are inferior to the whites in the endowment both of body and of mind."[14]

Most of the racial thinking in the United States grew out of contact with and speculation about blacks; Indians were focused on to a lesser degree. The discussion centered around whether all humans were part of the same species and therefore related to each other, or whether separate species of humans existed, of which blacks represented a distinct and inferior example. This theory of the polygenic origin of the races could have supplied the South with an excellent rationale for the defense of slavery. If blacks were a separate species of human beings, then they could be labeled as inferior and the treatment they received could be justified due to genetic difference. In fact, it could then also be argued that blacks were not really human and thus did not deserve to be vested with the same rights. In the literature of the period we find eloquently phrased arguments by blacks trying to prove that members of their race are, in fact, human. The following, written by Frederick Douglass in 1854, is an excellent example.

A very recondite author says that "man is distinguished from all other animals in that he resists as well as adapts himself to his circumstances." He does not take things as he finds them, but goes to work to improve them. Tried by this test, too, the Negro is a man. You may see him yoke the oxen, harness the horse, and hold the plow. He can swim the river; but he prefers to fling over it a bridge. The horse bears him on his back — admits his mastery and dominion. The barnyard fowl know his step, and flock around to receive their morning meal from his sable hand. The dog dances when he comes home, and whines piteously when he is absent. All these know that the Negro is a MAN. Now presuming that what is evident to beast and to bird cannot need elaborate argument to be made plain to men, I assume, with this brief statement, that the Negro is a man.[15]

Monogenic Origin of Races

On the other side, there was the view that all human races were descended from Adam and Eve. The problem for the South in accepting the polygenic argument was that they would have to reject this Biblical pronouncement, and Southerners balked at such a clear rejection of the scriptures.

The monogenists believed that all races had a common origin and that differences in color, body form, and intelligence were the result of adpatations to the environment over many generations. The monogenists did not accept the existence of pure races; instead they hypothesized that relatively permanent, distinct varieties of humans existed who were environmentally suited to different regions of the world. These localized differences were maintained through restricted mating.

Even with a belief in the single origin of the races, the monogenists were not egalitarians. The races, during centuries of development, had acquired characteristics that made it impossible for the monogenists to consider them all as being equal. Nothing seemed to contradict the assumption that blacks were anything but inferior. The Jeffersonians may have argued that all men were born equal; however, this provided no argument for the monogenists to believe

Liberian mother and child

that the races had remained equal. John Bachman, a major proponent of the monogenic argument, concluded that "we have been irresistibly brought to the conviction, that in intellectual power the African is an inferior variety of our species. His whole history affords evidence that he is incapable of self-government." [16] This supposed inferiority made it necessary for whites to support and protect blacks.

During the decades before Darwin, almost all of the racial theorists in Europe and America espoused racial differences and racial inferiority whether they believed that the races had a common origin or were created separately.

The Influence of Darwin

What ended the monogenist-polygenist debate was, of course, Charles Darwin's *The Origin of Species*. Darwin left no doubt that all races belonged to a single species. He wrote:

Although the existing races of man differ in many respects as in color, hair, shape of skull, proportions of the body, etc., yet if their whole structure be taken into consideration they are found to resemble each other closely in a multitude of points. Many of these are so unimportant or of so singular a nature that it is extremely improbable that they should have been independently acquired by aboriginally distinct species or races.[17]

The believers in the monogenic origin theory believed in a literal interpretation of the Bible. Darwin not only claimed that all humans were related, but also claimed that humans were related to the animals as well, through evolution. While the monogenic theorists were willing to accept the view that all humans were related to the white race, they were hardly ready to accept the whole animal world too.

Darwin showed that one species could give rise to another through natural selection and that all of evolution had been a process of the survival of the fittest. The greatest controversy arose from Darwin's assumption that humans had actually evolved from the apes.

The theory that the process of evolution resulted primarily from conflict and competition among the species, which culminated in the "survival of the fittest" and the disappearance of the unfit, had a great attraction to those who believed in the inequality of the races. In his later work, *The Descent of Man*, Darwin concluded that "At some future period, not very distant as measured by centuries, the civilized races of man will almost certainly exterminate and replace the savage races throughout the world."[18] Darwin's ideas gave rise to a new type of racial thinking. With the concept of the survival of the fittest, it could now be claimed that the inferior races were those that were unable to compete in the white world. Those who lost out in the struggle for existence were inferior specimens who were poorly adapted to their environment. The survivors were clearly of a superior stock.

Darwinism, by implying the disappearance of the "lower races," made the prospect of the extinction of blacks and Indians seem like a regrettable necessity of evolution rather than a tragedy due to white racism. Social Darwinism became a justification for policies of repression and neglect, particularly in light of the supposed failure of blacks during Reconstruction. "If blacks were a degenerating race with no future, the problem ceased to be one of how to prepare them for citizenship or even how to make them more productive and useful members of the community. The new prognosis pointed rather to the need to segregate or quarantine a race liable to be a source of contamination and social danger to the white community, as it sank ever deeper into the slough of disease, vice, and criminality."[19]

The Effect of the Eugenics Movement

Shortly after Darwin, a new science of heredity called eugenics developed in Europe, and the work of Gregor Mendel received great attention. Mendel's work demonstrated that certain characteristics could be transmitted from one generation to another. This process was governed by certain laws unrelated to the external life of the organism.

Sir Francis Galton, who was England's leading Darwinian scientist at the time, had been engaged in studies dealing with the inheritance of all sorts of human abilities and deficiences. Galton launched the eugenics movement, which was intent on bringing about human improvement through genetic control. Galton looked upon eugenics as both a science and a religion. He started to speak with evangelical fervor for the uplifting of humanity by breeding from the best and restricting the offspring of the worst. The betterment of society could only take place, he said, by improving the genetic qualities of the human race.

The old typological notion of there being superior species of humans was combined with Darwin's notions of natural selection (an idea suggesting that change in the species could be achieved by differential reproduction) to form the eugenics movement. Thus many scientists redirected their research toward a program of social salvation through selective breeding.

Suddenly genetics became a science and researchers were interested in showing that practically everything was inherited. Among the things that were considered to be inheritable were musical ability, pauperism, drunkenness, and criminal behavior. (Many people today still think of these things as being inheritable.) This new emphasis on genetic determination was very comforting to those people who were not paupers or drunkards, because they assumed that they and their children were safe from such unwelcome fates and obviously came from superior stock.

Effect on Immigration

Proponents of the eugenics movement were horrified at the immigration of large numbers of families from southern and eastern Europe. These families were often both large and poor. The eugenicists felt that the immigration of these "degenerate breeding stocks" would lead to the downfall of civilization. Madison Grant's purpose in writing *The Passing of the Great Race* was to alert Americans to this danger. Grant believed that the Nordic race was far superior to any other race and was the one on which the nation had to depend for "leadership, courage, loyalty, self-sacrifice and devotion to an ideal." Grant wrote:

. . . that the specializations which characterize the higher races are of relatively recent development, are highly unstable and when mixed with generalized or primitive characters tend to disappear. Whether we like to admit it or not, the result of the mixture of two races in the long run, gives us a race reverting to the more ancient, generalized and lower type.[20]

Grant suggested a number of remedies for the evils of race degeneration. First of all, the country had to strengthen the laws against miscegenation. He urged that the fit be encouraged to have more children and the unfit, fewer. Those individuals who had deficiences that could be passed on to their children had to be sterilized. For some, sterilization would not be enough. "The laws of nature require the obliteration of the unfit and human life is valuable only when it is of use to the community or race," he wrote. A "mistaken regard for what we believed to be divine laws and a sentimental belief in the sanctity of human life," is what is preventing us from doing what is necesary to save mankind.[21]

Grant's book did not come out until 1916 and, while well received, it did not have a great influence at the time because the United States was about to enter the war in Europe. The main thesis of *The Passing of the Great Race* was immigration restriction. However, immigration had declined to neglible numbers because the war made transportation by ship an unavailable alternative for aspiring immigrants. Consequently, it was not until after the war that Grant's ideas received great support.

Once the war had ended and immigration resumed, the campaign for restricted immigration gained power. Congress began a series of hearings on the issue. These hearings were packed with eugenicists who came to testify on the genetic inferiority of a large proportion of the immigrants who were entering the United States. It was claimed that these people were genetically incapable of adjusting to a free democratic society and that their children would also be incapable of doing so.

The Immigration Act of 1921 was set up under a "national origins quota." This quota limited the number of immigrants admitted from any European country to 3 percent of the immigrants from that country who were living in the United States in 1910. The law was considered as being too liberal and was changed in 1924 to 2 percent of the immigrants in the United States in 1890. This change favored the older immigrant stocks, such as the English, Irish, German, and Scandinavian, over the southern and eastern Europeans, who were newer immigrants. In addition, the Japanese were excluded altogether.

President Coolidge, on signing the bill, stated that "America must be kept American." Senator David A. Reed, who introduced the Senate version of the bill, explained that "the races of men who have been coming to us in recent years are wholly dissimilar to the native-born Americans."[22]

Extreme racist thinking continued through the 1920s and into the 1930s and was fueled by the academic community. Psychologists and geneticists were the leading spokesmen and proponents of the view of the superiority of the Nordic race. When it became clear that Hitler was exterminating vast numbers of people and when German refugee scientists came to the United States, a change started to take place. Then race became a negative concept and pamphlets and books appeared in the 1940s claiming that there really were no important differences among the human races. The whole attitude of the scientific community became one of antiracism and antieugenicism. Those who have grown up since the 1940s have come to accept this as the typical attitude of academics. In the late 1960s and in the early 1970s the old racist attitudes of a certain segment of the academic community came to the fore again. Several scientists tried to legitimize the belief in the inferiority of certain races. This fact comes as a great surprise to many people, but it is less surprising if we review the history of academic attitudes toward race, nationality, criminality, and poverty. As a result of the horrors of Nazi Germany, there was a temporary twenty-five year reversal in racist thinking. The race and intelligence debate is the latest branch of the eugenics movement and will be explored in the next chapter.

Notes

1. J. S. Mill, *Principles of Political Economy*, vol. 1, p. 390.

2. E. A. Ross, *Social Psychology*, p. 3.

3. Quoted in A. L. Kroeber and T. T. Waterman, *Source Book in Anthropology*, pp. 3–7.

4. T. F. Gossett, *Race: The History of an Idea in America*, p. 6.

5. Ibid.

6. Ibid., p. 16.

7. Ibid., p. 4.

8. Ibid., p. 11.

9. M. D. Biddiss, *Father of Racist Ideology; the Social and Political Thought of Count Gobineau*, p. 120.

10. Ibid., p. 174.

11. Gobineau, *Essai sur l'inégalité des races humaines par le comte de Gobineau*, pp. 852–853.

12. Cited in J. Newman, *Races: Migration and Integration*, p. 56.

13. Gossett, *History of an Idea*, p. 349.

14. Ibid., pp. 42–44.

15. F. Douglass, "The Claims of the Negro Ethnologically Considered" in H. Brotz, ed., *Negro Social and Political Thought, 1850–1920*, p. 229.

16. Gossett, *History of an Idea*, p. 63.

17. Ibid., p. 67.

18. G. M. Frederickson, *The Black Image in the White Mind*, p. 230.

19. Ibid., p. 255.

20. Gossett, *History of an Idea*, p. 359.

21. Ibid., p. 360.

22. Ibid., pp. 406–407.

Chapter Four
Race and Intelligence

Many comparisons depend upon tests, but
they also depend upon *our* intelligence, our
good will, and our sense of responsibility to
make the proper comparison at the proper
time. . . .

— *J. A. Fishman et al. "Guidelines for testing minority group children"*

Since 1969 the academic community and the public have been engaged in an extended and often emotionally charged debate over the relationship between intelligence and race. Several academics have become closely identified with each side of the issue and in this chapter we hope to clarify their respective positions. As we saw in the last chapter, the discussion of racial differences has been quite extensive both in Europe and the United States. Have the modern day eugenicists come up with some new findings or are today's studies simply more sophisticated versions of the old arguments?

So-called mental tests were first introduced in the United States in the 1890s. The first use that was made of these tests was to determine if there were any differences that could be correlated to race. Psychologist R. M. Bache tried to measure the quickness of sensory perception and compared twelve whites, eleven Indians, and eleven blacks. The Indians had the fastest reactions, the blacks were second, and the whites were the slowest. However, these results did not stop Bache from proclaiming that the test had proved that whites were the superior group. He maintained that they "were slower because they belonged to a more deliberate and reflective race than did the members of the other two groups."[1] While these tests were not yet intelligence tests, the pattern of proving white superiority and black inferiority had already begun before the IQ concept was even developed.

In 1905 Alfred Binet and Theodore Simon working in France developed a series of tests that were designed to measure intelligence. These tests were to be used to distinguish among various levels of feeblemindedness. The concept of mental age was also introduced so that children could be compared with others of the same age group. Three years later the tests and the mental-age concept were refined further and a second Binet-Simon scale was introduced. Even in these early days of intelligence testing Binet and Simon admitted that environment and educational opportunity would invariably affect the scores and concluded that the tests would only be appropriate for comparing children from closely similar environments.[2] However, many psychologists ignored the warning and looked on the tests as measures of hereditary intelligence that were virtually unaffected by the environment.

In 1912 William Stern introduced the intelligence quotient, which is popularly referred to as IQ. This score was obtained by comparing a person's mental age with the actual chronological age. All the pieces were now present for comparing the average IQs of the various racial and ethnic groups.

When Binet died, the intelligence-testing research laboratories were moved to the United States and came under the control of psychologist Lewis Terman. In 1916 the Stanford-Binet scale was introduced and the idea that intelligence could be expressed in numbers began to intrigue not only the psychologists, but the general public as well.

It will be remembered from the last chapter that Madison Grant's book, *The Passing of the Great Race,* also appeared in 1916. Intelligence and the lack of it had been common themes in racist arguments. Now the eugenicists were allied with a powerful school of psychologists to develop an impressive array of what appeared to be "positive and objective proof" of the superiority of one race over another. The well-known psychologist E. L. Thorndike observed that with sufficient research we would be able to determine what innate differences existed in the intelligence of the various races. He assumed that this could lead to the development of a scale that would rank the various races on the basis of this trait.[3]

When the United States entered the war in 1917, Robert M. Yerkes was asked to devise a series of tests to determine the intelligence and general aptitude of the men entering the armed services. More than 1,700,000 men were tested. Dr. Yerkes concluded that the tests proved the intellectual inferiority of blacks. Furthermore, this conclusion was "in the nature of a lesson, for it suggests that education alone will not place the negro race on a par with its caucasian [sic] competitors."[4]

Carl C. Brigham took alpha and beta test information from the army records and analyzed it further. To Brigham it was a foregone conclusion that blacks had a lower IQ than whites. What he was primarily concerned with was comparing the average IQ scores of the various immigrant groups with each other and against the native-born population. First, he categorized the foreign born according to how many years they had been in the United States. The five groups that were established were based on the number of years spent in the

Talmud religious school for immigrant children in New York City's Lower East Side

country: (1) five years or less, (2) six to ten years, (3) eleven to fifteen years, (4) sixteen to twenty years, and finally (5) twenty years or more. Brigham was surprised to find that the average IQ scores increased with the number of years spent in residence so that immigrants who had been in the country twenty years or more had an average IQ that was the same as the native-born population. The immigrants who had been here the least amount of time had the lowest IQs. Most people would not consider these results to be particularly surprising and would conclude that a person's mastery of the language and familiarity with American culture would improve relative to the length of time spent in the United States. These factors, in turn, would certainly help to raise a person's IQ score. However, Brigham viewed the results differently and concluded:

Instead of considering that our curve indicates a growth of intelligence with increasing length of residence, we are forced to take the reverse of the picture and accept the hypothesis that the curve indicates a gradual deterioration in the class of immigrants . . . who came to this country in each succeeding year period since 1902.[5]

Table **4.1**   Percentage of immigrants from each country who exceed the average native-born American in IQ

Country	Percentage	Country	Percentage
England	67.3	Belgium	35.3
Scotland	58.8	Austria	28.2
Holland	58.1	Ireland	26.2
Germany	48.7	Turkey	25.3
Denmark	47.8	Greece	21.3
Canada	47.3	Russia	18.9
Sweden	41.7	Italy	14.4
Norway	37.3	Poland	12.2

SOURCE: Carl C. Brigham, *A Study of American Intelligence* (Princeton: Princeton University Press, 1923, © 1922 by Carl C. Brigham), p. 210.

According to Brigham, the new immigrants were really less bright than those who had arrived during the earlier years of immigration. Although such an analysis might be dismissed today, this study was used as evidence to prove that the more recent immigrants were of a poorer genetic stock than the earlier arrivals.

Brigham also analyzed the results to show what percentage of the immigrants from the various countries exceeded the average IQ of native-born Americans. If 100 is considered as the average IQ, then Table 4.1 supposedly tells us the percentage of immigrants from the various countries that scored above this number. The implication in the table is that the superior immigrant groups are at the top of the list and the least desirable ones, at the bottom.

Brigham's study led him to the conclusion that extensive action was necessary to save the United States from inevitable decline. The "defective immigrants" would mate with the native population and bring about a general lowering of intelligence.

According to all evidence available, then [,] American intelligence is declining, and will proceed with an accelerating rate as the racial admixture becomes more and more extensive. The decline of American intelligence will be more rapid than the decline of intelligence in European national groups, owing to the presence here of the Negro. These are the plain, if somewhat ugly, facts that our study shows. The deterioration of American intelligence is not inevitable, however, if public action can be aroused to prevent it. There is no reason why legal steps should not be taken which would insure a continuously progressive upward evolution.

The steps that should be taken to preserve and increase our present intellectual capacity must of course be dictated by science and not political expediency. Immigration should not only be restrictive but highly selective. And the revision of the immigration and naturalization laws will only afford a slight relief from our present difficulty. The really important steps are those looking toward the prevention of the continued propagation of defective strains in the present population. If all immigration were stopped now, the decline of American intelligence would still be inevitable. This is the problem which must be met, and our manner of meeting it will determine the future course of our national life.[6]

In many ways these views are very similar to those of Gobineau that we discussed in the last chapter. The end of Brigham's statement hints that even more extensive measures are needed to stop the decline of American intelligence since so many of the "defective" strains are already in the country. Whether these measures should include deportation, sterilization, or extermination is left to the imagination of the reader. In any event, the extremely restrictive Immigration Act of 1924 was passed one year after Brigham's book was published.

Race, Intelligence, and Heredity

There are three key terms in the race and intelligence discussion that keep reappearing and it would be useful to define them. The first one is *race*, the concept of which has already been discussed in the last two chapters. The other two are heredity and intelligence. *Heredity* refers to individual characteristics that are passed on from one generation to the next through the genes. An individual may possess as many as 10 million genes. Countless numbers of genes would be involved in passing on such traits as intelligence or abstract thinking. *Intelligence* is a very difficult term to define. It is so difficult, in fact, that very recently psychologists still defined it as that which intelligence tests measure. In addition, there is considerable confusion over what intelligence tests are supposed to measure. Three major traits have been mentioned by various researchers.

Some claim that intelligence tests measure the potential to do well in school. Comparisons of school performance with intelligence test scores were first made by Binet. Today we still find that there exists a correlation between the scores and grades in school. Consequently, there is justification to assume that intelligence tests measure educability through traditional means.

Others have claimed that intelligence tests measure innate potential. The assumption here is that this potential exists before the individual interacts with the environment and sets the upper limit for what the particular individual can achieve in school and later life. Even among ardent racists it is difficult to find individuals who still believe that intelligence test scores are totally a product of innate genetic factors. Now the question that is being raised is, What percentage of the intelligence test score is genetically determined?

It has also been claimed that intelligence tests measure general intelligence, or the ability to benefit from experience and to engage in abstract thinking.

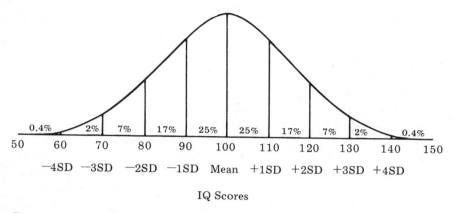

| 0.4% | | 2% | 7% | 17% | 25% | 25% | 17% | 7% | 2% | | 0.4% |

| 50 | 60 | 70 | 80 | 90 | 100 | 110 | 120 | 130 | 140 | 150 |

| | −4SD | −3SD | −2SD | −1SD | Mean | +1SD | +2SD | +3SD | +4SD | |

IQ Scores

Figure **4.1**   Normal curve showing the expected percentage of IQ scores within each range — percentages add up to more than 100 because of rounding. (SD stands for standard deviation.)

However, there is a problem in obtaining a valid measurement of this ability. An individual's intelligence can be broken down into verbal and nonverbal components, and we are able to devise tests that can measure just the social IQ, or the spatial IQ, or the numerical IQ. Consequently, the general intelligence score is really an average of the several abilities that are measured to get the IQ score.

One might rightly ask how there can be such a furor over the whole issue if we have not yet determined the actual definition of intelligence.

What Do Intelligence Test Scores Mean?

When we take data from the social sciences and plot them on a graph, we often find that they assume the shape of what has been called the *normal curve*. (See Figure 4.1.) People tend to think of any distribution that is bell shaped as forming a normal curve. However, there are some specific mathematical properties associated with such a distribution. The normal curve is usually broken down in terms of standard deviations from the mean. Figure 4.1 shows us that a fairly specific percentage of the cases usually fall between selected points on the curve. The normal curve can also be used to evaluate IQ scores. A score of 100 is the mean and each ten-point deviation from the mean is equivalent to one standard deviation. So by looking at the curve, we would know that an IQ score of 120 would be two standard deviations above the mean and would be a score that would be higher than the score achieved by 90 percent of the population.

While IQ scores approximate the normal curve, they do deviate very slightly

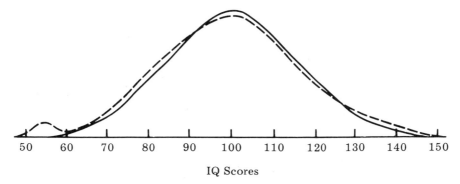

Figure **4.2**   Theoretical "normal" distribution of IQs (dark line) and actual distribution in population (broken line).

at the outer extremes and somewhat near the middle. This deviation is demonstrated by the curve shown in Figure 4.2, which is exaggerated slightly to make the point clear. The dark line represents the normal distribution; the broken line represents the actual distribution of scores in the population. There are more very low scores than would be expected in a completely normal distribution. There are also more scores at the upper end than would be expected. In addition, an excess of scores appears in the range from 70 to 90. However, aside from these minor differences, IQ scores do approximate the normal curve very closely.[7]

Arthur Jensen

The present-day race and intelligence controversy is an outgrowth of a paper written by the educational psychologist Arthur Jensen called "How Much Can We Boost IQ and Scholastic Achievement?," which appeared in the winter 1969 edition of the *Harvard Educational Review*.

Jensen first wrote about the inheritability of intelligence in a paper that was published by the National Academy of Science in 1967. Following the publication of this paper, he gave a talk in San Diego on how schools should be modified to take into account diverse mental abilities. In April of 1968, the editors of the journal *Harvard Educational Review* invited Jensen to write an article elaborating on the ideas presented in the San Diego talk.[8] Jensen accepted the invitation. As a result of the article, the press focused on the issue of race differences and IQ, and the furor began. The *New York Times Magazine* and *Life* quickly followed with popular versions of the article.[9]

Most of these popular versions played up the racial aspect of Jensen's article rather than his analysis of the interrelationship of heredity, environment, and intelligence.   The implication was that Jensen's main point was that blacks were genetically inferior to whites.   In many respects Jensen has become the most talked about and least read writer since Marx, a situation that has greatly contributed to the emotional fervor with which each side enters the discussion. For us to understand what the controversy is all about, we will briefly review some of the main points in Jensen's paper and leave the criticism of the ideas until later in the chapter.

Failure of Compensatory Education

Jensen begins his article with the line "Compensatory education has been tried and it apparently has failed."   He comes to this conclusion after completing a review of several nationwide studies of large federally funded compensatory education programs.   From this review he concludes that these special programs have produced no significant improvement in the intelligence or scholastic performance of the children enrolled.   He claims that if we continue to apply these same approaches, we will not be helping the disadvantaged students or the people paying for the programs.   Conseqently, we must question the assumptions, theories, and practices of these programs to find more fruitful approaches.   The programs he is referring to are those in which disadvantaged children are put in special educational environments in the hope that their intelligence test scores or school readiness will improve.

Jensen feels that the children have been blamed for the failure of these programs, when actually the schools should be held accountable.   The schools have not been tailoring their programs to take into account the problems of individual differences in developmental rates and diversity of learning skills. Instead the schools have assumed that all children are average in their mental capabilities, and hence have attributed the cause for any differences among them that might arise during the school years to cultural factors and home influences.   The compensatory programs have continued to be directed toward making up these environmental deficits as quickly as possible by providing appropriate experiences, cultural enrichment, and training in basic skills.[10]

Jensen does not advocate abandoning efforts to improve the education of the disadvantaged, but rather urges that an emphasis be placed on a diversity of approaches to discover the methods that work best.   While the conclusions that Jensen draws in this regard are critical, they are by no means very controversial. The real impact of Jensen's article begins with the next discussion.

Intelligence and Genetics

A large portion of Jensen's paper is devoted to proving that differences in intelligence are basically due to genetic differences and that environmental factors play a small role in the variance.   Jensen believes that an average of 80 percent of the variability in IQ scores can be attributed to genetic factors.[11]

Jensen tries to prove this point by examining studies of identical twins whose

Table **4.2**   Summary of studies of IQ correlations between related and unrelated individuals

Relationship	Number of studies	Average correlation coefficient
Unrelated persons		
Children reared apart	4	−.01
Foster parent and child	3	+.20
Children reared together	5	+.24
Blood relations		
Second cousins	1	+.16
First cousins	3	+.26
Grandparent and grandchild	3	+.27
Uncle (or aunt) and nephew (or niece)	1	+.34
Parent (as adult) and child	13	+.50
Parent (as child) and child	1	+.56
Siblings and twins		
Siblings reared apart	3	+.47
Siblings reared together	36	+.55
Dizygotic twins, different sex	9	+.49
Dizygotic twins, same sex	11	+.56
Monozygotic twins, reared apart	4	+.75
Monozygotic twins, reared together	14	+.87

Adapted from Arthur R. Jensen, "How Much Can We Boost IQ and Scholastic Achievement?" *Harvard Educational Review* 39 (Winter 1969), p. 49.

genetic development is theoretically the same since they both develop from a single fertilized egg.   In one study psychologist Sir Cyril Burt and geneticist J. A. Shields studied one hundred pairs of identical twins who had been reared apart from each other.   These separated twins were, on the average, only six points apart in IQ.   (Two people chosen at random from the population will be eighteen points apart.)   Jensen presents a summary of this type of information, which can be seen in Table 4.2, and believes that it provides strong evidence that IQ is basically genetic.   The more closely two people are related, the more similar their IQs will be and the higher will be the coefficient of correlation. (However, there is some recent evidence that has indicated that Burt's data may have been contrived.)

Jensen also deals with the relationship between socioeconomic status and intelligence.   It has generally been assumed that people in the upper classes have higher IQs than those in the lower classes.   Many people have claimed that this discrepancy is due to the enriched environment that accompanies higher incomes. However, from Jensen's article we are led to believe that the environmental influence is much smaller than we assumed and that the difference among the classes is genetic. Consequently, no matter what social class an adopted child is raised in, the child's IQ will be closer to that of the natural parents than to that of the adoptive parents.

Genetic and environmental factors are not necessarily in opposition to each other. Nor does their relationship represent an either-or proposition. Jensen believes that the critical issue is not whether a particular characteristic is due to heredity or environment, but rather what proportion of the characteristic is due to each factor. However, Jensen does believe that the variation in intelligence test scores of individuals is to a large extent due to genetic factors:

To be more specific, all major facts are comprehended quite well by the hypothesis that somewhere between one-half and three-fourths of the average IQ difference . . . is attributable to genetic factors and the remainder to environmental factors and their interactions with the genetic differences.[12]

Race Differences

If Jensen had confined his study to evaluating the faults of compensatory education or merely to showing that there was a strong genetic component in intelligence test scores, there would not have been such a great controversy over his monograph. However, Jensen proceeded into the area of race differences in IQ.

Jensen claims that groups that have been geographically and socially isolated from each other over many generations have different gene pools and are likely to exhibit differences in traits that are highly heritable. "These genetic differences are manifested in virtually every anatomical, physiological, and biochemical comparison one can make between representative samples of identifiable racial groups. . . . There is no reason to suppose that the brain should be exempt from this generalization."[13]

Jensen notes that there have been over four hundred major studies comparing the intelligence test scores of whites with those of blacks. The results indicate that "on the average, Negroes test about one standard deviation below the average of the white population in IQ, and this finding is fairly uniform across the 81 different tests of intellectual ability. . . ."[14]

To convince us further that the IQ difference between whites and blacks is genetic, Jensen notes that the IQ difference is still present even when social class differences are taken into account. Children of blacks in the highest income brackets have a lower average IQ than children of whites in the lowest income category. Jensen maintains that this finding cannot be explained by purely environmental theories or differences in prenatal and postnatal care.

Jensen also observes that the American Indian is more disadvantaged than blacks or any other minority group, for that matter. Indians have a lower average income, more unemployment, poorer standards of health care, shorter life expectancy, and higher rates of infant mortality than blacks. Yet their ability and achievement scores in the famous Coleman study of 1966 averaged half a standard deviation higher than the scores of blacks.[15]

These facts lead Jensen to conclude that:

. . . all we are left with are various lines of evidence, no one of which is definitive alone, but which, viewed together, make it a not unreasonable hypothesis that genetic factors are strongly implicated in the average Negro-white intelligence difference. The preponderance of evidence is in my opinion, less consistent with a strictly environmental hypothesis than with a genetic hypothesis, which, of course, does not exclude the influence of environment or its interaction with genetic factors.[16]

Jensen's Recommendations

Jensen believes that to bring about effective education we must first understand the mechanisms of effective education. To Jensen the disparity between black and that the difference between the average white and black IQ scores is due to equalizing educational opportunities is insufficient. He hopes that his work will provide the impetus for research and action in this area.

Jensen feels that the ideal of educational opportunity has to mean more than equality of facilities and teaching. Schools must provide a wide range of educational methods, programs, and occupational training. Rather than asking the children to fit into one type of educational system, the schools must be held accountable for adjusting to the various educational needs of a heterogeneous population. Educational failure can no longer be blamed on the children's inability to learn, but rather on the inflexibility of our educational structure.

Most of the proposals associated with the last part of Jensen's paper have been ignored. This may be due to the fact that the criticisms of the educational system are rather vague and very few specific proposals are offered as remedies. Instead, critics have assumed that Jensen's main goal was to show that the average IQ difference between whites and blacks is genetic. All of the attention has been focused on this area of the monograph

Reactions

Jensen's 123-page article was addressed to the academic community. Consequently, most people learned about his ideas through press interpretations or from other secondary sources. In this process numerous distortions, misstatements, and omissions occurred. Angry letters flooded editorial offices; Jensen was compared to Hitler and was accused of advocating all kinds of discriminatory policies.

Back at the University of California campus at Berkeley, Jensen was denounced and harassed by students and faculty members. Members of the Students for a Democratic Society disrupted his classes with heckling and bomb threats; two body guards had to be assigned to protect Jensen. The furor continues today and criticisms have been leveled against Jensen's paper for a number of reasons that we will explore shortly.

Hans J. Eysenck

Soon after Jensen's paper appeared, the psychologist Hans J. Eysenck focused further attention on the race and intelligence controversy with a generally subjective book designed to support the Jensen argument. He offers very little that was different from what Jensen presented in his monograph and generally does not do as good a job of presenting it.

Eysenck's main thesis is that intelligence is a highly heritable characteristic and that the difference between the average white and black IQ scores is due to genetic differences between the two races. In addition, Eysenck proposes that United States blacks are a nonrandom, lower intelligence sample taken from the African population. He reaches this conclusion for a number of reasons. First of all, he hypothesizes that the more intelligent members of the West African tribes would have managed to escape the slave traders, leaving the duller ones to be caught. In addition, he assumes that the tribal chiefs sold their less intelligent followers into slavery. Once the slaves were brought to the United States, the more intelligent slaves may have rebelled against their status and were killed as a result. Slave owners wanted dull submissive slaves who would be willing to work without thought or complaint. Eysenck claims that:

Thus there is every reason to expect that the particular sub-sample of the Negro race which is constituted of American Negroes is not an unselected sample of Negroes, but has been selected throughout history according to criteria which would put the highly intelligent at a disadvantage. The inevitable outcome of such selection would of course be the creation of a gene pool lacking some of the genes making for higher intelligence. [17]

Eysenck carries this idea of selective migration further to point out that other ethnic minorities in the United States also represent inferior specimens of the general population in their native country.

It is known that many other groups came to the U.S.A. due to pressures which made them very poor samples of the original populations. Italians, Spaniards, and Portuguese, as well as Greeks, are examples where the less able, less intelligent were forced through circumstances to emigrate, and where their American progeny showed significantly lower IQ's than would have been shown by a random sample of the original population. [18]

The fact that much of this reasoning is speculation does not stop Eysenck from treating it as if it were fact. We could have devoted an entire chapter to studies disproving these two passages we have quoted.

Eysenck believes that understanding the way in which intelligence is influenced by heredity is a prerequisite for developing educational programs for individuals with low IQs.   He maintains that a high IQ is essential for academic success and that it is unreasonable to disregard the importance of this fact:

It makes no sense to reject the very notion of such abilities as being important . . . and at the same time demand access to institutions closely geared to the view that such abilities are absolutely fundamental to successful study. [19]

Consequently, he is opposed to college and university programs that are geared to achieve proportional racial representation.

. . . even if there were no Negroes or other minority groups in a country, there would still be bright and dull children, and the problems posed by their existence would be equally great, although the emotion invested would perhaps be less. [20]

Eysenck is someone who makes a much greater effort to proclaim his nonracist intentions than Jensen ever did, but then proceeds to present information and interpretations that are more extreme than Jensen's.   Eysenck claims to be pained by having to delve into research that challenges his original assumption that no genetically determined differences exist between the races and then seems to enjoy speculating on the causes of these differences.

Richard Herrnstein

Harvard professor Richard Herrnstein became involved in the whole race and intelligence controversy by writing an article, "IQ," for the *Atlantic*.   He suggested that society was moving toward what he called a "hereditary meritocracy" in which social stratification was based on innate differences. [21]

Herrnstein's argument runs as follows.   First of all, mental abilities are inherited, and people close to one another in IQ tend to marry.   Secondly, success depends on IQ, and success produces financial and social advantages. The end result is that social status will be concentrated among those with high IQs.   Supposedly, this trend will become more prevalent as society becomes more egalitarian and artificial barriers and discrimination are eliminated. When that point is reached, natural ability will become the sole determinant of social rewards.

Herrnstein believes that the society of the future will be one in which intelligence will be more and more under the control of heredity.   Since social mobility is related to intelligence, it too will be controlled by heredity.   Consequently, those with high IQs will be concentrated at the top of the social-class ladder while those with low IQs will be at the bottom.   Therefore, the realization of our vision of an egalitarian society with no discriminatory barriers will result in a virtual caste system based on inborn traits passed on from one generation to the other.

Herrnstein points out that there is an ironic difference between the effects of a closed caste system and an open class system. Traditional castes are based on inherited characteristics and limit social mobility. Because of this, there is IQ heterogeneity at all levels, since many high-IQ people are restricted to lower castes, while many low-IQ individuals are maintained artificially at the top. In the open class system those with high IQs rise to the top of the class ladder, while those with low IQs stay at the bottom. Heredity plays an increasingly important role in the intelligence differences between those at the top and those at the bottom. Consequently, true social equality leads to inequality based on inherited traits.

Even though Herrnstein never discussed race, he has been accused of being a racist because of the argument he advanced. Critics are disturbed about the potential use of the argument to justify racial discrimination. There is concern that the privileged might use it to claim innate superiority over other segments of society.

The conclusion that causes the greatest problem is that wealth and power will be concentrated in a hereditary meritocracy based on mental ability. However, it could also be argued, as Noam Chomsky does, "that wealth and power tend to accrue to those who are ruthless, cunning, avaricious, self-seeking, lacking in sympathy and compassion, subservient to authority, willing to abandon principle for material gain."[22] These would be the traits that are inherited and would form the basis for the meritocracy.

A number of criticisms can be leveled against Herrnstein's views. The IQ scores of children do not exactly correlate with the scores of the parents. For example, two parents each having an IQ of 135 will not necessarily produce a child with an IQ of 135. Based on studies that have been conducted with high-IQ parents, a more accurate prediction is that the child's IQ would be lower than that of the parents in a reasonable number of cases. In this particular case, the IQ of the child would probably be closer to 120. Conversely, two parents with low IQs (say, 90) can produce a child with an IQ higher than that of either of the parents (105). Because of this situation the rigid caste system based on IQ with little mobility that Herrnstein envisions would not come about, since the upper segments will continue to produce offspring that are downwardly mobile while the lower segments will produce offspring that are upwardly mobile.

Herrnstein acknowledges that factors other than IQ, such as motivation and personality, also contribute to success or lack of it. A lower-class individual with a high IQ and an alcoholism problem, for example, may pass on genes for high IQ to a future generation, thus leading to upward mobility for that off-spring. In the same way, middle- or upper-class parents may produce high-IQ children with personality problems that cause them to be downwardly mobile. Consequently, fluidity would again be introduced into the social system and Herrnstein's premise would not hold up.

Finally, to accept Herrnstein's argument, we must assume that people work primarily for financial gain and that the satisfaction derived from a particular job is not a sufficient inducement for working. Just because the starting salary for a trash collector in New York City might be higher than that for an elementary school teacher does not mean that individuals with higher IQs will start to gravitate toward the first occupation as opposed to the second. Many people do not engage in their profession because it maximizes wealth, but because it may be interesting, challenging, or intrinsically rewarding. Consequently, Herrnstein's caste system would again break down because high-IQ individuals would still be distributed throughout the social classes because of selective employment.

William Shockley

William Shockley, a professor of engineering science at Stanford, is highly qualified in his specialty. In fact, he won the Nobel Prize as the coinventor of the transistor. However, he has little recognized expertise in the areas of race relations, genetics, education, or psychology, contrary to his claims. He takes a more extreme position than the other writers, since he speculates about discriminatory action while the others do not. Shockley has launched a one-man crusade to warn the country about the evils of "dysgenics," a term that refers to disproportionate mating among genetically inferior individuals. Shockley is of the opinion that the average IQ of the general population is going to continue to decrease because lower-IQ individuals have more children than higher-IQ individuals. The fact that this argument is an old one that has been disproved for a variety of reasons does not stop Shockley. Unlike any of the other authors mentioned so far, Shockley clearly states that blacks are genetically inferior and wants to do something about it. He proposes what he calls "thinking exercises" such as a voluntary sterilization program for genetically defective and low-IQ individuals. For example, Shockley proposes that we take individuals with IQs below the average and offer them $1,000 for each IQ point they are below 100 as an incentive to be sterilized.

Shockley's writings and statements are so unscientific and blatantly racist that he warrants very little attention from serious students of race and heredity. He has come to national attention because of the controversial nature of his views and his willingness to speak in public.

The fact that a Nobel Prize winner or others of outstanding academic backgrounds engage in what may seem like racist activities is not new. There is again ample evidence from history to indicate that members of the academic community have been all too willing to accept these types of arguments. We have already discussed the history of racist thinking in American academia. If we look at Germany during World War II, we find numerous Nobel Prize winners and internationally known scholars writing unscientific tracts to support the view that the Germans were genetically superior specimens of the human race while Jews were genetically inferior. For example, Philipp Lenard, who also won the Nobel Prize in physics, was one of the first scientists to become a follower of Hitler. He began to spread the idea that there were two types of physics — a pure type of German physics (*Deutsch Physik*), and a totally reprehensible type of Jewish physics represented by the work of Albert Einstein.[23]

Johannes Stark, another famous German physicist, won the Nobel Prize in 1919. At the inauguration of a Lenard Institute at the University of Heidelberg on December 13, 1935, Stark declared:

Jewish physics which . . . came into being during the last three decades and has been made and publicized both by Jews and by their non-Jewish pupils and imitators appropriately found its high priest in a Jew, in Einstein. Jewish advertising wanted to make him the greatest natural scientist of all times. Einstein's theories of relativity, however, in essence were nothing but a heaping of artificial formulae on the basis of arbitrary definitions and transformations of the space and time coordinates.[24]

The list of noted scholars who have taken extreme positions on racial questions in both the United States and the rest of the world is seemingly endless. We have chosen two fellow Nobel Prize winners in physics to show that Shockley's credentials are by no means unusual.

Criticisms

While we have already mentioned some of the faults in IQ research, we have left the real criticisms of the various theories of intelligence differences between whites and blacks until now. No doubt the reader has probably been able to suspect what some of the criticisms might be from the discussion so far. The following is a summary of the general types of objections that have been raised.

IQ as a Statistical Index

The various authors mentioned have tended to use the IQ score as if it were a behavioral entity, when in fact it is merely a statistical entity. In other words, the IQ score is merely a score that is used to summarize performance on a test. To begin with, there may be some severe problems with the applicability of the test to the population in question or with the conditions under which the test is being administered. This was clearly the case with the Army tests mentioned earlier that were administered to immigrants who were unfamiliar with the American culture and English language. If, for one reason or another, a test is not suitable for the population to which it is being administered, the resultant scores are going to be inaccurate and invalid. Even Jensen noted that when he worked in a psychological clinic and gave tests to children from an impoverished background, the children always seemed brighter than the tests would indicate. He then had the children come in on two to four different days and did nothing more than get acquainted with them.   As soon as the children seemed comfortable he tested them again.   As Jensen put it, "A boost of 8–10 points or so was the rule; it rarely failed . . ."   Just feeling comfortable with the examiner is in itself an important variable.

Intelligence is also a very complicated concept.   This fact became evident in our discussion about the difficulty in defining the term.   Intelligence can be broken down into several components, and each individual could receive scores for verbal IQ, nonverbal IQ, social IQ, and so on.   Therefore, the IQ measure that we are receiving is only a partial measure of the individual's total intelligence.   To be really accurate, we would need scores for the various types of intelligence.   Intelligence involves diverse mental abilities.   Intelligent behavior can be manifested in a wide variety of forms, with each individual having certain areas of intellectual strength and other areas of intellectual weakness.   For example, Stodolsky and Lesser did a study of four mental abilities (verbal ability, reasoning, number facility, and space conceptualization) among first-grade Chinese, Jewish, black, and Puerto Rican children.   Each group seemed to do better on one ability than on another.   The authors were able to conclude that ethnicity fosters the development of different patterns of mental abilities.   Consequently, a composite IQ score does not take into account these differences in mental abilities and may penalize those groups that are weak on abilities emphasized in IQ tests.[25]

Jensen has claimed that blacks have difficulty with the abstract thinking that is so necessary for a high IQ.[26]   Jazz music is clearly based on abstract forms. It is ironic that this art form that represents one of the blacks' main contributions to American culture is dependent on an ability that they supposedly lack.

Finally, we should also note that the IQ test is misleading because it implies that all intervals on the scale are equivalent; that is, a ten-point difference in a score at one point on the scale is the same as a ten-point difference at some other point on the scale.   This is not the case.   A difference of ten points between two people at the extremes of the scale may not be an indication of as great an intellectual difference as a ten-point difference between two people in the middle of the scale.   In addition, no one can really tell us what a five- or ten-point difference is really going to mean in terms of intellectual ability or educational performance.   Personality factors and motivation are important variables that cannot be ignored.   Herrnstein notes the danger in trying to draw far-ranging conclusions from the results of IQ tests.

An IQ test can be given in an hour or two to a child and from this infinitesimally small sample of his output, deeply important predictions follow — about schoolwork, occupation, income, satisfaction with life and even life expectancy.[27]

Extent of Heritability of Intelligence

Many people who favor a totally environmental explanation of IQ differences have made a grave error by trying to claim that genetic factors play no role whatsoever. The extreme environmentalist position can be seen in the follow-ing quotation from the famous psychologist John B. Watson.

Give me a dozen healthy infants . . . and I'll guarantee to take any one at random and train him to become any type of specialist I might select — doctor, lawyer, artist, merchant, chief and, yes, even beggar-man and thief, regardless of his . . . abilities . . . [and] race of ancestors.[28]

Taking a totally environmental position leaves one very vulnerable to the proofs of the geneticists. The famous biologist Dobzhansky believes that the environmentalists have made a major error in failing to understand that to be equal is not the same thing as being alike. Equality is a sociological ideal, not a biological one. We can grant equality of opportunity to people, but we can-not make them alike. Furthermore, if everyone were genetically identical, equality would become meaningless. We should deal with people on the basis of their individual potentialities and accomplishments, and not according to race or color.

The assumption that intelligence involves a genetic component has merit. However, the relative importance of this component is open to question. One thing that is often misunderstood about Jensen's assertion that 80 percent of an individual's intelligence is genetic is that this figure represents an average. The figure is not meant to apply equally to every person. For some people, envi-ronment may be a major factor, for others, a minor one. The 80-percent fig-ure is merely an average of many studies in which the heritability percentage ranged from 60 to 90 percent. Even Jensen notes that all the studies on the heritability of intelligence have been based on European and North American whites. These results cannot be unequivocally applied to American blacks. Jensen notes that we would have to conduct heritability studies with American blacks to find out if IQ tests are measuring a genetic component to the same ex-tent in both populations.[29]

A partial answer to this question can be found in a study by Sandra Scarr-Salapatek. The assumption that has usually been made about the interplay be-tween environment and genetics is that the two factors act independently of each other to bring about increments or decreases in IQ. For example, it is as-sumed that the two factors affect IQ, but that they do not necessarily affect each other in the process. Dr. Scarr-Salapatek does not agree with this. She claims that certain environments may be more favorable to a strong genetic compo-nent than others. Genetic factors may have a stronger effect on people who develop in favorable and stimulating environments and may have a less influ-ential effect on people raised in unfavorable environments. Differences in IQ among children in favorable environments are more likely to be due to genetic factors, while differences among children from deprived backgrounds are more likely to be due to environment. Therefore, someone who may be carrying genes that could potentially bring about high IQ may never reach that potential in a poor environment, and would consequently seem no different from some-one who is carrying genes that might bring about an average or low IQ.

To prove this hypothesis it would be necessary to show that the heritability of intelligence is less among disadvantaged socioeconomic groups. Dr. Scarr-Salapatek did a study with children in the Philadelphia schools and was able to prove the hypothesis. She concluded that her study:

> . . . shows that the percentage of genetic variance and the mean scores are very much a function of the rearing conditions of the population. A first look at the black population suggests that genetic variability is important in advantaged groups, but much less important in the disadvantaged. Since most blacks are socially disadvantaged, the proportion of genetic variance in the aptitude scores of black children is considerably less than that of the white children.[30]

Consequently, this study seems to indicate that intelligence is much more a function of genetics among whites than it is among blacks due to the disparity in their environments.

Inadequate Treatment of Environmental Variables

The environmental variables in the comparison of racial groups and social classes are so diverse and varied that maintaining control over them in an experimental sense becomes a major problem. Most investigations fail on precisely this point. Environmental differences with respect to nutrition, health, child-rearing practices, mental stimulation, and opportunities for interaction with the cultural environment are all known to be relevant variables. Just controlling for socioeconomic status does not imply that these other measures have also been adequately taken into account.

It is difficult to imagine that the status of blacks and whites could be compared in a meaningful way. The very existence of racial discrimination makes it impossible to say that the two groups are comparable. It is known that many black schools are inferior to white schools, and there are wide variations within each social class as well as between classes. It has been claimed that the social-class level of blacks is lower on the average than that of whites, even within the same social class. Therefore, middle-class blacks would not be the same as middle-class whites.

Thomas Sowell points out that Jensen never dealt satisfactorily with the fact that in studies of high-IQ black children females outnumber males by ratios ranging from 2.7 to 1 to 5.5 to 1. In the general population high IQs are fairly equally distributed between males and females, with males having a slight edge. If both black males and females have the same genetic backgrounds, then it is very difficult to explain this discrepancy through heredity. Consequently, environmental factors must be having different effects on black females than on black males.

Sowell also notes that first-born children are over-represented among high-IQ students. A recent study of the National Merit Scholarship finalists showed that in families having two to five children, more than half of the finalists were first-born. In families with five children, first-born children represented 52

percent of the winners, while fifth-born children represented only 6 percent of the winners. This disparity of 52 to 6 occurs between individuals who are supposedly genetically similar.[31] The environmental factor here is psychological. There seems to be a major personality difference between being the first-born or fifth-born child within the same family. We can also assume that there are major psychological differences between being reared in a poor black family as compared with a poor Indian family or a poor white family.

Professors Rosenthal and Jacobson of Harvard University have been studying for a long time the effects of the expectations of teachers on the actual performance of students. These studies are important indicators of how subtle the environmental factors often are that cause differences in IQ scores. In one study IQ tests were administered to several classes of students in an elementary school. Then about five "spurters" were randomly picked in each class. The teachers were told that these students had the potential to do very well academically, when in actual fact the students were in no way different from the rest of their classmates. The results of the study indicated that the children who were singled out actually did make more significant gains in their IQs than did the other children. The teachers were also asked to describe their students. The spurters were described as being more likely to succeed in later life, happier, more curious, more interesting, and better adjusted than the average students.

The teachers were also asked to describe the other students, many of whom had also gained in IQ. Children who gained in IQ when no improvement was expected were described negatively. In fact, the more they gained, the less favorably they were viewed. The most unfavorable ratings were of children in low-ability classes who made large improvements in IQ. "Evidently it is likely to be difficult for a slow-track child, even if his IQ is rising, to be seen by his teacher as well-adjusted and as a potentially successful student."[32]

This study has important implications for IQ research. It indicates that there is a self-fulfilling prophecy at work in the classroom. Students who are expected to do well receive subtle encouragement from the teacher through tone of voice, facial expressions, and comments. All of these mannerisms influence the student's own self-concept. If teachers expect students to do poorly, this information is also subtly transmitted and has its effect. In addition, the Rosenthal and Jacobson study suggests that certain students might well be negatively reinforced for showing improvement when none is expected.

Even though a trait may show a high degree of inheritability, the trait may be changed substantially by environmental intervention. For example, a large increase in height among adults in Western countries during the last 200 years has been noted. This increase has been due to improved nutrition and health conditions. Yet from studies on twins it has been determined that about 90 percent of height is hereditary — in other words, the genetic influence over height is greater than that over IQ. Therefore, height should be even less susceptible to environmental intervention than is IQ. If we assume that something that is hereditary to a large extent cannot be changed, we are making a grave error.[33]

How Important Is IQ?

In addition to the criticisms of the race and intelligence theorists that we have just discussed, a number of other facts are implicitly true.

1. The actual variation within any population will be greater than the actual difference between populations.

2. It is not a question of certain genes being absent or present in certain populations. The difference is merely in the relative frequency of a given set of genes.

3. The variation among races is not sharp, and racial mixing has been quite extensive.

The whole discussion of race differences with respect to IQ is not important in itself. It only assumes importance if people have racist views and want to use the arguments as ammunition for their cause. If we found that hair color and height were correlated and hereditarily transmitted, it would be no more than a scientific curiosity and would certainly not be the basis for years of controversy. It would merely be a discovery that one partially hereditable trait was tied in with another partially hereditable trait. Consequently, the whole discussion of intelligence and race seems to be of limited scientific value. A better idea might be to investigate the intellectual significance of devoting so much energy to this topic and to determine what end result is possible without violating the values of American society. A correlation between race and intelligence would be important only in a society where people are dealt with as members of a racial category, rather than as individuals. Herrnstein also mentions a possible correlation between height and IQ. However, this seems to be of no importance since we do not tend to discriminate according to height. If we did not discriminate according to race, the whole race and intelligence debate would be equally unimportant. The fact that intelligence is partially genetic should have little impact on a nonracist society. [34]

The importance of IQ and education has also been overemphasized with respect to the effects they have on future success. Christopher Jencks in his book *Inequality* has shown that education has little effect on income distribution in society. Jencks concludes that such factors as amount of schooling, family background, and test scores account for only about one-half of the difference among males in occupational status. The other 50 percent is controlled by personality factors and just plain luck.

If Jencks's hypothesis is correct, then individuals with similar test scores, family background, and schooling will still get jobs differing widely in status. Therefore, just knowing that one individual or group differs from another with respect to IQ scores does not really tell us anything about the potential for future accomplishments.

The whole race and intelligence discussion must also be viewed in terms of the implications for society. Jensen has chosen to ignore these implications and assumes that the investigation can proceed without having to take into account the sociopolitical aspects of the problem. He writes as follows:

. . . Unnecessary difficulties arise when we allow the scientific question to become mixed up with its possible educational, social, and political implications. The scientific question and its solution should not be allowed to get mixed up with the socio-political aspects of the problem. For when it does we are less able to think clearly about either set of questions. The question of whether there are or are not genetic racial differences in intelligence is independent of any questions of its implications, whatever they may be. [35]

However, this assumption is naive, a fact that became quite evident in a reply to the original Jensen article that was made by William F. Brazziel in the *Harvard Educational Review* in 1969. He noted that five days after Jensen made headlines in the Virginia papers, the issue of integrating the Greenville and Caroline County schools was discussed in the Federal District Court. Those against integration quoted heavily from Jensen and concluded that "white teachers could not understand the Nigra [*sic*] mind" and that all black children who did not get a certain score on a standardized test should be sent to an all-black remedial school where "teachers who understand them could work with them."[36]

Even Eysenck believes that one of Jensen's greatest faults lies in his failure to recognize and deal with the social consequences that might arise from his monograph. It is very easy for a reader to assume that an advocate of the existence of innate intellectual differences between races might also be in favor of segregation based on these differences. As Eysenck puts it:

A psychologist should perhaps be particularly aware of the likely social consequences of his actions. This is particularly true in such a field where emotions are strongly involved, and where the great and grievous injustices which white people have over the centuries done to black people would seem to require more than simple justice now. Some desire for restitution, some acknowledgement of past (and present) guilt, some realization and explicit statement of intent to see that never again would the sins of the whites be visited upon the blacks should perhaps accompany any statements on such matters as the genetic component in racial diversity. It is probably the absence of such evidence of humane and socially responsible considerations in Jensen's book which is in part responsible for the reception it has received.[37]

The whole discussion of race differences with respect to intelligence is basically a fruitless debate given the stated values and ideals of American society. Even if all the accusations of racial inferiority are correct (which they are not), what do we want to do with that information? A society based on freedom, justice, and equality should not be concerned about these issues since no course of action is possible that would not violate our most precious values. Genetic diversity is a desirable, not an undesirable, trait and society has a multitude of diverse positions to be filled. Individuals will arrange their lives according to their own definitions of happiness and their contributions will be different in kind and in magnitude. To attempt to establish behavior toward a group on heritability studies is contrary to the basic ethics of humanity.

Notes

1. T. F. Gossett, *Race: The History of an Idea in America*, p. 364.
2. Ibid., p. 365.
3. Ibid., p. 366.

4. Ibid., pp. 368–369.

5. C. C. Brigham, A *Study of American Intelligence*, pp. 110–111.

6. Ibid., p. 210.

7. A. Jensen, "How Much Can We Boost IQ and Scholastic Achievement?" *Harvard Educational Review* (Winter 1969): 24–25.

8. R. Mack, ed., *Prejudice and Race Relations*, pp. 35–55.

9. L. Edson, "Jensenism," *New York Times Magazine*, 31 Aug. 1969; J. Neary, "Jensenism: Variations on a Racial Theme," *Life*, 12 June 1970.

10. Jensen, "IQ and Scholastic Achievement," p. 4.

11. There is some indication that more recently Jensen has retreated somewhat from this view and is now willing to attribute a greater share of the variability to environmental factors. See *Boston Sunday Globe*, July 17, 1977, pp. 1, 9.

12. Jensen, "IQ and Scholastic Achievement," cited in A. Montagu, *Race and IQ*, p. 60.

13. Ibid., p. 80.

14. Ibid., p. 81.

15. Ibid., p. 85.

16. Ibid., p. 82.

17. H. J. Eysenck, *The IQ Argument*, p. 42.

18. Ibid., p. 43.

19. H. J. Eysenck, cited in Montagu, *Race and IQ*, p. 80.

20. Ibid., p. 81.

21. R. J. Herrnstein, "IQ," *The Atlantic Monthly*, September 1971, pp. 43–64.

22. N. Chomsky, "IQ Tests: Building Blocks for the New Class System," in *Annual Editions: Readings in Sociology: 73–74*, p. 91.

23. M. Weinreich, *Hitler's Professors: The Part of Scholarship in Germany's Crimes Against the Jewish People*, p. 11.

24. Ibid., p. 12.

25. S. Stodolsky and G. S. Lesser, "Learning Patterns in the Disadvantaged," in M. L. Goldschmid, *Black Americans and White Racism*, p. 171.

26. A. R. Jensen, *Educational Differences*, p. 246.

27. R. J. Herrnstein, "IQ," *The Atlantic Monthly*, September 1971, cited in Montagu, *Race and IQ*, p. 88.

28. J. B. Watson, *Behaviorism*, p. 24.

29. Jensen, *Educational Differences*, pp. 349–350.

30. S. Scarr-Salapatek, "Race, Social Class, and IQ," *Science* (24 Dec. 1971): 1294.

31. T. Sowell, *Race and Economics*, pp. 244–245.

32. R. Rosenthal and L. F. Jacobson, "Teacher Expectations for the Disadvantaged," *Scientific American* 218, no. 4: 22.

33. Montagu, *Race and IQ*, pp. 139–140.

34. Chomsky, "IQ Tests," pp. 94–95.

35. A. Jensen, "Do Schools Cheat Minority Children?" *Educational Research* (Nov. 1971): 25.

36. W. F. Brazziel, *Harvard Educational Review* (Spring 1969): 200.

37. H. J. Eysenck cited in Montagu, *Race and IQ*, pp. 29–30.

Part Two

INTERGROUP CONTACT

Chapter Five
Migration and Intergroup Contact

. . . race relations and all that they imply
are generally the products of migration and
conquest.

— *Robert E. Park* Race and Culture

Historical periods, as well as nations, religions, and social movements, have
their symbols. The barbarian Goth calls to mind the fifth century, and the
tenth century is represented by the Viking chieftain perched on the bow of his
long boat and plundering the coast of Europe. The intrepid explorer ex-
emplifies the spirit of the fifteenth century, while the armored knight serves as a
fitting symbol of the feudal period. These symbols focus attention on the
events, ideals, aspirations, and values of a particular era. They can also be
symptomatic of a sick and feverish age, and register its struggles, disappoint-
ments, and failures.

Generations from now, what will be the symbol used to represent the salient
events and concerns of the twentieth century? It seems unlikely that the artist,
the saint, or the scholar will serve as the symbol of our time. Nor will it be the
statesman or scientist, even though their roles have been of crucial importance.
The symbol for our era may well prove to be the refugee. The refugee is the
perfect embodiment of the instability of the twentieth century, of the anxieties and suspicions, of the racial prejudice and the fanatical nationalism, of
power struggles and the devastation of total war. Ours could be called "The
Century of the Homeless."

Since World War II there have been over 40 million refugees. Most of these have been physically driven from their homes in countries they have often occupied for hundreds of years.

At the end of World War II, 12 million Germans were expelled from Poland, Czechoslovakia, and Hungary and were forced to return to Germany. At this time Germany's territory had been reduced by 20 percent.

In 1947 India was partitioned into a Hindu India and a Moslem Pakistan and 14 million people became refugees within a few months; 8 million Hindus fled from Pakistan while 6 million Moslems fled from India.

Also in 1947 Finland was forced to give up one-eighth of its territory and simultaneously 500,000 Finnish refugees were expelled by the Soviet Union. In 1950 Bulgaria expelled 150,000 Turks. In 1972 Uganda forced 25,000 Asians to leave under threat of death.

During World War II it was the lucky ones in the Jewish population who became refugees; the rest were murdered by the Germans. Those that were able to escape settled in any corner of the world that could provide protection.

These are only some of the more notable examples of the massive forced migration that has taken place in the twentieth century. We have begun our discussion with these examples of forced migration, which has seemed to take precedence over the more peaceful types of migration in this era. However, all migration is not of this type and we should backtrack lest we forget that the origins of most forms of migration are more peaceful, although no less spectacular in outcome.

Race Relations and Migration

Migration is an important factor in understanding race and ethnic relations. (For a diagrammatic illustration, see Figure 5.1.) It could be argued that race problems are a consequence of the movement of peoples over the earth. If societies were content to live by themselves, in isolated, self-sufficient communities, there would be no interracial conflict, no clash of cultures, no race prejudice, and no necessity for ethnic groups to adjust their differences. The societies would have their problems, to be sure, but not the so-called race problems that afflict our heterogeneous modern nations.

No doubt, in years past, there were many such isolated societies, and even today they have not entirely vanished. Explorers periodically report the discovery of primitive tribes that have had little or no contact with the outside world. The Kreen-Akarores of Brazil are such a tribe.

When in the 16th century the Portuguese began colonizing Brazil, four million Indians stood in their way. The newcomers showed them scant mercy, brushing them aside by any means they could. Even in modern times, certain greedy civilizados have machine-gunned them, dynamited them from the air, and given them poisoned food.

Today Brazil can identify only about 200,000 pureblood Indians. Some of these —

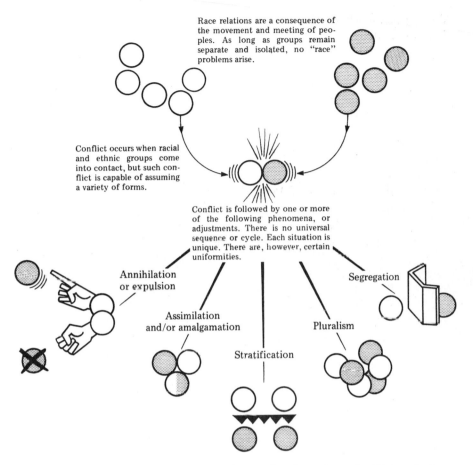

Race relations are a consequence of the movement and meeting of peoples. As long as groups remain separate and isolated, no "race" problems arise.

Conflict occurs when racial and ethnic groups come into contact, but such conflict is capable of assuming a variety of forms.

Conflict is followed by one or more of the following phenomena, or adjustments. There is no universal sequence or cycle. Each situation is unique. There are, however, certain uniformities.

Annihilation or expulsion

Assimilation and/or amalgamation

Stratification

Pluralism

Segregation

Figure 5.1 Race relations constitute a theme played on these five "strings." In a sense, each is a "solution" of race and ethnic problems.

the Kreen-Akarores are among them — live in forests only now being penetrated by pioneer rubber trappers, loggers, missionaries, and above all, the road builders who are opening Amazonia with a network of highways.

To overcome the savage hostility of these innocents, Brazil formed the National Foundation for the Indian, called FUNAI for short. . . .

The road that borders the Kreen-Akarores territory is FUNAI's great fear, for it exposes them, too much and too fast, to civilizados whose diseases they are not equipped to resist. In time FUNAI hopes it can persuade all the Kreen-Akarores to go willingly to Xingu National Park, a large reservation set aside for wild tribes.[1]

We need not look very far, however, for examples of isolated communities. There are remote and isolated communities in the mountains of Kentucky, Virginia, and Tennessee, and in the Ozarks of Missouri and Arkansas, where the disrupting influences of modern technology, science, and urbanization have barely been felt. For better or for worse, such isolation is rapidly becoming a thing of the past due to modern means of travel and communication.

Early Migration Patterns

We must not suppose that contact between racial and ethnic groups is a phenomenon only of the modern world. Moving from place to place was a way of life for many of our ancestors. Changes in climatic conditions and food supplies often were the cause of numerous migrations.

Throughout most of their career humans have subsisted by gathering the wild products that nature provided, by hunting, or by fishing. There are societies today whose economy is still built on these ancient practices, and even the most civilized societies preserve these activities either for commercial or sentimental reasons. It was only a few thousand years ago that humans learned to domesticate animals and to practice agriculture, thereby making a more settled life possible. Of course, there have been societies that depended on hunting and fishing and that managed to avoid a nomadic existence. On the other hand, pastoral nomads are quite a familiar type, and even agricultural nomads are not unknown. However, the hunting-fishing-gathering type of economic activity, which has been most characteristic of human existence, makes it necessary to keep on the move.

There are abundant reasons for believing that preliterate, prehistoric peoples roamed widely over the earth and came into contact and conflict with strangers who differed from themselves both racially and culturally. The evidence for these prehistoric migrations is of several types.

1. *Archaeological evidence*   Just as we leave behind on our city dumps and refuse piles the evidences of our type of civilization, so have prehistoric peoples left behind material witnesses to their cultures. The archaeologist digs these up, and with them seeks to reconstruct the history of ancient and departed societies. By studying the distribution of various types of artifacts, designs on pottery, ruins of dwellings, forms of art, and so on, the archaeologist often is able to trace a people to its original home, follow its routes of migration, and make inferences as to its contacts with other civilizations. Archaeology offers indisputable evidence that, long before the dawn of history, primitive people were continually on the move, invading the territory of others, borrowing ideas from enemies and from strangers, constructing dwellings to ensure safety from marauders, and often mixing their blood with that of the conquerors or their victims.

2. *Linguistic evidence*   Similarities in languages also reveal to the philologist the fact that certain peoples have migrated. Thus in North America most of the Athabascan-speaking Indians lived in Canada, but some of them had gone elsewhere. The Navajo and Apache of New Mexico and Arizona reveal in

their speech the fact that they came originally from Canada. In all parts of the world, similarities of speech reveal to the trained ear the evidences of human migrations.

3. *Folklore*   The oral traditions of primitive peoples often include stories about their migrations and their conflicts with strangers. The Hebrews passed on the stories of their origin, of their years of slavery in Egypt, of their wanderings over the Sinai Peninsula, of their eventual entrance into the Promised Land and their wars with the tribes already settled there. Preliterate peoples also transmitted their traditions. The Aztecs, for instance, told stories of their place of origin "in the North," of their invasion of Mexico, and of their conquest of the native tribes they found there. Incidentally, linguistic evidence gives support to these traditions.

4. *Biological evidence*   To the biological scientist, the presence of blond hair, blue eyes, or other racial features in a population not generally possessing those features is evidence of migration and contact. The racial features of the American Indian indicate Asiatic origin and kinship to other Mongoloid peoples; the blondness found among certain Berbers of North Africa suggests an early migration of Nordics from Europe; and the Hottentots of South Africa give evidence of their migration from northeastern Africa, where they had mixed with the Hamitic peoples of that region.

5. *Cultural evidence*   The possession of certain traits of culture by a preliterate society often suggests that group's origin in some distant place. For example, certain customs of cattle-raising observed by the Yakuts of northeastern Siberia indicate to the anthropologist that these people migrated from farther south; and the wide distribution of Inca pottery in South America testifies to the expansive habits of that tribe. This type of evidence, however, must be used with caution, for culture traits are able to diffuse apart from the migration of peoples. The smoking of tobacco spread quickly over the earth and was adopted by people who had never seen American Indians, who invented the custom. We ourselves take delight in many a feature of our civilization that we owe to far-away peoples with whom we have never come into direct contact.

The dawn of the historical period furnishes additional support to the theory that migration and intergroup contact are ancient phenomena. We know that the Germanic tribes migrated from Asia Minor into western and southern Europe, that the Greeks invaded the Mediterranean region at the end of the second millennium before the Christian era, that the Magyars moved into Hungary, that the Slavs superseded the Finnish people of Russia, that the Mongolians invaded Europe, and that the Bulgarians migrated from the region of the Black Sea into the Balkan Peninsula. Our knowledge of the African continent is by no means comparable to our knowledge of Europe, but linguistic, traditional, and anatomical evidences point to the frequency of population movements there also. Abyssinia was peopled by Semitic invaders, the Arabs swept over northern Africa, and the Bantu tribes spread over the greater part of the continent, and presumably supplanted an old pygmy population.

The Case of the Jews

To illustrate the phenomenon of migration, no better group could be selected than the Jews. Because of Christian intolerance and insistence on keeping the Jews in a subservient position, the Jewish existence has been a migratory one throughout history, and the title of "the wandering Jew" is well earned. When first encountered, the Jews were a tribe of desert dwellers, seeking a more comfortable homeland for themselves in that pleasant strip of land known as "The Fertile Crescent," lying between the Persian Gulf and the Mediterranean Sea. They eventually succeeded, after much conflict, in winning a foothold in that portion of the Crescent called Canaan. This was not for long, however, for famine struck and they were forced to move on to Egypt. There they lived through several unhappy centuries until, under the leadership of Moses, they set out once again for Canaan. Before reaching their destination, they endured many years of wandering around the Sinai Peninsula; but eventually they reached their "promised land," only to find other claimants settled there, against whom they had to wage a series of bloody wars. In time, however, they established themselves, and flourished as a united nation. Then came conquering armies from the East, destroying their cities and carrying away the Hebrew people as captives. From these captivities many never returned; but in 538 B.C. those who did find their way back to Jerusalem, proceeded to rebuild the city.

The years following were by no means free from contacts and conflicts with other peoples and cultures, for the Greeks came, under Alexander the Great, and later the Romans. These incidents, while they had profound effects on the psychology and the culture of the Jews, did not force them to leave their homes. In 70 A.D., however, came the Great Dispersion, when the Roman Titus captured and burned Jerusalem, slaying more than a million Jews in the process. Many of the survivors were enslaved and sent to labor in the mines of Egypt; others were taken as captives to march in a triumphal procession through the streets of Rome; and still others were driven to the corners of the earth. Even before this time there were large communities of Jews in Alexandria, Rome, Athens, Antioch, Babylon, and many other ancient cities. But after 70 A.D., with the destruction of their temple in Jerusalem, further dispersion occurred and Jews continued to pray for a return to this homeland in Palestine for centuries.

It is not possible here to trace their subsequent migrations, nor even to enumerate the most significant events. Frequently the Jews were offered inducements to settle in this land or that, but more often persecution forced them to leave the country in which they resided and seek a new home, if one could be found. The triumph of Mohammedanism, for instance, in the eighth century caused many Jews to flee, for the Moslems turned upon those people who steadfastly refused to accept the new faith. The Crusaders of the eleventh, twelfth, and thirteenth centuries presented many Jewish communities with the alternatives of flight or death. In 1290 every Jew was ordered to leave England,

and between sixteen and seventeen thousand had to flee. It was not until 1654, when Oliver Cromwell rescinded this order, that Jews were permitted to return. They were expelled from France in 1306; and at one time or another they were ordered out of Vienna, Cologne, Nuremberg, Hamburg, Wittenberg, and many another city, province, or state. In 1492, the very day before Columbus set sail for America, the Jews were expelled from Spain.

Occasionally monarchs would invite Jews to settle in their realms, but seldom for reasons of tolerance or pity. The King of Denmark, for instance, observing the commercial talents and wealth of the Jews in the Netherlands, opened the doors of his kingdom to them. In the fifteenth century, the Jews found a welcome in Poland. The rulers of that region looked with favor upon their coming, for the land was barbaric and sparsely settled; a population of educated, urbane, commercial people such as the Jews was coveted.

The eighteenth century ushered in an era of tolerance that gave promise of marking the end of Jewish persecution and expulsion. In America political leaders were saying that all men are created free and equal, and in France they were shouting, "Liberty, Equality, and Fraternity." In 1782 Joseph II of Austria issued his famous "Edict of Toleration"; in 1791 France abolished all laws directed against Jews; Holland and Prussia followed in granting civil liberties to their Jewish citizens.

These hopes for a brighter day for the Jews, however, were soon shattered. A reaction occurred, and the nations of Europe began to slip back into their old ways. In Germany there were massacres and expulsions. Some countries repealed the laws that had granted freedom to the Jews. In Russia they were made the scapegoats for the assassination of Alexander II and suffered ghastly cruelties. In France the resurgence of anti-Semitism found its expression in the famous Dreyfus case.

World War II and the atrocities of the Nazis brought about further attempts at massive migration; however, few countries were humane enough to offer sanctuary, and the bulk of the Jewish population in Europe was slaughtered. Those who were able to save themselves traveled to the United States, South America, Palestine, and the Orient.

In Russia the harassed Jews had revived their ancient hope of finding a homeland in Palestine; but it remained for a Western European Jew, Theodor Herzl, to translate this dream into the actuality of modern Zionism. Against nearly insurmountable obstacles Israel finally became a reality and hundreds of thousands of Jews began to wend their way back to their original homeland.

The Expansion of Europe

An entirely different type of migratory movement is that known as the Expansion of Europe. One of the most amazing spectacles of history is the way in which the people of Europe began, in the fifteenth century, to overflow their

Immigrants leaving Ellis Island to start new life in the United States

boundaries and set out to explore, convert, conquer, and colonize every corner of the earth. For the student of race relations, no other historical event can compare in importance with this movement of white Europeans into other continents that involved their coming into contact with members of other races and different cultures and creating problems of conflict and adjustment. As a migratory movement, the Expansion of Europe differs radically from the wanderings of the Jews.

It is customary to date this movement from the early fifteenth century, when Portuguese sailors began to venture forth on the uncharted seas, or from the discovery of the New World in 1492. Also, it has not been uncommon to attribute the initiation of the movement to some individual, to the genius of Prince Henry the Navigator or the courage of Christopher Columbus; or to seek its cause in some incident, such as acquisition of the compass by European navigators. The fact is, however, that the Expansion of Europe was the result of a combination of factors — personal, social, technological, and economic. Its roots may be traced back long before the fifteenth century.

Europeans in ancient times had been in touch with the peoples of the East, but these contacts were broken by the barbarian invasions and, somewhat later, by the incursions of the Moslems. In the ninth century, however, adventurous seamen from the ports of southern Italy began to trade with the cities of the eastern Mediterranean, and soon other Italian cities, such as Venice, Pisa, and

Genoa, entered this lucrative commerce. Europeans began to acquire a taste for the fabulous products of Asia, and the Crusades provided a great stimulus to the development of these new wants.

The wealth of the East was, indeed, dazzling to the Europeans. Theirs was a monotonous diet, and the spices from Asia made a world of difference to them in the enjoyment of their meals. Then there were the precious stones, the silks and satins, the beautiful rugs, the shawls and tapestries, the glass and porcelain. In return for these, the Europeans had little to offer, other than rough woolen cloth, copper, lead, tin, and a few other base materials. They needed gold and silver, therefore, to pay for their imports, and their supply of these precious metals was inadequate. Small wonder, then, that Europeans seemed greedy for the gold that they later discovered in the possession of Aztecs and Incas, and that they suspected other Indian tribes of having.

The eastern shores of the Mediterranean were the gateway for most of the trade with the East. The Spanish and Portuguese, accordingly, were not well situated to participate. They had developed the same tastes as their fellow Europeans, but they resented the high prices they were forced to pay. They were eager, therefore, to discover some new route to the East. They had reasons for believing that there were routes to the "Indies," for their knowledge of geography and navigation was not as primitive as many suppose. Their scholars knew that the world was round and had even made a fairly accurate guess at its size, and the navigators of that century were familiar with the compass, the astrolabe, and other instruments that made their vocation less hazardous.

In 1415 the Portuguese began to expand by capturing Ceuta, across the Strait of Gibraltar, in Morocco. Then, under the leadership of Prince Henry the Navigator, and with the support of the King, they began their explorations of the western coast of Africa. Fifty years later they had reached the Guinea coast; in 1488 Bartholomew Diaz sailed to the southern tip of Africa; and before the close of the century Vasco da Gama had rounded the Cape and sailed on to India. In the meantime the Spanish, under Columbus, had discovered the New World; the British, under John Cabot, had reached the Canadian coast; and the Italian, Amerigo Vespucci, had made a voyage to Brazil and had written a letter in which he referred to "the new world." Others who participated in this initial expansion of Europe are familiar to all and too numerous to mention.

Exploration and trade, however, were not the only interests of the Europeans. They went out sometimes to conquer and subdue the native peoples and sometimes they went as settlers. They laid claim to all the lands they touched, and fought among themselves for their possession. They despoiled and exploited the peoples they met, and set about to supplant what they regarded as heathen customs with their own civilization. Missionaries introduced the Christian religion and traders developed a market for European products. The population of Europe increased at an incredible rate, and fifty million people crossed the seas to find a better place to live. This expansion of

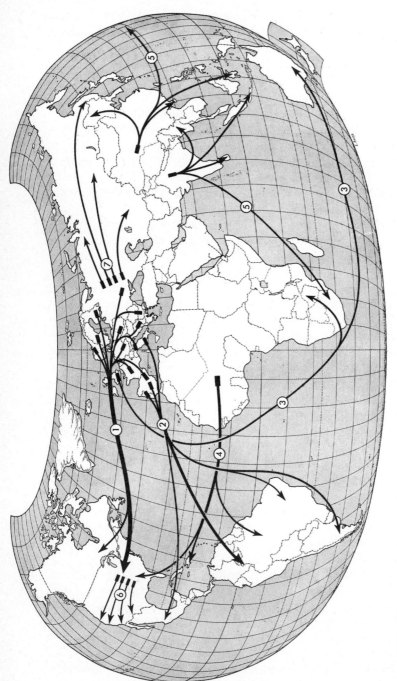

Figure 5.2   Major intercontinental migratory currents in modern times.

"The main currents of international migration since the beginning of the sixteenth century have been: (1) from all parts of Europe to North America; (2) from Latin countries of Europe to Middle and South America; (3) from Great Britain to Africa and Australia; (4) import of slaves from Africa to America.   Another current (5), partly intercontinental, partly intracontinental, has flowed from China and India. The most important internal migration has been (6) westward in the United States and (7) eastward in Russia."

W. S. Woytinsky and E. S. Woytinsky, *World Population and Production.* © 1953 by the Twentieth Century Fund, New York. P. 68.

Europe has continued to the present day, with the result that the English-speaking peoples of North America and Australia far outnumber those in England, Spanish-speaking peoples of South and Central America are more numerous than those of Spain, and people of European descent are found living in every quarter of the globe. The "Europeanization" of the whole world has proceeded apace and continues today.

Major Population Shifts

Woytinsky and Woytinsky have described several major shifts of population in the twentieth century.[2] These migrations have accounted for most of the population interchanges and all have occurred since the sixteenth century. Figure 5.2 shows these population shifts.

Europe to North America Between the seventeenth century and World War II 45 million people emigrated from Europe to the United States and Canada. Many of these returned, but 25 million remained permanently. Today approximately 150 million people in North America can trace their ancestry back to this migration.

Europe to Central and South America Approximately 20 million Europeans emigrated from Spain, Portugal, and Italy to Central and South America. Today nearly 50 million people in these areas have European ancestry.

Europe to Africa and Australia Approximately 17 million people in these areas can trace their ancestry to the colonization of Africa and Australia by the British and the Dutch. In many cases the Europeans brought diseases with them that were unknown to the native population and killed off large numbers of the original population.

Africa to the Americas The slave trade, which began in the sixteenth century, brought an estimated 15 million blacks to the American continent. Less than a million came in the sixteenth century; 3 million, in the seventeenth; 7 million, in the eighteenth; and 4 million, in the nineteenth.

Types of Migration

It is apparent from the cases reported thus far that many different kinds of movements of people are included under the term *migration*. To understand race relations it is necessary to recognize the fact that contacts between different racial and ethnic groups occur under a wide variety of circumstances. Often they are made at the point of the sword, while at other times they are entirely peaceful; they may be voluntary or involuntary, on the part of either or both of the races; the motives leading to the contact may be selfish or altruistic; the interests of the two groups may be antagonistic or complementary. Our language contains a great many terms that indicate the variety of circumstances under which different peoples come together. The following classification of the types of migration is based on the typology of William Petersen.[3]

Primitive Migration

Primitive migration results from ecological and environmental changes that make it difficult for people to survive. The people move because they are unable to cope with the natural forces. Food supplies may deteriorate, weather conditions may become intolerable, or competition for a limited number of resources may put certain groups at a disadvantage. Often a food-gathering or hunting tribe cannot survive on what is available in one area and moves back and forth within a certain area. On another occasion a drought or an attack of locusts may eliminate the potential food supply and force migration.

Forced or Impelled Migration

While ecological pressures serve as the activating agent in primitive migrations, social institutions or the government are the cause in *forced* or *impelled migrations.* Thus the Moors were expelled from Spain in 1609; the Jews, as we saw, have been forced to leave one country after another throughout their history. Huguenots were driven from France in the seventeenth century; Gypsies were expelled from England by Henry VIII; and the Acadians, heroes of Longfellow's *Evangeline,* were uprooted and scattered among the English colonies of North America. The Governor of Missouri, in 1838, issued an order expelling the Mormons from that state. The slave trade, which we will discuss presently, and the penal colonies, which have been established in Australia and elsewhere, are also examples of forced migration.[4]

Lest we conclude that forced migration is a cruel relic of the past, we might be reminded that the twentieth century has already witnessed a forcible expulsion of peoples on a scale hitherto unapproached. Today we know these people as "refugees" and "displaced persons." On the eve of World War I tens of thousands of Bulgarians had to flee from Turkey, and an equal number of Turkish Moslems had to flee from Bulgaria. Later on, thousands of persons in the Balkans were more or less forcibly removed under a program known euphemistically as the "transfer of minorities." To be sure, most of this transfer of populations was done under high-sounding treaties, which were supervised by commissions "to insure justice"; but the fact remains that most of the victims were reluctant to emigrate, and they were not happy to exchange their property for the redeemable government bonds they were forced to accept, and which, not surprisingly, promptly declined in value. Consequently, no small amount of compulsion had to be applied.

World War I cut millions adrift. During the war Turkey embarked on a mass expulsion of its Armenian minority, sending many refugees into Europe, the Middle East, and the United States. Half a million found refuge of a sort in Russia. Between the two world wars the stream of refugees continued. The civil war in Russia stimulated a mass emigration, estimated at 2 million.

The victory of Franco in Spain led to a mass flight across the border. The Republican army, together with a throng of civilians, retreated into French territory. Some of these eventually found their way to North Africa or to Mexico, while 200,000 remained in France.

World War II set in motion a refugee flood of astronomical proportions. When the Germans overran Poland, they pushed 300,000 refugees out of the country. Shortly thereafter the Soviet government insisted on the transfer of some 400,000 German ethnics from the Baltic states, on which the Soviets had designs, and Hitler obligingly "recalled them to the Fatherland." When the Germans moved westward, hordes of Dutch and Belgian civilians streamed into France. The same sort of thing happened when the Germans invaded Russia and the Balkans. Finally, when the tide of battle turned, hordes of fearful Russians, Ukrainians, and Balts joined the retreating Germans. Thirty million, they say, were displaced. Many of these, of course, subsequently returned to their homes; but there were millions who, for one reason or another, dared not return.

Petersen used impelled migration to refer to situations in which the migrants retain some power over deciding whether or not to leave. With forced migration they do not have this power. In Nazi Germany the years 1933 to 1938 were years of impelled migration when Jewish emigration was brought about by various anti-Semitic acts and laws. In the period from 1938 to 1945 Jews were herded into cattle cars and transported to concentration camps. Consequently, impelled migration can develop into forced migration.

The reasons for forced and impelled migration can vary. On the one hand, a country may want to rid itself of a certain group of people. On the other hand, the process may occur because a country wishes to import needed laborers against their will. The slave trade years in which Africans were captured and sent to various countries provide an example of this second reason.

Impelled migration, where groups of people flee a country because of impending difficulties, has been an important form of population exchange throughout human history. In many instances the weaker former occupants of an area have fled as a stronger group invaded the area. For example, as the North Vietnamese took over more and more areas of South Vietnam, large groups of people fled to the non-Communist controlled areas.

Free Migration and Mass Migration

In the types of migration discussed so far, the people, for the most part, are responding to adverse conditions over which they have little control. There is another type of migration, *free migration*, in which the migrants are making a decision to move not just because of survival, but because of a whole host of reasons all of which involve an unforced choice on the part of the people. Many Europeans came to the United States because of idealistic aspirations rather than unbearable circumstances.

Free migration usually involves trailblazers and individuals strongly motivated to seek novelty and improvement. Very often others follow their example, and a small trickle of migration can become a broad stream. When this happens, we then speak of it as *mass migration*. Mass migration is largely a phenomenon of the modern world, especially of the nineteenth and twentieth centuries. It is a peaceful movement, between well-established countries that are on friendly terms, or at least are not hostile, and one of which is old and densely populated while the other is new and less thickly settled. Unlike the movements described heretofore, mass migration is primarily an individual undertaking, or a "collective drift," rather than the organized movement of an integrated group, although whole villages have been known to migrate piecemeal to another country, and governments often do control, regulate, direct, and encourage or discourage the process.

Colonization is a form of free migration. This type of population movement occurs when a well-established society sends out some of its citizens to settle certain specified localities. Such a transplanted fragment remains closely tied to its mother country, politically, economically, and culturally. The migration is often an undertaking of the state itself; but sometimes private groups have established colonies in pursuit of their interests as they see them. In these latter cases, however, the sanction of the state is usually involved, although not always.

Colonization is an ancient type of population movement, practiced by the Chinese, Greeks, Romans, Phoenicians, and many other peoples. It has taken a variety of forms, too; and many classifications of colonies have, accordingly, been made. We can distinguish between the farm type and the plantation type of colony. The farm colony arises where the soil and climatic conditions are similar to those of the country from which the settlers came, rendering acclimatization easy, permitting the migration of whole families, promoting independence and individual enterprise, and often resulting in the colonists' transferring their primary allegiance from their old home to the new. Such, for instance, was the settlement of Canada, most of the United States, South Africa, New Zealand, Tasmania, and Australia. The plantation colony, on the other hand, arises where the geographical conditions are quite different from those of the homeland. The colonizers are predominantly male, and their ties with the native country remain strong. Agriculture takes the form of a highly specialized crop, produced by a large operating unit. Labor is a major problem, for the native populations can seldom be induced to work for wages and some system of forced labor must be resorted to. Many of the most crucial problems of race relations have arisen under such conditions. This type of colonization was characteristic of the Portuguese in Brazil, the Dutch in Java and Sumatra, and the British in the Malay Peninsula and the Caribbean.

Table 5.1   Classification of migratory movements

Origin	Migratory force	Class of migration
Relation between peoples and nature	Ecological push	Primitive
Relation between peoples and state, or equivalent, social institution	Migration policy	Forced / Impelled
Norms and values	Higher aspirations	Free
Collective behavior	Social momentum	Mass

SOURCE: William Petersen, "A General Typology of Migration," *American Sociological Review* 23 (1958), p. 266.

Petersen's classification can be summarized in Table 5.1. In the first column, we see the origin for the movement. In the second column, we see the actual migratory force; and in the third column, we see the classification of the exact type of migration.

Internal Migration

Still another form of movement that is often significant in race relations is that known as *internal migration*. There have been times, of course, when there was very little movement of people within the borders of a state. Under serfdom, for instance, one did not have the right to move; and, even with the disappearance of serfdom, the individual was still not endowed with independence of action, for he or she was a member of the commune, which regulated many aspects of one's life. Now, however, internal migrations are going on continually in all civilized countries. One of the most important of these is the drift of population from the city to the suburbs. Internal migration has been a conspicuous feature of American society, profoundly affecting its history, its institutions, and its culture, as well as the relations between racial and ethnic groups. First, there were the migrations of the Indians, both before the arrival of Columbus and since. Then there was the westward march of the American people, expanding the young nation from the Atlantic to the Pacific. Other important internal migrations in our country were the flight of the Mormons from New York to Utah, the rush of gold-seekers to California in 1849, the interstate migrations of recent years, the seasonal migrations of laborers, and, especially, the great migration of blacks from the rural South to the industrial cities of the North and the West. Table 5.2 shows the growth and distribution of the black population.

Table 5.2   Growth and distribution of the black population

State	1910	1930	1960	1970
Alabama	908,282	944,834	980,271	903,467
Alaska			6,771	8,911
Arizona	2,009	10,749	43,403	53,344
Arkansas	442,891	478,463	388,787	352,445
California	21,645	81,048	883,861	1,400,143
Colorado	11,453	11,828	39,992	66,411
Connecticut	15,174	29,354	107,449	181,177
Delaware	31,181	32,602	60,688	78,276
District of Columbia	94,446	132,068	411,737	537,712
Florida	308,669	431,828	880,186	1,041,651
Georgia	1,176,987	1,071,125	1,122,596	1,187,149
Hawaii			4,943	7,573
Idaho	651	668	1,502	2,130
Illinois	109,049	328,972	1,037,470	1,425,674
Indiana	60,320	111,982	269,275	357,464
Iowa	14,973	17,380	25,354	32,596
Kansas	54,030	66,344	91,445	106,977
Kentucky	261,656	226,040	215,949	230,793
Louisiana	713,874	776,326	1,039,207	1,086,832
Maine	1,363	1,096	3,318	2,800
Maryland	232,250	276,379	518,410	699,479
Massachusetts	38,055	52,365	111,842	175,817
Michigan	17,115	169,453	717,581	991,066
Minnesota	7,084	9,445	22,263	34,868
Mississippi	1,009,487	1,009,718	915,743	815,770
Missouri	157,452	223,840	390,853	480,172
Montana	1,834	1,256	1,467	1,995
Nebraska	7,689	13,752	29,262	39,911
Nevada	513	516	13,484	27,762
New Hampshire	564	790	1,908	2,505
New Jersey	89,760	208,828	514,875	770,292
New Mexico	1,628	2,850	17,063	19,555
New York	134,191	412,814	1,417,511	2,168,949
North Carolina	697,843	918,647	1,116,021	1,126,478
North Dakota	617	377	777	2,494
Ohio	111,452	309,304	786,097	970,477
Oklahoma	137,612	172,198	153,084	171,892
Oregon	1,492	2,234	18,133	26,308
Pennsylvania	193,919	431,257	852,750	1,016,514
Rhode Island	9,529	9,913	18,332	25,338
South Carolina	835,843	793,681	829,291	789,041

Table **5.2** continued

State	1910	1930	1960	1970
South Dakota	817	646	1,114	1,627
Tennessee	473,088	477,646	586,876	621,261
Texas	690,049	854,964	1,187,125	1,399,005
Utah	1,144	1,108	4,148	6,617
Vermont	1,621	568	519	761
Virginia	671,096	650,165	816,258	861,368
Washington	6,058	6,840	48,738	71,308
West Virginia	64,173	114,893	89,378	67,342
Wisconsin	2,900	10,739	74,546	128,224
Wyoming	2,235	1,250	2,183	2,568
Total	9,827,763	11,891,143	18,871,831	22,580,289

Source: *Bureau of the Census, Statistical Abstract of the United States, 1976*, Washington, D.C., Bureau of the Census, p. 32.

Causes of Migration

We have already hinted at some of the motives that cause people to leave their homes and to set out to invade, to conquer, to colonize, or to settle in a strange land. The motives must be overpowering, for the hazards and discomforts attendant upon migration have always been great. Accustomed as we are now to means of transportation that are rapid, cheap, safe, and convenient, we are likely to overlook the dangers and difficulties the emigrant of a century ago had to endure. Nor was transportation the only obstacle. Often there were legal barriers to be overcome, and by no means unimportant is the fact that most people have sentimental ties, not lightly broken, to bind them to their native soil.

Many myths and legends have arisen to explain the motives underlying migration. We have been led to believe that our own land was settled by persons who were impelled by a desire to worship God as they pleased, or by a love of freedom, or by rebellion against the oppressive Old-World society. Such lofty motives were dominant at least with the earlier settlers, we are told, while less worthy motives of an economic nature prompted the later immigrants. Far less admirable were the interests of those who conquered and settled the Latin American countries, obsessed as they were with a greed for gold.

Economic factors are certainly of great importance in stimulating migration. Anthropologists are of the opinion that the movements of primitive tribes are induced by some kind of economic pressure — changes in climate, desiccation of the country, depletion of the soil, overpopulation, or exhaustion of natural resources. The magnificent ruins in Mesa Verde National Park, in Colorado, bear witness to the fact that years of drought forced the inhabitants of those cliff-side cities to abandon the region they and their ancestors had inhabited for many centuries.[5] The folk tales of many primitive peoples relate how, when their numbers increased to the point where game and other resources were taxed, some of the tribe were forced to wander off in search of new sources of food. The Missouri, Iowa, and Oto Indians used to account in this manner for the fact that their ancestors, centuries earlier, had split off from the Winnebago tribe in Wisconsin.

Economic factors were of primary importance in the expansion of Europe and in the peopling of the United States. The phenomenal growth of Europe's population, doubling its size between 1700 and 1800, not only aroused the concern of Thomas Malthus and other thinkers, but undoubtedly helped to put the idea of emigration into the popular mind. So, too, did the series of crop failures and the famines that afflicted one section of Europe or another from time to time. Similarly, economic conditions in America reflected themselves in the fluctuations of immigrant tides, decreasing in times of depression and mounting in times of industrial activity.

This is not to say that there have been no other motives. Religious persecution has unquestionably been a factor in promoting emigration. Jews have often had to flee in the face of intolerance; the Germans who came to Pennsylvania in 1683 were religious refugees; Huguenots were driven from France; the Armenians, who were Christian, suffered at the hands of the Mohammedan Turks, and sought refuge elsewhere. William Penn advertised his colony as a home for those who wanted to escape religious persecution, with the result that Quakers, Presbyterians, Mennonites, and many others came in considerable numbers to settle there.

Political and social conditions have also served as stimuli for migrations. In 1866, when Sweden established high property qualifications for voting, considerable discontent appeared among those who were disfranchised, and interest in emigration was aroused. Letters from Swedes who came to the United States in that period make frequent and favorable reference to the social and political equality they enjoyed. The failure of the revolutionary movement of 1848 gave the stimulus to the pioneers of the Bohemian immigration to America. Political discontent looms large in the history of Irish emigration, and operated also in the migrations of Russians, Poles, Finns, Hungarians, and many others. Discontent with the rigidity of Old-World society or with the class and caste systems, and desire to escape compulsory military service have motivated many to seek homes in another land.

But migration is not adequately explained in terms of impulses spontaneously aroused by conditions in the immigrant's homeland. Stimuli have also been artificially induced and introduced from the outside. The transportation of immigrants grew into a lucrative business, and agents for the steamship companies used to go about planting the idea of emigration in the minds of credulous peasants, often with little concern for the welfare either of the individual or of the nations affected. Labor agents, too, despite the fact that their operations were illegal, were responsible for considerable migration. The most important of all the influences from the outside, however, were the immigrants themselves, whose letters to relatives and friends in the Old World were eagerly devoured, were circulated throughout the village and beyond, and were often printed in local newspapers. When they returned to their native communities, as they often did, boasting of their success and displaying their wealth, these fortunate ones encouraged many others to emigrate who would otherwise have resisted the temptation.

Migrations and American Society

A large and important portion of the history of the United States is concerned with the migrations of various peoples to these shores; and most of what the sociologists have regarded as the study of race relations has dealt with the meeting, the conflicts, the adjustments, and the amalgamation of the heterogeneous groups that have gone into the making of our nation. The United States has experienced all the types of migratory movements we have described. Let us take a look at a few of the most significant.

The American Indian

We have been guilty of virtually ignoring the Indians in our histories. Artists, novelists, and entertainers have not neglected them, but many students of the American scene have dismissed them with a few paragraphs. The truth is, however, that the presence of the Indians has profoundly affected our history and our culture. They played a part in the sheer matter of survival; for many a struggling colonial settlement would have been wiped out by starvation had not friendly Indians proffered aid. The Europeans had neither the knowledge nor the experience to found successful colonies. The Indians taught them what to plant and how to cultivate it; they shared with the whites their knowledge and skills of woodcraft; they blazed the trails that were later to become roads and highways. They have participated in all our wars. They even played a role in the development of American democracy; for many of the colonists had hopes of planting on this continent the European system of castes and classes, only to find that the rugged and dangerous life of the frontier was not conducive to such a social system.

The Indians were objects of mystery and speculation for the Europeans from the very beginning of their contact. It was once widely believed by the whites that the Indians were the descendants of the Ten Lost Tribes of Israel. Another legend held that Modoc, a Welsh prince, sailed westward in 1170 A.D. and discovered the New World. He returned to his homeland, outfitted a second expedition, and set sail, but was never heard from again. Some Indians, it was thought, were descended from Modoc's colony.   Still other theories derived the Indians from the Egyptians, the Japanese, the Irish, the Polynesians, refugees from the "lost Continent of Atlantis" or from the continent of Mu, which is supposed to have existed once upon a time in the Pacific.   These theories were based upon the flimsiest kinds of evidence, such as similarities in language, myths, or customs.

Considerable research has been done on the origin of the American Indians, and there is little doubt now that they came from Mongoloid stock and wandered into the Americas from Asia.   The time of their coming is more difficult to determine; but most scientists believe that they lived here at the close of the last glacial epoch, and possibly as long as 15,000 to 25,000 years ago. We may be certain that America was not originally settled by a single group of people, nor within a short span of time.   This was no sudden settlement, or mass migration.   Primitive bands of Asiatic hunters presumably came over in successive waves, probably across Behring Strait, and remained.   As they multiplied, they continued to spread, until eventually they were living in the greater part of both American continents.

Blacks

The black presence in the New World is the result of a series of events entirely different fom those which operated in the case of the Indian; and relations with the other races that they encountered have always been affected by the circumstances under which the contacts occurred.   For centuries the relationship was one of slavery, the consequences of which are still felt, long after the institution itself has been abolished.

Blacks, as a matter of fact, were among the first to arrive in America in modern times.   Tradition has it that the pilot on Columbus' flagship was "Alonzo, the Negro"; and history testifies that blacks accompanied Balboa, Cortes, Velas, Pizarro, and many other conquistadores.   One of them, Estevanico, was a distinguished explorer in his own right.   These black pioneers, however, had little effect upon subsequent trends in race relations.

When Europeans began to exploit the New World they had discovered, their greatest problem was to secure a labor supply.   At first they attempted to make use of the Indians.   Enslavement and a variety of other devices were used to get them to work, but these attempts were failures.   The English, accordingly, began to look eagerly on the hordes of poor whites in their own country, inducing them to cross the Atlantic as indentured servants and to pay for their passage with a term of service.   They also raided the jails and even resorted to kidnapping children, women, and drunken men.   None of these sources proved satisfactory, and it was at this juncture that Africa seemed to offer what appeared to be an adequate and inexhaustible labor supply.

Blacks were not total strangers to the inhabitants of Europe.   That they were known to the ancient Greeks and Romans is proved by objects of art portraying negroid features and by references in the literature. But there is no indication that the white peoples of ancient Europe had a prejudice against blacks or that they attached any social significance to their racial features. It is probable that blacks from Africa occasionally found their way into Europe throughout the historical period. Their numbers were small, and they were not looked on as a solution to any of the problems of the time.

The story of modern black slavery, and of black transport to America, begins in 1433. In that year, a Portuguese ship exploring the coast of Africa brought back two natives from Rio de Oro. Successive explorations resulted in the purchase or capture of other slaves, so that within five years one thousand blacks had been taken to Portugal, and by 1460 seven or eight hundred were being imported annually. In the fifteenth and sixteenth centuries the Portuguese were confronted with a manpower shortage. The long wars with the Moors had depleted their population and colonization and exploration were making serious demands on them. In addition their growing commerce attracted rural people to the cities, with the result that agricultural labor was in short supply. Black slaves, therefore, were especially welcome to the Portuguese. Spain was not long in following the example of Portugal.

Black slaves were employed as early as 1502 by the Spanish settlers in the West Indies, but they were not regarded as the solution to the labor problem in the New World. Instead, the Indian seemed at first to be the answer. An insitution known as the *encomienda* was established. This was a grant of land, with accompanying unpaid, forced, Indian labor for life. Another Spanish institution designed for the proper development of the colony was the *repartimiento*, which was a grant of Indian forced labor for use either on the land, or in mines, factories, monasteries, or for public works. Since the labor supply was supposed to be unlimited, the Indians were worked to death. So terrible was their life that they were driven to mass suicide and infanticide, with the result that their numbers declined with disastrous rapidity.

The Indians had one friend, Bartolome de Las Casas, Bishop of Chiapas. We cannot here recount his many labors on their behalf and the opposition he encountered from the Spanish colonizers and even from his own clergy. In a desperate effort to halt the annihilation of the Indians, Las Casas went to Spain in 1517, appeared before Charles V, and pleaded the cause of these unfortunate people: "At my first arrival in Hispaniola, it contained a million inhabitants, and now (twenty years later) there remain scarce the hundredth part of them." He urged that black slaves, whom he regarded as more robust and better adapted to agricultural operations, be sent out to provide the necessary labor. His suggestion met with approval; and thus a tremendous impetus was given to the African slave trade. One European country after another entered this new and lucrative occupation.

In the present United States, the beginnings of black slavery go back to the year 1619, when a Dutch ship unloaded "twenty Negars" at Jamestown. The Virginians, like the Spaniards in the Indies, were desperate for laborers. These blacks, however, were not purchased as slaves, but were accepted as indentured servants — a status with which the English were more familiar. The institution of slavery in the 13 colonies was the product of a long, continuous development. Africa came to be regarded by them, too, as the most satisfactory source of workers for the task of developing a new continent.

After this beginning, the African continent was raided to supply the demand for laborers in the New World for nearly four centuries. No accurate figures are available on the number of blacks transported to the Americas, and the estimates vary widely. The demand was certainly not uniform over the four centuries, and the restrictions on the traffic were more severe at one time than another. Some scholars have thought that 30 million blacks were brought from Africa to America in the course of the slave trade. For Brazil alone the estimates vary from 3 to 18 million, with 5 million being a reasonable and conservative guess. No one doubts that the total figure would run into many millions. When we consider that, for every slave who succeeded in crossing the Atlantic, there were a number who were killed in the raids or who died in passage, the impact of the traffic on the African continent assumes enormous proportions.

The Atlantic Migration

Yet neither the wanderings of the early Indians nor the forced migration of blacks from Africa equals in magnitude or importance the flood of European emigrants who came to the United States to settle. Biologically, historically, and culturally the people of the United States are European. We are one of the results of the Expansion of Europe. Most of us, if we could trace our complete ancestry, would come upon Irish, German, English, and numerous other antecedents. Our American civilization itself is a patchwork quilt composed largely of the contributions of the various European peoples. Sociologists and historians have long been interested in the background of the heterogeneous groups that crossed the Atlantic to settle this nation, and in the conflicts and adjustments that resulted from their meeting here.

More than 45 million people left their homes in Europe, crossed the Atlantic, and came to settle in the United States. We cannot quote the precise figure, for it was not until 1820 that records began to be kept. Possibly 2 million came as colonists before the Revolutionary War, and it is estimated that another 250,000 came between 1776 and 1820. With the beginning of World War I in 1914 a sharp decline in immigration occurred, and shortly thereafter Congress placed drastic restrictions on the number of persons permitted to enter the country. The Atlantic Migration, accordingly, reached its greatest proportions in the century between the close of the Napoleonic wars in 1815 and the opening of the World War in 1914. During that period more than 30 million immigrants entered the United States from Europe.

The flow of immigration was not uniform throughout this period, however, but fluctuated from year to year. Periods of economic distress in Europe would force large numbers to seek a home across the seas; at other times political disturbances or religious persecution would stimulate emigration. On this side, periods of industrial activity and prosperity would create a demand for labor, while depressions and wars would divert the flow of emigration elsewhere. There were times when other countries proved to be more attractive to the European emigrant than the United States. The tropics always held a certain appeal, and in the decade of the 1820s Brazil loomed as the land of greatest opportunity. Hence the flow to the United States varied greatly. We find that in 1816 about 8,000 immigrants entered the United States, while in the following year the number jumped to 22,400. In 1820 only 8,385 came, but in 1832 there were 60,482. The year 1891 saw more than half a million enter the country, but in 1898 there were only 229,299. The peak year was 1907, when 1,285,349 arrived; and we received more than a million also in the years 1905, 1906, 1910, 1913, and 1914. Not all of these immigrants, of course, were from Europe; but approximately 85 percent were, while another 11 percent entered from other American countries, principally Canada; and relatively few from the rest of the world.

Not only did the number entering the United States vary from time to time, but the ethnic composition also changed. For nearly three centuries most of our immigrants and colonists came from the countries of northern and western Europe — Great Britain, Ireland, the Scandinavian countries, Germany, the Netherlands, France, and Switzerland. This is known as the "Old Immigration." In the 1880s, however, immigrants from southern and eastern Europe, belonging to what is referred to as "New Immigration," began to arrive in noticeable numbers. In 1896, for the first time, the latter outnumbered the former, and they held to their numerical superiority until 1921, when Congress deliberately set about to reverse the trend. This is not to say that people from eastern and southern Europe were not among the earliest settlers. The fact is that in the colonies there were persons of Italian, Greek, and Russian ancestry, and many of them played conspicuous roles in the Revolutionary War. The New Immigration, however, was relatively light until the last quarter of the nineteenth century. Italian immigrants, for example, numbered only 439 in the decade of the 1820s and 9,231 in the 1850s, but there were 307,309 in the 1880s, and 2,045,877 in the first decade of the twentieth century. A similar trend is characteristic of the Greek, Russian, Austrian, Hungarian, and other eastern and southern European nationalities.

Much of the history of the United States is intertwined with the arrival and settlement of these multitudes, and the nation today is biologically and culturally the product of the meeting and mixing of these diverse peoples. America has, indeed, been a melting pot; but the process whereby the melting has taken place is by no means as simple and automatic as we have been led to suppose.

Refugees and Displaced Persons

The people of the United States like to think of their country as a haven of refuge, where those who are persecuted for racial, religious, or political reasons might find freedom and security. While we recognize that most immigrants have come for economic gain (which we regard as less praiseworthy), we recall with pride that many peoples, from the Pilgrims on down, have sought these shores for the sake of their spiritual ideals.

We even overlook the fact that certain other countries also have opened their doors to the victims of religious, racial, and political persecution. Great Britain, despite her periodic economic difficulties, has frequently welcomed refugees. So have Switzerland, Austria, West Germany, Greece, Belgium, the Netherlands, and the Scandinavian countries. France, especially, has long served as a magnet for refugees from every part of the world, and probably, more than any other nation, deserves to be called the "Land of Asylum." France has never taken steps for the systematic assimilation of her foreign population, nor has she opposed their formation of ethnic colonies or the expressions of their national cultures. Yet, the psychological climate of France being what it is, experience has shown that foreigners, including refugees, tend to become assimilated.

Nevertheless, since World War I the United States has received hundreds of thousands of refugees and displaced persons. Unlike the immigrants of the nineteenth century, these people have reluctantly and unwillingly left their homes, not for economic gain, but because of the ravages of war, or because their political opinions or their religious or ethnic affiliations made them the objects of persecution.

The most severe blow to the United States' image as a haven for refugees occurred during World War II. Millions of people, particularly Jews destined for extermination, wanted to flee the wrath of the Nazis and Fascists. Americans overwhelmingly disapproved of and were appalled at the treatment of the Jews in Germany during that period. However, an isolationist Congress and the fear of having to care for millions of penniless refugees made it impossible to pass acts to allow these individuals to enter the United States. By September of 1939 when the war had shut off immigration, England had admitted 9,000 refugees without permits; Holland, 2,000; France, 600; Sweden, 250; and the United States, 240. This cut back is even more disturbing in light of the fact that there were some one and a quarter million unfilled places on the United States immigration quotas for various countries between 1933 and 1943.

The main blame for this travesty must go to the State Department under the leadership of Cordell Hull. President Roosevelt must also share some of the blame because of his unwillingness to take executive action and his great concern for political expediency. It appeared that a change had come over the country, and America could no longer be thought of as a sanctuary for the oppressed. [6]

In recent years the United States has been more willing to pass special acts to speed up the immigration of oppressed groups. This policy was put into effect when twenty-five thousand Asians were expelled from Uganda and when the North Vietnamese took over South Vietnam.

The migration of large groups of people affects the communities they are leaving and the communities they are entering. American society has many permanent traces of its history of extensive immigration and migration. For example, the American national character has been affected. The history of movement has made Americans individualistic and self-sufficient, since migration makes it difficult to depend on family and kin for support. It could also be claimed that migration has made Americans more tolerant of disorder and more optimistic, since both of these traits are also prevalent in a society of migrants. These ideas are hard to test since it is difficult to collect empirical evidence to support them. However, few would doubt that migration has been very influential in shaping the American value system.

Problems of race relations, then, arise from the fact that peoples move from place to place, and in so doing they come into contact with others who differ from them racially and culturally. Such contacts almost invariably lead to a conflict of interests, to hostility, prejudice, and a struggle for dominance or survival. That is not all, however. Despite their disagreements, groups who are in contact will have a mutual effect upon each other, and seldom if ever do they fail to interbreed. Eventually they may succeed in reaching some sort of modus vivendi. In this whole process, however, the circumstances under which the groups came into contact are of utmost importance. It makes a world of difference whether they come together as conquerors and conquered, as masters and slaves, or as immigrants and hosts. People's memories are long, and the pattern of race and ethnic relations that emerges from the contact never fails to reflect the fact that the initial meeting was a voluntary or an involuntary one, an invasion or a conquest, or that the newcomers were met with a welcome rather than a sneer.

Notes

1. W. J. von Puttkamer, "Requiem for a Tribe," in *National Geographic* (Feb. 1975): 256, 268.

2. W. S. Woytinsky and F. S. Woytinsky, "World Migration Patterns," in C. B. Nam, *Population and Society*, pp. 298–313.

3. W. Petersen, "A General Typology of Migration," *American Sociological Review* 23, no. 3 (June 1958): 256–266.

4. J. J. Senturia, "Mass Expulsion," *Encyclopedia of the Social Sciences*, vol. 10, pp. 185–189.

5. For a somewhat different interpretation, see S. C. Jett, "Pueblo Indian Migrations," *American Antiquity* 29, no. 3 (Jan. 1964): 281–300.

6. L. H. Carlson and G. A. Colburn, *In Their Place: White America Defines Her Minorities, 1850–1950*, pp. 290–291.

Chapter Six
Conflict

. . . conflict and cooperation are not separable things but phases of one process which always involves something of both.

— *Charles Horton Cooley* Social Process

Seldom have the members of diverse races met under more favorable circumstances than those that surrounded the initial contacts of white Europeans and brown Hawaiians. It was on the morning of January 18, 1778, that the natives of the island of Kauai awoke to find Captain James Cook's two vessels, *Discovery* and *Resolution*, standing offshore. Accustomed to nothing more than small canoes, the natives were greatly impressed. "These are forests that have drifted out to sea," they exclaimed, as they marveled at the lofty masts. They called the strange objects *moku*, islands, not knowing that they were but small ships, of less than five hundred tons.

The men aboard impressed them no less than the ships. They thought Captain Cook was their god, Lono, and they accorded him royal honors and prostrated themselves before him as he passed. They were eagerly curious about their visitors and all they possessed, and were desirous of obtaining, by hook or crook, anything they could lay hands on.

Word spread rapidly about the mysterious creatures who had come on their huge, floating islands. "Fire and smoke issue from their mouths," so the rumors ran. "They have openings in the sides of their bodies into which they thrust their hands and draw out iron, beads, nails, and other treasures; and their speech is unintelligible." Natives on the other islands, of course, were properly skeptical of these wild tales, but they lost no time in taking to their canoes and .setting out to glimpse these remarkable beings. They were convinced, too, when they actually saw smoke coming from the mouths of the sailors, and saw and heard the fire belching from the portholes of the ships with a noise like thunder.

Captain Cook did not take undue advantage of their credulity. As a matter of fact, he was a humane and tolerant man, especially so if we compare him with other explorers of that era. He commented on the Hawaiians' pleasant dispositions, and admired them for their neatness and ingenuity. His intentions were honorable. He had come not to enslave or exploit them, but only to advance knowledge of geography and astronomy. Sometimes he would capture a few of the natives, take them aboard ship, treat them well, load them with presents, and set them ashore. He was determined that they not misunderstand his good intentions. Before he reached the Hawaiian Islands he had had some unfortunate experiences with the natives of other islands in the Pacific, and had been forced to shoot a few. But he always deplored such occurrences, and justified them on the ground that he had to convince the savages that he intended them no harm. In short, he believed that he was a man of good will, and he had come to a land of friendly, curious people.

The records agree that relations were most cordial. The old king gave Cook a beautiful featherwork cape, and received in return a linen shirt and the Captain's own sword. The Hawaiian priests were especially generous, and sent to the ships endless supplies of meat and vegetables, for which they demanded nothing in payment. The historian of the expedition records that the instances of kindness and civility on the part of the natives were too numerous to mention. So generous were they, in fact, that after a time the islands began to run short of food. The king, accordingly, was forced to inquire politely and tactfully when his white friends planned to depart. When they told him the date, huge quantities of tapa, hogs, and vegetables were presented as farewell gifts.

These idyllic relations, unfortunately, came to an end. Shortly before the whites took their leave, a Hawaiian stole a blacksmith's tongs and chisel, and dived overboard with them. Pareah, a chief, went ashore at once to recover them, and he returned, not only the two articles, but other stolen goods as well, which had not been missed. An officer of the expedition insisted, however, on taking a canoe as additional punishment for the theft, and to this Pareah objected. A scuffle ensued, and the hostility of the Hawaiians began to mount. The next night one of the *Discovery*'s boats was stolen for the nails it contained, which the Hawaiians highly prized. Captain Cook thereupon resolved to make use of one of his favorite expedients, seizing the king and making him a hostage until reparation should be made. So he went ashore, accompanied by a band of marines, and demanded that the king return with him to the ship. Cook failed to appreciate the loyalty that the natives felt for their king, and a battle ensued. As the party retreated to its boats, Cook received his death blow from a club in the hands of one of the chiefs. The whole affair was a tragedy of misunderstanding.[1]

Small wonder, then, that there are many who insist that conflict is an *inevi-table* consequence of the meeting of peoples.   Says Donald Young: "Group an-tagonisms seem to be inevitable when two peoples in contact with each other may be distinguished by differentiating characteristics, either inborn or cul-tural, and are actual or potential competitors."[2] Bogardus, Park, and Brown, who posit a natural cycle of steps or stages in race relations, invariably include conflict as one of them.   We saw in Chapter 5 that even before the dawn of history primitive bands were moving over the face of the earth, encountering strange peoples, and trespassing on their lands.   Archaeologists suspect that these prehistoric contacts resulted in wars and bloodshed, and in the destruc-tion and displacement of one group by another.   Historic evidence supports such guesses, and indicates that conflict of some sort is a common occurrence when unlike peoples meet.   Many people today regard as the very essence of the race problem the elimination, reduction, and control of these persistent ten-sions.   Certain it is that these conflicts are the phases of the race problem that make the headlines and force on people's minds the subject of race relations.

Contact Without Conflict

There are reports, however, of unlike groups that dwell together in peace and harmony.   Let us consider some of these, for they may offer a clue to the way in which conflict might be reduced or prevented.   At the least, they will cast doubt on the generalization that conflict is an inevitable and universal accom-paniment of the contacts of racial and ethnic groups.

Tungus and Cossacks

On the western border of Manchuria two unlike groups live together, trade and associate with each other, and for generations have managed to avoid conflict. They have been visited by Ethel John Lindgren, who has published a report on what is unquestionably a remarkable situation.[3] She declares that during her period of residence among these peoples (1) she never heard a Tungus or a Cossack indicate that he regarded the other group with hatred, contempt, or fear; and (2) she was unable to discover any tradition or record that the relations between the two groups have ever been other than amicable, although she searched for such evidence in the memories of the oldest living persons in both groups.   The Tungus, she says, will criticize the Cossacks for their thieving habits, but will commend them for their sobriety, while Cossacks will extol the scrupulous honesty of the Tungus although deploring acts of violence they commit while under the influence of drink.   The Tungus, moreover, will frankly confess that they prefer to live in their tents in the forest rather than in the Cossack village with its stuffy homes that they consider injurious to health. In brief, here is no blind and sentimental love of neighbor, for each group prefers its own way of life and regards that of the other with a critical but realistic tolerance.

Racially and culturally, the two groups are quite different. The Tungus have Mongoloid physical features, while the Cossacks are Caucasoid. Apparently, however, they attach no significance whatsoever to the color of their skins or the type of their hair, and it never occurs to either group that the Tungus ought to have some fellow-feeling for the Chinese simply because they share certain superficial physical characteristics with them.

Culturally, the Tungus and the Cossacks are far apart. The Tungus are an illiterate, nomadic, primitive people, dwelling in tents, depending on their domesticated reindeer and on hunting for their subsistence. Nominally they are Christians, and they used to pay an annual visit to a church for baptisms and weddings; but lately they have been cut off from priests and churches, and their Christian affiliations have been limited to hanging ikons in their tents and placing crosses on graves. Their ancient primitive religious beliefs are persistent, and their medicine men enjoy great prestige for their skill in curing disease, predicting the future, and communicating with the spirits.

The Cossacks are proud of their Russian background. In all probability they are the descendants of Russians who invaded and conquered Siberia early in the seventeenth century. Later some of them left Siberia for Manchuria, where they founded agricultural settlements and where they were visited by Lindgren. Christianity has deeper roots in their culture than in that of the Tungus, and they zealously participate in the ceremonies of the church. At the same time, they are not without their superstitions and folk beliefs. They are village-dwellers, and their homes are more substantial and impressive than the rude shelters of the Tungus. It is their practice on cold nights to close doors and windows and keep their stoves hot, much to the amusement and discomfort of the Tungus, whose practice it is to sleep in partly open tents, lightly covered, and let the fire go out. The Cossacks rely for their subsistence on agriculture and raising livestock, although hunting squirrels and wapiti assumes some importance in their economy, and they carry on an extensive trade with the Tungus.

The Cossacks speak Great Russian, and never bother to learn the Tungus language. On the other hand, the Tungus are bilingual, and all the men and most of the women understand Russian quite well. This would seem to give the Tungus a distinct advantage in their trade relations, for they can consult together in the markets in a language that no trader can understand. The Cossacks, however, have one asset that tends to compensate for their linguistic limitations. They alone can read, write, and reckon. The Tungus culture is sadly deficient in mathematical skills, and even the simplest problems of addition are too difficult for most of them. Thus the advantage in trade that the Cossacks gain through their literacy and their monopoly on arithmetic is partly counterbalanced by the superior linguistic talents of the Tungus. In this sphere of life, as in others, the inequality between the two groups is not so great that respect ceases to be mutual.

Lindgren points out that contacts between these two are numerous and frequent, and there are ample opportunities for clashes. First, there are markets. During the winter months, when the Tungus are busy hunting squirrels, Cossack traders will travel up the frozen rivers on horse-drawn sledges in order to trade; and in summer the Tungus will come with their reindeer to the Cossack village for the same purpose, at which time they are often entertained in the homes of their trader friends. Second, there are chance encounters in the forests. Both Tungus and Cossacks enjoy hunting, and frequently their trails cross. Third, there are extended visits, for one reason or another. Young Tungus men will often remain for a time in the Cossack village after the close of the summer markets. Then, some years ago, when an epidemic took their reindeer, the Tungus migrated to the Cossack settlements, and became hired laborers in homes and fields, until they had saved enough to purchase new herds. Clearly, the absence of conflict is not to be explained on grounds that the two groups are strangers to each other.

How, then, can we account for these halcyon relations? The cause cannot be found in the temperament of the peoples, for both have contacts of quite a different sort with other groups. Among the plausible reasons suggested by Lindgren's report are the following:

1. The numbers of the two groups have always been small and about equal in size. Some fifty years ago the Tungus numbered about 850, and the Cossacks approximately the same. At the time of Lindgren's visit (1932), smallpox had reduced the Tungus to 160. The Cossacks with whom they traded numbered about 150 individuals, though there were other Russians in the region.

2. There has been no competition for land and resources. The Tungus nomadize over a territory of 7000 square miles, giving the very low population density of about .02 per square mile. Only the fringes of this large area have been invaded by Russians, Chinese, and others.

3. Outside influences have been of such a nature that they tended to draw Tungus and Cossacks together, rather than drive a wedge between them. About 1908 the Chinese government became interested in the frontiers as possible sources of tax revenues, but the Tungus proved too elusive. Later they imposed taxes upon the fur trade of the Cossacks, thus tapping both groups in one stroke. This oppression by people whom they regard as outsiders has served to strengthen the bonds between Tungus and Cossacks.

4. In many respects the two cultures happened to be supplementary rather than antagonistic. Economically, the trade in furs has been highly profitable to the Cossacks, and has brought to the Tungus many new items they have learned to prize. Furthermore, the attitudes they have held with regard to religion, marriage, land, and property could harmonize rather than clash; and neither group brought to the contact situation beliefs in racial superiority. Lindgren thinks that the social organization that has characterized the two peoples, one in which the values of freedom, individualism, and equality are emphasized, goes far toward explaining the absence of conflict.

Whether these conditions still prevail, or will continue, we cannot say. It is not inconceivable that certain developments, such as depletion of the game supply, population changes, or interference with the fur trade, might operate to destroy the amicable relations between the Tungus and the Cossacks, and to promote discord and strife.

Indians and *Ladinos*

Another instance of race relations without conflict has been reported by Dr. John Gillin.[4] The community he describes is the town of San Luis Jilotepeque, in eastern Guatemala. The population of more than three thousand is composed of *ladinos*, who make up about one-third of the total, and Indians of the Mayan stock, who make up the remainder. Dr. Gillin maintains that these two racial groups are quite different, are in close physical contact, practice a mutual tolerance of each other's mode of life, and are remarkably successful in avoiding overt conflict, even though there is a good deal of contempt on the part of the *ladinos* for the Indians.

Differences between the two groups are great, although not as great as those separating Tungus and Cossacks. The *ladinos* are lighter in color, and some are blonds, but many of them are as dark as the Indians. Consequently, physical features are not reliable as symbols of status, and it becomes necessary to note such items as dress and mannerisms. Indian women wear a picturesque costume consisting of a wrap-around skirt, embroidered blouse, bright beads, and head shawl. The men wear the typical peon costume of white shirt and short white trousers, which stop slightly below the knee. Neither wears shoes, although the men, on dress occasions, when they adopt clothes of European design, may put on sandals. The dress of the *ladinos* follows European patterns, even including neckties, which Indians never wear.

The two groups show innumerable other cultural differences, so that it would be correct to think of them as distinct ethnic groups. *Ladinos* speak only Spanish, while the Indians are bilingual. While both groups are nominally Catholic, religion is rather superficial for the *ladinos*, while for the Indians it is an important and integral part of their lives and includes many aboriginal features and ceremonies that have been grafted onto the Christian faith. Dr. Gillin shows that *ladinos* and Indians are different not only on the surface but even in deeper matters of beliefs and attitudes. Regarding such things as the value of money, the soil, work, family, and relatives, the two groups have distinct cultures. For example, the *ladino* measures prestige by money and wealth, and the things that money will buy; but in the Indian community one achieves prestige through wisdom, experience, and character, none of which can be bought. Even so, the *ladinos* constitute the upper class of the village. They own most of the land, hold most of the important political posts, occupy the desirable residential sites, and they demand and receive from the Indians the respect and courtesies due to their superior social position.

One would expect, under such an unjust and inequitable system, that there would be continual strife and bickering. However, just one act of violence is recorded, and even this came about only when a *ladino* politician plied Indians with liquor and incited them to attack his *ladino* rival. The fact is that the Indians are not seething with resentment and do not feel that they suffer from exploitation and discrimination. Rorschach tests indicate that aggression is far less characteristic of the Indian than of the *ladino*.

Dr. Gillin's explanation of this surprising absence of conflict is that the Indians have developed a culture that adequately satisfies their drives, wants, and desires, and they do not therefore consider the pressure from *ladinos* as being onerous or unendurable. Their kinship system gives them a feeling of social security and of belonging. Their religion, although it may seem superstitious to the outsider, does serve to reduce their worries and anxieties. Their medical folklore, while it may not cure, does bring peace of mind to the sufferer. Work on the land they regard as honorable rather than degrading, as the *ladinos* do. Finally, the Indians enjoy a certain freedom. They may, if they feel oppressed, cease to be Indians and become *ladinos* by abandoning the Indian customs, adopting the clothes and manners of the upper class, putting on shoes and a necktie, and, if necessary, moving to another village. Thus in many ways the lot of the Indians is more enviable than that of the *ladinos*. Frustration and boredom are virtually unknown to them, while they are the major problems of the *ladino* community.

The Basques of Idaho

Coming nearer home, we have reports of intergroup contacts here in the United States from which the element of conflict is lacking. One such recent report concerns the Basques of Idaho.[5] J. B. Edlefsen, the author of this report, states that he is a native of Idaho, attended the schools and colleges there, and had many Basques as fellow students. Later, as a businessman he had many relations with these immigrants; and, finally, as an instructor in a college in Boise, he had several Basque students in his classes. He insists that from the earliest days of the Basque immigration there has been "an almost complete absence of prejudice and conflict."

The Basques are an ancient, proud, and independent people whose native land is in the Pyrenees region of Spain and France. Their origin is clouded in mystery, and their language unique. Some of them came to America in the 1860s and early 1870s, settling in the Nevada area. Others followed, migrating to Oregon and Idaho in the 1880s. There are no accurate statistics as to their number in the United States at the present time, although estimates are placed as high as fifteen thousand. There are approximately three thousand in the state of Idaho.

When the Basque newcomers began to arrive in Idaho, says Edlefsen, they attracted little attention except for the fact that they used a language totally unintelligible to the other residents of the area. Sheep owners and ranchers gave them employment. This was their traditional occupation, and they readily proved their worth. Their industry and dependability immediately resulted in an economic welcome being extended to others of this strange group, and their numbers grew. Those who had been married before emigrating arranged for their families to come, while others married young Basque women who came to the area with relatives and friends.

The Basques, however, tended to segregate themselves by establishing their own communities. Edlefsen maintains that such segregation was not forced on them, for the older American residents did not regard the Basques as inferior, nor did they persecute them or discriminate against them in any way. He thinks that their segregation resulted from their strong racial pride; their determination to preserve their traditions; the nature of the occupation in which most of them engaged; the fact that they were Catholics in a predominantly Protestant environment; and, most important, their fierce pride in, and stubborn retention of, their language.

Even so, they began to mix more and more and to become assimilated. Some of them moved into other occupations. Many established themselves as independent sheep owners and earned the reputation as leaders in the industry. Most achieved economic security and high status in the area. The men began to learn English, and their children, attending the local schools, became rapidly Americanized. Then they began to move out of their segregated residential areas, and to purchase homes wherever they chose, for there was no opposition to their doing so. As a matter of fact, says Edlefsen, they were welcomed as equals. Soon they abandoned their separate church and affiliated with the other Catholic group in the community. Increasingly, they became naturalized citizens. Second- and third-generation Basques are tending to marry non-Basques, and the author says there is little doubt that, in time, amalgamation and assimilation will be complete.

There are still other accounts of intergroup relations that have not magnified the element of conflict. There are Indian tribes that boast that their relations with whites have never been other than friendly. Dr. Irving Goldman has described the coming of the whites to the country of the Alkatcho Carrier Indians of British Columbia and concludes, "There seems to have been not the slightest physical conflict."[6]

The Concept of Conflict

Those who insist on the inevitability of conflict when unlike groups enter into relations with one another will be critical of the cases we have reported. They will say, for instance, that the hostility between white and Indians was nowhere more severe than in Guatemala, if we look back into the records to the early days of contact. The present peaceful arrangements, they will say, are simply an instance of accommodation that follows conflict. They may say, too, that the seeds of conflict are present, and the probability of their blooming is neither impossible nor remote. Lindgren, as a matter of fact, suspects that the harmonious relations between Tungus and Cossacks are a delicate adjustment that may be upset if there should be a depletion of the natural resources, or if the population ratio should become distorted. In the case of the Basques, Edlefsen drops the hint that the notorious hostility of cattle and sheep owners might on occasion have been directed toward these newcomers.

The crux of the matter really lies in our definition of conflict. Many instances of race relations without conflict might be discovered if we choose to define conflict narrowly, so as to include only its violent, overt forms. But if we recognize the fact that conflict involves also those subtle, restrained forms of interaction wherein one seeks to reduce the status of one's opponents, and not to eliminate them entirely from the conflict, then perhaps it is true that conflict invariably occurs when unlike peoples meet.

Coser has defined conflict as "a struggle over values or claims to status, power, and scarce resources, in which the aims of the conflicting parties are not only to gain the desired values but also to neutralize, injure, or eliminate the rivals."[7] Bernard claims that "conflict exists between groups when there is a fundamental incompatibility in their values, goals, interests, etc.[8] Many of the nineteenth-century sociologists were very much concerned with social conflict in their theories. Conflict is the key explanatory variable in Marxian thought. Marx believed that the unequal allocation of scarce resources determined social relationships. Marx felt that the potential for social conflict was inherent in social situations that caused people to compete with each other for desirable assets. Therefore, the potential for conflict exists between groups if they feel that their access to scarce resources is being threatened by the presence of the other group. We could look on the cases of contact without conflict that we have just presented as instances in which the groups did not think of each other as competitors who had to be eliminated.

Kriesberg believes that conflict exists because groups of people believe that they have incompatible goals. These incompatible goals may force them to see each other as competitors. Conflict may occur from competition over any one of a number of scarce resources ranging from territory and status to power and income.[9]

Some disagreement has arisen over whether it is necessary for parties to be aware that there is an incompatibility between them before a conflict can exist. The early sociologists all assumed that a consciousness by the parties that they are in contention with each other is an essential element in conflict. For example, Park and Burgess wrote that "Conflict is always conscious."[10] However, it is also possible for two groups to be unaware of the competition that exists between them. In this instance, we would have a latent conflict, which has the potential of developing at some later point. In Table 6.1 we can see the various situations that are possible when two groups come together.

In (1) in the table we have the traditional type of situation that we usually think of when a conflict exists. Both parties believe they are at odds with each other and this is actually the case. In (2) both parties are at odds with each other, but only one party perceives the disagreement and acts on that belief. The other party assumes that there is no real problem, and believes that the

Table **6.1**   Varieties of social conflict

	Parties' beliefs about conflict situation		
Actual fact	*Both believe conflict exists*	*One believes and other does not*	*Neither believes conflict exists*
Conflict	(1) Balanced conflict	(2) Unbalanced conflict	(3) Latent conflict
No conflict	(4) Unrealistic two-party conflict	(5) Unrealistic one-party conflict	(6) Harmonious contact

Modified from Louis Kriesberg, *The Sociology of Social Conflicts* (Englewood Cliffs, N.J.: Prentice Hall, 1973), p. 5.

first party is acting irrationally. In (3) we have the latent conflict situation. Here there is real disagreement and competition present between the parties, but neither perceives it nor acts on it. The potential for a conflict to erupt is always present and it may actually be realized at some point in the future. In (4) we see an instance of an unrealistic conflict. Both parties believe that they are in contention with each other, but in actual fact no conflict exists. In (5) no conflict exists, but one party misperceives the situation and believes a conflict to exist. In (6) a conflict-free situation exists.

Intensity of Conflict

The fact that two parties are in conflict with each other does not mean that automatically there will be an armed battle between them. Various levels of intensity of conflict are possible, and it is important for us to discuss them. The intensity of the conflict will depend on the degree of motivation of each party to coerce or defeat the other. The situation will be considered in the light of the various deterrents that may hinder each party from acting on its hostility. For example, a group may be deterred from acting by the fear of retaliation or the belief that the action will not really accomplish the goals and will lead only to further difficulty. Another aspect that will decrease the intensity of violence in a conflict is the extent to which the groups are integrated into the society. As Lewis Coser puts it:

The more integrated into the society or group are the parties to the conflict, the less likely will the conflict between them be violent. The greater the degree of integration, the higher the likelihood that the conflicting parties will choose weapons that will not permanently menace their common bonds. Violent class struggles or class wars are likely to give way to less militant means, such as institutionalized strikes or regularized contests. . . .[11]

As the two groups come to the realization that they have common bonds because of their membership in a larger society, they will not let their differences cause them to act in such a way that they might destroy each other. The differences will be there, but the intensity of their conflict will be diminished. For example, even though the Irish Catholics may be engaged in violent conflict with the Protestants in Ireland and the Arabs and Israelis may be at great odds with each other in the Middle East, when members of these opposing groups live in the United States, they no longer engage in open warfare with each other even though their animosity for each other may still exist.

Another factor that will determine the intensity of the conflict is the degree to which the participants in the conflict are collectively oriented or individually oriented. In other words, are they engaged in a struggle that transcends their own individual goals, or are they engaged in a struggle only to help themselves? If they are engaged in a struggle that involves a broad ideological base, they are more likely to use extreme measures than if they are merely trying to help themselves. One feels greater freedom to kill someone in the name of democracy or communism than to eliminate a competitor who is interfering with personal goals. The ideological end often seems to justify the means and gives the individual a clear conscience to act more radically and mercilessly.[12]

Individual Conflict Versus Group Conflict

As the reader may have guessed from the last paragraph, we must draw a distinction between individual conflict and group conflict. For example, some people would think that group reactions merely represent the total of the individual reactions to a particular series of events, so that the action of a group is the expression of the views of its 100, 500, or 5 million members. With this view one assumes that improving the individual interpersonal relations of the members of each group will improve or eliminate the potential for conflict. However, there is a basic fault in this view and Jessie Bernard describes it very well:

In brief, a thousand friendships between members of two groups — German and American scientists, for example, or a thousand love affairs between soldiers and forbidden enemy women — will not add up to friendly group relations. Nor conversely, will a thousand quarrels between American tourists and French taxidrivers add up to a Franco-American conflict.[13]

For the most part, laws that govern interpersonal relations are not always the same as those that govern intergroup relations. Therefore, group conflict has to be analyzed differently than individual conflict. Many of the Nazis during World War II who were engaged in an all-out effort to exterminate the Jews had individual Jewish friends whom they assisted in escaping from ultimate destruction. Group conflict must be analyzed from a group perspective; it is not merely the outcome of thousands of individual prejudices and disagreements.

Conflict includes, in addition to wars and riots, such peaceful activities as picketing, boycotting, ridicule, laughter, and insolence. These patterns of conflict change from place to place and from time to time, and each has its own history. Some are ineffective and futile, while others succeed remarkably in achieving their objectives. They are not limited, of course, to race and ethnic relations, but occur also in the conflicts between other groups — labor and management, nation and nation, class and class, sect and sect. Let us consider now some of the forms conflict between racial and ethnic groups has assumed.

Patterns of Conflict

Lynching

Lynching is a pattern of conflict that has undergone considerable change in the course of its history. It involves execution by a mob, without trial and regardless of the existence of regular courts of law, of an individual who is suspected, convicted, or accused of a violation of laws or mores. It is a form of violence that has been especially characteristic of the United States in the recent past. It was most prevalent in the South, in rural and small-town communities; the victim was usually black, and the participants lower-class whites. (See the map of lynchings from 1882 to 1963 in Figure 6.1.)

It has not always been so, however. The origin of lynch-law is clouded in mystery, but it is commonly believed to have originated with a certain Charles Lynch, a Virginia Quaker, whose religious scruples forbade his taking human life even during wartime. Charles Lynch was born near the present city of Lynchburg, Virginia, in 1736. Although his sympathies were with the colonists in the revolution, he was unwilling himself to participate in the fighting. In his frontier community the Tories were active, especially in stealing horses for the British armies; and the officers of the law, and the courts of justice, were totally incapable of coping with the situation. Lynch and several of his compatriots therefore decided to take the matter into their own hands. They apprehended the thieves, held court in the Lynch home, brought witnesses and accusers face to face with the suspects, and meted out punishment to the guilty, usually to the tune of 40 lashes across the bare back; but they did not resort to execution. They came to be respected as loyal patriots, and in October, 1782, the Virginia Legislature passed an act completely exonerating Lynch and his associates.[14]

Following the Revolutionary War, the pattern of lynching spread over the country. Especially on the frontier did the custom take hold of using extra-legal procedures in dealing with horse thieves, wife beaters, protectors of runaway slaves, gamblers, and murderers. Often there was a semblance of a trial, sometimes resulting in the acquittal of the accused. Punishment in the form of execution was far exceeded by fines, flogging, and tarring and feathering. Blacks were seldom the victims.

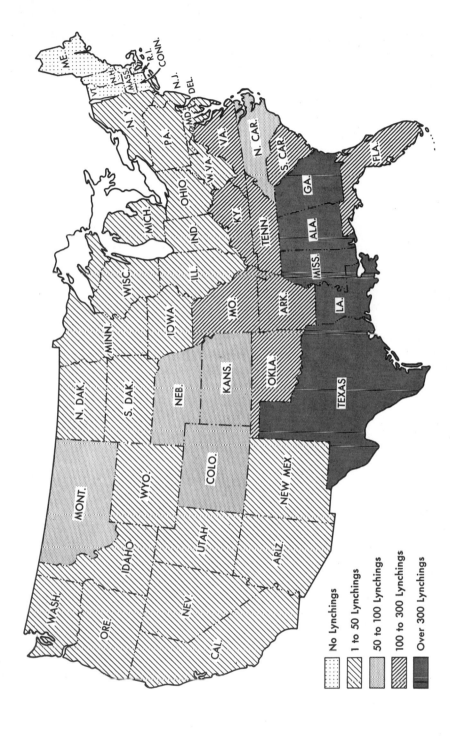

Figure 6.1 Lynchings (1882–1963).

No Lynchings

1 to 50 Lynchings

50 to 100 Lynchings

100 to 300 Lynchings

Over 300 Lynchings

It was in the decades immediately preceding the Civil War that lynching began to acquire its modern character. White people in cotton states grew desperately afraid of slave revolts, and resorted to lynch-law to suppress abolitionists, agitators, and rebellious blacks. Finally, the period of the Civil War and the Reconstruction saw the pattern of lynching firmly established: courts of law, although in full operation, were circumvented; no effort was made to determine the guilt of the accused; punishment was invariably death, often accompanied by torture; and the victim was usually black.

Statistics on the extent of lynching are not reliable. There is some difference of opinion as to just when a homicide should be classified as a lynching; and the laws of the various states are not in agreement. Minnesota, for example, defines it as the killing of a human being by the act or procurement of a mob, while in Kentucky and North Carolina the victim must first have been in the hands of the law. The *Chicago Tribune* made an annual summary between 1882 and 1917; and Tuskegee Institute has attempted to keep accurate statistics since 1889. From these data it appears that lynching has claimed more than five thousand victims since 1882.[15] What the number would be if we included the years prior to that date, and the victims of mobs in the Wild West, is anybody's guess.

Nine-tenths of the recorded lynchings have occurred in the Southern states, and four-fifths of the victims have been blacks. Only the six New England states can boast of no lynchings. The victims, other than blacks, have included Indians, Mexicans, Italians, Swiss, Japanese, Chinese, Jews, Bohemians, and Filipinos.[16] The crimes with which they have been charged are as varied as the groups victimized. Homicide leads as the crime for which most victims of lynching mobs have been accused, while rape takes second place. When we consider, however, the relative frequency of these two offenses, we find some basis for the general belief that there was a relationship between sex and lynching, and that violation of a white woman was a major incentive to mob action, as well as the commonest rationalization given by white people for lynching. While murder, rape, arson, and assault were the principal grounds for lynching, many others existed, including some most trivial. Among these were theft, insulting a white man, writing insulting letters, poisoning cattle, throwing stones, drunkenness, circulating radical literature, jumping a labor contract, organizing sharecroppers, asking a white woman in marriage, and refusing to give way to white persons.[17] Of course, these cannot be regarded as the *causes* of lynching; they are but the occasions, the excuses, or the incidents that arouse the mob. The causes lie much deeper, and would include the frontier heritage in American culture and the general attitude toward the law as well as various other complex social and economic factors.[18]

The peak in lynchings was reached in 1892, when 235 lynchings occurred. Lynching was especially prevalent during the 1890s, when there was an annual average of 154.1 executions. In the decade of the 1920s, there were 315 lynchings, 33 in the 1940s, and 6 in the 1950s. One lynching was reported in 1961. Some feel that the decrease in lynching is only apparent; that lynching has been "driven underground"; and that certain substitutes have arisen to take its place, such as "quick justice," killing of accused persons by police officers, and murder by quiet, small groups, rather than by noisy mobs.[19] Perhaps the truth is that lynching as a form of conflict is simply giving way to other forms more in keeping with the times.

Race Riots

Unlike lynching, rioting is an ancient and universal form of conflict. Riots occurred in the Greek city-states, and throughout the Roman Empire they were a familiar phenomenon. They are a conspicuous feature in the history of all modern nations. A riot is an outbreak of temporary, spontaneous, violent mass disorder. Racial antagonisms are by no means the principal occasions for inciting riots; political, economic, religious, and other types of dissatisfaction have been far more important. Labor disputes, anticlericalism, royalism, anarchism, socialism, strikes, unemployment, and poverty have produced infinitely more riots than has race prejudice. The race riot, however, is a pattern of conflict that causes serious concern to the residents of all the biracial and multiracial areas in the world today.

A race riot is different from a lynching in that the action is two-way. A lynching is a one-sided form of conflict, in which the victim is hopelessly overpowered. A riot, on the other hand, sees the opposing forces more evenly matched; the minority fights back, inflicts damage on the aggressors, and feels that it has some hope of defending itself. Whereas in this country lynching tends to be a Southern, rural type of conflict, the riot is an urban phenomenon, and tends somewhat to be more Northern than Southern. Riots are different, too, from insurrection, rebellion, and revolution, in that they involve no intention of overthrowing the existing political order, although they are often preliminary to social movements of greater scope.

A typical race riot is the one that occurred in South Africa in January, 1949, which was described as follows:

On January 13 hate and fear coalesced and exploded in Durban. Over the "bush telegraph" came a rumor that a young Negro had been attacked and injured by an Indian in Durban's downtown market. Some of the city's 100,000 Negroes, most of them Zulus, did not wait to verify the report (later proved untrue). Chanting Zulu war songs and hurling bricks and stones, they moved against the sections where about 120,000 Indians live and work. In four days, while the savage cry of *bulala!* (kill!) resounded through Durban, 83 Negroes, 53 Indians and one European died by violence.

The riots grew out of an old complex of racial hates and abuses. The Union of South Africa's 2,300,000 white "Europeans" mortally fear and sternly repress the country's 7,750,000 Negroes, and the 280,000 expatriate Indians fare little better. The Indians, in turn, often exploit the helpless Negroes, creating a criss-cross of enmities which have been intensified by the extremist racial policies of Dr. Daniel Francois Malan's new nationalist government. Fearing the whites, Durban's Zulus had struck blindly at the more vulnerable Indians.

The Indians killed some Negroes; before the outbreak was crushed, even more were killed by white police and troops. . . .

The Durban riots began in the heart of the city and then spread to the suburbs as police attacked the Zulus with clubs and whips. In an outlying Indian colony the frustrated rioters burned blocks of Indian homes, seven of the eleven occupants dying in one flaming house. Repeated volleys from machine guns, which killed many Negroes, finally ended the uprising. . . .

Hunted Indians fled from Durban to a wooded valley near the city, looking only for a place to hide from the enraged mobs. The government posted guards around the area while troops and the police fought the pillagers in the city.

In the week following the Durban riots there were racial flare-ups in other South African cities, but there was no indication that the government would modify its repressive measures against "non-Europeans."[20]

The riot has long been a feature of interracial conflict in the United States. In 1837 there was one in Boston in which the Irish were involved and in which fifteen thousand persons participated. The three decades prior to the Civil War witnessed many in Northern industrial centers, growing out of the competition between blacks and various immigrant groups for jobs. Abolitionist riots were frequent also during the same period. At the time of World War I a wave of rioting swept through a number of cities. One of the worst was in 1917 in East St. Louis, Illinois, in which 39 blacks and 8 whites were killed and hundreds were estimated to have been more or less seriously injured, 70 having received treatment at one hospital alone. The year 1919 was an especially bitter period, prompting W. E. B. DuBois to say:

That year there were race riots large and small in twenty-six American cities including thirty-eight killed in a Chicago riot of August; from twenty-five to fifty in Phillips County, Arkansas; and six killed in Washington. For a day, the city of Washington, in July, 1919, was actually in the hands of a black mob fighting against the aggression of the whites with hand grenades.[21]

There was a flare-up of rioting also during World War II. On February 27 and 28, 1942, a riot occurred in Detroit over the occupation of the Sojourner Truth Homes, a federal low-rent housing project designed for black defense workers. The Ku Klux Klan burned crosses the night before the tenants were to move in, and the following day the project was picketed by whites who lived nearby and a mob of 1,000 sought to prevent moving vans from delivering furniture. Before the riot ended, 25 had been seriously injured and 110 blacks arrested.[22] The next year there was another riot in Detroit, in which 34 were killed and more than 1,000 were wounded, the details of which have been given by two sociologists who made their observations on the scene.[23] Widely publicized also was the notorious "zoot-suit riot" in Los Angeles on June 7, 1943. Although local newspapers and authorities denied that this occurrence constituted a race riot, subsequent reports established the fact that the participants were white servicemen and civilians, on the one side, and Mexican and black youths on the other.   Other serious riots of the 1942-to-1944 period occurred in New Orleans, Mobile, Beaumont, Newark, Seattle, and elsewhere.

Numerous so-called race riots occurred in the late 1960s in various cities throughout the United States.   In most of these riots blacks were usually engaged in violent confrontation with law enforcement officers.   A few of the disturbances involved minority groups other than blacks.   Few of these riots, however, were between members of different ethnic or racial groups who were acting as representatives of that group.   For the most part, the riots involved a protest against the establishment from those who felt alienated from it.   In this sense the protests were not really riots, but rather insurrections or rebellions.

In 1968 the United States Department of Labor issued a profile of individuals arrested in the 1967 Detroit riot.   The typical person involved in the riot

was a single man just over thirty years of age, a Protestant, but not a regular churchgoer.

He had dropped out of school by the eleventh grade.   His birth place was the South and he had lived in Detroit for fifteen years or more.

He was a blue-collar worker in a manufacturing plant, where he earned $120 a week. He was currently employed, but he had experienced more than five weeks of unemployment during the previous year.   He had not participated in a government training or poverty program.

He believed that conditions, both for himself and the Detroit Blacks generally had improved during the last five years.   He was also hopeful that Blacks would someday have everything the White man had.[24]

The fact that many of the riot participants felt that the general status of blacks would be improving in the future and that the riots came at a time when advances were being made in the area of race relations in the United States is very interesting in that it follows a traditional pattern.   It appears that periods of rising expectations produce a great deal of frustration in people.   Just when it seems that things are getting better, the frustration of not having all the expectations satisfied becomes unbearable.   Past history has shown that oppressed people usually do not rebel when the situation seems hopeless.   Revolution, as de Tocqueville has noted, usually occurs during periods of change and improvement.

Nations that have endured patiently and almost unconsciously the most overwhelming oppression often burst into rebellion against the yoke the moment it begins to grow lighter. . . .   Evils which are patiently endured when they seem inevitable become intolerable when once the idea of escape from them is suggested.[25]

Several requirements must be met before a riot situation with collective violence will occur.   Obviously, first there must be general frustration and resentment to provide the motivation.   However, the real factor that will determine whether or not the action will take place is the potential for retaliation by the group that bears the brunt of the riot.   The feeling that one might be punished for disruptive actions is lessened by being in the presence of a large number of people. The participants seem to feel that it would be impossible to apprehend and imprison everyone involved in the law breaking. Consequently, when large numbers of people are engaged in actions that are violations of the law, an individual may act in a way that would never be considered when alone. If a crowd feels that the establishment is unable or unwilling to use the force necessary to quell the disturbance, the temptation to enter the quarrel becomes even greater.

Pogroms

This pattern of intergroup conflict has been associated particularly with the Jews of Russia. Pogrom literally means *destruction*. The Jews, of course, have long been the victims of massacres, riots, and persecutions of all sorts; but pogroms are somewhat different. They often appear to have started spontaneously, but actually they are organized from higher administrative levels. Fearing revolutionary movements of peasants and workers, unscrupulous governments attempt to divert the grievances of the people from political and economic affairs and direct them against the Jews. The first pogrom occurred in 1881. The Czar Alexander II had been assassinated, and the bureaucracy and the landed aristocracy were afraid that the widespread discontent with the government might get out of hand. Although there were no Jews among the murderers of the Czar, the Jews were chosen as the scapegoat. Rumors were circulated, and people were even told that it was the imperial wish that on Easter the Jews be punished for their many faults. Peasants and city rabble, motivated as much by a desire for loot as by their prejudices, joined in the attack. The facts that these outbursts occurred simultaneously in many cities, and that the police and the military stood by until the third day, proved that the pogroms were organized and directed from above. Others were to follow. After a few months of calm, the "summer pogroms" began, spreading to many of the cities that had been spared at Easter, and in March, 1882, they began again. After some years of peace, the Minister of the Interior, Von Plehve, organized an appalling number of pogroms, beginning with that of Kishinev in 1903. The Jews were attacked in more than six hundred towns, villages, and cities. Thousands were killed, and the damage to property was tremendous. The Jews fled from Russia in droves. Many of them came to the United States and others went to South America, Africa, or Palestine, while penniless ones sought refuge in the various cities of Europe.[26]

Other Forms of Violence

There are many other patterns of violence that human conflict has assumed, among them being wars, insurrections, rebellions, and revolutions. They are sufficiently different to warrant our having the individual words in our vocabulary, although distinctions between them are not easily made. *War* is defined nowadays as armed conflict between sovereign states, but the term is used metaphorically in many other connections, and in times past, conflict between any groups regarded as organic unities has been so designated. An *insurrection* is a movement involving the use of armed force against the established order; and such a movement, should it enlarge its scope, would be called a *rebellion* or a *revolution*. [27]

Whatever the differences, however, all these forms of conflict have characterized the relations between racial groups. The struggles that formerly prevailed between the whites and the Indians in the present United States are properly referred to as *wars*, for the Indian tribes were theoretically treated as though they were sovereign powers. [28] The so-called Sepoy Mutiny was in reality an *insurrection* on the part of Hindus and Mohammedans against British domination and British disregard for the mores of the native peoples. The uprising in Haiti under Toussaint L'Ouverture, whereby the blacks succeeded in driving out their white masters, is properly designated a *revolution*, for it was directed toward a radical modification of the political and social order.

Insurrections

Insurrections have been frequent in the history of the relations between racial groups. Contrary to the popular belief that blacks stoically accepted their slave status, the truth is that they were continually taking up arms against their masters. There were numerous slave insurrections in Brazil, [29] and hardly an island in the Caribbean fails to show in its record at least one serious revolt of blacks against slavery and the plantation system. In the United States blacks were continually plotting rebellion; and while these risings never seriously threatened the institution of slavery, they did put fear and trembling into the white population and some of them assumed considerable proportions. [30] Most notable were the insurrections led by Denmark Vesey and Nat Turner.

Denmark Vesey purchased his freedom in 1800. He established himself as a carpenter in Charleston, South Carolina, and for twenty years lived as a respectable "free Negro" and enjoyed a relatively comfortable existence. He was, however, a sensitive person, and he was unhappy over his own freedom and success while others of his race were in slavery. He therefore set about to plot a revolt. His plans were carefully laid, and his associates were chosen with utmost scrutiny. Over a period of years they collected their weapons — daggers, bayonets, and pike heads. The second Sunday in July, 1822, was set as the date for the revolt. The whites, however, were informed, and Vesey hastily moved the date ahead one month. His assistants, scattered as they were for miles around Charleston, did not all get the word, and the insurrection was readily quashed. Estimates of the number of blacks involved in the plot ran as high as 9,000. About 139 were arrested, 47 of whom were condemned. Four white men were imprisoned and fined for implication in the plot and for encouraging the blacks.

Nat Turner was a slave who belonged to a Virginia planter, Joseph Travis.

Turner was a mystical, superstitious person, who felt a divine call to free his people. The solar eclipse of February, 1831, convinced him that the time had come for him to deliver the slaves from bondage. The date was to be the Fourth of July; but Turner became ill, and he postponed the date until he should see another divine sign. On August 13, 1831, it seemed to him that the sun turned "a peculiar greenish blue," and he therefore chose August 21 as the date for the revolt. He and his followers began by killing their master and his family, and then roamed the countryside destroying other whites. Within twenty-four hours a total of sixty whites had been killed. State and federal troops were called, and the slaves were speedily overwhelmed. More than one hundred slaves were killed in the encounter, and thirteen slaves and three free blacks were immediately hanged. Turner himself was captured two months later and was promptly executed.

Strikes and Boycotts

These weapons, long used the world over in labor disputes and by indignant consumers, have also been employed by ethnic groups in their conflicts with each other. Instances are continually reported in the press. For example, in 1975 it became known that Arab governments had drawn up a blacklist that included approximately two thousand industrial concerns that did business with Israel. The list also included banking houses and other businesses that were owned or operated by Jews. Any firm on the blacklist was discriminated against when it came to Arab investment.

There was resistance to the Arab boycott. For example, the investment company Merrill Lynch, Pierce, Fenner and Smith refused to capitulate to Arab demands to drop the United States branch of Lazard Frères, a partially Jewish-owned firm in Paris, in a deal to raise 5 million dollars for the Mexican government and 25 million dollars for a car manufacturer. With these actions the battle between Arabs and Israelis had spread beyond the Middle East.

American blacks have often resorted to the boycott as a weapon in their struggle for job opportunities. During the depression of the 1930s large numbers rallied to the slogan, "Spend Your Money Where You Can Work," refusing to patronize merchants and institutions that refused to employ black labor. More recently, blacks have used the boycott with great effect in Montgomery, Alabama. The incident began on December 1, 1955, when Mrs. Rosa Parks, a black seamstress employed by a downtown department store, refused to give up her seat when told to do so by the bus driver. At the time, there were 26 blacks and 10 white persons seated in the 36-passenger bus. Bus drivers were, at that time, required by Alabama law to segregate passengers, but they could use their discretion in determining where the line should be drawn. When the driver asked Mrs. Parks and three other blacks to give up their seats, a number of white persons were about to board. He declared later in court that he was trying to "equalize" seating facilities. Seeing that Mrs. Parks was adamant, the driver called a police officer who led her off the bus

and escorted her to the police station. There she was booked on a charge of violating the city's segregation law. Subsequently the charge was changed to read a violation of state law, which gives the bus drivers the power to assign and reassign seating. The law makes it a misdemeanor for anyone to disobey the driver's orders. Mrs. Parks, when asked why she had refused to move to the rear of the bus, said, "It was a matter of dignity; I could not have faced myself and my people if I had moved." She was found guilty in the City Recorder's Court and fined $10. Her attorney filed notice of appeal.

In the meantime a movement on the part of the Montgomery blacks to boycott the buses had begun. On the day of the trial three-quarters or more of the usual black riders stayed off the buses. The extent of the protest was noticeable, for the fifty thousand blacks who live in Montgomery constitute about 40 percent of the city's population and made up nearly 75 percent of the bus passengers. There was no widespread absenteeism from work that day; blacks went to their jobs by taxis, wagons, or on foot over long distances.

That evening, after the court had rendered its judgment, a mass meeting was held in a local church. The five thousand persons, including forty-seven black ministers, who attended this meeting were urged not to ride the buses. A resolution was adopted to continue the boycott indefinitely; those present were urged to make their cars available in assisting others to get to work; the Montgomery Improvement Association was formed, and the Reverend Dr. Martin Luther King was elected chairman. In addition, the three following proposals were addressed to the Montgomery City Lines as a basis for ending the boycott: (1) More courteous treatment of black passengers; (2) seating on a first-come, first-served basis, with blacks continuing to sit from the rear of the bus and whites from the front; and (3) black bus drivers to be employed on predominantly black runs.

The following morning black patronage was estimated to have been down 90 percent and subsequently it approached 100 percent. The boycott continued month after month. When the boycott moved into its second month, the bus company declared that it was operating at considerable loss, curtailed its services, and petitioned for an increase in fares, which the City Commission granted. Negotiations were attempted, but were broken off when it became apparent that compromise was impossible.

On February 21, 1956, the grand jury returned eleven true bills, indicting ninety blacks, including twenty-four ministers. The indictments were based on an Alabama law, enacted in 1921, which states, "Two or more persons who, without a just cause or legal excuse for so doing, enter into any combination, conspiracy, agreement, arrangement or understanding for the purpose of hindering, delaying or preventing any person, firm, corporation or association of persons from carrying on any lawful business, shall be guilty of a misdemeanor." On March 22, 1956, Dr. King was found guilty of leading an illegal boycott against the bus company. He was fined and sentenced to 386 days in jail, but notice of appeal suspended the sentence.

The boycott continued, and the case moved slowly through the courts. On November 13, 1956, the United States Supreme Court rendered its decision, declaring invalid the Alabama law and the city ordinance requiring segregation of races on interstate buses. The Supreme Court affirmed a ruling by a lower court, which had held that the challenged statutes "violate the due process and equal protection clauses of the Fourteenth Amendment to the Constitution of the United States." Officials of several Southern states, where there were segregation statutes, indicated that they would continue, by some means or other, to enforce segregation on buses despite the court's decision. The blacks of Montgomery, feeling their case had been won, voted to end the boycott on December 21, 1956.

Following the Montgomery affair blacks in many cities and towns, in both the North and the South, were encouraged to employ the boycott (sometimes referred to as "selective patronage"). The technique is not infallible. In many instances it has failed miserably, but frequently it has succeeded in winning major concessions from the dominant group.

White Resistance Groups

White people in both the North and the South have also organized in their efforts to prevent integration of the schools and similar encroachments on the pattern of traditional race relations. The organizations began to be established following the ruling of the United States Supreme Court in 1954 that segregated schools were unconstitutional. These so-called White Citizen's Councils were set up in Mississippi and spread throughout the South. Their slogan was "Segregation or Economic Boycott." The National Association for the Advancement of Colored People accused the movement of being a "dressed up Ku Klux Klan," but its leaders, many of whom were prominent citizens, insisted that they did not believe in violence, and denied that there was any attempt of reviving the methods of the old Klan. One who was instrumental in promoting the movement explained the plan of operation as follows:

If I had a Negro working for me, and he belonged to the NAACP or some similar group, I'd do the same thing I'd do to any Negro working for me who wanted to cause trouble — I'd just let him go. . . . When the Negro tried to obtain work elsewhere in the region, he would find no jobs available. When he tried to borrow money, or even buy food in the stores, he would be met with a curt, "We don't have any money to lend," or "That item is not in stock." No law will be broken. There are volumes of court cases to back up every move that will be taken.

There can be no doubt that the economic sanctions employed by these Councils had considerable effect. Black teachers lost their jobs, farmers were boycotted by wholesalers, signers of desegregation petitions had their names published in newspapers. Even white people who held unorthodox racial views were threatened, and white ministers who were outspoken on racial matters lost their parish assignments.

In 1974 the Boston Public Schools were forced to institute a large-scale busing program to desegregate their schools. This program was the final recourse, after many years of resistance by school officials and after every possible legal option had been tried. The local white groups responded with boycotts and violence, and hundreds of police had to be stationed at the schools to avert outright clashes. Groups such as Restore Our Alienated Rights, or ROAR for short, were set up to fight the school busing program. The city of Boston and the state of Massachusetts had to spend millions of dollars to keep order. The depth of the white resistance to the school busing program can be seen in the following statements by high school students who were about to be bused to integrated schools.

Nobody's gonna go on any bus, said . . . a senior at South Boston High School. "It's like Russia, like Socialism: the state telling you where to go to school, saying you here and you there, without giving the kids or the parents a say. . . .

[Another student said] he believes the balance plan is tokenism. It's no solution to the racial problem. A few blacks here and a few whites there — on buses or not — isn't going to solve the problems of blacks and whites not getting along, and it's not going to solve the problems of bad education. . . .

It's the way you were brought up. I don't know why I feel uptight around blacks, but I do. It's in me. It's in my background. My parents never said blacks are this or that. But there aren't enough blacks in South Boston for us to know any — personally, on a one-to-one basis.[31]

The resistance of the whites in Boston to busing was comparable to any resistance that occurred in the South during earlier periods of desegregation. This reaction was particularly interesting because during the earlier era many Northern whites often looked with contempt on the resistance actions of Southern whites.

Nonviolent Resistance

The Reverend Dr. Martin Luther King was very much committed to the technique of nonviolent resistance in combating racial discrimination. Other individuals and organizations working toward progress in race relations have also advocated and used this method. Dr. King, however, espoused and employed the technique of nonviolence with astonishing success. He exhorted his followers, "Face violence if necessary, but refuse to return violence." He insisted that they display no attitude and commit no act that would give offense to the whites. He concluded his mass meetings with the injunction, "Let us pray that God shall give us strength to remain non-violent though we may face death."

This method of nonviolence, or noncooperation, or passive resistance, as it is sometimes called, is especially associated with the name of Mohandas K. Gandhi, and Dr. King and others who have proclaimed it frankly acknowledged their indebtedness to him. It is, however, far older than Gandhi. Its origins go back to the ancient religions and philosophies of the East. The practice entered Europe as an aspect of Christianity; there is an element of it in stoicism; Tolstoy, Thoreau, and many others have espoused it in one form or another. Gandhi was certainly influenced by all of these. He was a keen student of the Bible and the Hindu scriptures; he read Thoreau's essay on *Civil Disobedience* when he was a young man, and he corresponded with Tolstoy.

By 1890 some 150,000 Indians had migrated to South Africa, most of whom had settled in Natal. The whites were strongly prejudiced against them, had imposed on them numerous discriminations, and sought to prevent further immigration. In 1893 Gandhi was called to Pretoria on an important case. He was a young lawyer, having recently returned to India from three years of study in England. He was a person of some importance, and was accustomed to being treated with courtesy and respect. In South Africa, however, he suffered all the insults and indignities to which the members of his racial group were habitually subjected. He resented such treatment bitterly, and looked forward to the completion of his mission so that he might return to India.

When he was ready to leave, however, he learned that a bill was being proposed that would deprive the Indians in South Africa of the franchise. He resolved, accordingly, to remain there and to take up the cause of his unorganized, demoralized people. This meant the sacrifice of a lucrative law practice, which was bringing him at that time about $25,000 to $30,000 a year. Nevertheless, Gandhi espoused a life of poverty, and for the next twenty years remained in South Africa fighting the battle for his fellow Indians.

He first used his legal talents to prove the illegality of the Exclusion Act. He founded a newspaper, organized the Indians, sought to promote education, taught the doctrine of nonresistance, and urged his followers to remove themselves from the society of the whites, to boycott all public services, to eschew violence altogether, and to return good for evil. Gandhi himself was the embodiment of this ideal. When the whites faced a crisis, Gandhi would come to their aid. During the Boer War he organized an Indian Red Cross; and when a plague broke out in 1904, he organized a hospital. For these services he was rewarded with medals and honors, which he subsequently returned in protest against the actions of the government. He met with some measure of success in relieving the oppression of the Indians in South Africa, and in 1914 he returned to India to champion the cause of the Indian people against the British. His career there and his success in winning independence for India are too well known to bear repeating.[32]

Gandhi's method of nonviolence has had tremendous influence on minorities throughout the world. If the Indians, without resort to arms, can prevail against the mighty British Empire, who is to say what other subordinate people might hope to achieve? Many others have taken a lesson from Gandhi's techniques, eschewing violence, and relying on peaceful methods to achieve their ends.

Art as a Weapon in Conflict

Conflict between racial groups is not limited to the violent and militant forms that we have been discussing, although they receive the greatest attention. There are subtle weapons that are no less effective than insurrections, riots, strikes, and boycotts to which oppressed peoples in their despair frequently resort. The fiction and autobiography of Richard Wright, for instance, doubtless deliver telling blows to the discriminatory system under which blacks suffer. Other artists, too, have used their skills. Poets, painters, sculptors, actors, and musicians, too numerous even to list, have joined in the protest.[33] American blacks, deprived of other weapons and appreciating the futility of armed conflict, began very early to employ the arts. Many of the famous spirituals gave voice to their defiance, and the last few decades have seen a great multiplication of protest art.

Consider, too, the wide variety of literary forms, devices, and styles that artists employ. James Weldon Johnson, Richard Wright, and James Baldwin may be in agreement on their basic purpose, but their literary products are quite dissimilar. Langston Hughes and Paul Robeson both used art as a weapon of protest, but their techniques are worlds apart.

In 1967 a show on Harlem opened at the Metropolitan Museum of Art that caused a great furor among whites. The show included both paintings and sculpture and a thirteen-room multimedia sight and sound exhibit of Harlem life. Much of the protest developed because the show was not considered "art," but as the *New York Times* described it, "an amateur exercise in social evangelism." Another problem was that the show had many anti-Semitic overtones that brought out a great Jewish protest. The main result was that the two minorities fought feverishly with each other over the exhibit, while the rest of white society ignored the statements in the exhibit.

Humor

A misconception has often prevailed that a sense of humor is more highly developed with some groups than with others, and that certain unfortunate ones are altogether devoid of it. The fact is, however, that humor is universally appreciated and is commonly used by racial and ethnic groups in their conflicts with one another. Those who have lived among a strange people long enough to appreciate the nuances of their language testify to the fact that all peoples have their humor and that they use it not merely for amusement, but also to vent their hatreds. American Indians enjoy many laughs at the white person's expense, and anthropologists report that primitive people delight in mocking and ridiculing the customs of missionaries, traders, and colonial administrators. It is gratifying to make opponents appear ludicrous to themselves, but where that is not possible much satisfaction is still to be derived from making the opponents ludicrous in one's own eyes. This is one of the functions of humor in conflict situations. Witness the innumerable jokes about Jews, blacks, Italians, Irish, Chinese, Japanese, and Mexicans. An examination of black periodicals will reveal a plethora of jokes and cartoons, most of them, to be sure, having no relation to the racial struggle, although many of them bear witness to the fact that blacks derive pleasure from seeing whites get the worst of it.

White people, on the other hand, have shown a fondness for stories that lampoon the ignorance and pomposity of black preachers, black fondness for chicken and watermelons, the hardness of their skull or the blackness of their skin, and the easy virtue of their women. Needless to say, these hold little or no humor for the blacks.

Minority groups also use humor in an aggressive fashion with each other. This is a way of releasing the frustration and hostility that is generated from discrimination by the majority group. Black teenagers often engage in a verbal battle known as "playing the dozens." In this exchange each participant takes a turn at insulting the other. No one really wins or loses and success is measured by the originality or novelty of the insult. Roger Abrahams presents many interesting examples of black humor in his book, *Positively Black*. The following example of playing the dozens is taken from it.

Now dig. Your home is so small, the roaches have to walk sideways through the hallways.

Your mother is so small she can do chinups on the curb.

Your mother is so fat she has to have a shoehorn to get in the bathtub.

Man, you're so dark, you need a license to drink white milk.

If electricity was black, your mother would be a walking powerhouse.

You look like death standing on the street corner eating a life saver.[34]

As can be seen from such an exchange, the insults often involve the very traits that provide the basis for discrimination by the larger society. In this instance, the intensity of blackness becomes a central focus. In others, poverty, illegitimacy, or the sexual promiscuity of one's mother become the subject of the insult.

Litigation

In many parts of the world, where racial groups smart under the domination of others, the privilege of fighting for justice in courts of law is not enjoyed by the minority. If they resent their status and wish to change it, or if they are simply driven to take out their resentment on their oppressors, the only weapons at their disposal are the various forms of violence or the subtler methods of propitiation. It was formerly so in the United States. Blacks could not fight the institution of slavery by argument in the courts, nor could the Indians take out an injunction against the invasion of their territory or their removal to a reservation. All these disabilities, however, have been ostensibly removed in this country. The Fourteenth Amendment to the Constitution declares that "all persons born or naturalized in the United States . . . are citizens" and that they are entitled to the privileges of life, liberty, and property, and to the protection of the laws of the country.

In spite of this nominal equality, it has frequently been pointed out by students of race problems that blacks, Japanese, Chinese, Mexicans, and European immigrants fall short of enjoying the ideal of American justice. One of the most flagrant violations was the treatment accorded American citizens of Japanese descent during World War II, when thousands of them were forcibly expelled from the Pacific Coast states, suffering great financial losses, and were herded into relocation centers. The only charge against them was the fact that they were of Japanese ancestry. Moreover, the wide prevalence of discriminatory laws, the biases of the police, miscarriages of justice (especially in the lower courts), and the devices for circumventing the law are well known.

Despite these shortcomings, however, it cannot be denied that minority groups in the United States have increasingly turned to litigation as a highly effective weapon in their struggle for equality. Consider, for example, the black fight for educational opportunity. Repeatedly, they have taken their case to the courts. In 1933 a black man brought action against the University of North Carolina in an effort to gain admission to the school of pharmacy, but he lost his suit on a technicality. Two years later another succeeded in his attempt to enter the University of Maryland law school. In 1936 Lloyd Gaines attempted to enter the law school of the University of Missouri, and when his application was refused he took his case to the courts. He lost in the state courts, but the United States Supreme Court decreed that a state must provide equal education for all of its citizens *within the state*. This decision caused reverberations throughout the South. Maryland and West Virginia thereupon permitted blacks to enter institutions that had theretofore been restricted to white students, while other states set about to provide graduate and professional education for blacks.

On June 5, 1950, racial segregation in the United States received a deadly blow in three memorable decisions by the Supreme Court. On that day the Court: (1) outlawed the Jim Crow segregation of blacks in railroad dining cars on interstate trips; (2) ordered the University of Texas to admit Herman Sweatt, a black, to its law school, on the ground that the black law school that Texas had set up was not the equivalent of the school for whites; and (3) ordered the University of Oklahoma to stop segregating black graduate student G. W. McLaurin in its classrooms.

In the Sweatt case the Court served notice that segregated law schools, however lavish their facilities, are inadequate; and it declared, in effect, that segregation and equality are incompatible:

The law school to which Texas is willing to admit petitioner excludes from its student body members of the racial groups which number 85 per cent of the population of the State and include most of the lawyers, witnesses, jurors, judges and other officials with whom petitioner will inevitably be dealing when he becomes a member of the Texas Bar. With such a substantial and significant segment of society excluded we cannot conclude that the education offered petitioner is substantially equal to that which he would receive if admitted to the University of Texas Law School.

In the McLaurin decision the Court insists the black students, once they have been admitted to graduate schools, must be treated with complete equality. McLaurin had been admitted to classes with whites, but had at first been put in a little anteroom. Later, along with other blacks at the University of Oklahoma, he had been simply seated in a different row from the whites. The Court declared that such practices impair the student's "ability to study, to engage in discussions, and exchange views with other students," and ordered that a black student "must receive the same treatment at the hands of the State as the students of other races."

Blacks continued to use the nation's courts in their fight for educational equality, with the result that on May 17, 1954, the United States Supreme Court ruled that "in the field of public education the doctrine of 'separate but equal' has no place. Separate educational facilities are inherently unequal." This ruling, however, has not brought an end to the matter, for an infinite number of obstacles have arisen in the implementation of the Court's decree. The important fact is that the courtroom has been chosen as the arena in which the contest will be waged and decided, and that argumentation is the principal weapon.

Similarly, in their struggle for equality in other areas of life American blacks have employed the weapon of litigation with increasing success. They have gone into the courtroom to win the right to play on municipal golf courses, to eat in restaurants, to travel on trains and buses, to sleep in hotels, to register and vote, to obtain employment, to use swimming pools, and even to be addressed as Mr., Mrs., Ms., or Miss.

Nor are blacks the only minority group who use legal processes in their struggle for justice and equality. American Indians have been finding that the courts are more effective than guns and tomahawks in settling their grievances against whites. Choctaws, Chickasaws, and Navajos have been eminently successful of late in securing their claims for millions of dollars from the American government.

The Ballot

Among the most powerful weapons in interracial conflict is the ballot. Leaders of minority groups recognize this fact and bend every effort to win for their members the right to vote. Then once it has been won, they put it to use. At the same time, the dominant races appreciate the importance of keeping this weapon out of the hands of those whom they wish to control. In South Africa, where a few million whites seek to maintain their superior status over four to five times as many blacks, the privilege of voting is zealously guarded.

In his study of colonialism, Dr. Raymond Kennedy observes that one common feature of all the systems, be they British, French, Japanese, or any other, is the retention of political control by the possessing power, leaving the natives with little or no share in the government of their own land.[35] The administration of colonies is directed from the ruling country, all important positions being held by representatives from the home government. Natives are often permitted to participate in advisory councils, and sometimes in legislatures, but the powers of such bodies are so circumscribed that decisions on all-important matters remain with the home government or its agents. Whenever native leaders do try to organize their people for effective political action, they are denounced as radicals, imprisoned, or exiled.

In Guatemala, according to Dr. Gillin, the *ladinos* have managed to retain control of the political machinery.[36] For a time, local officials were appointed by the central government, and it was only *ladinos* who were chosen, not only for the higher offices, but for all paid political jobs as well. A new democratic government, however, has come into being, under which municipal officials are elected, and the Indians may vote. They have not taken full advantage of the opportunity, but candidates for office have learned to pay respect to the wishes of the Indians. This development has split the *ladinos* into two factions — conservatives, who deplore the gains made by the Indians and predict dire consequences should they get out of hand, and liberals, who believe in playing the political game with the Indians.

The political history of the United States is replete with the struggles of minority groups to use the ballot in advancing their cause. The Irish very early mastered the technique, while the Polish and Italian groups have met with considerable success, at least on the state and local levels. The epic struggle, however, has been that of blacks. Prior to the Civil War blacks were disfranchised throughout the South, and most of the North as well.[37] The Fifteenth Amendment gave the ballot to the blacks, who set about immediately to make the best possible use of this new weapon. The whites were equally determined to curb its use; and by means of a variety of devices, such as the "grandfather clause," the poll tax, literacy and character tests, property requirements, and above all, the white primary, succeeded in virtually disfranchising blacks.

Blacks in the meantime, have sought to regain the ballot. The Supreme Court declared the "grandfather clause" void in 1915; and the bulwark, the white primary, has been successfully assaulted and declared illegal after a great many test cases were taken to the courts. The poll tax was continually under fire for many years, until in 1964 the requisite number of states approved the Twenty-fourth Amendment to the Constitution, which states:

The right of citizens of the United States to vote in any primary or other (federal) election . . . shall not be denied or abridged by the United States or any State by reason of failure to pay any poll tax or other tax.

Especially since the 1930s blacks have learned to make their political influence felt, and the major parties reveal in their platforms that they appreciate the strength of the black vote, especially in such crucial states as New York, Ohio, Michigan, Pennsylvania, and Illinois.

Direct Action

The Montgomery bus boycott convinced many blacks of their power to effect social change. At the same time impatience with the slow processes of litigation and the ballot began to mount. Especially did the younger blacks begin to resent the snail-like pace of desegregation and to long for active participation in the struggle. Accordingly, on February 1, 1960, in Greensboro, N.C., a group of black students took their seats at a lunch counter from which they had hitherto been barred, and they continued to sit quietly despite the fact that they were denied service. The affair received wide publicity in the press, and the sit-in movement spread rapidly to other communities throughout the country. Not only were lunch counters the objects of such demonstrations, but also churches, libraries, skating rinks, swimming pools, beaches, and parks, with the result that the public began to hear of kneel-ins, wade-ins, pray-ins, walk-ins, and lie-ins. The picketing of stores, city halls, construction projects, schools, churches, and offices of boards of education became daily occurrences.

In February, 1964, the members of CORE in San Francisco inaugurated a novel type of direct action that came to be known as the shop-in. The demonstrators would enter a supermarket, fill shopping carts with groceries, wheel them to the counter, have them checked, and then walk out, leaving the sacks and boxes piled in front of the clerks. The tactic aroused bitter resentment on the part of both blacks and whites. The local black newspaper denounced it as "a malicious idea," and many blacks declared that they would sever their connection with CORE if the practice continued.

It is difficult to evaluate the success of the direct-action technique. Daniel C. Thompson, who has studied the racial situation in New Orleans, says, "This strategy shocked the established leadership in New Orleans — both black and white. Individually, black leaders at first tended to criticize such methods of direct action and to underestimate their potential effectiveness. However, within two years after the Greensboro incident, sit-ins, or the threat to begin them, had brought about the desegregation of lunch counters in more than one hundred Southern cities. They served to arouse many blacks from their traditional apathy and passivity. And they dramatized for the whole nation black dissatisfaction with discrimination and segregation.[38]

Those sociologists who maintain that conflict is an inevitable and universal consequence of the meeting of unlike peoples certainly have abundant evidence to support their thesis, especially if they include those subtle and shadowy forms in which hostility often manifests itself. Moreover, it is apparent that the members of minority groups have sought in various ways to improve their lot and to subdue their oppressors. Some of the techniques that they have used have a long record of failure; yet even so they continue to be employed. Subordinate peoples have occasionally chosen their weapons with great care, and have recognized the importance of adopting the wisest possible strategy and the most promising techniques. Others, however, have struck out blindly, with little thought for the weapons they would use — if, indeed, they had any choice.

Notes

1. For accounts of the discovery of the Hawaiian Islands, see A. Kippis, *Narrative of the Voyages Round the World Performed by Captain James Cook*; A. Kitson, *Captain James Cook, The Circumnavigator*; S. D. Porteus, *Calabashes and Kings: An Introduction to Hawaii.*

2. D. Young, *American Minority Peoples*, p. 586.

3. E. J. Lindgren, "An Example of Culture Contact Without Conflict," *American Anthropologist* 40 (Oct.–Dec. 1938): 605–621.

4. J. Gillin, "Race Relations Without Conflict: A Guatemalan Town," *American Journal of Sociology* 53, no. 5 (March 1948): 337–343. Cf. R. Redfield, "Culture Contact Without Conflict," American Anthropologist 41, no. 3 (July–Sept. 1939): 514–517. This article draws some interesting comparisons between the Guatemalan and the Tungus-Cossack situations.

5. J. B. Edlefsen, "Enchantment among Southwest Idaho Basques," *Social Forces* 29, no. 2 (Dec. 1950): 155–158.

6. I. Goldman, "The Alkatcho Carrier of British Columbia," in R. Linton, ed., *Acculturation in Seven American Indian Tribes*, p. 372.

7. L. Coser, "Some Sociological Aspects of Conflict," in G. T. Marx, *Racial Conflict*, pp. 14–15.

8. J. Bernard, "The Conceptualization of Intergroup Relations with Special Reference to Conflict," in G. T. Marx, *Racial Conflict*, p. 26.

9. L. Kriesberg, *The Sociology of Social Conflicts*, p. 61.

10. Ibid., p. 4.

11. Coser, "Aspects of Conflict," p. 17.

12. Ibid., p. 17.

13. Bernard, "Conceptualization of Intergroup Relations," p. 27.

14. F. Shay, *Judge Lynch: His First Hundred Years*, pp. 20–25.

15. Cf. Shay, *Judge Lynch*, pp. 7–8; F. W. Coker, "Lynching," in *Encyclopedia of the Social Sciences*, vol. 9, pp. 639–643; G. B. Johnson, "Patterns of Race Conflict," in E. T. Thompson, ed., *Race Relations and the Race Problem*, p. 142ff.

16. J. E. Cutler, *Lynch-Law*, pp. 171–172; Young, *American Minority Peoples* p. 252ff; Shay, Judge Lynch, p. 153ff.

17. Shay, *Judge Lynch*, pp. 79–81; Coker, "Lynching," p. 641; Johnson, "Patterns of Race Conflict," pp. 144–145; G. Myrdal, *An American Dilemma*, vol. 1, p. 560ff.

18. Myrdal, *American Dilemma*, vol. 1, p. 563.

19. Myrdal, *American Dilemma*, pp. 566, 1350.

20. *Life*, 7 Feb. 1949, pp. 27–31. Copyright *Time*, Inc. This story accompanies some vivid photographs of the riots. Other pictures illustrating the racial situation in South Africa can be seen in *Life*, 10 March 1947, and 17 Sept. 1950.

21. W. E. B. DuBois, *Dusk to Dawn*, p. 264.

22. Photographs in *Life*, 16 March 1942, pp. 40–41.

23. A. M. Lee and N. D. Humphrey, *Race Riot*.

24. B. E. Griesman, *Minorities*, p. 285.

25. Ibid., p. 282.

26. J. W. Parkes, *The Jewish Problem in the Modern World*, pp. 63–66, 70, 74.

27. F. L. Schumann, "Insurrection," *Encyclopedia of the Social Sciences*, vol. 8, pp. 116–118.

28. C. Wissler, *Indians of the United States*, passim, but especially pp. 65–69, 164–169, 203.

29. D. Pierson, *Negroes in Brazil*, p. 7.

30. J. H. Franklin, *From Slavery to Freedom*, pp. 66–67, 73, 79ff., 299–311; H. Aptheker, *Negro Slave Revolts in the United States, 1526–1860*; J. C. Carroll, *Slave Insurrections in the United States, 1800–1860*.

31. Lucinda Smith, "The Busing News Hits South Boston," *Boston Evening Globe*, 2 July 1974, p. 8. Courtesy of the Boston Globe.

32. R. Rolland, *Mahatma Gandhi*. Translated by Catherine D. Groth; H. N. Brailsford, "Passive Resistance and Non-Cooperation," *Encyclopedia of the Social Sciences*, vol. 12, pp. 9–13.

33. A summary appears in Franklin, *Slavery to Freedom*, chap. 26.

34. R. D. Abrahams, *Positively Black*, p. 40.

35. R. Kennedy, "Colonial Crisis and the Future," in R. Linton, ed., *The Science of Man in the World Crisis*, pp. 306–346.

36. Gillin, "Race Relations Without Conflict," p. 339.

37. Mangum, *Legal Status of the Negro*, pp. 371–372.

38. On the strategies of the black revolution, see Thompson, *Race Relations and the Race Problem*, chap. 7; L. Killian and C. Grigg, *Racial Crisis in America*, pp. 18–26, 130–144; Jacqueline J. Clark, "Standard Operational Procedures in Tragic Situations," *Phylon* (Fourth Quarter, 1961): 318ff.

Chapter Seven
Steps, Stages,
and Cycles

In no two instances have the interrelations of
different ethnic groups run exactly the same
course.

— R. T. *La Piere* Sociology

Relations among racial and ethnic groups may seem to include an infinite variety of human experiences; to run the whole gamut of emotions; to involve all possible behavioral patterns; and to be utterly unpredictable, capricious, and irrational. They seem to engender attitudes that range from curiosity and hospitality, at the one extreme, to the bitterest hostility at the other. They include friendly cooperation and serious conflict. They may be highly emotional today, and tomorrow may betray cool and calculating deliberation. The motives that bring peoples together range all the way from selfish to altruistic, and include love of freedom, desire for economic gain, religious devotion, and sheer adventure.

This variability is all very disturbing to a scientist, who looks for order, consistency, and uniformity so that a problem may be better understood. Is it possible, however, to reduce the phenomena of race relations to any kind of order, to discover consistent patterns, or to make valid generalizations?

Race Relations Cycles

Some sociologists profess to have found a pattern of race relations. They deny that each situation where unlike groups have come together is a law unto itself, but insist that there are recurring phenomena that have a natural, chronological relationship. They maintain that there is a succession of events or processes, a series of steps or stages, certain uniformities and similarities in all situations where the races have met. They have expressed their generalizations in the form of a *race relations cycle*. We must bear in mind that the cycles these scholars have constructed are not the products of wild speculation, but were developed from observation and analysis of many concrete situations.

The Cycle of Robert E. Park

One of the greatest students of race relations was Professor Robert E. Park, who traveled widely and observed closely the behavior of various groups in their relationships with others. He reached the conclusion that "in the relations of races *there is a cycle of events which tends everywhere to repeat itself.*" First, he believed, groups come into *contact*; there invariably follows *competition*; eventually some kind of adjustment or *accommodation* is reached; and, finally, there is *assimilation* and *amalgamation*. Said Dr. Park:

The race relations cycle which takes the form, to state it abstractly, of contact, competition, accommodation, and eventual assimilation, is apparently progressive and irreversible. Customs regulations, immigration restrictions, and racial barriers may slacken the tempo of the movement; may perhaps halt it altogether for a time; but cannot change its direction; cannot, at any rate, reverse it. . . . It does not follow that because the tendencies to the assimilation and eventual amalgamation of races exist, they should not be resisted and, if possible, altogether inhibited. . . . Rising tides of color and oriental exclusion laws are merely incidental evidences of these diminishing distances. . . . In the Hawaiian Islands, where all the races of the Pacific meet and mingle . . . the native races are disappearing and new peoples are coming into existence. "Races and cultures die — it has always been so — but civilization lives on." [1]

Many a person who never heard of Dr. Park has reached similar conclusions. One frequently hears expressed the idea that, in the long run, the American Indians and the Jews will be completely absorbed and will disappear as distinct groups. Some even maintain that the blacks will, centuries hence, become fused into the general population. "A thousand years from now," said one anonymous philosopher, "we will all be a shade darker, sing better, and be ten percent more human." Underlying such simple, superficial predictions is the conviction that assimilation and amalgamation are inevitable results of the meeting of peoples.

The Cycle of E. S. Bogardus

Somewhat different is the cycle constructed by Professor Bogardus. He had in mind especially the relations of white Americans with the Chinese, Japanese, Filipino, and Mexican immigrants in California; and he believed that there were "sufficient recurrences in each case, as well as similarities in the behavior recurrences, to justify the label of a race-relations cycle."[2] The stages in this cycle are as follows:

1. *Curiosity* First arrivals are invariably the objects of amazement and curiosity. Their strange habits and customs invite passing comments, and a certain sympathy is generated for the lone stranger far away from home. The host group at first is not aroused or disturbed, and mechanisms and mores of defense do not make their appearance.

2. *Economic welcome* Employers are quick to tap these new sources of labor, and either directly or indirectly encourage further immigration.

3. *Industrial and social antagonism* Suddenly there arises a wave of opposition to the newcomers. At first there are sporadic outbursts of prejudice, followed by organized movements. Labor has usually taken the lead in protesting on grounds of unfair competition and the lowering of the American standard of living. Patriotic societies, protectors of the nation's traditions, offer their prompt cooperation to combat the alien threat. These two organized groups win the support of the native stock, whose fears can be easily aroused at the thought of the country's being overrun by foreigners. Neighborhoods resent the invasion of the conspicuous member of a strange racial or ethnic group, who seeks to find a better home by moving into a more desirable residential area.

4. *Legislative antagonism* Opposition rises to the next level, when bills are introduced into state legislatures and into Congress that would restrict the movements of the immigrants. The newcomers are openly, publicly, and viciously denounced. Politicians make capital of these attacks against the foreigners, who cannot vote, and courageously campaign in the defense of the community, the state, and the nation.

5. *Fair-play tendencies* Eventually, but invariably, a movement in behalf of tolerance and fair play will develop. Certain citizens, either because of friendship for the immigrants or because they recognize the injustice of the attacks, will initiate a countermovement. Such movements generally are not well organized, lack financial support, and are embarrassed by dreamers and zealots. However, they do serve to help the harassed immigrant retain confidence in the American tradition, and preserve the nation's democratic reputation in the eyes of the rest of the world.

6. *Quiescence* After the opposition has succeeded in obtaining the restrictive and prohibitive legislation that it desired, there is a slowing down of antagonistic activities. The organizations that have been in the forefront of the attack, assuming that the danger has been removed, will modify their attitudes, will profess beliefs in tolerance and sympathy for the immigrants, and will espouse programs to secure justice for their erstwhile enemies.

7. *Second-generation difficulties* Finally, problems of the second generation emerge, when the American-born children of the immigrants begin to react to

their social situation. Their problems arise from the fact that they have lost touch with the culture of their parents, and are not entirely accepted by the Americans, with the result that they become a "lost generation" of cultural hybrids, uncertain and insecure.

The Cycle of W. O. Brown

Even more cautious in the construction of a cycle has been Professor W. O. Brown, who recognized the fact that "not all cases of race conflict fit the pattern," but who believes, nevertheless, that race relations do have a natural history, do pass through a series of stages, and do manifest a certain cycle of development. He proposes the following:[3]

1. *Initial contacts of a symbiotic, categoric sort*   At this stage there is some exchange of goods and services, a minimum of actual social contact, very little overt hostility, and some uncertainty, fear, and curiosity.

2. *Emergence of conflict*   Clashes at first are concerned, not with status, but with land, resources, and physical survival.

3. *Temporary accommodations*   Occasionally, but rarely, the conflict of the preceding stage will result in the destruction of the weaker group; but usually the two opposing groups will come to terms, with the conquered accepting subordination or isolation in preference to destruction. If its numbers are small, it may even be absorbed into the dominant group, thus bringing the cycle to an end. In the event, however, that the weaker group continues to threaten the stronger or the latter effectively resists fusion, the accommodations will be only temporary and the fourth stage of the cycle will appear.

4. *Struggle for status*   The culture of the conquered group begins to disintegrate, for seldom can a social system live through conquest, domination, and forced isolation. The members of the subordinate group have no choice, therefore, but to try to penetrate the society of their masters, to adopt their culture, and to seek to satisfy their needs and interests in terms of the civilization of the dominant group. Such an invasion, of course, by a supposedly inferior people is resisted, with the result that there emerges a conflict for rights, for status, and for the privilege of participation in the social order.

5. *Mobilization*   As the struggle for status grows in intensity, each group mobilizes its forces. The dominant ones develop myths and ideologies to support the status quo and formulate policies and programs to defend it. The subordinate race begins to manifest race consciousness and race pride, and supports movements and organizations calculated to win status and rights for the underprivileged. Race prejudice emerges and race becomes an obsession with both groups.

6. *Solution*   Theoretically, Brown thinks, there are three possible outcomes of racial conflict. Complete isolation of the races would be a perfect solution; but

this is not practicable, for isolation menaces the interests of the stronger group and arouses the anger of the weaker. Subordination is another possibility; but this becomes increasingly difficult, for the diffusion of democratic ideals rouses subordinate peoples and makes them unwilling to "keep their places" meekly and peacefully. The third possible solution is assimilation and fusion. Brown thinks this last is "perhaps ultimately inevitable, but immediately improbable." Hence he predicts that "race problems will continue to harass mankind and intrigue sociologists."

The Cycle of Clarence E. Glick

One of the more recent attempts to present race relations as a series of steps or stages is that of Professor Clarence E. Glick.[4] He is aware that there are unique features in each situation where unlike groups are brought together, but feels that it is possible and useful to abstract from the many situations certain common and recurrent elements, and "to look at race relations as typically involving a sequence of phases."

1. *The precontact phase* Prior to the expansion of Europe there existed in most parts of the world folk societies that were characterized by a slow rate of social change, but a high degree of cultural integration and institutionalization.

2. *The contact and predomination phase* This period is characterized by contacts between members of the indigenous folk society and persons, such as traders, from the invading "foreign" society. The native society often becomes severely disrupted, especially when the invaders attempt to establish domination over it. Normal modes of life and conduct are abandoned. New types of native leaders may arise, including persons who under the traditional system had no prospects of rising to positions of leadership, and who express more realistically than the hereditary leaders the feelings of resentment, hope, and despair that the members of their society share.

3. *The domination phase* The conflict of the second period generally gives way sooner or later to some form of accommodation, wherein the invading group establishes itself as the dominant political power in the area. The natives may become peons or landless squatters, working for the new dominant group; or they may become apathetic "wards" in a native reserve. Some of the natives accept the new power pattern and cooperate with the dominant group, and some become "professional natives," dancing and singing for the tourists. Assimilation proceeds apace. Missions or government agencies establish schools and health centers, and the cities attract natives as a source of labor. The values of the dominant group enjoy prestige, while those of the native group lose their appeal. Here we have the genuine beginnings of *race relations*, for the "educated natives" appear and feel that their inferior status in the new society is determined by their race, not by their culture, which they share with the dominant group.

4. *The postdomination phase*   When the status system established during the domination phase begins to break down we come to the postdomination phase. In this period two types of challenges may be identified. (a) Nationalistic movements. Increasing numbers of natives seek to remove the members of the dominant group from their position in the top stratum of the hierarchy. A variety of organizations make their appearance, either actually or ostensibly set up for other objectives. If the dominant group permits these organizations to function openly, they provide the native intellectuals with a niche for themselves. (b) Integration. Under certain circumstances, especially where there has been extensive assimilation of the dominant culture by the natives, movements toward integration will appear. Those in the subordinate group will seek to solve the status dilemma by bringing the whole society to the point where it will eliminate race or color as the categorical basis for determining status. The phase will also see the establishment of interracial movements, drawing their support from both the dominant group and the minority, and affording members of the minority an opportunity to enjoy a status approximating equality with members of the dominant group who are participating in the movement. At the same time a cleavage appears in the dominant group, some still thinking in terms of a superior racial group and others thinking in interracial or nonracial terms.

The Cycle of Stanley Lieberson

Another cycle of race relations is that proposed by Professor Stanley Lieberson.[5] He recognizes the fact that there are "wide variations between societies in the nature and processes of race and ethnic relations," and admits that a multiplicity of factors operate to produce these differences. He is critical of the cycles other sociologists have constructed. As for Park's, he insists that "neither conflict nor assimilation is an inevitable outcome of racial and ethnic contact," and regarding the cycles of Bogardus and others, he says they were "narrowly confined to a rather specific set of groups or contact situations."

Lieberson maintains that the most crucial factor in determining the course of race relations is the relative power of the groups involved. When two populations, he says, begin to occupy the same habitat, but do not share a single economic-political-social order, each group endeavors to preserve that order with which it was familiar prior to the contact. Events will largely depend on which group dominates, the newcomers or the indigenous people.

When a people migrating to a new territory is superior to the indigenous population in technology (especially weapons) and is more tightly organized, warfare and conflict are likely to appear early. The local inhabitants suffer a numerical decline, their economic and political institutions are undermined, they may come slowly to participate in the institutions of the dominant group, racial consciousness and a sense of unity often arise, and they succeed in dispossessing their overlords in some instances. Africa offers numerous illustrations of this.

On the other hand, when the newcomers are subordinate and the indigenous people wield the power, the course of race relations is quite different. There is less conflict in the early stages of contact, and it is limited and sporadic when it does occur. Threats of demographic and institutional imbalance are reduced because the host society is able to control the numbers and character of the migrants. Hostility is minimized, for the migrants usually fare better in their new home than they did in their old, and they have the option of returning if they wish to do so. The host society places great emphasis on assimilation, perhaps even by exerting pressure, with the result that the newcomers tend to become integrated with relative ease and rapidity. However, differences do appear, as occurred in Australia with its Italians and Germans, depending on the conditions prevailing at the time of the entry of the newcomers.

The Cycle of Graham C. Kinloch

Professor Graham C. Kinloch has developed a theory that uses a multilevel conceptual framework.[6] That is, his theory tries to explain race relations without limiting itself to only the psychological, sociopsychological, or sociological levels. Kinloch believes that race is a social definition that evolves out of a society's historical development. The definition will undergo change with the passage of time, particularly with industrialization, resulting in redefinition of both the majority as well as the dominant elite. Kinloch looks on race relations as being dynamic and changing rather than static. Hence they must be analyzed in terms of changes in the social structure and society.

Kinloch begins with the assumption that the differences in race relations between societies will depend on the degree to which the structure of the society is colonial. A *colonial* type of society is one in which the ruling elite is made up of a small, migrant, white, Anglo-Saxon, Protestant group. This group controls and exploits the local population and imports others under conditions similar to slavery for the principal purpose of economic advantage. Such an elite normally defines the local population in negative terms and sets up a social structure based on institutionalized racism. This definition is based on instances where whites have tried to colonize the less developed areas of the world.

Kinloch believes that the more colonial a society's structure is, the more conflict ridden the initial contact between the elite and other racial groups will be. In addition, the more colonial a society is, the more racist and rigid the intergroup relations will be. This situation will lead to conflict and to an eventual accommodation between the two parties.

As economic development takes place, the minorities will begin to reject the negative definitions that have been applied to them by those in power. The governing group will try to suppress this reaction. However, any form of suppression will only increase the minority pressure for change and will lead to some new system of racial interaction. The minority eventually increases its power and becomes independent of the governing group.

The major implication of this theory is that race relations are the outgrowth of the particular societal arrangements that evolve from certain historical, social, and economic circumstances. For the elite to increase its economic development and protect its power monopoly, it must define certain groups in a negative way. The new social definition affects interracial behavior on both the group and individual levels. According to Kinloch's theory, only a change in the structure of society will bring about a change in race relations. This change comes about when the oppressed group rebels against the elite.

The Uniqueness of Each Situation

If it is true that the relations among racial and ethnic groups follow some universal and inevitable pattern, it would be well for us to know it; and the sociologist who discovers the cycle would indeed perform a useful service. We should then be able to predict the course of events, perhaps to control it, and certainly to mitigate some of the painful features of the process. At the present stage of our knowledge, however, it hardly seems possible even to sketch the bare outlines of such a race relations cycle. Dr. Bogardus makes no claim of universality for the cycle he has constructed; Dr. Brown confesses that his does not fit all situations; and Dr. Glick offers his cycle as merely a "heuristic device" for understanding various social roles and types. Dr. Park's theory is open to doubt, for assimilation and amalgamation may not be inevitable, and certainly there are instances of racial contact where conflict and competition have been conspicuously lacking. Some scholars, therefore, question the existence of any universal pattern, and lean rather to the belief that so numerous and so various are the components that enter into race relations that each situation is unique, and the making of generalizations is a hazardous procedure. As LaPiere has expressed it, *"In no two instances have the interrelations of different ethnic groups run exactly the same course."* [7] Let us look at some of the evidence on which this statement is based.

Race Relations in Brazil

In many respects the components that went into the making of the racial situation in Brazil were similar to those present in the United States, but the resulting patterns have been quite different. Brazil, like our own nation, was colonized by a heterogeneous mass of Europeans. Early in the sixteenth century Portuguese adventurers, shipwrecked sailors, and deserters began to settle there. They were followed by undesirables, who had been banished from Portugal for religious or political reasons, or for crimes they had committed. Among the early settlers, also, were impoverished nobles who hoped to recoup their fortunes in the New World, and ambitious young men who, because of their physical fitness, were chosen to secure the colonial garrisons.   Orphan girls were sent over by the Crown to become the wives of the settlers.   To complete the picture, there were prostitutes and clergy, Jews and Jesuits, Gypsies and government officials, and a few hardy peasant families.

These white Europeans were met in Brazil by an Indian population. Bloody wars ensued, in which many of the Indians were killed, some were enslaved, and others were driven westward into the interior.   Indian women were appropriated by the white men, first as concubines, later as legitimate wives; eventually a large mixed-blood element arose.   The trend has been toward the absorption of this mestizo population by the dominant white group.

At an early date the importation of black slaves from Africa began.   Sugar came to be recognized as the principal crop and the plantation system was eminently suited to its production; but inexpensive labor was needed, and neither the white Europeans nor the Indians proved equal to the demands.   Accordingly the black slave, as in North America, came as the answer to the problem in Brazil, and millions of blacks were imported before 1877, when slavery was abolished.

Brazil, then, like the United States, has been the meeting place of white, red, and black peoples.   The adjustments of these groups to one another, however, have been quite different in the two countries.   In the United States color prejudice has been very strong, discrimination and segregation have prevailed, and a system of color caste has emerged.   In Brazil, on the other hand, amalgamation has been the dominant policy and has become firmly fixed in the mores of the people. Pierson states, "To individuals from all classes of the population this eventual amalgamation and assimilation of diverse ethnic units is a matter of pride and self-commendation."[8]   The race problem, as the Brazilian sees it, is *not* one of "preserving racial purity," but rather one of overcoming the resistance that a group occasionally offers to absorption.   Hence there has been some opposition to Japanese immigration, for fear that these newcomers might constitute a group difficult to assimilate.   Furthermore, Brazil has not followed the practice of racial segregation.   Pierson reported that in Bahia, the city that was the basis of his study, families of whites, mixed bloods, and blacks dwell side by side.   Nor is one excluded from professions, occupations, or social clubs on account of racial features.   This is not to say that Brazil offers to underprivileged groups a democratic utopia, for Pierson himself confesses that prejudice exists there, and he points out that the upper classes are predominantly light in color while the lower classes are black.   He is supported in these observations by Brazilian sociologists, one of whom declares that "color prejudice and discrimination exist to some extent," but who present evidence to prove that "public opinion is always on the side of the opponents of any kind of racial discrimination."[9]   In these, and many other details then, the course of intergroup relations has moved along quite different lines in Brazil and the United States.

Students of the Brazilian pattern of race relations have suggested the following factors as being especially influential in shaping the events in that country:

1. In the early days of the colony relatively few European women came to Brazil, with the result that the Portuguese men took Indian women as mates and wives. Both state and church gave approval to these unions. A century later, when women did begin to migrate from Europe, the process of race mixing had become too firmly established to be readily checked.

2. The Portuguese themselves brought to Brazil a certain tolerance of color that facilitated interracial marriage. Pierson has the ingenious theory that Portugal, having been dominated by the Moors for five hundred years, had come to regard dark skin as a symbol of prestige, and to consider it an honor and an improvement of status to have a mate darker than oneself.[10]

3. Portuguese folkways of sex and marriage have contributed to the continued amalgamation of the races. Among these customs is that of concubinage, or *mancebia*. This is a rather common type of union in which the men often have a legal family at the same time, and the women involved are usually mulattos, rarely blacks. Also, family ties are tenacious, transcending the loyalty one feels for church or state. Strong attachments hold parents to their offspring.

The future of race relations in Brazil cannot be predicted with complete assurance. The probability is that amalgamation and assimilation will proceed; the blacks will continue to be absorbed by the mixed bloods, who, in turn, will continue to be absorbed by the predominantly European population. There are some indications, however, that Brazilians are growing more race conscious. Closer contacts with other nations, where color prejudice holds high value, may conceivably affect the existing attitudes. Pierson reports that large-scale European immigration of the past century, especially into the southern states of São Paulo, Santa Catharina, and Rio Grande do Sul, has had a modifying influence on the racial opinions that formerly prevailed in those areas.[11] He notes also that the rise of prejudice in the city of Rio de Janeiro was responsible for the organization in 1935 of "The Brazilian Movement against Race Prejudice." The fact that blacks in São Paulo are becoming race conscious and are resentful of discrimination is confirmed by the establishment of black literary and recreational clubs, women's organizations, and several black journals.

The Hawaiian Islands

Race relations on the Hawaiian Islands have followed a course quite different from that in either Brazil or the United States. There are similarities in all three of these areas, to be sure, but the total Hawaiian configuration has been amazingly distinctive. A heterogeneous population of more than seven hundred thousand makes its home on the 6,449 square miles of these volcanic

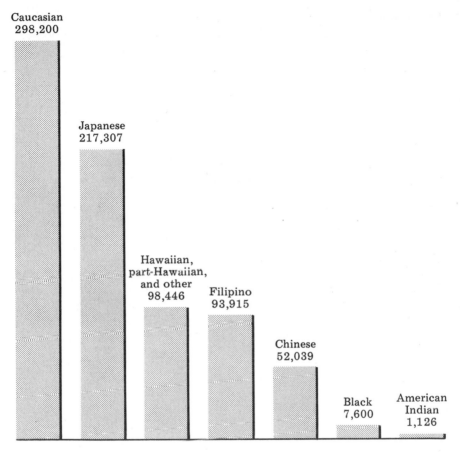

Figure 7.1   The principal racial and ethnic groups of Hawaii, 1970.

Figures from U.S. Bureau of the Census, *Statistical Abstract of the United States, 1976.*

islands.   A more variegated aggregation could not be found anywhere, for Hawaii includes among its citizens persons of American, British, Norwegian, German, Spanish, Puerto Rican, Portuguese, black, Chinese, Korean, Japanese, Filipino, Hindu, Danish, Micronesian, and Polynesian stocks, plus many other groups, and an infinite variety of mixtures of all of these.   (Figure 7.1 shows Hawaii's principal racial and ethnic groups.)

Bringing together peoples of such different racial and cultural backgrounds would seem to be an invitation to endless strife and hatred, but the remarkable fact is that Hawaii has gained a reputation as a "polyracial paradise."   The islands have been referred to as "the world's most successful experiment in mixed breeding," and as a "melting pot, unmatched in today's world for interracial tolerance and affection."   This reputation is certainly not without good foundation, but more discerning and objective writers have insisted that tensions do exist there, that upper-class whites often pay mere lip service to tolerance, and that beneath the calm surface one will find instances of inequality, prejudice, bitterness, and discrimination.

Granted, however, that race relations in Hawaii have not been without blemish, there is no denying that the mores of equality have prevailed. Discrimination and segregation, as we know them on the mainland, have been conspicuously absent there. Titles of respect are given to persons of all races. There are no restricted sections in the theatres, and hotels and restaurants will not refuse service to anyone because of color. If one visits the schools, one may perhaps find that the principal is black or American Indian. The police force includes members of many racial stocks. At social functions persons of all ethnic groups can be seen engaging in friendly conversation with one another. Whites will be found working for employers of darker complexion, and taking orders from them, without feeling that such behavior is improper. A person's status depends more on ability and character than on racial antecedents. Intermarriage is quite common, as it has been from the earliest days of contact, and persons of pure ethnic stock are becoming fewer and fewer. The prediction, based on careful analysis of vital statistics, has been made that "by the end of the century, it may well be that a majority of the inhabitants will be persons of mixed blood, and Hawaiian blood will be found probably in the majority of these."[12] However one feels about all this apparent equality, tolerance, and racial intermixture, in Hawaii it is considered a breach of good manners to voice one's disapproval.

How did all these diverse peoples find their way to this tiny spot in the Pacific? To begin with, a thousand years ago primitive Polynesians paddled their canoes to the islands and settled there. Centuries later, in the middle of the 1500s, two Spanish ships were wrecked nearby, and those among the crew who survived took local wives, remained there, and left numerous progeny. It remained, however, for Captain James Cook to "discover" Hawaii on his third Pacific voyage in 1778. Thenceforth close contact was maintained between the islands and the rest of the world. For a time Honolulu served as a way station in the international fur trade. Soon the sandalwood trade with China assumed commercial importance, until the islands were stripped of this natural resource. Then whalers began to use the islands as a supply station. Finally, when the whaling industry began to decline, the inhabitants turned more and more to agriculture. Sugar cane had long been known there. As early as 1802 a Chinese resident had found that the soil was eminently suited to cane production, and in 1835 American settlers had planted it extensively. But in the 1850s, the commercial possibilities of sugar loomed in the islanders' minds.

These economic activities, of course, brought in people from many lands. White people came from far and wide, many of them took local women for wives, and reared families. Missionaries arrived from New England in 1820. Blacks are known to have been there early in the nineteenth century,[13] as were representatives of many other races and nations.

The cultivation of cane, however, greatly stimulated immigration, for the planters soon faced the problem of a labor supply since the native Hawaiians were not disposed to perform the monotonous tasks demanded by the cane fields. In addition, their numbers had been declining seriously following their contacts with the world. There were probably 300,000 of them at the time of Cook's discovery, but they were rapidly decimated by mumps, measles, and whooping cough until they had dropped to the all-time low of 57,000 in 1872. The Hawaiians sought to rebuild their native stock by inducing Polynesians to come from other islands of the Pacific, and a few responded. The sugar planters, however, were more interested in cheap labor than they were in racial homogeneity, and they turned to Chinese coolies, large numbers of whom were imported as contract laborers. Toward the end of the nineteenth century the residents began to fear that Hawaii would become a Chinese colony, and a different source of labor was sought. Several thousand Portuguese were recruited, with other European peoples, but the demand could not be satisfied.

Then attention was directed to Japan. A few Japanese had been brought in as early as 1868, but thousands were introduced in the years following 1885. The Japanese government insisted that each shipment include a sufficient number of women. The fear then arose that Hawaii would become a Japanese community, and still other sources of labor were explored. Early in the twentieth century 5,000 Puerto Ricans and approximately 7,000 Koreans came to the islands. More Portuguese were induced to come, and eventually Filipinos were imported to work on the plantations.

How can we account for the fact that, with such diverse and numerous ethnic groups, and such keen competition for status, conflict has been kept to a minimum, tolerance and amity have been amazingly conspicuous, and assimilation has proceeded apace? The reputation the islands have won for interracial harmony and equality is richly deserved. What factors have contributed to the development of such a situation?

Without professing to know *all* the significant factors, we may say that certain characteristics of the native Hawaiians were decisive. Unlike the aborigines of Brazil and the United States, the peoples of Hawaii were never enslaved, confined to reservations, driven into the interior, or reduced to subservient status. Instead, they maintained their position and actually set the pattern race relations would take.

The Hawaiians, at the time of their "discovery," were a simple preliterate people, carefree and tolerant. They had no knowledge of such an institution as slavery, had no feeling of inferiority, and were not averse to marrying outsiders. Although their culture was of a primitive, Stone Age type, they did possess the skills that enabled them to produce an abundance of vegetables, meat, fruit, timber, and salt — articles highly desired by the trading vessels plying the Pacific in the eighteenth and nineteenth centuries. Moreover, they were immediately attracted to the iron implements and weapons, the cotton goods, and various other articles the Americans and Europeans had to offer. Thus trade was possible and quite acceptable to all parties concerned.

The Hawaiians, moreover, were not loosely and inadequately organized, as one might expect a primitive people to be, but throughout most of the contact period were united under strong and shrewd rulers. The white traders who came to the islands found it expedient to respect the authority of these chiefs, and to deal with them and their subjects as equals. These rulers, too, were able to secure the services of a number of whites, who took up their residence on the islands, and who brought to the Hawaiians the technical knowledge of the civilized world. These whites were accorded positions of honor, were regarded as chiefs, married individuals of high rank, and set about to give the islands their mixed-blood population. Thus in Hawaii the hybrid from the beginning has enjoyed an enviable status, being descended from men and women of good position whose unions were socially approved. It has been quite otherwise in other areas where the races have met, and where miscegenation occurs on the fringes of the population and among the least respectable members of the two groups.

This pattern of tolerance and respect, established early in the period of contact, was accepted by the later arrivals. Thus, when the New England missionaries appeared in 1820, they were doubtless shocked by many of the customs of the natives, and they certainly came with a desire to convert the "benighted heathen" to their own "superior" moral code. They were forced, however, to make compromises. Permission to settle on the islands had to be obtained from the king, and he was somewhat reluctant to grant it. Finally he referred the problem to one of his advisers, a white who had lived in Hawaii thirty years and who had a native wife and a family of mixed-blood children. His advice to the king was that they be allowed to remain, and the missionaries, accordingly, could hardly forget their indebtedness to him, however much they disapproved of his conduct. The arrival of these strait-laced New Englanders, with their own wives and children, might very well have introduced into the situation traditions of racial superiority and inferiority. Instead, the missionaries were impelled to accept the local mores of equality, to treat the natives as equals, and to show respect to those in authority. Somewhat later, when the white residents and transient sailors on the islands had grown numerous and strong and were in a position to challenge the local authorities and to overturn the social system, the missionaries came to the support of the natives and helped them to preserve order and to defend themselves against their would-be exploiters.[14]

No doubt there were many other factors that operated in the development of the unique pattern of race relations that we find in Hawaii today. W. C. Smith believes that the multiplicity of ethnic groups has been an important influence, making it difficult for any group to single out another as a target for a long and concerted attack.[15] He holds also that the large hybrid population, enjoying the prestige that it does in Hawaii, has played a significant role. Most important, however, was the character of the natives, the features of their culture at the time of the early contact, and the peculiar circumstances under which the first relations with the outside world occurred.

Race relations in Hawaii have many features in common with those in Brazil. In both regions we have a meeting of peoples who were widely different, both physically and culturally. There was the same mixing of blood and blending of cultures. There was a struggle for dominance, in which the efforts on the part of some to exploit others was met by a show of resistance by the subordinate groups. In both areas we find evidence of the existence of prejudice, discrimination, inequities, and conflict.

At the same time, it is apparent that the course of race relations has not been identical. Where the Indians were annihilated or driven into the interior, the Hawaiians held their own, in status if not in numbers. The plantation system was introduced very early in Brazil, but it was generations after the initial contacts before the plantation made its appearance in Hawaii. Slavery was quickly adopted by the Portuguese to solve their labor problem, and blacks were forcibly transported to Brazil; but Hawaii never resorted to the institution of slavery to meet its demand for labor. Certainly the story of race relations as it unfolds in Brazil is not duplicated in Hawaii.

The factors that entered into the two situations were quite unlike. For one thing, the Hawaiians presented to the whites upon their arrival a much more united front than did the Indians in Brazil. Then, too, the motives leading to the contact of the races were quite different. Brazil's Indians faced a heterogeneous group of adventurers who came to conquer and colonize, while the Hawaiians' first contacts were with sailors whose interest lay in trade and who were not bent upon dominating, exterminating, or dispossessing the natives of the islands. Of major importance, however, were the values and traditions the various racial and ethnic groups brought to the situation. The value the Portuguese attached to pigmentation, their familiarity with the institution of slavery, and their attitude toward concubinage were certainly important in shaping the events that were to follow in Brazil. The value system of the native Hawaiians, as well as that of the whites, helps explain the course of race relations in the islands. Thus while some similarities between the two cases can be found, the differences make it clear that it is dangerous to generalize narrowly.

American Indians

To illustrate the thesis that "in no two instances have the interrelations of different ethnic groups run exactly the same course," we cannot do better than to consider the contacts between the whites and the various Indian tribes in our own country. Such a comparison has been made in a volume edited by Professor Ralph Linton[16] that describes the effects that the coming of the white man had on the Puyallup, Shoshoni, Ute, Arapaho, Fox, Carrier, and San Ildefonso Indians. The story is quite different for each of these groups, as two extremes will illustrate.

The Puyallup

This tribe, for instance, was a loosely organized people living on Puget Sound, near the site of the present city of Tacoma. Fishing was the basis of their economy, but important also were hunting and the gathering of berries and other wild products. A high degree of specialization of labor had been developed in the pursuit of their various economic, religious, artistic, and military activities. They lived in large communal dwellings, but it was custom and necessity that dictated this practice rather than any strong group feeling. In fact, their society was highly competitive and was characterized by intense jealousies and suspicions.

The whites descended on the Puyallup in an avalanche. Prior to 1832 contacts had been few and indirect, and the influences of whites on the Puget Sound Indians were negligible. In that year, however, retired employees of the Hudson's Bay Company established a permanent settlement on Nisqually Bay at no great distance from the Puyallup, and whites began moving into the region, taking up land and engaging in agriculture. The discovery of gold in California in 1849 gave a tremendous impetus to the influx. Here was a ready market for building materials and food, and the homesteaders on Puget Sound set to work busily to meet that demand. The white population grew rapidly.

This was no country for white women, however. The bachelors who migrated there, accordingly, took Indian wives. This arrangement proved quite satisfactory, for the Puyallup had long been accustomed to seeing their women marry outside the tribe, and the women, in turn, were prepared to find that marriage called for a complete change in the way of life. They took readily, therefore, to the customs of their white husbands, and reared their mixed-blood children in much the same manner as other pioneer children were reared. Puyallup men, too, were not adverse to doing manual labor for their white neighbors. They were good and skillful laborers, and quickly learned to use the tools and to perform the tasks demanded by their employers. The whites were extremely careful to deal with the Indians justly, making no distinctions in the wages they paid for labor and the prices they charged for goods. The Puyallup continued to fish and to gather berries and their new neighbors offered a ready and eager market for their products. Under such conditions, where the Indian and the white dealt with each other on a basis of equality, amalgamation and assimilation moved along rapidly, with a minimum of overt conflict.

Such was the situation prior to the 1860s. Says Linton:

It would be hard to imagine better conditions for the acculturation of a native people than those which existed during the early part of Puyallup-white contact. The Indians were accepted on terms approaching social equality, with many legal intermarriages and the mutual recognition of relationship claims in both groups. Indians and whites worked side by side at the same tasks and for the same wages, and the only direct attempts to change the native culture were those connected with the abandonment of the communal houses and the introduction of Christianity. Even the latter seems to have been in the hands of intelligent and sympathetic missionaries. The individualistic patterns of the native culture made it easy for certain Indians to take on white habits without waiting for the rest of their group to assume them. The result of all this was the rapid assimilation of the Indians into the white population, and all distinctions would probably have disappeared if it had not been for certain later developments.[17]

Following the American Civil War, however, great numbers of white people flocked to the region. Between 1880 and 1886 the population of the state of Washington increased nearly 300 percent. The cities around Puget Sound experienced rapid growth. Tacoma flourished, and the Puyallup were right in the center of this development. Moreover, the newcomers did not share the attitudes toward the Indians that the pioneers had displayed. On the contrary, they were reluctant to intermarry with them and disposed to discriminate sharply. The Indians became addicted to liquor, which they could now purchase easily and which contributed greatly to their demoralization. The most signicant change, however, was the sudden wealth that came to the Puyallup, as their lands skyrocketed in value and the white settlers and the railroad companies scrambled to purchase them.

The Indians were not prepared to cope with the wealth that had so unexpectedly fallen into their hands. Their scale of values became upset and distorted. They would see a tribal peer whom they had never respected suddenly acquire this new power, while a leader whom they had always revered was passed by in this new dispensation. In their earlier introduction to white money, it was the able and industrious who succeeded in acquiring it, just as success had always been the lot of the deserving one in aboriginal times. But it was no longer so; money was flowing freely and easily, and the undeserving were sharing equally in it. Disputes arose over the ownership of the land and the disposal of estates, and cases were taken to the courts. The age-old suspicions and jealousies were fanned into flame. Feuds and murders took a heavy toll. The Puyallup population declined rapidly, and the small remnant left today will doubtless be absorbed into the white community eventually.

The Fox

A complete contrast is offered by the experiences of this group. Theirs has been one long struggle against absorption and domination by the whites, and against the adoption of the white culture. In these efforts they have met with a surprising degree of success.

The contacts of these Indians with Europeans date back to the early part of the seventeenth century. Father Allouez visited them in 1669, and found them using metal tools, which testified to their familiarity with the traders. At that time they were living near Green Bay, in what is now Wisconsin. Formerly, they had inhabited southern Michigan, and subsequently they were to dwell in various places in the upper Mississippi Valley. These were village Indians, subsisting by hunting and cultivating their crops of corn, beans, squash, and pumpkins. They tapped the maple trees and made sugar and they gathered berries, nuts, and numerous other wild plants. Part of the year they lived in their permanent villages, and part they spent roaming the country on long hunting expeditions.

War was one of the major interests in the life of a Fox man. The tribe had to fight, of course, to protect its hunting grounds against trespassers, and to acquire new territory as its numbers increased. Tribal members would fight, also, to avenge the death of one of their own group. More especially, though, they fought because they enjoyed warfare and because of the prestige it brought them. Older warriors would continually boast of their exploits and martial success brought honor and respect. Fox boys could hardly restrain themselves until the age of fifteen or so, when they could join a war party.

The Fox were continually at war with other Indian tribes. During the historical period they numbered among their enemies, at one time or another, the Ojibwa, Sioux, Pawnee, Winnebago, Ottawa, Menominee, and many others. Hostility to the French also arose at an early date. Tradition attributes this antipathy to their dislike for the beards Frenchmen wore, but the truth probably is that some of their tribe were mistreated by the French in Montreal in 1671, and the Fox never forgave them for it. They were continually preying on the French, frustrating all their plans, and disrupting their trade. The French, in fact, so despised the Fox that they wanted to annihilate them, and made numerous efforts to do so. The British, to be sure, nurtured this hostility between the French and the Fox. They offered bribes to the Indians, and gave them a better price for their furs than the French were disposed to offer. In the Revolutionary War, the Fox took the side of the British, but subsequently came to terms with the new government of the United States.

Eventually, after many unwilling cessions of their lands and the signing of numerous treaties, they settled in what is now Iowa. They were determined to have as little as possible to do with the whites, but they were unable to isolate themselves. Settlers pushed into their territory and poached on their lands or took lead from their mines. Finally in 1842 they reluctantly ceded their Iowa lands to the whites and agreed to migrate to Kansas.

They loathed Kansas, however. The flat, treeless plains had no attractions for people who loved the green hills, woods, and water. The Sauk and Kickapoo tribes had also been removed to Kansas and were no happier there than the Fox. These three groups, however, reacted to their new situation in different ways. The Kickapoo moved on to Mexico, where some of their descendants have remained to this day. The Sauk decided that the proper course for them was to adopt the ways of the white culture, which they proceeded to do. The Fox, on the other hand, were determined to return to Iowa and to continue their resistance to assimilation. Accordingly, they took a step without parallel in the history of Indian-white relations — *they purchased land from the whites*. They began by selling their ponies, which brought sufficient funds to enable them to buy eighty acres in central Iowa. They added to this, as other funds became available, until at the present time they own more than three thousand acres. Here they have continued to live, shutting themselves off from their white neighbors as completely as possible and perpetuating their Indian culture insofar as they can.

Compromises, of course, have been inevitable. The Fox have had to suppress their warlike traditions. Farming, formerly a repugnant idea, has become the mainstay of their existence. They have learned to appreciate money. Some of them can speak English. They do not hesitate, moreover, to take over from the whites any items of culture that they feel will suit their purposes. Thus they have adopted automobiles, tractors, and other farm machinery. The men shave with razors, and the women have learned to can food, although they continue to preserve much of it by the ancient Indian methods. When they go to town, they patronize the movies and the pool rooms. They borrow from the banks when they need credit to run their farms. Insofar as possible, however, they have remained faithful to the Fox culture. Christianity has never succeeded in gaining a foothold among them. Their native language is used by all. Old ceremonies are still preserved. The ancient social organization still functions. At one time there was considerable intermarriage with whites, but this has virtually ceased. In short, the Fox have made certain necessary adjustments to the surrounding white community, but have been amazingly successful in their determination to resist amalgamation and assimilation.

Reasons for the Differences

How may we account for the fact that the various Indian tribes, in their relations with the whites, have not followed any common pattern nor gone through a similar process of steps and stages, but instead have displayed a wide variety of reactions and experiences? No doubt there are innumerable factors responsible for these differences, but the following have certainly been instrumental:

1. *The initial contacts*   Some tribes came suddenly to feel the full impact of European culture, while others had the good fortune to learn about it gradually. Those who inhabited the Atlantic coastal regions, for instance, were confronted almost overnight by a host of strange peoples and even stranger gadgets and customs, while those who lived farther inland, such as the Cherokees, were spared this traumatic experience. The former were overwhelmed by the multiplicity of new ideas, habits, and material objects, to say nothing of devastating diseases, while the latter were able to become acquainted with a few at a time, to ponder them, to accept or reject, and to integrate into their own culture those they chose to adopt. Moreover, the initial contacts were in some instances honest, equitable, and friendly so that a pattern of harmonious relationships was established; while in other instances the first knowledge the Indians had of the whites was acquired through dealings with dishonest, brutal, and unscrupulous individuals, leading inevitably to the formation of hostile and prejudicial attitudes.

2. *Tribal solidarity*   Some Indian tribes were closely knit, politically united, and possessed a strong sense of solidarity.   The Indians of the southwestern Pueblos, for instance, maintain themselves as closed groups, admitting few aliens and censuring their own members who do not strictly conform.   Various mechanisms are used to preserve the exclusive character of the society.   Rituals are employed for initiating members into the in-group; cleansing ceremonies are performed to reintroduce members to the group after an absence; there are secret activities for members only; and knowledge of the group's customs and values, and participation therein, are shielded from aliens.   Tribes in which these conditions prevailed were in a better position to withstand the encroachments of white people and their culture.   On the other hand there were tribes that were loosely organized, with only tenuous systems of leadership and authority.   Strangers were not infrequently "adopted" into the tribe, and there were few secrets from which outsiders were guarded.   The Puyallup, for instance, were highly individualistic, and felt no need to wait for others in the group to join in the adoption of the white's folkways.

3. *Natural resources*   The effect of the coming of the whites on the natural resources on which the Indians relied differed from tribe to tribe.   Often the result was complete destruction of the economic base of tribal life, as by the depletion of buffalo herds.   In some cases the Indians were forcibly removed to a new and strange environment.   In either case, established ways of life were radically altered and difficult new adjustments had to be made.   Other tribes, for one reason or another, were not subjected to so painful an ordeal.   The Indians of San Ildefonso, for example, suffered no important changes in their natural environment through the arrival of the whites.   True, there was some destruction of the game, but agriculture, rather than hunting, was the foundation of their economic life, and this was not disturbed by either the Spaniards or the Americans.

4. *Values*   Each tribe had its own hierarchy of values, and these conflicted sharply with the values of the whites in some instances, whereas in other situations the two systems were complementary or at least compatible.   Thus those who made warfare a virtue and regarded martial glory as the only avenue to the achievement of status inevitably found themselves at odds with the whites, who were bent on the establishment of peace and order.   Those who cherished a nomadic life, too, could not avoid conflict with the sedentary whites.   Not all Indians, however, were nomadic, and many of them regarded war as a nuisance or a calamity.   Some tribes placed the highest value on religion, or the acquisition of wealth, or the performance of ceremonies, and these values could be carried over easily into a world dominated by the whites.

5. *Attitudes of the whites*   The attitudes of the white people who came into contact with the Indians were of crucial importance in determining the course of race relations.   There were traders, who had no desire to see the Indian way

of life radically changed, but who had, instead, a vested interest in the perpetuation of the prevailing culture. Others came as permanent settlers, determined
to take or to purchase the land. Missionaries, of course, were primarily concerned with changing the Indian; some were tolerant, sympathetic, and patient,
while others had no appreciation for the Indians' virtues and sought to produce
a complete and immediate change. Then there were those whites who approached the Indians with preconceived ideas of racial superiority and aloof-
ness, while others were devoid of such attitudes.

6. *Marriage and sex mores* The various Indian tribes, as well as the whites,
differed widely with respect to their mores on sex and marriage. Some were
strictly endogamous, while others had traditions of tribal exogamy. Some
placed a high value on chastity, and others did not. The Fox and the Puyallup
illustrate the two extremes. It can be readily seen that under one system of sex
mores assimilation and amalgamation would be accelerated, while under another system they would be prevented or retarded.

These are not the only variables, of course, that served to make the course of
race relations different from one tribe to another. We cannot overlook the role
played by certain outstanding individuals, some of whom were hospitable to the
whites while others were adamant in their resistance. Important, also, was the
fact that certain tribes were strongly ethnocentric, glorifying their own history
and customs, while others had slight regard for their simple culture and readily
acknowledged the superiority of the whites. Tribes differed, too, in their power
structures. There were those, for instance, who bestowed great respect and authority on the aged, the very ones who would be most inclined to manifest fear
and suspicion of the new and unfamiliar ways of the invaders.

Uniformities

Even though the course of race relations is not identical in any two situations,
we must not conclude that there are no similarities. As a matter of fact, certain phenomena are virtually universal in those areas where racial and ethnic
groups have come together. Conflict, although perhaps not inevitable, is often
a universal accompaniment of the meeting of diverse peoples. Biological mix
ture is another, for there seems to be no exception to the rule that, when peoples come into contact, a mixture of blood results. The give and take of elements of culture is still another consequence, although wide differences occur
in the rate of such exchange and the length to which it goes. The domination
of one group over the over usually follows when peoples meet, and those in the
subordinate group react in certain familiar ways. In the succeeding chapters
we consider these widespread, if not universal and inevitable, phenomena.

Notes

1. R. E. Park, "Our Racial Frontier on the Pacific," *Survey Graphic* 9 (May 1926): 196. Reprinted in R. E. Park, *Race and Conflict*, p. 150.

2. E. S. Bogardus, "A Race-Relations Cycle," *American Journal of Sociology* 35, no. 4 (Jan. 1930): 613.

3. W. O. Brown, "Culture Contact and Race Conflict," in E. B. Reuter, ed., *Race and Culture Contacts*, pp. 34–37.

4. C. E. Glick, "Social Roles and Types in Race Relations," in A. W. Lind, ed., *Race Relations in World Perspective*, p. 239ff.

5. S. Lieberson, "A Societal Theory of Race and Ethnic Relations," *American Sociological Review* 26, no. 6 (Dec. 1961): 902–910.

6. G. C. Kinloch, *The Dynamics of Race Relations*, pp. 205–209.

7. R. T. LaPiere, *Sociology*, p. 429.

8. D. Pierson, *Negroes in Brazil*, p. 344.

9. E. Williams, "Racial Attitudes in Brazil," *American Journal of Sociology* 54, no. 5 (March 1949): 402–408.

10. Pierson, *Negroes in Brazil*, pp. 116–117.

11. Ibid., pp. 342–343.

12. B. L. Hoormann, "Racial Complexion of Hawaii's Future Populations," *Social Forces* 27, no. 1 (Oct. 1948): 71.

13. L. L. Lee, "A Brief Analysis of the Role and Status of the Negro in the Hawaiian Community," *American Sociological Review* 13, no. 4 (Aug. 1948): 422.

14. An interesting account of the coming of the missionaries is given in R. E. McKee, *The Lord's Anointed: A Novel of Hawaii*.

15. W. C. Smith, "Minority Groups in Hawaii," *The Annals of the American Academy of Political and Social Science* 223 (Sept. 1942): 41.

16. R. Linton, ed., *Acculturation in Seven American Indian Tribes*.

17. Ibid., p. 37.

Part Three

PATTERNS OF INEQUALITY

Chapter Eight
Techniques of Dominance

The sad truth is that whatever modifications
have been affected . . . are due to great and
incessant pressure.

— *James Baldwin* Nobody Knows My Name

In 1670 a small band of Englishmen made the first permanent settlement in
what was to become the state of South Carolina. Theirs was a perilous and
precarious venture and the foothold they gained on the coast was not solid.
The Indian tribes were justifiably suspicious, and the Spaniards to the south
were anything but hospitable. For their own security, the English welcomed
immigrants to their colony and offered every possible inducement. Others
from Britain soon joined them and the settlement grew in numbers and
strength. Presently there began to arrive groups of thrifty, pious French Huguenots, who were harried and persecuted at home and were attracted to Carolina by the promise of religious freedom. The English were glad to see them.
There was land aplenty for all, and the Huguenots were skillful, hard-working
citizens. But they spoke a strange language, their customs were queer, and
their religion was not of the approved Anglican variety. There were no objections to their settlement in Carolina; but the English wanted it understood that
they were to stay "in their place." They could own land, earn wealth, work,
and worship; they could not aspire to the status of the English, enter the government, or establish their language or faith.

Years later, when it was proposed that the Huguenots be permitted to send
delegates to the Assembly, the English raised the cry, "Shall the Frenchmen,

who cannot speak our language, make our laws?" The answer, obviously, was negative.

Time healed the wounds, however. In 1696 the Assembly granted to aliens living in the colony "all the rights, privileges, powers and immunities whatsoever, which any person born of English parents may, can, might, could or of right ought to have, use and enjoy." Assimilation proceeded rapidly. The French language began to disappear. Huguenot clergymen sought ordination in the Anglican church, and most of the Huguenot churches became part of the established society. The process, to be sure, was not without discord. The Huguenots exploded when their English neighbors insisted that they had not been properly married and that their children were, therefore, illegitimate. Furthermore, the British laughed at the awkward efforts of the French to speak English and were shocked at their practice of receiving the sacrament sitting down, their dispensing with godparents, and their refusal to make the sign of the Cross. The historical records abound with numerous instances of conflict and misunderstanding. But all that was years ago. The Huguenots, as a group, have long since ceased to be. One of their churches, the only Huguenot church in the United States, still stands in Charleston. French surnames are not uncommon to this day, and the names of streets testify to their former residents. The processes of assimilation and amalgamation, however, have run their entire course.

Much the same thing happens whenever racial and ethnic groups come into contact. The group that enjoys the greater prestige and wields the power is invariably jealous of its status, will not surrender its prerogatives without a struggle, and is determined to defend its own values and its culture against competing and conflicting systems. The lesser group, at the same time, is no less attached to its traditions and values, is not satisfied with a subordinate "place," and is determined to improve its status. The noted sociologist Robert E. Park has referred to the struggle for status as the very source of race problems. He notes that racial groups are tolerated as long as they "know their place." It is when they seek to improve their position in society that they are resented.[1]

Here, then, is the very crux of the so-called race problem. The underprivileged minority conceives of the problem as one of achieving a more desirable status, of removing the stigma of inferiority, of casting off the disabilities and handicaps imposed on it, and of acquiring power and status equal to that of any other group. To the dominant group, on the other hand, the race problem is seen essentially as one of maintaining its position of dominance, of holding on to its power and prestige, and of preserving its way of life. A docile, subservient, industrious racial or ethnic minority can be very useful, even indispensable; but such a minority becomes a menace when it grows restless, seeks to change its status, and aspires to play new roles. Dominant groups, then, must devise techniques, agencies, and policies of social control. Indeed, they have often long foreseen the inevitable uprising and have taken steps to prevent it.

Crude methods of physical force, important though they be in achieving dominance over others, are not in themselves adequate for maintaining a position of superiority. To be sure, force must always be held in reserve and be readily available in an emergency; but effective domination depends on techniques more subtle and efficient than guns and bombs. As a matter of fact, dominant racial and ethnic groups are often greatly outnumbered by the peoples over whom they exercise control, and their power and prestige would be insecure indeed if they rested only on physical force. In South Africa, for instance, less than 4 million whites lord it over more than 17 million natives; in Hawaii, the *haoles* (whites of American and European origin), who enjoy the greatest power and prestige, are decidedly outnumbered by those of other racial stocks; and in Jamaica, the whites, in control, are a mere 2 percent of a population that consists of 85 percent black, 13 percent Asian and East Indian, a scattering of Chinese, and others. In many parts of the world, then, the dominant racial group cannot rely on its numerical strength, but must look to other techniques to insure its dominance. Even where it does have the advantage of numbers, and where its power is undisputed, symbolic means of control are employed. In the United States, although blacks are outnumbered nine to one, whites use many devices other than physical force to maintain supremacy.

Control of Numbers

Among the devices employed by dominant peoples is that of regulating the numbers of those who threaten to upset the status quo. Benjamin Franklin was disturbed by the thought of large numbers of foreigners flocking to Pennsylvania, and in 1750 he wrote to a friend asking

why the Pennsylvanians should allow the Palatine Germans to swarm into our settlements, and by herding together to establish their Language and Manners to the exclusion of ours? Why should Pennsylvania, founded by the English, become a colony of Aliens, who will shortly be so numerous as to Germanize us instead of our Anglifying them?[2]

The fears expressed by Franklin were shared by others in his time, but many years were to pass before they would affect the immigration policy of the nation.

Elsewhere, however, the practice of regulating and restricting the number and type of immigrants has long been in force. Canadians, for instance, have never looked on their country as a haven for the surplus population of foreign lands or as a refuge for the poor, oppressed, and underprivileged. They regard immigration as a purely domestic problem.

Nevertheless, Canada is eager to experience population growth, and continues to welcome — and to seek — immigrants. In the ten years following World War II Canada received more than a million newcomers, quite a feat for a nation of then 15 million. This country has accepted a goodly share of the world's refugees from communism. Even so, a third of these newcomers were of British stock, and almost another third were from France, Germany, the Netherlands, Austria, and the United States. Canada's policy of keeping the numbers of immigrants manageable, and of ensuring their assimilability, remains in force:

Since the end of the Second World War it has been the policy of the Government of Canada to stimulate the growth of the population by selective immigration. Efforts are made to choose immigrants of prospective adaptability to the Canadian way of life and to admit them at such times and in such numbers as employment conditions warrant.[3]

The "White Australia" Policy

Australia has long been determined to keep itself a white British commonwealth, and racial and ethnic groups that would be likely to endanger such a goal have been consistently excluded. The result is that Australia's population is approximately 95 percent British. When the United States adopted its quota system in the 1920s, Australia took immediate action and empowered its Governor-General to prohibit the entry of those persons deemed undesirable because of their "presumed unassimilability." This action was aimed especially at immigrants from southern and eastern Europe and its purpose was to prevent their seeking a home in Australia when the United States had closed its doors against them. So effectively has the color bar been enforced that only 1 percent of the population is nonwhite, and many of these are the offspring of persons who were already in Australia when the rigid immigration laws were enacted.

An editorial in the *West Australian* described the rationale behind the restrictive immigration laws:

The purpose of the immigration laws is to build up a homogeneous community and to avoid the creation of mixed racial problems. It is also to avoid any development of substandard economic conditions.

Australia has to live with Asia by reason of geography. We want to be friends with Asians but Australians are essentially of European stock. We cannot become Asians and we do not wish to.[4]

This "White Australia" Policy has its critics, both within and without the commonwealth. The peoples of overpopulated Asia deeply resent the policy which excludes them from a continent almost the size of the United States, sparsely settled by a mere 13,000,000 people. Australia hopes to have a population of 20,000,000 within the next two decades, but insists that only whites be permitted to enter.

Sir Keith Wilson is an ardent supporter of the White Australia Policy and has described the reasons for not admitting "unassimilable" minorities as follows:

We do not want Australia to be a little Italy, a little Germany, a little Greece or a little any other country. We want our immigrants to become Australians and our immigration system is based on admitting people who, having come here, want to become Australians.[5]

The emphasis in Australia's immigration policy is on admitting people who can adapt to and assimilate the white Anglo-Saxon tradition in which the nation evolved.

Within the country there is some criticism of the policy of racial exclusion. The Communists have adopted the issue as an ideal one for their purposes, and certain religious groups have sought to have the laws relaxed. Their efforts, however, have been to no avail. All governments — Labor, Liberal and Conservative — have supported the policy since 1901, as have the press and public opinion.

In recent years there have been minor modifications of the laws to make it possible for some non-Europeans to become citizens. However, the basic goal is still to maintain the ethnic identity of Australia.

Hawaii

Hawaii affords another instance of a society in which the dominant element has attempted to protect its interests by controlling the influx of competitive groups. Early in the nineteenth century the sugar industry began to loom large in the economy of the islands, and the *haoles* readily gained control of this lucrative business. As we have seen, they desperately needed labor on their plantations and found the native Hawaiians were not disposed to engage in so monotonous a task. The *haoles*, accordingly, began to import large numbers of Chinese from Canton. The Hawaiians themselves, more interested in racial homogeneity than in sugar production, would have preferred to rebuild their shattered population by inducing other Polynesians to migrate to the islands; but the *haoles*, whose primary concern was a labor supply, preferred the Chinese and their preference prevailed. Before long, however, when many of the Chinese left the plantations, moved into the cities, and began to compete with the *haole* merchants and artisans, vociferous opposition to them arose. The royal cabinet investigated the issue and reported:

The excessive proportion of Chinese in the kingdom, and their rapid encroachment upon the various businesses and employments of the country, require adequate measures to prevent the speedy extinction in these Islands of western civilization by that of the East, and the substitution of a Chinese for the Hawaiian and other population.

Chinese immigration, accordingly, was at first restricted and then stopped altogether. The demand for labor, however, was still pressing, and the *haoles* turned next to Portuguese and Japanese. When the Japanese, in turn, became dangerously numerous, the tension was relieved by the importation of Koreans, Puerto Ricans, Spanish, and still more Portuguese.

Immigration Policies of the United States

The policies of the United States with respect to immigration have undergone considerable change over the years. From its inception as a nation until 1882, its policy was almost one of free and unrestricted admittance. While this country has never made a practice of soliciting and assisting immigrants, as have British dominions and certain South American countries, the United States did encourage their coming during the first century of its history. This was regarded as the land of the free, a haven for those oppressed by tyrants, and a place of opportunity for all who were willing to labor. The words of Emma Lazarus, inscribed on the Statue of Liberty, were indeed appropriate:

Give me your tired, your poor,
Your huddled masses yearning to breathe free,
The wretched refuse of your teeming shore,
Send these, the homeless, tempest-tossed to me:
I lift my lamp beside the golden door.

To be sure, there were those who had misgivings about foreigners. George Washington wrote to John Adams in 1794: "My opinion with respect to immigration is that except for useful mechanics and some particular descriptions of men or professions, there is no need of encouragement"; and Thomas Jefferson was even more emphatic in expressing the wish that there might be "an ocean of fire between this country and Europe, so that it would be impossible for any more immigrants to come hither." Such fears, however, were not widely felt. There was the West to be opened, railroads had to be built and canals dug, there was land to be had for the asking, people were pouring across the mountains, and the young nation was eager for population.

Opposition to immigration did begin to crystallize, however, in the 1830s. It was suspected, with good reason, that various European countries were in the habit of dumping their paupers and criminals onto these shores; several of the states took steps to prevent the landing of these undesirables. The proper type of legislation was difficult to frame. The states all wanted immigrants of good quality and did not want to divert the stream elsewhere. It was no easy task, therefore, to word the laws in such a way that they would exclude the undesirable types without also discouraging the desirable ones. In the end it became obvious to everyone concerned that state control of immigration was neither feasible nor constitutional, and the whole problem was turned over to the federal government.

There were other reasons, besides dislike of paupers and criminals, that lay back of the growing opposition. In the discussions of the time there appeared the familiar arguments about the dangers of a heterogenous population, the difficulty of assimilating certain ethnic groups, the tendency of foreign groups to segregate themselves in colonies, the congestion in the cities, and the political corruption to which the foreign-born, often unwittingly, lent themselves. Much was said, also, about the effect of immigrants on the wages of native workers, their willingness to adopt a lower standard of living, to do more work for less money, and their readiness to function as strike-breakers. Finally, there was hatred and fear of the Roman Catholic religion, the faith to which the majority of the Irish and many of the Germans adhered.

From these circumstances there arose two political movements. One was the Native American party, centered largely in the cities of Massachusetts, New York, and Pennsylvania, and coming into prominence for the first time about 1835. Rioting, destruction of property, and anti-Catholic demonstrations were among the techniques whereby the adherents of the party gave vent to their opposition, but it was in politics that the movement sought to make its influence felt. The party held a national convention in 1845 and adopted a platform that called for repeal of the naturalization laws and the appointment of none but native Americans to office. They did succeed in electing eight members to Congress, where numerous bills and resolutions were introduced; but no positive measures can be traced to the party.

The other movement took the form of a secret organization that probably started in New York City in 1850. Its name was The Supreme Order of the Star Spangled Banner; but since its members were in the habit of answering all questions about their organization by saying, "I don't know," it came to be known as the Know Nothing party. The society grew very rapidly, and by 1854 had discarded most of its secret character. It openly endorsed candidates for public office and even put forth candidates of its own. The following year the movement claimed to have among its members the governors of seven states, the majority in a number of state legislatures, numerous other public officials, and forty-three representatives and five senators in Congress. In 1856 a national convention was held, and Millard Fillmore was chosen as its nominee for the presidency. The principles of the party, as embodied in its platform, were: Americans must rule America; only the native-born should hold office in federal, state, and municipal governments; the naturalization laws should be changed to require twenty-one years of continued residence as a prerequisite for citizenship; paupers and criminals should be excluded; Romanism and all papal influences should be resisted; all military organizations composed of foreigners should be forbidden. The Know Nothings, despite their political strength, had little influence on legislation. The events immediately before the Civil War diverted the public interest to slavery, immigration itself declined after 1854, and the Know Nothing party passed out of existence. In 1855 Abraham Lincoln wrote:

Our progress in degeneracy appears to me to be pretty rapid. As a nation we began by declaring that "all men are created equal!" We now practically read it, "All men are created equal, except Negroes." When the Know-Nothings get control, it will read, "All men are created equal, except Negroes and foreigners and Catholics." When it comes to this, I shall prefer emigrating to some country where they make no pretense of loving liberty — to Russia, for instance, where despotism can be taken pure, and without the base alloy of hypocrisy.[6]

After the Civil War immigration began once more to climb steadily. In fact, immigrants were actually in good favor for a time. The war had taken a shocking toll of life. Moreover, Congress had passed in 1862 a homestead act having liberal and generous features; as a consequence, many people were drawn to the West. Accordingly, nobody felt cramped by the presence of the immigrants. The first federal law dealing with immigration, passed in 1864, far from restricting it, actually gave it encouragement. Among other things, this law provided for the appointment by the President of a Commissioner of Immigration, who was to be under the direction of the Department of State. Further, it provided for the protection of immigrants from fraud and imposition, and for assistance in helping them reach their ultimate destination in this country. At the same time the steamship was supplanting the sailing vessel as a means of transportation. This greatly mitigated the perils and discomforts of the steerage passengers and it contributed also to the great increase in immigration from southern and eastern Europe.

A crucial date in the history of immigration is 1882 for it marked a radical change in the American policy from one of freedom to one of *federal regulation*. This transition was not, however, sudden or surprising. Decades earlier, as we have seen, there had been loud and organized opposition to the immigrant, but it had never succeeded in getting itself expressed in federal legislation. Congress did place a ban on the entrance of convicts and prostitutes in 1875, and the following year the Supreme Court rendered a highly significant decision declaring unconstitutional all the state laws pertaining to the regulation of immigration. In the meantime the feeling had been growing that the United States no longer needed foreigners in its labor force, and competition between native laborers and immigrants was ceasing to be regarded with equanimity. More pertinent, however, was the bitter antagonism that Californians were showing toward the Chinese. On August 3, 1882, accordingly, Congress passed its first general immigration law, inaugurating a period of federal regulation, control, and selection, which continued to 1921. A vast and complicated body of federal immigration laws came into existence. Chinese laborers were at first excluded for a ten-year period, and later, indefinitely; head taxes were imposed; defectives, idiots, lunatics, and convicts were excluded; provisions were made for deportation of undesirables; paupers and persons suffering from loathsome diseases were forbidden to enter; the doors were closed to epileptics, anarchists, polygamists, professional beggars, chronic alcoholics, vagrants, stowaways, and persons who advocated overthrow of the government by force or violence.

The year 1921 is another landmark in the nation's immigration history because it marks the inauguration of a policy of *restriction*, as distinct from the policy of selection that preceded it. In that year Congress passed an emergency measure, limiting the total immigration for any year to 358,803, and stipulating that "the number of aliens of any nationality who may be admitted under the immigration laws to the United States in any fiscal year shall be limited to three percent of the number of foreign born persons of such nationality resident in the United States, as determined by the United States Census of 1910." This was a deliberate attempt to keep out immigrants from southern and eastern Europe, and to favor those from the countries of northern and western Europe.

This restrictive and discriminating legislation was the climax of a long period of agitation. For more than twenty years prior to the passage of the quota act, immigration had been a vital national issue. Between 1900 and 1907 immigration was debated primarily from an economic, and only incidentally from a racial or ethnic, viewpoint. Restriction was urged to protect the American standard of living, and to prevent pauperism, crime, bossism, and the decay of democratic ideals. Between 1907 and 1914, as we saw in Chapter 3, the arguments shifted to racial and eugenic grounds. Immigrants from southern and eastern Europe were declared to be "unassimilable," doubts were cast on the ability of the Anglo-Saxon stock to survive, and heterogeneity was accused of undermining the strength of the nation. Many bills designed to restrict immigration by imposing a "literacy" test were introduced into Congress. Several of these passed one house or the other, and some passed both houses only to be vetoed in turn by Presidents Cleveland, Taft, and Wilson. Cleveland characterized them as "a radical departure from our national policy relating to immigration," as indeed they were; and both Taft and Wilson rejected them on the grounds that their purpose was really restrictive and not selective, as they professed to be. Nevertheless, Congress did enact a bill over President Wilson's veto on February 5, 1917. Its provisions, seemingly innocuous, would merely exclude "all aliens over sixteen years of age, physically capable of reading, who cannot read the English language, or some other language or dialect."

Actually, however, the literacy test was a deliberate attempt to limit the number of immigrants, to discourage the "new" immigration, and to favor the "old." The act also included a "latitude and longitude test," forbidding immigration from the South Sea Islands and various parts of Asia not already covered by the Chinese Exclusion Act and the "gentleman's agreement" with Japan, and thereby allaying the fears of many Americans who envisioned a great influx of Asians to the Pacific coast. Finally, this Act of 1917 designated meticulously the various classes of persons who would be denied admission to the United States. Thus under the guise of individual selection, there were introduced into the American immigration policy the somewhat more questionable principles of group selection and restriction. (Figure 8.1 shows immigration trends from 1820 to 1973.)

The Quota System

The Quota Act of 1921, in preparation for which the Immigration Act of 1917 had served as an entering wedge, was frankly a temporary measure that was adopted to meet an emergency. When World War I ended, it became obvious that Europeans were on the verge of resuming the migration to the United

Thousands

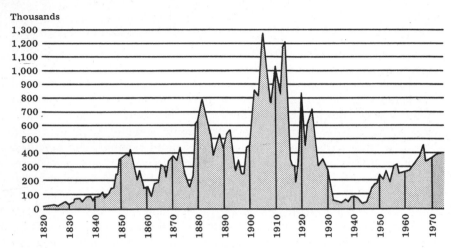

Figure 8.1   Trends of immigration to the United States, 1820–1973.

From U.S. Bureau of the Census, *Statistical Abstract of the United States, 1975*, p. 101.

States that had reached such tremendous proportions in the early years of the twentieth century. The Quota Act was an attempt to stem the tide, and at the same time to tip the scales in favor of those ethnic groups for which the American people had a preference. This temporary measure was superseded, finally, by the permanent Immigration Act of 1924. Under this law the number to be admitted each year was limited to 2 percent of the population of the particular nationality that was resident in the United States according to the census of 1890, the total number under this plan not to exceed 164,667. Beginning in 1929 a new method of computing the quotas on the basis of *national origins* was put into effect. The total number to be admitted each year was 150,000 and the quota for each country would be based on the proportionate number of that nationality living in the continental United States in 1920 in relation to the total population for that year, except that a minimum quota of 100 was established. For example, if 8 percent of the people living in the United States were of Swedish birth or origin then 8 percent, or 12,000, would be the yearly quota for Sweden. Since the minimum quota for any country was 100, the total was slightly more than 150,000. In 1944 the Chinese, who had long been excluded altogether, were brought within the system and were assigned a quota of 105; in 1946 India was assigned a quota of 100 and the Philippines were allowed 100.

On the surface, the quota system appears to be just and impartial. Actually it discriminates decidedly in favor of the "old" immigration, allotting about 25,000 annually to the countries of southern and eastern Europe, and more than five times that number to the nations of northern and western Europe. The quotas, however, give no clear indication of the realities of immigration to

the United States since their adoption. During the 1930s immigration declined to a mere trickle. In fact, the year 1932 saw 35,600 arrivals and
103,300 departures; and 1933 saw 23,100 arrivals against 80,100 departures.
During 1943 only 23,735 aliens entered the country as immigrants. In some
years the greater part of the quotas go unused, while in other years the demand
for admission far exceeds the number permitted to enter.

Moreover, those who hoped that this new policy would make for a more homogeneous population were in for disappointment. Under the provisions of
the law, certain parts of the world were subject neither to total exclusion nor to
a quota. This unrestricted area included all the independent nations of North,
Central, and South America, and the West Indies. There were no limits
placed on eligible native-born citizens of those countries who might choose to
enter the United States. Therefore, when immigration from Europe was drastically reduced, there developed a partially, compensatory movement of peoples
from Canada, Mexico, and other American countries, and from our own territories, especially Puerto Rico.

The McCarran-Walter Act

The McCarran-Walter Act, a highly controversial piece of legislation enacted
by Congress in 1952, did not appreciably change the country's immigration
policy. The quota system, based on national origins, remained intact. The
bill was designed to bring thousands of piecemeal immigration statutes and regulations (accumulated since 1789) into one compact code. It removed some
glaring inequities; for example, all Asiatic immigrants would be eligible for citizenship, where previously Japanese and certain others had been barred. It
placed under the quota system certain nations whose citizens had previously
been excluded. In short, it accepted the principles of quotas and national origins without reservation. Table 8.1 gives the immigration quotas provided for
in that law.

1965 and 1968 Changes

A number of changes in the immigration regulations took place in 1965. The
quotas under the 1952 Act were continued, but a new preference system was
instituted. In addition, until July 1, 1968, any unused places were transferred
to an immigration pool. This pool was used for those individuals who wanted
to enter the country, but could not get visas because the quota for their country
had already been filled. The allocations from this special pool could not
exceed 170,000. The parents, spouses, or children under 21 of United States
residents were admitted without regard to quotas. There were also certain categories of special immigrants who also did not fall under the quota system.

In July of 1968 a ceiling of 120,000 was set for the Western Hemisphere natives who would be admitted on a first-come basis with no limit on the number
coming from any one country. In December of 1968 a limit of 170,000 was

Table **8.1**   United States immigration quotas, 1921–1965

Country	Quota	Country	Quota
All countries	154,657	*Europe* (cont'd)	
Europe	149,667	Norway	2,364
Austria	1,405	Poland	6,488
Belgium	1,297	Portugal	438
Bulgaria	100	Rumania	289
Czechoslovakia	2,859	Spain	250
Denmark	1,175	Sweden	3,295
Finland	566	Switzerland	1,698
France	3,069	Turkey	225
Germany	25,814	U.S.S.R.	2,697
Great Britain	65,361	Yugoslavia	933
Greece	308	Other Europe	1,534
Hungary	865	*Asia*	3,215
Iceland	100	*Africa*	1,400
Ireland	17,756	*Australia, New Zealand*	
Italy	5,645	*and other Oceania*	600
Netherlands	3,136		

SOURCE: Bureau of the Census, *Statistical Abstract of the United States*, Washington, D.C., Bureau of the Census.

set for natives of the Eastern Hemisphere, with no more than 20,000 being allowed to come from any one country. The selection process for Eastern Hemisphere immigrants gave preference to family reunification and to individuals with skills and talents that were in short supply. (For actual numbers of immigrants by country, see Table 8.2.)

Assimilation

Dominant peoples, jealous of their way of life and eager to preserve it, have often looked on assimilation as the solution to their problem, and have sought to impose their culture on the foreign elements in their midst. Thus assimilability has sometimes been regarded as the crucial test to be applied to those who would enter the society. Australia's policy of carefully selecting her immigrants is based on such an assumption.

Assimilation has also been the policy of the United States, although not so consciously and systematically pursued as in Australia at present. As we have seen, there prevailed in this country for a long time the comfortable belief that

Table **8.2**   Immigrants by country of last permanent residence

Country	Total, 155 years (1820–1974)	Country	Total, 155 years (1820–1974)
Europe	35,888,309	*Europe* (cont'd)	
Belgium	200,138	Other Europe	298,919
Czechoslovakia	135,728	*Asia*	2,145,676
Denmark	362,491	China	478,602
Finland	32,411	Hong Kong	130,406
France	740,626	Japan	386,582
Germany	6,948,299	Korea	122,381
Austria	4,311,191	Philippines	236,770
Hungary		Turkey	381,253
Great Britain	4,839,562	Other Asia	409,682
Greece	619,550	*America*	8,172,883
Ireland	4,719,358	Canada	4,037,114
Italy	5,259,026	Cuba	369,049
Netherlands	355,527	Mexico	1,849,399
Norway	854,965	West Indies	614,880
Poland	499,176	Other America	1,302,441
Portugal	399,845	*Africa*	98,553
Spain	243,761	*Australia and New*	
Sweden	1,269,462	*Zealand*	108,756
Switzerland	345,795	*All other countries*	298,548
U.S.S.R.	3,349,313		
Yugoslavia	103,166		

SOURCE: Bureau of the Census, *Statistical Abstract of the United States, 1975*, Washington, D.C., Bureau of the Census, p. 101.

assimilation was an inevitable, automatic process, and that the various ethnic minorities would of their own accord adopt the dominant pattern of living if left to their own devices.   Such optimism, however, was hardly justifiable, nor was it shared by all.   As a matter of fact, there were certain ethnic groups in early nineteenth-century America who envisioned quite a different course. German intellectuals, for instance, pondered various schemes for concentrating their people and perpetuating their social heritage in the New World.   Some of them even proposed that the Germans take over one of the American states and adopt German as the official language.   At one time the Irish petitioned Congress for a land grant in the West on which they might settle certain of their fellow nationals.   Congress wisely rejected the petition on the ground that it would be undesirable to concentrate alien peoples geographically and thereby

encourage the formation of a nation that would be a patchwork of foreign settlements. This action proved that the United States was committed to a policy
of assimilation rather than one of Balkanization. Even so, there were times
when the English language held but a scant advantage over the German. So
important was the Teutonic element in Illinois before the Civil War that
Abraham Lincoln, astute politician that he was, tried to master the German
tongue, and for a time was the owner of a German-language newspaper. A
great influx of British settlers, however, was sufficient to tip the scales.

America has indeed shown adeptness at molding into one nation a wide variety of peoples. The motto, "E Pluribus Unum," is not altogether an idle
boast. Some of the minority groups, however, have had insurmountable obstacles placed in their path, even when they themselves desired to become assimilated; and many other groups, although more fortunate, have also encountered discrimination.

Discrimination

Dominant peoples everywhere have resorted to various devices for restricting
economically, politically, and socially the racial and ethnic groups over whom
they have set themselves. The term commonly applied to such practices is *discrimination*, which F. H. Hankins has defined as the "unequal treatment of
equals, either by the bestowal of favors or the imposition of burdens." Discrimination touches on every phase of life. Subordinate groups are often restricted in their use of hotels, restaurants, transportation, and such public facilities as parks, playgrounds, swimming pools, and libraries. Churches and
hospitals are often closed to them; intermarriage is opposed; and social contacts
between master and servant are hedged about with an elaborate system of etiquette. In the economic realm members of minority groups are barred from
trade unions and professional associations; they are effectively excluded from
many occupations; they are the "last to be hired and the first to be fired"; and,
where they are permitted to work, they are kept down by the imposition of a
"job ceiling." One function of these discriminations is to isolate the dominant
and subordinate groups and to limit contact and communication between
them. Isolation and segregation, accordingly, help to preserve the status quo,
impede the process of assimilation, and, in fact, serve to *dull the appetite for
status* on the part of the underprivileged group.

Reluctance to Educate "Inferiors"

More important, discriminatory policies make it difficult for oppressed groups
to acquire the knowledge, skills, and tools with which to improve their status.
Dominant peoples have often refused to place firearms in the hands of those
beneath them. Here in the United States, the whites, even when their backs

were to the wall in the Revolutionary and Civil Wars, were reluctant to arm blacks. Among the colonial powers France alone imposed conscription for military duty on subject peoples, although Great Britain did draw a fair proportion of the armed forces from dependencies, especially India. The potential military strength of colonial areas is vast, but, significantly enough, the ruling powers have avoided training many of their subjects in warfare. The truth would seem to be that they are afraid to do so, for fear the natives might turn their arms on their masters. More dangerous than rifles, however, are two other weapons that dominant groups have jealously guarded or grudgingly and warily shared, namely, *education* and *the ballot*.

Colonial powers have been notoriously tightfisted in their support of education for their subjects. Even France, committed to a policy of assimilation, never developed an adequate system of schools; nor have the British, Dutch, Portuguese, Japanese, Belgians, or any other imperialistic power done so. Financial reasons are commonly offered as the excuse, although other social services, such as agricultural, veterinary, and public health programs, often receive a fair degree of support. The simple truth is that ruling groups realize that education of the natives would blast the whole system of control. Even where there is some development of schools, emphasis is placed on practical and useful technical subjects -- not on the barren social sciences and the effete humanities.

It has been so in the United States. Prior to the Civil War there was strong sentiment against the education of blacks, both slave and free. This philosophy prevailed, even in the North, while in several of the states of the South, the teaching of blacks was forbidden by law (although frequent violations are recorded). So effective were the barriers, however, that very few blacks were literate when they were granted their freedom. On emancipation, accordingly, blacks manifested a keen desire for education, a fact that Booker T. Washington explained as their natural curiosity to discover just what there was about books that made them so dangerous.

Black leaders have always realized that there were two keys that could open the doors to racial equality — education and the ballot. Some regarded the former as the more important, some the latter, and others insisted that both were essential. The whites, in the meantime, showed little enthusiasm for the education of their onetime slaves. However, their own value system would not permit them to deny educational opportunities altogether to blacks, and they compromised by seeing to it that such opportunities be inferior and inadequate. The areas in which this was apparent were the following: (1) The money spent per pupil was less for blacks than for whites. (2) There was great discrepancy in the value of school properties. (3) The length of the school term was shorter for blacks. (4) Less was spent for transportation. (5) The pupil-teacher ratio was more favorable in the white schools. (6) Teachers in the black schools were less well prepared, and their salaries were lower, than those of the whites.

Discrimination against blacks in education was not limited to the South, although the method whereby it was accomplished differed from one region to another.   Some Northern cities practiced a type of extralegal segregation in their school systems, gerrymandering of school districts was not unknown, and, most important, the residential segregation imposed on blacks resulted in virtually segregated schools.   So it was at the higher levels.   There was, for instance, a quota system that placed restrictions on not only blacks, but Jews, Italians, and members of various other minorities as well.   Some colleges and universities excluded blacks altogether, while others made it extremely difficult for them to enter, and accepted only a limited number from the many applicants.   Thus in devious ways have dominant groups guarded the possession of the knowledge and skills requisite for acquiring and retaining prestige and power.

For many years the black struggle to acquire educational equality was handicapped by the application of the "separate but equal" principle.   This principle had been given legal sanction in the famous case of *Plessey* v. *Ferguson* (1896). In that case the United States Supreme Court *sustained* a Louisiana statute requiring separate railroad accommodations for blacks and whites, and in support of the decision, referred to the accepted practice of segregation in the public schools.   This action of the Court was interpreted as giving the green light to those who wanted separate schools for the two races.   For two generations thereafter, accordingly, the philosophy of "separate but equal" prevailed in the South, even though it was obvious that the schools were indeed separate, but far from equal.   Churches and philanthropic organizations attempted to equalize the educational opportunities by establishing schools of their own and providing various kinds of subsidies, but the task was too great for them.   Black lawyers, in representing their clients, were often able to prove that the opportunities were not equal, and steps had to be taken to provide a semblance of equality.   Finally, in the 1950s, the principle of "separate but equal" was itself challenged and the Supreme Court handed down its decision that "separate educational facilities are inherently unequal."

The Court's ruling, however, did not solve the problem.   The proponents of segregation resorted to a variety of means to nullify or circumvent the decision. One device was that of giving county and city boards of education authority to assign pupils "so as to provide for the orderly and efficient administration of the public schools."   The State of Georgia made it a felony "for any school official . . . to spend tax money for public schools in which the races are mixed," and South Carolina amended its constitution to provide for the elimination of the provision for a liberal system of free public schools. In the Northern states residential segregation, plus a certain amount of gerrymandering of school districts, accounted for a high degree of *de facto* school segregation.   More than twenty years after the original Supreme Court decision the Boston Public Schools were under court order to eliminate segregation in the city's schools.   The violence and political chicanery rivaled anything seen in the South during the 1950s. The road toward equal education and integrated schools has been long and difficult with numerous setbacks and frustrations.

The Ballot

The ballot is still another weapon which dominant peoples have shared with others only under pressure. Kennedy finds that one of the common features of colonial systems is the retention of political control by the possessing power, leaving to the natives little or no share in the government of their own land. There are many ways in which this can be done, even while giving the appearance of a certain degree of self-government. Natives, for instance, are permitted to have advisory councils, but crucial decisions are always made elsewhere; local leaders are retained in office, but if they express opinions hostile to their real rulers, they are quickly spirited away to remote penal areas.

In the Caribbean, as we have seen, many of the familiar techniques of domination are absent. Jim Crow and lynching are not in evidence; segregation is not practiced in schools, theaters, restaurants, or public conveyances. White, black, and brown meet together in the same churches, and are buried side by side in the cemeteries. But when it comes to the ballot, blacks, until very recently, found themselves deprived of it; and mulattos joined with whites to keep it from them.

In the United States the whites have never lost sight of the fact that the ballot would be a powerful instrument for social change in the hands of blacks. At the beginning of the Civil War even the free blacks were disfranchised throughout the South, and in most of the Northern states as well. There were only six states, in fact, that did not discriminate against blacks at the polls. After the war, the South lost no time in enacting discriminatory legislation, designed to perpetuate white supremacy. This legislation, the so-called Black Codes, was instrumental in bringing about the adoption of the Fourteenth and Fifteenth Amendments, which put an end to all the various constitutional and statutory provisions that the southern states had devised to limit the elective franchise to the whites.

The South thereupon set about to circumvent the Constitution and to prevent by other means black use of the ballot. The whites stooped to fraud, bribery, threats, and violence; they resorted to stuffing ballot boxes, to the employment of more boxes than were necessary, and to the surreptitious removal of the polls at the last moment. Such fraudulent and illegal devices, however, were not deemed adequate, and the whites began to cast about for some legal means of excluding blacks from the suffrage. They adopted the famous "grandfather clause," subsequently declared unconstitutional; they excluded those who had been convicted of crimes of a kind to which blacks were peculiarly vulnerable; they insisted that one must be "of good character to vote," or that one should be able to read, understand, and explain the Constitution; and they administered the tests of these abilities so as to discredit blacks.

Most effective of these devices, however, was the *poll tax*. The poll tax not only disfranchised blacks, but also disqualified many of the whites, and it played neatly into the hands of commercial and industrial interests, political machines, and demagogues. Several Southern states proceeded to abolish it of their own accord, until, by 1964, it was retained only in Texas, Arkansas, Mississippi, Alabama, and Virginia. In that year the requisite number of states approved a measure to add the Twenty-fourth Amendment to the Constitution, according to which the right to vote in any primary or other federal election may not be denied by reason of failure to pay a poll tax.

Restrictive Legislation and Repressive Action

The use of legislation and threats of violence or punishment have often been used to keep a group in a subordinate position. This kind of action can be initiated within government channels or it can spring from vigilante groups. When such action is sanctioned by the government, anything that is thought to pose a threat to the status quo will be legislated against and penalized. The penalty may take the form of a mere fine or it can include severe punishments and execution. Banishment or segregation are other forms of repressive action that have frequently been used.

Governmental action is often tied to control by numbers. First, the subordinate group is kept so small that it is relatively weak in comparison to the majority group. Then any disruptive actions can be dealt with severely and swiftly to make it impossible for the minority to bring about changes that appear undesirable to the majority. In this way restrictive legislation takes over where immigration quotas and other measures of population control leave off.

The condition of the Japanese in the United States provides us with an interesting example. Most Japanese immigration to the United States occurred between 1900 and 1930. During this time a paranoia swept the country, particularly the coastal areas of the West, that a massive Japanese invasion was taking place and that the Japanese had a secret plan to take over the country by sheer numbers through immigration. This idea was obviously unsubstantiated. The Japanese have never represented more than 0.1 percent of the United States population and never more than 2.1 percent of the California population. Nevertheless, the belief in a Japanese invasion was widespread and people responded as if it were true. In 1908 President Theodore Roosevelt made a "gentleman's agreement" with Japan that they would restrict and control the immigration of Japanese laborers and farmers to the United States. However, this measure did not solve the problem and the Japanese in this country continued to acquire land and become farmers. To make matters worse, they were outproducing white farmers. In 1913 the government enacted the Anti-Alien Land Act. This act restricted ownership of land for agricultural purposes to individuals who were eligible to become United States citizens. The Japanese had already been classified as "aliens incligible for citizenship" and were obviously singled out as a target for the application of this law. However, they were able to circumvent the law and make it ineffective. First of all, many already owned land and the law was not retroactive. In the second place, they

could lease the land and still compete with the native farmers. And finally, they could buy the land in the name of children who were born in the country and were citizens by birth.

In 1924 Congress passed a law against the immigration of aliens who were ineligible for citizenship. The only group to which this law was applicable was the Japanese. Consequently, no Japanese were allowed to enter the United States until after World War II. The final blow came in 1942 when all Japanese citizens and noncitizens in three western coastal states were sent to ten "relocation centers" to protect the rest of the population against possible acts of espionage and sabotage.

Groups often put into effect repressive actions that are not within their legal bounds. We are all aware of the violent actions of the Ku Klux Klan and their use of extralegal measures to punish those who violated what they thought of as proper race relations. In addition, there have often been riots and pogroms where members of the majority group invaded the residential areas of the minority, destroyed property, and caused injury and death to the inhabitants. Throughout history there have been many instances where the authorities have looked the other way and not punished those responsible for these actions. Therefore, the fear of this kind of retaliation has also been an effective measure in keeping a minority group in a subordinate position.

The dominant group has a number of measures at its disposal to maintain its position and control over the majority. Some of the more obvious ones have been discussed in this chapter We will be going into greater detail on these various measures throughout the following chapters.

Notes

1. R. E. Park, "The Nature of Race Relations," in E. T. Thompson, ed., *Race Relations and the Race Problem*, p. 23ff.

2. Quoted in W. C. Smith, *Americans in the Making*, p. 394.

3. *Canada Year Book, 1963–1964*, p. 198.

4. H. I. London, "Non-white Immigration and the 'White Australia' Policy," *West Australian*, p. 40.

5. Ibid., p. 29.

6. A. J. Beveridge, *Abraham Lincoln, 1809–1858*, vol. 3, p. 354.

7. R. Kennedy, "The Colonial Crisis and the Future," in R. Linton, ed., *The Science of Man in the World Crisis*, p. 308ff.

Chapter Nine
Social Stratification

All good people agree,
And all good people say,
All nice people like Us are We
And everyone else is They . . . .

—*Rudyard Kipling*

Stratification is the division of society into ranks, grades, or positions, and involves unequal distribution of privileges, material rewards, opportunities, power, prestige, and influence. Apart from the area of race relations, this process of arranging the individuals and groups of a society on horizontal levels operates wherever people try to work out a common life together. Perfect equality prevails nowhere, except in the dreams of utopian philosophers. The fact is that in every society there are various jobs that have to be done, and very early in human history it was discovered that specialization and division of labor resulted in greater efficiency. Furthermore, some of the functions that had to be performed were more difficult than others, some more appealing, and some downright repulsive. The problem, therefore, every society has to solve is this, How is it possible to distribute these various functions? How can we assign people to their special roles?

Material rewards and prestige act as incentives for the filling of certain positions. Therefore, people will be willing to endure the hardships involved in training for important occupations because of the rewards they receive in return. An important goal of society, then, is to motivate people to want to fill certain positions and, once they are in these positions, to encourage them to fulfill the responsibilities attached to them.

If all jobs were equally pleasant, equally important to society, or required the same amount of ability, it would not matter who was in which job. However, this is not the case; some jobs require a greater ability than others, some are more pleasant, and some are more important to society. Because of this, a society must find some rewards that will act as an incentive. In addition, some way of distributing the rewards differently according to the various positions must also be found. The distribution of rewards gives rise to social stratification.

What kinds of rewards does a society have at its disposal? There are material rewards, which will contribute to greater comfort, well-being, and power. Also there are intangible kinds of rewards that contribute to self-respect and ego enhancement. People usually admire someone who is in a position of great importance, great power, or great wealth.

If we apply this reasoning to the medical profession, we will see a good example of how the system is supposed to work. It requires a great deal of training and endurance to become a medical doctor. In addition, it is very important to society that we have enough qualified practitioners. Individuals comtemplating a career in the medical profession have a number of incentives urging them on. The position is accorded a great deal of prestige with ample financial rewards in our society. There is also a great deal of ego enhancement involved, since the individual can feel that he or she is serving a useful and important function in society.

There are two ways in which stratification can occur: (1) permit everyone to *compete*, in the hope that all will come to perform the functions to which their interests and abilities are best suited; and (2) *assign* everyone to some societal role or roles, using as a basis for the assignment some easily ascertainable characteristic such as sex, age, family, or skin color. Both these methods have been widely employed, and both get a society's work done. The former is the essence of *democracy* — equal opportunity for each individual to compete for the role and status deserved, regardless of race, religion, sex, or family. The second method, carried to its logical extreme, is that of *caste*, wherein the status, role, and various other aspects of an individual's life are determined by birth and remain fixed throughout life. The fact of the matter is that no society operates entirely on either of these principles. Even the most democratic, like our own, makes a practice of ascribing some roles and statuses; and the most caste-ridden societies have a certain amount of plasticity.

Whenever racial and ethnic groups come into contact, the process of stratification operates to resolve the conflicts that arise and to adjust the disturbing differences. The *form* the stratification takes, however, varies widely from one situation to another, and from time to time. The relations between groups may assume the discriminatory features of *slavery*, the arrogance of *caste*, the craftiness of *peonage* or other forms of *forced labor*, the flexibility of class, and the subtlety of *discrimination*. Stratification may result in the creation of wide and impassable barriers between racial and ethnic groups, or it may involve a pattern of differentiation so slight that it is readily overcome and goes unnoticed.

Types of Stratification

Jamaica

The island of Jamaica, 90 miles south of Cuba, holds a certain fascination for sociologists. British colonists settled this territory, as they did the United States, and they imported black slaves to perform the labor on their plantations; but quite a different pattern of race relations has emerged.

Jamaica was occupied first by the Spaniards in 1509. The Indian population gradually withered away, and eventually became extinct. The British acquired the island in 1670, and took over the operation of the sugar plantations which flourished there. At the end of the century there were in Jamaica approximately ten thousand whites and forty thousand black slaves. Seventy-five years later there were eighteen thousand whites and a quarter of a million slaves. By 1844 the number of whites had fallen to about sixteen thousand, and it has remained at approximately that level ever since. The white population includes a community of Jews, and there are also smaller, but important, groups of Syrians, Chinese, and East Indians.

Many of the white plantation owners preferred to live comfortably in England rather than on the island; others sent their children to Europe for their education and the children often failed to return. The sex ratio of the white population was, accordingly, heavily masculine, and the practice of concubinage was common. The decrease in the white population was a crucial fact in the developing social system. Because of the continual departure of the dominant whites, a vacuum was created in positions of intermediate responsibility, and the free mixed bloods moved into this vacuum. Thus a differentiation developed between the mulatto and the black, lightness of skin color came to be valued as a promise of higher status, and status itself came to be equated with lightness. Smith found that the whites were far ahead of the other racial groups in education, wage earnings, and farm land tenure; the mulatto population came next; and the blacks were in a very disadvantageous position.[1] These groups, to be sure, are not rigid castes; there are black lawyers and doctors, but their numbers, in proportion to the black population, are small in comparison to those of lighter skin. The whites dominate polite society, and control most of the large estates, the finance, and the shipping activities.

The whole society has somewhat the characteristics of a layer cake, although the layers are not so precisely distinguished, and the situation is manifestly a fluid one.

In intimate social relationships and personal intercourse, color is all important. White skin has become a mark of social status. This all-pervasive color consciousness not only isolates whites from blacks, but erects a barrier between blacks and mulattos, and prevents any development of cohesion and group loyalty within the mixed group itself. The mulattos, accordingly, despise their black ancestry, covet the status of whites, are more prejudiced against black skin than are the whites, and are anxious to receive recognition from white society.

The situation in Jamaica, therefore, has more the features of flexible, open social class than of rigid castes and strict segregation. It is possible for an able and ambitious black individual to marry a white or mulatto person, to enter the high-status occupations and professions, to accumulate wealth, and thereby to climb the social ladder.

The Caste System in India

For untold centuries India has experienced wave after wave of invaders and conquerors, each seeking, often with success, to set itself up in a dominant position over the peoples already there. Within historic times there have come Persians, Greeks, Scythians, Arabs, Huns, Portuguese, and British; and long before the dawn of history there were invasions of Negritos — pygmies with dark skins and "peppercorn" hair, Australoids, and many other nameless peoples. The earliest invasion of India of which we have any sort of record was that of the *Aryans,* somewhere about 1500 B.C. These people are known to have used an Indo-European language, and probably had fair hair and blue eyes. They first occupied and settled the northwest portion of India and later established colonies elsewhere on the peninsula. They were desirous of maintaining their dominant position and of preserving their fair color; and it is supposed that soon after their invasion of India they prohibited intermarriage with the aborigines. Their efforts to prevent amalgamation did not succeed, although to this day the higher castes of India generally have lighter skins and narrower noses than the lower castes, there being many exceptions to the rule.

This is not to say that the Aryans *invented* and superimposed the caste system or created it out of whole cloth. The system was, as a matter of fact, the product of a long period of development that has never ceased and it grew out of a body of customs, taboos, ideologies, and patterns of social organization already present both among the Aryans themselves and among the native peoples they conquered. Long before the invasion the inhabitants of India had surrounded themselves with many food and occupational restrictions, were characterized by strong tribal cohesion, and had learned to follow their own customs and to manifest a spirit of compromise and tolerance for strange ideas and practices. Into this situation the Aryans brought their own social organization, consisting of a class system that included the ruling or military class, the priestly, and the commonalty. Out of these ingredients, and others, the system of caste was formed and it gave to the relationships among the ethnic groups of India a rigid, stable, immutable character that is unmatched in other biracial and multiracial situations.

It should be noted, that the Hindus themselves have never placidly accepted the caste system. Students of Hinduism have frequently noted the continuous changes going on during the centuries of the caste system's development. Individuals have occasionally been able to pass for members of a higher caste. Even today modifications of caste rules are still taking place.

Sociologists have been in the habit of using the term *caste* to describe the stratification pattern that developed following the Civil War. Early in the present century W. I. Thomas and Charles H. Cooley were pointing out the castelike nature of race relations in the United States[2]; in recent years a great many studies of the American race problem have given a prominent place to the concept of caste in their analyses.

Stratification Through Forced Labor

Often dominant peoples have resorted to some form of *forced labor*. When the Spaniards arrived in the New World they imposed on the Indians two institutions — *repartimientos* and *encomiendas* — both of which placed the natives under a peculiar type of bondage and resulted in the rapid depletion of the native population. When these institutions were abolished toward the end of the colonial period, the whites contrived new methods of holding Indian and *mestizo* labor under some form of involuntary servitude. One of the most common was that of *peonage*, whereby members of the subordinate group were encouraged to become deeply involved in debt. It then became necessary to render service to discharge the obligations incurred; but by means of low wages and high interest rates, it has frequently been possible to make of peonage a system of perpetual debt bondage, the indebtedness even being passed on from father to son. Various other methods of forced labor have been and still are employed whereby native peoples and minority groups are maintained in a subordinate position. Among them is the device used by the whites of South Africa to make available the black manpower needed on the plantations and in the gold, coal, and diamond mines. Theoretically, the Europeans and the natives have chosen *segregation* as the basic form of accommodation to govern their relations with each other. Political parties declare their loyalty to a policy of *apartheid*, or "separateness," and set up as a goal an "absolute territorial division between European and native so that ultimately there would be in South Africa a region in which no native, and another in which no European, would be regarded as a permanent inhabitant." However, poll taxes and "hut taxes" have been levied on the natives, with the result that the poverty of their territories and the pressure of population force many of them to leave home and work in mines and on farms to earn enough to pay the taxes. The whites frankly admit that the chief purpose of this system of taxation is to obtain native labor.

Stratification and Levels of Power

What we see from these examples is that social stratification need not be based solely on economic factors, even though they are often the basis for stratification. Frequently, economic factors have been emphasized because of their close relationship to power, which is of crucial importance in determining

dominance.   Whenever two distinct racial or ethnic groups come together and interact for an extended period of time, one group ends up assuming the dominant role.   In theory we might assume that two groups could come together and develop an egalitarian relationship.   However, there are few cases of racial groups in advanced societies establishing egalitarian relationships because there are few cases in which the relationship between racial groups has been based on complete equality of power.   Differential power is a key factor in race relationships in advanced societies.   The greater the discrepancy between the power held by the individual groups involved, the greater the extent and scope of racial domination will be.

Why should different levels of power lead to the domination of one group by another? Gerhard Lenski has suggested that humans have an insatiable desire for goods and services. No matter how much is produced or consumed, people are never completely satisfied. In addition, there is a status value attached to the goods and services consumed. Consequently, demand will exceed supply and Lenski claims that "a struggle for rewards will be present in every human society." The outcome of this struggle and the relationships that are developed as a result of it will be based on the different levels of power between the racial groups.[3]

If we apply Lenski's argument to race relations, we can see that the efforts of one racial group to dominate another racial group may, in some cases, be motivated by a desire to control goods and services. When a racial group is placed in a subordinate position, it may be eliminated as a competitor or, as we will see with the example of slavery in America, it may be used to enhance the supply of goods and services for the dominant race.

We will now examine the institution of slavery in America and the changes in the status of blacks after the abolition of slavery. During the discussion we will see that the power differences were not just between whites and blacks, but also between Northerners and Southerners. Slavery in the United States was controlled by a small but powerful group of Southern plantation owners who had great control over patterns of social thought and political institutions. Most Southern families did not own any slaves and those that did usually had less than five slaves. The vast majority of the slaves were on large plantations and were owned by a small portion of the population. Even so, slavery was supported by the nonslaveowning Southerners. It will be seen from the following examples that the Southerners lost their power to maintain the system of slavery when the Civil War was lost. Slavery was not profitable to the North and consequently there was no interest there in maintaining the institution. The years since the end of slavery have seen a change in the power of blacks with a consequent change in their relationship to the whites who form the numerical majority.

The Black Experience

Indenture and slavery   In 1619, when the first twenty blacks were unloaded from a Dutch man-of-war at Jamestown, Virginia, they were given the status of indentured servants, since apparently it did not occur to the Virginians at the time to make slaves of them. Slavery, of course, is a very old institution, can be traced back to prehistoric times, and has had a worldwide history. Many preliterate peoples have been familiar with it, and the ancient civilizations of Sumeria, Egypt, Greece, Carthage, and Rome regarded it as a natural and normal phenomenon.[4] In the early part of the seventeenth century slavery was well established among the Portuguese, Spaniards, and Arabs, but it had not taken firm hold on the British. The Virginians, therefore, had no precedent for enslaving these twenty blacks. They were familiar with the institution of indenture, a system whereby individuals would contract to serve a number of years in return for their ocean voyage. Unlike slavery, servitude under indenture was neither lifelong nor hereditary. The British settlers were desperately in need of labor; but in a region where resources are abundant and population is scanty, it is impossible to induce a sufficient number of people to work for wages. At the same time, there were in the British Isles great numbers living in "penurie and want," who were willing to try to improve their lot in the New World if someone would pay their passage. It is estimated that half of those who settled in the thirteen American colonies came as indentured laborers.[5] Even so, the demand for labor could not be met by this system.

The first blacks, then, were assigned to the status of indentured servants, the presumption being that after they had performed the service called for in their contracts, they would be free. They did not enjoy this status very long, however, and because of their powerlessness they began to be treated with more severity than were other indentured servants. The punishment meted out to them for violations of laws and customs was greater than that for others in the servant class, and sexual relations with blacks were regarded as especially debasing. Gradually, by a series of laws enacted, court decisions rendered, and attitudes and mores developed, the status of blacks changed to one of hereditary, lifelong servitude that is better known as slavery. The change had come about well before the close of the century. The underlying factor, of course, was the demand for a labor supply. Blacks were preferable to white indentured servants for several reasons. For one thing, their ineradicable racial features made it difficult for them to escape; the women could be put to work in the fields, which was not the custom for white women; their services were available for life, while white servants were available only for a few years; and their children, unlike the children of whites, were also valuable property. All things considered, the black slave was well worth the additional cost. Blacks, therefore, eventually displaced white indentured servants in the cotton and tobacco colonies.

For years most whites and blacks in the United States interacted only as owner and slave. There were, to be sure, free blacks, whose number rose to nearly half a million by 1860. Most of these had been set free by their owners for reasons of sentiment or ideals, or because of some meritorious service performed while in slavery. Others were the descendants of free mothers (white or black), or of unions between Indians and blacks; and some, by their own thrift, had earned enough to purchase their freedom. There were few of them in the regions of the large plantations, but they were numerous in the tidewater sections of Virginia and Maryland and in the Piedmont of North Carolina and Virginia. For the most part, however, they were an urban people who were concentrated in the seaboard cities of New Orleans, Mobile, Charleston, Boston, New York, Philadelphia, Baltimore, and Washington. Their status was a peculiar one. Some amassed considerable wealth and even owned slaves themselves. In the southern cities they engaged in the skilled trades, and followed a wide range of occupations. Among them were hotelkeepers, milliners, storekeepers, teachers, clerks, and architects. In the North they had a more difficult time gaining a foothold in the economy. Frazier says:

The free Negroes in the North did not form an intermediate stratum in a stable stratified society as did their brothers in the South. They were concentrated in cities where a great industrial civilization was coming into existence. They saw themselves disfranchised where universal suffrage was extended to the male population. They were generally excluded from public education which was becoming the right of all citizens. More important still, they were restricted in their efforts to make a living. [6]

The status of the free blacks suffered many changes throughout the period of slavery and varied greatly from place to place; it is therefore difficult to generalize. For the most part, however, it was precarious and inhospitable. They found considerable discrimination in the courts, at the polls, in education, in industry, and in freedom of movement. Franklin speaks of them as "quasi-free Negroes" and says that "toward the end of the slave period the distinction between slaves and free Negroes had diminished to a point that in some instances was hardly discernible." [7]

After the Civil War   The Civil War marked the end of slavery for blacks, but a new status was not immediately forthcoming. For thirty years a bitter conflict raged to determine just what the new "place" of blacks would be. There were those who were determined to give them a status in no way different from that of other American citizens; but such an objective was abhorrent to the South and had slight appeal to the North. Even President Lincoln never formulated a clear conception as to what the status of blacks should be. The South, however, had its own ideas; and immediately after the war one state after another enacted laws, known as Black Codes, which practically reinstituted slavery. Limitations were placed upon the ownership and rental of property, possession of firearms, testimony in court, freedom of speech and movement, choice of occupation, and voting privileges for blacks. Heavy penalties were levied for vagrancy and breach of contract that were tantamount to a system of forced labor. The North, motivated more by political and economic considerations than by concern for black welfare, used the Black Codes as an excuse for imposing military rule on the South for the ostensible purpose of insuring black citizenship rights. Historians have debated and recounted at great length the events of the succeeding decade, the Reconstruction Period, and its final culmination in the Compromise of 1876, when the question of black status was discarded as a national issue and turned back to the South. There followed several decades of further conflict, and finally a new pattern of accommodation emerged. This new pattern is commonly spoken of in the South as *white supremacy*, and blacks refer to it as *second-class citizenship*. Its features are well known. Blacks were virtually disfranchised. Their economic opportunities were severely limited, with many occupations being closed to them and a "job ceiling" established in those areas in which they were allowed to work. The educational facilities provided for them were definitely inferior to those provided for whites. They were barred from most hotels, restaurants, theaters, barber shops, auditoriums, parks, and playgrounds; the accommodations provided for them on trains, streetcars, and buses were separate, but seldom equal. They were restricted and exploited as homeowners or tenants. The medical facilities available to them were limited, with the result that they suffered high mortality rates. In courts and at the hands of the law, they did not enjoy the same treatment accorded whites.

Revolt against the system   There have been many changes over the years and indeed the condition of blacks has never remained static, even during the period of slavery. Nor is it correct to say that blacks meekly accepted their subordinate status. There have always been rebels among them, although for three hundred years their efforts bore little fruit and those who rallied behind them were few and far between.

During World War I, however, blacks began to break the barriers of the system as they slowly started to gain power. Their horizons were lifted when some 400,000 of them moved from the rural South to the urban North to fill the employment vacuum created by the cessation of immigration from Europe. President Wilson's stirring assertions about democracy doubtless had their effect. Nearly 350,000 entered the Armed Services and 100,000 served overseas. Blacks from various parts of the country were brought together, creating new insights and aspirations. They began to demand their rights as citizens, with the result that during and immediately following the war there were outbreaks of race riots in Washington, Chicago, Omaha, Knoxville, and scores of other cities and towns throughout the country. Blacks not only made demands, but were prepared to fight for them.

The United States Supreme Court, too, which had long sanctioned the white supremacy and separate but equal philosophies, began to render verdicts favorable to the black cause. In 1915 the court invalidated the Oklahoma *grandfather clause*, one device that had been employed for the disfranchisement of blacks. In 1917 the Court ruled that a Louisville, Kentucky, ordinance providing for racial residential segregation violated the Fourteenth Amendment. Beginning in 1927 with the case of *Nixon* v. *Herndon* there was forthcoming a long series of rulings that destroyed the white political primary device; and in 1938 in the case of *Gaines* v. *Canada* the first crack appeared in the wall of school segregation.

The Great Depression of the 1930s weighed heavily on blacks as it did on the entire country, but many of the New Deal measures provided opportunities that had never existed before. Some blacks received cash benefits under the various agricultural acts and blacks and whites voted together on the establishment of marketing quotas. Electricity was brought to many homes for the first time through TVA and REA. Many blacks were assisted in purchasing farms through FSA and others became homeowners with the assistance of HOLC. Public housing projects enabled some to escape from the slums, and many learned skills and continued their education with the assistance of NYA. In 1935 there was organized the Congress of Industrial Organizations (CIO) which adopted membership policies more liberal than those of its rival organization, the American Federation of Labor.

World War II saw an acceleration of the movement toward equality. The number of black officers in the armed services grew from five to seven thousand. President Roosevelt's Executive Order No. 8802 forbade racial discrimination in defense industries and inaugurated the Fair Employment Practices Committee. The Supreme Court, too, continued to hand down decisions favorable to the black cause.

Changes have come continually since World War II. President Truman in 1947 established the Committee on Civil Rights, and the following year saw the publication of its significant report, *To Secure These Rights* Executive Order No. 9981, in 1948, led to the integration of the armed services. In 1945 New York State adopted a Fair Employment Practices law, and many other states followed in passing similar legislation. The Supreme Court continued to render decisions favorable to blacks in the areas of voting, interstate travel, restrictive covenants, and education. Finally, on May 17, 1954, and on May 31, 1955, the Court handed down its historic decisions pertaining to separate educational facilities.

The changing status of blacks was manifested by their prominence on Olympic teams and in radio, television, and the movies. Black novelists, poets, and artists were winning international acclaim and black scholars began to receive appointments in the leading universities. Their political power began to be used effectively, and the major parties vied for their vote. Big business became aware of their economic importance and began to compete for their patronage.

The black demands for equality grew more insistent than ever in the 1960s and 1970s. They grew impatient with the slow pace of school integration and became disillusioned when they observed how the rulings of the courts and the acts of Congress were circumvented. Unemployment, brought on by increasing automation, fell heavily on them. Their leaders grew more aggressive. The older organizations, the NAACP and the Urban League, adopted bolder techniques; CORE (Congress of Racial Equality), which arose in 1942, gained in prominence; and new movements — Student Nonviolent Coordinating Committee (SNCC or "Snick") — came into being. "Freedom Rides," demonstrations, marches, sit-ins, boycotts, and numerous other forms of protest became daily occurrences throughout the country. Blacks had finally become powerful enough to fight against their second-class status.

Throughout their history in America the status of blacks has been related to their power. When their power was nil, they were ripe for exploitation. As their power increased, there have been proportionate advances toward equality.

There are many ways of attaining power. For blacks, an important, but often forgotten, source of power has been the discrepancy between the stated

Blacks protesting against the white establishment

values and goals of equality and the reality of day-to-day interactions. If Americans wanted to maintain a benevolent self-image consistent with their egalitarian ideology, they had to do away with the type of discrimination which contradicted it. Since the 1960s black leaders have been very effective in forcing Americans to see the inherent racial discrimination in their actions.

Even so, there remains a broad hiatus between the position of blacks in American society and that of whites. Their wages are lower, their unemployment rates are higher. They have less formal education and its quality is poorer. While their life expectancy has improved, so has that of other groups. It has been very difficult for blacks to break out of the ghetto. They are still confined, partly by educational inadequacies and partly because of discrimination, to low-paying service and semiskilled occupations.

The Status of Hybrids

The process of stratification, operating as it does when racial and ethnic groups come into contact, invariably encounters the problem of the hybrid. What should be the status of those of mixed blood, one of whose parents comes from the dominant group and the other from the subordinate? The problem arose very early in colonial America. In the hope of avoiding it, Virginia levied heavy penalties for miscegenation; but as we have seen, these did not prevent the rise of a mulatto element in the population. In 1662, accordingly, a law was passed that imposed the mother's status on her children — that is, the children of a black woman slave and a white man would be slaves for life, and the father would pay a fine double that for other fornication. Other laws quickly followed. One specified that, should a white woman marry a black or a mulatto man, she would be condemned to five years of servitude if a servant and would be banished from the colony if she were free. The children issuing from such an alliance were classified as bastards and were bound, as were other bastards, to a term of apprenticeship until they were thirty years of age. In due course, further laws of a similar nature were passed; and Virginia was followed by Maryland, Massachusetts, Connecticut, Pennsylvania, New York, and the other colonies in an effort to prevent miscegenation and to fix the status of the offspring of mixed unions. It became the practice to regard a person as a black who had any known black ancestry. Sinclair Lewis made this the theme of his *Kingsblood Royal*, a novel, which, incidentally, would seem utterly incredible to those in other societies where mulattos hold a status quite different from that assigned to them in the United States.

Hybrids in Other Societies

The status of the hybrid is quite different in other societies. Often it is distinctly lower than that of either of the parent stocks. Reference has been made repeatedly to the Anglo-Indians, who are rejected alike by British and Indian forebears and who have been condemned to an anomalous and unenviable status. It was not always so, however, and need not remain so in the future. In the early days of contact the Anglo-Indian stood much higher in the social system and enjoyed many privileges denied to the native people. Another area where the hybrid has low status is East Africa. Dr. E. Kalibala, a native of Africa and a member of the Grasshopper clan of the Ganda tribe, told the author several years ago that there are mulattos among his own people who are regarded with condescension and contempt and are considered something of a problem. At one time, the plan was discussed of relegating them to an island in Lake Victoria, where they might live out their lives in complete isolation.

Elsewhere, the hybrid has been assigned a position intermediate between the dominant and subordinate groups. So it is in South Africa, where there are over a million mixed bloods, known as the Cape Coloured. They are a mixture of Portuguese, Hottentot, Dutch, Malay, Bantu, and of black slaves imported from West Africa and Mozambique. Thousands of them over the years have passed into the white group, but most have some tell-tale racial features that make passing impossible. Some are agricultural laborers or farmers, but the majority live in the cities where they are engaged in the less desirable occupations. They take pride in their white blood, but despise their black ancestry. They identify themselves in every possible way with the dominant whites, who are careful not to accept them as equals, and continually try to place as wide a gulf as they can between themselves and the natives, who doubtless would accept them if they chose to cast their lot with them. In the meantime they constitute an intermediate caste, a buffer group, separating whites and native peoples; and the former, so greatly outnumbered by the latter, appreciate the support of the Cape Coloured.

The status of hybrids, therefore, varies greatly from place to place. In some situations they are despised outcasts, and in some they are forced into the status of the subordinate group from which they are descended. Often, however, they are assigned to an intermediate position — as in South Africa, the islands of the Caribbean, and Java — but even this intermediate status may be barely superior to the lower one, and may mean merely clinging to the fringes of the dominant group. In Haiti, to cite only one instance, the elite of the society are mulattos. These differences in the status of hybrids are the result of a complex of economic, demographic, historical, and cultural factors.

American Mestizos [8]

In the eastern United States there are some two hundred communities of people whose racial ancestry is uncertain and whose lives are profoundly affected by that uncertainty. Most of them insist that they are white and covet the prestige and status accorded to white people. The whites, however, suspect that there is some black ancestry, however small and remote, and are unwilling to accept them. The mixed bloods vehemently deny black ancestry but will often confess to the presence of an Indian strain. Indians — those, at least, who enjoy some official recognition as such — are skeptical of the mixed bloods' claim and acknowledge it only reluctantly.

The names given to these groups are usually anathema to the people who bear them. There are exceptions, however. The Nanticokes of Delaware and the Narragansetts of Rhode Island are proud of those ancient Indian names and strive continually to gain wider acceptance for them. So it is with the Shinnecock, the Poosepatuck, the Montauk, and the Matinecock, all of Long Island, the Waccamaws of North Carolina, and the Chickahominy and other Indian groups in Virginia. These are all strongly suspected of having little Indian blood, and they have retained almost nothing of their ancient language and culture; but there is an unbroken thread that binds them to the past, and they cling tenaciously to their tribal identity, guarding their old Indian names as priceless possessions.

Not so with the others. Worst of all, as these folk see it, are those names that explicitly identify them with blacks. Thus the Jackson Whites loathe the term "Blue-eyed Negroes," which they sometimes hear; the South Carolina Brass Ankles detest "Red Niggers"; and the Virginia hybrids cringe at the sound of "Issues," a shortened form of "Free Issues," a name by which the free blacks, before and after the Civil War, were differentiated from those blacks whose freedom derived from the war.

Occasionally the name applied to these people is descriptive of some physical characteristic they possess or are thought to possess. Thus there are the Brown People of Virginia, the Yellowhammers of South Carolina, and the Black Andersons, who live in the North Carolina mountains.

Those who have studied these hybrid groups are at a loss to know what to call them. One hesitates to use the popular, local names, so offensive are they. Many writers simply refer to them as mixed bloods, racial hybrids, or mongrels. The term *triracial isolates* has enjoyed a certain vogue, and in the literature they are often called "raceless people," "racial orphans," "mystery people," "half-castes," "half-breeds," or merely "breeds." The term *mestizo* has been proposed and seems to be gaining acceptance. It has the advantage of being noncommittal. Literally it means "mixed," and these folk readily admit that they are mixed. The term is widely used in Latin America, where it is applied to those of European and Indian ancestry, but is often applied to other mixtures as well. In the Philippines it is used for those of Chinese and native racial ancestry. The dictionaries define *mestizo* as "a person of mixed blood," so it would seem, therefore, to be a fitting label for the folk we are describing.

The origin of these American mestizos is unknown. There is evidence that they were present in colonial times, and some of them participated in the Revolutionary War. General Thomas Sumter used them effectively in his guerilla assaults on the British, and after the war allowed them to settle on his estate, where their descendants still reside. The records show that in 1790 a group of mestizos petitioned the South Carolina House of Representatives for exemption from certain laws applicable to blacks, and their petition was granted. There is documentary evidence, though admittedly scanty, that before the Civil War there were groups of people here and there who set themselves apart from both the black and the white populations.

Most mestizo groups, in all probability, represent an amalgam of Indians, adventurers, traders, runaway slaves, outlaws, deserters, and deviants of all types, both white and black. The Lumbees are a case in point. In the 1730s, when the first European settlers arrived in that region of North Carolina now known as Robeson County, they found living there a race of mixed bloods. These people lived in houses, not wigwams, cultivated crops, spoke an English dialect, and had the manners and customs of the frontier. In a document written in the year 1754 no mention is made of Indians living in the territory, but it is stated that "a mixt Crew, a lawless People, possess the Lands without patent or paying quit rents." White settlers moved in nevertheless, and the two races had as little to do with each other as possible. In time they developed a pattern of coexistence and managed to live together harmoniously, except when some crisis arose to disrupt the truce; for instance, the mestizos were allowed to vote and to send their children to schools with the whites, even though they were designated in the census as "free persons of color." However, when the state constitution was revised in 1835, the mestizos were denied the franchise and were excluded from the white schools. Resentment mounted, for they insisted that they had rendered service in both the Revolutionary War and the War of 1812. Thereupon they set about to build their own schools and to hire their own teachers. Another crisis developed during the Civil War, when the Confederacy, in its desperation, drafted the mestizos, not to bear arms but to do manual labor along with slaves and free blacks. This they refused to do, with the result that three of them were captured and executed as deserters. There followed many years of turmoil until, in the 1880s, the mestizos embarked on their long and arduous struggle to establish their identity as Indians.

Mestizo communities are not expected to disappear in the near future. The most viable, and the most likely to survive, are those that are large enough to support a community life, where there is an adequate economic base, where there is a body of tradition to give cohesion and a name of which they can feel proud, and in which the obstacles to acceptance by whites have not been surmounted.

Special Statuses

Very often members of the dominant group will select certain members of the subordinate group on whom they bestow special privileges and treatment different from others of that group. This situation occurs because the particular individuals possess special traits or abilities that are useful in increasing the wealth, power, or prestige of the dominant group. For the individuals selected, there will often be a personal gain since they will receive material rewards or prestige. The rest of the subordinate community may look up to them and they may be accorded powers within the group that are not granted to the ordinary members. In some cases the special status accorded to these few individuals leads to further subordination of the majority of that group. In other cases these individuals are able to gain privileges for the entire group. There have been many examples of this throughout history. We have chosen two cases to illustrate our discussion.

The Court Jew

During the seventeenth century Germany became much more tolerant of Jews and accepted them in large numbers. The Jews were granted the right to have their own communities and to practice their religion without interference from the majority. This policy was motivated by monetary considerations, rather than by an idealistic attempt at greater tolerance. The German princes of the period wanted to increase the population of their lands to gain taxpayers. Showing greater tolerance toward the Jews would attract them from those lands where they were persecuted and increase the wealth of the princes.

The German princes also needed help in administering their commercial and fiscal policies. They needed experienced financiers and organizers to carry out their political and economic goals. However, the bulk of the population viewed politics and economics with mistrust and animosity. Their belief in the theological and scholastic theories of the Middle Ages or the Lutheran ethical doctrine of economics made them unsuitable as advisors to the princes. The princes needed individuals who could deal with economic and political problems without religious or political biases. Jews were well suited for this task. However, they were a second-class minority and even under tolerant conditions did not have all the rights and privileges of the majority. The princes proceeded to choose certain qualified Jewish advisors from the local ghettos. These individuals received special privileges and rewards in return for their services.

The financial affairs of that period were closely tied to diplomatic and political affairs. Stern has described the role of the court Jew:

He was used in secret missions, political councils, armistice negotiations and military operations. Through his personal mediation, lands and positions were bought and sold. Through his financial transactions, electorates and crowns were acquired, and through his agents the latest news and most reliable information could be obtained. In this way the court Jew took over the functions of a secret agent and spy, of a reporter, consul and diplomatic courier. [9]

Consequently, the court Jew became an indispensable innovation. Nevertheless, he was still confined to the ghetto where all Jews had to live and was bound to its social and religious organization. On some occasions this special position was used to bring about actions that would benefit the entire community. On other occasions the court Jew would respond with arrogance and disdain toward the religious characteristics that kept him in a second-class position.

The House Slave

In any system of total domination the social and economic divisions are defined by the enslaving group. On the large plantations there were two types of slaves, the field slaves and the house slaves. The field slaves were usually poorly dressed and poorly fed and were engaged in the type of field work that was prevalent for the particular plantation. The house slaves were often known as servants and usually fulfilled functions directly related to the owner and the household. Many historians have spoken of the house slaves as a kind of slave aristocracy. They were usually of a lighter skin color than the field slaves. They were directly responsible to a housekeeper, the master, or the mistress. They were often addressed as "Mister" or "Miss" by their fellow slaves. Age was also an important factor; the older they were and the longer they had been in service to the household, the greater was the respect they commanded.

Some people have claimed that the house slaves were not in a superior position because they had to attend directly to the master or mistress and were constantly under close scrutiny. They had to be careful of every action or phrase lest it be considered disobedient or insubordinate. Consequently, it has been claimed that these slaves developed personality and speech disorders from the constant strain of this close contact. Nevertheless, the house slaves were in a privileged position and often identified more with the master than with the field slaves. The evidence for this strong association can be seen with repeated instances of slave uprisings and revolts being fouled by house slaves finding out about such plots and passing the information along to the master. For the most part, the division between house slaves and field slaves tended to further disunite the slaves and ensured against massive collective action taking place.

One consequence of the meeting of peoples, then, has been the subordination of the one and the assumption by the other of a position of authority, power, and domination. This pattern has been followed at least since the dawn of history and probably long before; and it has occurred on all continents and among all races. The form that such stratification takes, however, admits of wide variability, and ranges from a loose and flexible system of class to a rigid and immutable institution of caste. The members of a subordinate group may accept for a time their inferior status and may devise ingenious and satisfying rationalizations for it, but they will not indefinitely submit to its injustice. Accordingly, race relations take on a dynamic character, and astute students of race problems have insisted that they are basically and essentially a struggle for status and power.

Notes

1. "Social Stratification in the Caribbean," in L. Plotnicov and A. Tuden, eds., *Essays in Comparative Social Stratification*, pp. 43–76.

2. W. I. Thomas, "The Psychology of Race-Prejudice," *American Journal of Sociology* 9, no. 5 (March 1904): 609ff; C. H. Cooley, *Social Organization: A Study of the Larger Mind*, p. 218.

3. G. Lenski, *Power and Privilege: A Theory of Social Stratification*, p. 31.

4. B. J. Stern, W. L. Westermann, et al., "Slavery," *Encyclopedia of the Social Sciences*, vol. 14, pp. 73–92; B. Berry, "Slavery," *Encyclopedia International*, vol. 16, pp. 532–536.

5. C. Goodrich, "Indenture," *Encyclopedia of the Social Sciences*, vol. 7, pp. 644–647.

6. E. F. Frazier, *The Negro in the United States*, p. 79.

7. J. H. Franklin, *From Slavery to Freedom*, p. 215.

8. B. Berry, "American Mestizos," in N. P. Gist and A. G. Dworkin, eds., *The Blending of Races*, pp. 190–212, © 1972. Reprinted by permission of John Wiley & Sons, Inc.

9. S. Stern, *The Court Jew*, p. 9.

Chapter Ten
Cleavages

It is clear that boundaries persist despite a
flow of personnel across them.

— *Fredrik Barth* Ethnic Groups and
Boundaries

Throughout history minority groups have often had difficulty in improving their position because they did not present a united front and were hindered by cleavages, jealousies, and rivalries. As a matter of fact, dominant groups are known to encourage such cleavages, the better to maintain their own position. "Divide and rule" is a device well understood in the area of race relations.

Europeans who first settled this country were ably assisted in gaining a foothold by the fact that the Indians were continually at one another's throats. The Iroquois were a terror to other tribes for miles around, the Osage plundered Indian villages and white settlements alike, the Sac and Fox virtually wiped out the Missouri, and the Haida had no qualms about robbing and enslaving members of their own race if they happened to belong to hostile bands. It was the proud boast of the Pawnee that they never fought against the United States, but gladly joined with the whites on numerous occasions to annihilate other Indians. The English, Dutch, French, and Americans took advantage of these intertribal hatreds, pitting Indian against Indian, and easily winning red allies to help them destroy other red men. There were shrewd Indian chiefs who saw the folly of all this and attempted to bring about a union of the tribes to stem the flood of white men. Joseph Brant, a Mohawk chief, toured the country trying to persuade the Indians to band together in defense of their lands, as did King Philip, Pontiac, Black Hawk, Tecumseh, and many others. It need hardly be said that the gulf that separated tribe from tribe was too great to be spanned by the zeal and oratory of these prophets.

Minorities, to be sure, do occasionally close their ranks and present a solid front to their opponents. As a matter of fact, the pressure exerted by a dominant group often has an integrating effect on the minority. The persecution of the Jews has been a major factor in holding them together. Some have even claimed that the stereotypes long associated with Jews, which made them a distinct ethnic group, would fade away as the boundaries between them and non-Jews declined and anti-Semitism disappeared. Anti-Semitism has shaped the Jewish personality and has helped to create cultural traditions that provide a separate identity. Many of these traditions have had survival value and supposedly would no longer be necessary in an unprejudiced environment. For example, since ghetto Jews were excluded from a long list of trades and occupations, they were often forced into usury and then despised for it. These Jews were frequently accused of violating the host, of ritual murder, and of poisoning wells. Because they were suspected, scorned, segregated and intefered with, they developed certain protective traits. The hostility of the larger society made it necessary for them to develop a community that could satisfy all their needs. Consequently, the separateness and clannishness of which Jews were often accused was an outgrowth of their negative experiences with the larger society.

If the Jewish personality was formed by anti-Semitism, then the absence of it should also have profound effects. We are provided with a good example in the case of Israel. The Israeli personality has little resemblance to the personality of the fearful, anxious, and agitated Jew of the eastern European ghetto. However, hostility from outside sources still produces a high level of unity and identification even though the basic personality is changing.[1]

The growth of the Mormon religion was also influenced by hostility from the larger society. During the 1820s Joseph Smith, a young farmer from Vermont, claimed that he received visits from heavenly beings that enabled him to produce a six-hundred-page history of the ancient inhabitants of the Americas known as the Book of Mormon. Shortly after the establishment of the Mormon church, Smith had a revelation that "Zion," the place where the Mormons would prepare for the millennium, was to be established in Jackson County, Missouri. Within two years twelve hundred Mormons bought land and settled in Jackson County. The other residents in this area became concerned about the influx and in 1833 published their grievances in a document that became known as the "manifesto," or Secret Constitution. They charged the Mormons with: (1) trying to bring "free Negroes" into the state, (2) gaining the balance of power in elections, (3) keeping socially and religiously aloof from their neighbors, and (4) claiming that they were the rightful owners of Jackson County. Those who signed the document pledged to remove the Mormons from Jackson County. Several specific episodes of conflict followed that eventually forced the Mormons to move into an adjoining county. Their encounter with a hostile environment produced a sense of collective identity at a time when it was desperately needed. The Church was less than two years old and included individuals from diverse religious backgrounds. There was a great deal of internal discord and if it had not been for the unity that resulted from the conflicts with the townspeople, the group might have disappeared altogether.[2]

On other occasions minorities have often become unified by directing their animosity toward some distinctive trait in their opponent's culture, or by adopting as a symbol something of their own that sets them off from their oppressors. Thus the Poles made Catholicism the symbol of their nationalistic aspirations, for their enemies on one side were Russian Orthodox and, on the other, were German Lutheran. Similarly, the Irish and the Czechs have used their opponents' religion as an object of their antipathy. The Koreans, who in four thousand years had never developed or adopted any national religion and gave scant attention to missionaries, took eagerly to Christianity as a symbol for their Independence Movement once the Japanese had conquered their country and attempted to force assimilation on them. Language, too, has often served as a rallying point for an oppressed group, as Norwegians, Irish, Poles, and many other European minorities well illustrate.

Leaders of minority groups, appreciating the tremendous power that lies in unity, have sought from time to time to bring together not only their own people, but also others who suffer discrimination. Appeals are made to all minorities to band together to defeat some bigoted candidate for office, to support a liberal one, to invalidate restrictive covenants, or to promote the passage of legislation. In Europe minorities have often attempted to wring concessions from dominant groups by joining forces. It is a formidable task, however, to overcome the divisive forces that operate within and between racial and ethnic minorities and to get them to agree on goals and establish a permanent and effective organization, however great the advantages may be.

The stereotypes we carry around in our minds, then, do not admit of the wide range of differences that actually prevail. The "typical" black, Jew, or Italian does not exist, except in the imagination, on the stage, and in fiction. Stereotypes persist, however, by virtue of the fact that when we encounter individuals who depart radically from our mental picture of the "type," we dismiss them with the comfortable excuse that they are "not typical." The truth of the matter is that minority groups reflect an infinite range of personalities, philosophies, values, roles, and statuses. These differences help the dominant group, making it easier to maintain control and exercise power.

This is not to deny that dominant groups, too, are seldom of one mind. In South Africa where the whites constitute so small a minority, numerically speaking, one would suppose that they might form themselves into one monolithic group, the better to preserve their power and prestige. We are told, however, that there is a cleavage between Gentile and Jews; and between British,

English-speaking subjects, on the one hand, and those of Dutch descent, who speak Afrikaans, on the other. There are differences, too, with respect to racial policy. While the great majority of the whites are firm believers in white supremacy, and are supporters of the government's policy of apartheid, there are also the Integrationists, who insist that the Natives become Europeanized, bring their standard of living up to that of the whites, and share political power with the whites. The Integrationists look forward to a South Africa where equal rights will be granted to all civilized persons within the same political structure, irrespective of race and color. This proposal, of course, elicits only revulsion from the advocates of apartheid.

No doubt it is true everywhere that racial and ethnic groups that enjoy power and prestige are rent with internal differences and divisions. However, in this chapter we will examine the bases of cleavage that are common to minority groups and prevent their offering a united front in their struggle for status.

Intergroup Cleavages

Minority status alone has seldom been an adequate reason for bringing unlike peoples together. On the contrary, it frequently happens that the hatred one minority bears for another surpasses even its hatred for its oppressors. African natives, for instance, will vent their rage on the helpless Hindus rather than on the domineering whites. Cape Coloured are no less prejudiced against black natives than are whites; and Anglo-Indians have long shown a reluctance to identify their interests with those of Indians.

Blacks and Immigrants

The paths of blacks and immigrants have crossed frequently because the two groups often experienced similar problems of adjustment. Both have been the victims of exploitation, segregation, and discrimination. They have been forced to reside in the blighted areas of our cities, and to earn their living at the least desirable occupations. European immigrants and blacks were thrown into direct contact and competition with each other during the last century. They often lived near each other, worked at the same jobs, and sent their children to the same schools.

One would think that common interests would have created within them a strong fellow-feeling. Instead, blacks have traditionally manifested a bitter prejudice against foreigners, and the immigrants, in turn, have been quick to adopt the prevailing attitudes toward blacks. Most of the early race riots in New York City involved the blacks and the Irish. Drake and Cayton report that Chicago's blacks, at the turn of the century, viewed the influx of European immigrants with mixed emotions.[3] True, they often lived side by side in the slums of the city, and sometimes in the same buildings; and the blacks regarded

Immigrant family in their tenement apartment

the foreigners with a certain amount of understandable condescension. At the same time, they were not oblivious to the fact that these "aliens" constituted a potential threat to their jobs as butlers, barbers, maids, janitors, bootblacks, and waitresses. During the lean years of the depression the black press sounded the familiar note that it was unfair for "foreigners" to hold jobs while blacks were unemployed. Blacks complained that "foreigners learn how to cuss, count, and say 'nigger' as soon as they get here." The development of prejudice against blacks was usually one of the first lessons of Americanization. Even though their status was low in American society, the immigrants could feel superior to blacks. Myrdal has suggested that immigrant groups were probably more prejudiced, on the average, than native Americans in the same community.[4]

Many people often compare the immigrant experience of yesterday with that of today's blacks. They claim that since the immigrants were able to pull themselves up by their bootstraps, then blacks should be able to do the same. There are, however, numerous conditions that are not the same now as during the period of massive immigration and these changed conditions make a valid comparison difficult. For example, economic conditions have changed; unskilled labor is far less essential than before and blue-collar jobs are decreasing in number and importance. Because of this development, blacks who migrated to the city have found much less opportunity than did the earlier settlers. Barriers of racial discrimination have hindered further the economic adjustment of blacks.

The European immigrants also had greater political opportunities to help them escape from poverty. They usually settled in rapidly growing cities in which the political machines offered them various forms of remuneration for political support. Ethnic groups were often able to exercise control over certain occupations and were able to make their power felt in affairs that concerned the community.

By the time blacks arrived in the cities in large numbers, many things had changed. The political machines were no longer as powerful and could not guarantee them jobs and favors. The older immigrants were often unwilling to share the remaining political power with blacks and continued to control the areas even after their numerical majority had ceased. This was the case in Harlem, which was dominated by white politicians even after it had been a black ghetto for many years.

The immigrants came at a time when poverty and hard work for low pay was widespread and the relative deprivation between them and the rest of society was less acute. The American dream of working your way to success from poverty seems more difficult today than in the past, making for a defeatist attitude among many of today's blacks.[5]

In addition, nostalgia may have colored our present perception of immigrant life and the ease with which these individuals reached middle-class status. The immigrants experienced many adjustment problems and cases of alcoholism and family breakup were common. Irving Kristol describes it as follows:

> We tend to compare the Negro urban family of today with the white suburban family of today, rather than with the white urban family of yesteryear. Family life among the raw urban proletariat of 19th-century America, as in 19th century Britain, showed many of the "pathological" features we now associate with the Negro family. Statistics on broken homes and illegitimacy are impossible to come by for the earlier times. But anyone familiar with the urban literature of that period cannot but be impressed by the commonplace phenomenon of Mrs. Jones and Mrs. O'Hara raising her brood while Mr. Jones and Mr. O'Hara have vanished from the scene.[6]

Blacks and Jews

Francis Lewis Cardozo, one of the most powerful politicians in the late 1860s, was very significant in movements dedicated to the advancement of blacks. He was the illegitimate son of a mulatto woman and a Jewish father who was an apologist for the slave establishment. The father, Jacob Cardozo, was the editor and publisher of one of Charleston, South Carolina's leading newspapers, the *Southern Patriot*. The elder Cardozo wrote "that slaves enjoyed more wealth than free laborers." He also happened to be the South's most prominent economic theoretician.

Francis Cardozo was a white man in appearance, but became an outcast among his Jewish brethren because, according to South Carolina law, he was forced to assume his mother's black identity. Cardozo became a Presbyterian minister and was eventually instrumental in getting Congress to deny South Carolina readmission to the Union because of its treatment of blacks.[7]

The fact that Cardozo's dual heritage could not be reconciled and that his black identity made it impossible for him to be fully accepted by the Jewish community highlights the problem of black-Jewish contact. The view that Jews and blacks held of each other during the early history of the United States was affected by the institution of slavery and the considerable difference in their statuses. American slavery was based solely on color and virtually denied the humanity of the victim. However, Jews were considered to be white and suffered no more than any other ethnic or religious minority in the New World. In fact, throughout much of the history of the United States, Jews were socially more acceptable than Roman Catholics.[8]

As the slaves converted to Christianity an interesting phenomenon took place. They began to think of themselves as the descendants of "the Hebrew chillun," who were enslaved under Pharaoh in Egypt three thousand years earlier. The stories of the trials and tribulations of the Jews in the Old Testament exerted a strong influence on blacks. Countless Negro spirituals repeating the theme of Moses telling Pharaoh to "let my people go" and of Joshua "fighting the battle of Jericho" were sung and passed on from one generation to the next. The identification with the early Hebrews enabled the slaves to regain some sense of hope that had been destroyed under American slavery.

Most Jews, however, instead of viewing blacks as kin, simply responded to them as other whites did. Consequently, Jews were often bewildered when blacks claimed kinship with them and blacks became frustrated at the Jewish dismissal of this assumption.[9]

The attempts at assimilation by blacks and Jews were also received quite differently. As whites, Jews encountered the same difficulties as any other immigrant group attempting to gain access to the mainstream of American society. Blacks, on the other hand, have never been favorably received when attempting to integrate, even though, as Eric Lincoln describes in the following excerpt, they had fewer "disabilities," theoretically, than the new immigrants.

It did not seem to matter that they already spoke the language, having learned it over three centuries or so of intimate proximity and experience. The blacks had no unpleasant accents, only the approved regional inflections of indigenous old stock. Since they were already Methodists and Baptists by faith, there seemed little need to apostatize. . . .

Black people . . . shouldn't have had to worry about changing their names. They had good euphonious "American" names already, without any troublesome suffixes like "witz" or "berg" or "stein" or "ski" or "sky."[10]

While blacks and Jews have never been able to unite and see themselves as one minority group, there has been a great deal of contact and many alliances between them. Some prefer to describe it as a situation in which Jews have generously assisted blacks in their attempts to attain equal status. To a large extent, this is true.   Jews have been known for holding liberal universalist ideals and have historically harbored less antiblack feelings than Gentiles. They were among the founders of the National Urban League and the National Association for the Advancement of Colored People.   Numerous Jewish philanthropists have generously contributed to black causes.   Blacks, for their part, have often expressed a great admiration for the Jews and frankly envy them their success in overcoming the obstacles that have been placed in their path.   They have looked, sometimes with mixed feelings, on the achievements of the Jews, and on their success in becoming governors of states and justices of the Supreme Court.   Black intellectuals have frequently exhorted their people to study and emulate the Jewish techniques for fighting discrimination and prejudice.

However, it would be too simplistic to claim that the course of black-Jewish relations has always run smoothly.   The last ten years, in particular, have seen a breakdown in this relationship.   Anti-Semitism among blacks has recently become a matter of some concern.   It has been especially virulent in the cities of the North, where it is a relatively new phenomenon.   Blacks have engaged in boycotts of Jewish establishments and have disseminated anti-Semitic prop-aganda.   Black businesspersons have used anti-Semitism as a major weapon in their competition with Jewish merchants, and have made effective use of such slogans as "Spend Your Money Where You Can Work," "Sustain Black En-terprise," and "Patronize Your Own."

Much of black anti-Semitism is essentially antiwhite prejudice, for it so hap-pens that in the urban North the Jew is the representative of the white race who comes into closest contact with blacks.   Ironically, the fact that Jews are less prejudiced against blacks than are Gentiles makes them more willing to have business dealings with blacks, and these relationships, in turn, give rise to sus-picion and animosity.   Jews, for instance, are not averse to renting residential properties to blacks or to serving as agents and collectors.   Pawnshops owned and operated by Jews are a conspicuous feature of the black urban community. The Jew is often an employer of labor, and Jewish merchants dominate the business of the black ghetto.

In addition, as Gerald Stroeber notes, blacks often refer to whites they come in contact with as "Jews" even when that is not the case.

Thus, a black would refer to his "Jew landlord" even if the man's name were Kowalski or O'Brien, or to a Cadillac, even if black-owned, as a "Jew canoe." In black areas of cities, such as Detroit, white storekeepers were often called "Goldberg" though the ac-tual owner might represent any one of several non-Jewish ethnic groups.[11]

Jews often symbolize the white world of power and the hold it has on the black community.

Herbert Gans has pointed out that to a considerable extent black-Jewish conflicts have been related to succession, "the process by which members of one ethnic or racial group (the departing group) move up a notch on the socio-economic ladder and are succeeded in their old position by a less affluent group

Urban slum, New York City

(the successors)." Often the succession process involves no major problems, but problems can develop if the departing group does not make room quickly enough for the successors. During periods of economic recession, or when the departing group lacks the skill and desire to move on, large segments will stay put and block the road for the successors. For example, while several ethnic groups have been involved in organized crime, it has been the Italians who have been the least willing to give up their positions, thus blocking entry to other racial and ethnic groups desiring entry.[12]

Blacks have often entered a neighborhood after the Jews have moved on to a better area of the city. However, a departing group frequently retains ownership of tenements or stores that may still prove to be profitable. This retention is seen in communities that have changed from Jewish to black and has caused the blacks to assume that Jews were profiting from them and blocking their own entry into neighborhood business ventures. Most of the merchants and landlords involved are of the older generation; few younger Jews are succeeding their parents in these businesses. Therefore, these problems of succession will be temporary in nature.

Old-World Hates Transplanted

The bitter rivalries that have burned for centuries between the various nationalities of Europe are not extinguished by a passage across the Atlantic; and one
finds, accordingly, a persistence of these age-old antipathies among the ethnic
groups of the United States.   As Schermerhorn says, "Often a prejudice retained from the European environment has continued in the American scene;
residual Slovak hatred of Hungarians or Polish antagonism toward Germans
and Russians has continued unabated for long periods and made it possible for
employers to play these groups off against each other."[13]   Witness, moreover,
the chronic hatred of the Irish for the English.   Roberts even assigns to this
traditional attitude an important role in fomenting the American Revolution.
Because of oppressive laws enacted in Ireland in 1695, he says, a great number
of Irish schoolmasters emigrated to America, where they continued to follow
their profession, never losing an opportunity to add fuel to the smoldering fires
of resentment for the English whom they found in the colonies.   Similar in effect is the prejudice of the Finns for their erstwhile oppressors, the Swedes and
the Russians; the hatred of the Flemish for their fellow Belgians, the Walloons;
the Norwegians' jealousy of the Swedes; and the hostility of the Armenians
toward the Turks.   Czechs and Slovaks bear little love for each other, and insist
that, if their names must be joined together, it take the form of Czecho-
Slovakia rather than Czechoslovakia.   Serbs, Croats, and Slovenes have never
been on friendly terms, despite their political union into the nation of Yugoslavia, and those who have come to America have brought their ancient jealousies
with them.   It is even reported that Irishmen from County Cork, building
railroads in America, quit their jobs rather than work alongside Irishmen from
County Connaught.

Ethnic communities have often lived side by side and believed that they had
nothing in common even though they both were suffering the same kinds of
problems that are peculiar to immigrants.   Competition for jobs has brought
about clashes, as when Finnish miners fought with Irish.   Most groups also
had great animosity for the Chinese and Japanese and in California Irish labor
leaders were prominent in the attack.   The Irish were involved on many occasions in intergroup conflicts.   In many parts of America, they were the first
to enter during the nineteenth century and wished to defend their gains against
the encroachment of newer groups.   Because of their prominence in politics,
they attracted the hostility of the later arrivals, such as Germans, French-
Canadians, and Poles.[14]

Intragroup Cleavages

However serious the enmities racial and ethnic groups bear for one another,
they are no less an impediment to united action than are the cleavages within
such groups.   The bases for such intragroup divisions are numerous and varied,
but the principal ones follow the lines of color, status, age, and social class.

Color

In various places where blacks have held second-class positions to whites, stratification systems have emerged within the black community that are based on shades of color. The islands in the Caribbean have a history of placing a high market value on white skin. While this trend is diminishing, it is clearly far from disappearing. The following description by Eric Williams shows how extensive these color distinctions were just a short time ago.

Between the brown-skinned middle class and the black there is continual rivalry, distrust, and ill-feeling, which, skillfully played upon by the European people, poisons the life of the community. Where so many crosses and colors meet and mingle, the shades are naturally difficult to determine and the resulting confusion is immense. There are the nearly-white hanging on tooth and nail to the fringes of white society, and these, as is easy to understand, hate contact with the darker skin more than some of the broader-minded whites. Then there are the browns, intermediates, who cannot by any stretch of the imagination pass as white, but who will not go one inch toward mixing with people darker than themselves. And so on, and on, and on. Associations are formed of brown people who will not admit into their number those too much darker than themselves, and there have been heated arguments in committee as to whether such and such a person's skin was fair enough to allow him or her to be admitted, without lowering the tone of the institution. Clubs have been known to accept the daughter and mother, who were fair, but to refuse the father, who was black. A dark-skinned brother in a fair-skinned family is sometimes the subject of jeers and insults and open intimations that his presence is not required at family functions. Fair-skinned girls who marry dark men are often ostracized by their families and given up as lost. There have been cases of fair women who have been content to live with black men but who would not marry them. . . . The people most affected by this are people of the middle class who, lacking the hard contact with realities of the masses and unable to attain to the freedoms of a leisured class, are more than all types of people given to trivial divisions and subdivisions of social rank and precedence.[15]

Among American blacks there was also once a system of cleavages based on various shades of color, but it never reached the extent just described. For the most part, these distinctions disappeared during the era of race pride in the late 1960s.

In addition, it is not universally true that Caucasoid features take precedence over Negroid. In Africa it is often the other way around and the offspring of whites and blacks find themselves handicapped in their tribal life.

Age

Age, too, has often been a source of intragroup conflict, particularly during the era of mass immigration and assimilation.

Sociologists have long been aware of the conflicts that rage between immigrants to the United States and their American-born children. Immigrants bring with them their customs, traditions, attitudes, and values. They make constant and desperate attempts to preserve and perpetuate them, and to inculcate them in their children. The new generation, however, often remains apathetic, or even antagonistic, preferring instead to adopt the ways of the dominant group. There are certain bases for conflict between parents and children even under the best of circumstances, but in the case of immigrant minorities the occasions for conflict and misunderstanding are greatly multiplied. Children come to regard their parents as "old-fashioned"; they despise them for their Old-World origin, their lack of education, their unfamiliarity with the English language, and their ignorance of American standards. They reject their advice and authority, and thereby reverse the usual relationship that prevails between the generations.

The following quotation from a second-generation Japanese woman displays some of the problems:

In regard to the young people's socials where dancing is involved, our first generation usually disapprove by saying it is not becoming for respectable young men and women to be seen in each other's arms. . . . Since our parents have never experienced dancing themselves, and have never seen it in Japan, when they are explosed to it here they think dancing indecent.[16]

The problem was not just among the Japanese. A similar cleavage between first- and second-generation Poles also occurred. In 1934 Brunner described it as follows:

Harmonious relations between parents and children are exceptional. In these exceptional cases the parents have got away from traditional modes of behavior and show openmindedness in accepting new values. They have adopted a higher standard of living, speak the English language well, and are willing to disregard traditional standards of a religious and moral nature. They do not persist in holding to national solidarity as a duty, and are desirous of having business and social contacts with Americans. Wherever this is not the case, antagonism is inevitable. . . . It shows itself in a defiant attitude, a disrespect of the parents and repeated cases of friction. A girl said to her mother, who asked her not to go out so late at night, "The old lady is crazy; shut up!" Parents speak of their children as "these American children" with an air of resignation.[17]

In another early book a Russian immigrant girl described the conflict created by being a part of two worlds.

You see, we young people live in two worlds, and learn the ways of both worlds — the ways of our parents and the ways of the big world. Sometimes we get mixed up and fight, we fight our parents and we fight the big world. Sometimes I feel I am not much of an American. I was raised by Russians, I understand Russians, I like Russians. At other times I think I am not much of a Russian. Except to my parents, I never speak Russian, and all my friends are Americans. Well, I am an American; we live in America — why shouldn't we take their ways? When my parents object to my American friends, I say, "I work with them. I do everything with them; why shouldn't I go out with them?" Then they come back at me and say, "Why don't you sleep with them?" They think they would disgust me with Americans, but I get mad and say, "Well, I will!" and they have nothing more to say. . . . I have learned American ways. I can't go against my friends and do the Russian way. . . .

Many times I get mad, and then I leave the house. You see, I don't want to hurt my parents and still I want to live like I see is right — that is, right according to American ways. They can't see it my way, and I can't see it their way.[18]

Old and New Settlers

A certain degree of prestige seems always to be derived from long residence in a particular place. There are, to be sure, other determiners of status, but one who can remember "way back when," or who can trace his lineage to the first settlers, or who bears the surname of one of the old families enjoys considerable advantage in the struggle for social position. Thus the First Families of Virginia, the Daughters of the American Revolution, the Mayflower Descendants, and the Daughters of Texas Trail Drivers cherish the peculiar possession that is theirs and look with some condescension on those whose forebears arrived at a later date.

It is not surprising to find similar attitudes prevailing among the members of ethnic minorities. The old settlers feel superior to newcomers, ridicule their awkward and ignorant ways, blame them for lowering the group's status, and are reluctant to become identified with them.

A cleavage of the same sort prevailed for many years within the Cherokee Nation of Indians, producing a condition of smoldering civil war. On the one side were the Old Settlers, including those who, early in the nineteenth century, had gone more or less voluntarily to the Indian Territory that is now the state of Oklahoma. Opposing them was the other faction of the tribe, far more numerous than the Old Settlers, known as the Cherokee National Party, under the leadership of a great chief, John Ross. This latter group was composed of those who had been forcibly expelled from their home in the mountains of North Carolina, Tennessee, and Georgia, and had been driven to Indian Territory. Both factions desired to heal this tribal wound; but the Army, which had jurisdiction over Indian Affairs until 1849, had a different idea. One of the Army's devices for controlling the Indians was the technique of "divide and rule." Lines of cleavage were carefully felt out in the various tribes and the dissensions were aggravated so as to prevent any strong cohesion and resistance on the part of the Indians. In the case of the Cherokees, the Army prodded and encouraged the Old Settlers, with the result that for a decade the tribe was split into two hostile camps.

American Jewry also manifests this familiar cleavage between early and later arrivals. Jewish immigration to the United States may be divided into four major periods. The first, corresponding roughly to the colonial period, brought Jewish immigrants chiefly of Spanish and Portuguese origin. As early as 1654 (thirty-four years after the Mayflower brought the Pilgrims to Plymouth), a band of twenty-three Jews, under the leadership of Asser Levy, arrived in New Amsterdam, as New York was then called. Four years later fifteen Jewish families settled at Newport, Rhode Island. This latter community grew and prospered, and in 1763 it built a handsome synagogue, which is still standing. Jews are known to have been living in Pennsylvania in 1657; and in the same year the records of Maryland testify to the presence in that colony of "ye Jew Doctor," Dr. Jacob Lombrozo. Other colonial records establish the fact that Jews were living in Virginia, South Carolina, Georgia, and Connecticut in the seventeenth and eighteenth centuries. The second wave of immigration, beginning in 1815 and reaching its peak around 1848, brought chiefly German Jews of a white-collar and professional class. The third and largest wave stemmed from eastern Europe and began in 1881, when the Jews in Russian Poland and the Ukraine were threatened with persecution and extinction. Others followed from Hungary, Rumania, Slovakia, and Bohemia, until nearly 2 million, mostly skilled and unskilled workers and tradespeople, had entered the country. The fourth period covers the years between the two world wars. In the 1920s many fled from Europe to escape the postwar economic dislocations, until their number was drastically reduced by the immigration laws of 1924; and in the 1930s many came from Germany, Austria, Poland, and other central European countries to escape the Nazi persecutions.

Rivalry between the Jews of western Europe and those of central and eastern Europe traces back many centuries. Says Wirth:

Quite early in the medieval history of the Jews there grew up partisan camps in the larger Jewish community. On the one hand were the Spanish, or Sephardic Jews, who prided themselves on the purity of their stock and the superiority of their status; on the other hand were the German Jews, or Ashkenazim, whose ghetto history considerably lowered their status.[19]

The order of their arrival in America, far from allaying this attitude, served only to stimulate it. Those colonial pioneers of Spanish and Portuguese stock held themselves aloof from their coreligionists from Germany, and those from Germany in turn felt themselves superior to Jews from Russia. One of the earliest symptoms of this rift was seen in the secession of the Ashkenazic element from the Jewish community of Philadelphia in 1802 and the formation of a separate congregation and the establishment of separate benevolent and educational activities. This set the pattern for other communities. "The first Jewish settlers of Chicago," says Wirth, "were Bavarian Jews. . . . The Bavarians considered themselves the earliest settlers, and looked down upon the Poles as an inferior caste."[20]

Social Classes

Minorities, too, have their social classes, which serve further to prevent cohesion and cooperation. To illustrate this fact we will consider American blacks whose class structure has received far more attention from sociologists than that of any other racial or ethnic group.[21] The phenomenon of social class is admittedly a difficult one to study, for it is only in a few societies that people fall neatly and precisely into well-marked strata. Instead, class lines are usually vague and flexible, the criteria of status are numerous and subtle, and the demarcation of class lines is somewhat arbitrary.   Accordingly, social scientists are not in complete agreement as to just how many classes there are or just where to draw the distinctions between them.   It is customary and convenient, however, to use a threefold classification of upper, middle, and lower.

The black lower class is the largest of the three.   It is hazardous, of course, to generalize about so large a population, scattered as it is over North and South, and living under both rural and urban conditions.   The various studies, however, do warrant some cautious descriptions of this class.   It consists largely of unskilled laborers, farm hands and sharecroppers, household servants, janitors, porters, laundresses, and bootblacks.   Extreme poverty is common, there is little or no ownership of property, incomes are low and uncertain, and in times of economic crisis many of this class are on relief.   Family life is often disorganized, illegitimacy and desertion are common, and the family tends to be centered around the mother and is even matriarchal.   There is little education, and the older members of the class are either illiterate or practically so.   Books, newspapers, and periodicals play an insignificant role in their lives.   Instead, religion and recreation are the interests, with Baptist, Methodist, Holiness, and Spiritualist churches predominating.   Delinquency and crime rates are high, and aggressive and violent behavior is not rare.   This class falls far below the American minimum standards in housing, food, and clothing.

The black upper class presents an entirely different picture.   It is a small group, about 10 percent of the total.   It includes the owners of sizable farms, professionals (doctors, lawyers, druggists, professors, artists, writers, and some teachers, ministers, and civil service employees), and the owners and operators of substantial businesses (banking, insurance, contracting, real estate, and service establishments).   The income of this group is well above the average for blacks, but it is not comparable to that of upper-class whites. Home ownership is important, and often there is ownership of other property as well.   Family background is stressed, legal marriage is essential, illegitimacy and desertion are regarded as disgraceful, and the family tends to follow the paternalistic pattern.   Education is highly important, more so even than wealth, and is much more a determinant of status than in white society.   Members of the upper class will try to shield their children from contacts with lower-class blacks and from humiliating experiences with whites.   Adults themselves will keep their contacts with whites to a minimum and to that end their recreational activities are centered in the home, including such diversions as dinner parties and bridge.   The boisterous, "shouting" forms of religious expression are eschewed, and church membership, insofar it prevails, tends toward the Episcopal, Congregational, and Presbyterian.   This group insists that its ministers be men of refinement and education.   In fact, decorous behavior is virtually an obsession with the upper class, great stress being laid on good manners, strict morals, correct speech, cultural attainments, and respectability.   In certain Southern cities, as a matter of fact, the black upper class adheres to a strict puritanical code.   Light skin color and Caucasoid features are disproportionately represented in this class, and a certain bias against black racial features has even been reported. The black class structure, however, is a dynamic, not a static, phenomenon; and both the criteria of status and the composition of the classes are undergoing constant change.

Between these two extremes stands the middle class. It is larger than the upper class, but smaller than the lower. Here are found the small business owners, professionals with limited practices, successful farm tenants, skilled and semi-skilled industrial laborers, schoolteachers, social workers, salespersons, office workers, clerical employees in the civil service, police officers, and fire fighters. Theirs, in short, is regular, but low-paying, employment. For the most part, this group has attained primary or secondary education, but few of them other than teachers, have attended college. Education, however, they hold in high esteem and they look forward to sending their children to college. Here is a group striving to better its condition and especially that of the children. Prominent among its social types are the "strivers" and the "strainers." It holds aloft the symbols of respectability and success. High among its values are thrift, independence, honesty, and industry. They are obsessed by a drive to get ahead, "to lay a little something by," to have a nice home, to wear good clothes, and to live in a decent neighborhood. Family life tends to be stable, although common law marriages are not unknown. They are the pillars of the Baptist and Methodist churches, and a large portion of lodge membership comes from this class.

Between these social classes there is not the best of feeling. The upper class condemns the lower as boisterous, stupid, and sexually promiscuous. Its members are described as loud in their conversation, disgusting in public, without ambition, and disposed to have large families they cannot support. The middle class is equally severe in its criticism of the lower.

The lower class, in turn, is contemptuous of the upper, referring to them as "big shots," "dicties," "stuck-ups," "muckti-mucks," and accusing them of being disloyal to their race ("sellin' out to the white folks"), extremely selfish and snobbish, unbecomingly proud of their Caucasoid features and light color, and ever ready to exploit their black patients and customers. The middle class they accuse of being sanctimonious, greedy, miserly, pretentious, and hypocritical. Those in the middle criticize the upper class for their card playing, lewd dancing, irreligion, and insincerity; and these, in reply, wound their inferiors with the "unkindest cut of all," saying that they are "nice, respectable, and honest — but nobody."

Thus the cleavage between the black social classes magnifies the difficulty for this racial minority, large though it is, to present a united front to its oppressors. The existence of social classes, furthermore, serves to disperse black discontent with their lower status, for if *some* have succeeded in acquiring wealth, education, and position, does it not follow that the way is open for *other* blacks to improve their lot if they make the effort? If there is ignorance and poverty, is it not the individual who is at fault, rather than the system? Thus dominant groups, in their own selfish interests, prove themselves shrewd when they temper their rule with a modicum of generosity and opportunity.

Minority groups, then, are invariably rent by cleavages of one sort or another, a fact that plays conveniently into the hands of dominant groups. Such cleavages, we have seen, follow many different lines. The rule of divide and conquer is nowhere more true than in the area of minority relations.

Notes

1. G. Friedman, "Jews as a Product of History," in D. E. Gelfand and R. D. Lee, *Ethnic Conflicts and Power*, pp. 135–137.

2. V. D. MacMurray and P. H. Cunningham, "Mormons and Gentiles," in Gelfand and Lee, *Ethnic Conflicts and Power*, pp. 206–209.

3. St. Clair Drake and H. R. Cayton, *Black Metropolis*, pp. 57–83.

4. G. Myrdal, *An American Dilemma: The Negro Problem and Modern Democracy*, p. 603.

5. Kerner Commission, "The Racial Ghettos and the Immigrants," pp. 227–231.

6. I. Kristol, "The Negro Today Is Like the Immigrant of Yesterday," in P. I. Rose, ed., *Nation of Nations: The Ethnic Experience and the Racial Crisis*, p. 206.

7. L. Berson, *The Negroes and the Jews*, pp. 11–13.

8. R. G. Weisbord and A. Stein, *Bittersweet Encounter: The Afro-American and the American Jew*, p. 7.

9. Berson, *Negroes and Jews*, p. 31.

10. Weisbord and Stein, *Bittersweet Encounter*, p. x.

11. G. S. Stroeber, *American Jews: Community in Crisis*, p. 132.

12. H. J. Gans, "Negro-Jewish Conflict in New York City: A Sociological Evaluation," in Gelfand and Lee, *Ethnic Conflicts and Power*, p. 219.

13. R. A. Schermerhorn, *These Our People*, p. 498.

14. P. Taylor, *The Distant Magnet*, pp. 232–233.

15. E. Williams, *The Negro in the Caribbean*, pp. 64–66.

16. E. K. Strong, *The Second-Generation Japanese Problem*, p. 259.

17. E. de S. Brunner, *Immigrant Farmers and Their Children*, pp 239–240.

18. P. V. Young, *The Pilgrims of Russian Town*, pp. 114–115.

19. L. Wirth, *The Ghetto*, p. 84.

20. Ibid , p. 160.

21. For reports on the class system of blacks, see Myrdal, *American Dilemma*, p. 689ff; Drake and Cayton, *Black Metropolis*, pp. 495–715; M. R. Davie, *Negroes in American Society*, pp. 415–433; H. Powdermaker, *After Freedom*, passim; A. Davis, B. B. Gardner, and M. Gardner, *Deep South: A Social Anthropological Study of Caste and Class*, pp. 228–251; E. F. Frazier, *Black Bourgeoisie*, and *The Negro Family in the United States*, p. 295ff; C. S. Johnson, *Patterns of Negro Segregation*, pp. 231–235; M. M. Gordon, *Assimilation in American Life*, pp. 166–173.

Chapter Eleven
Prejudice

Prejudice, like race, has only marginal rele-
vance to race relations.

— *Carey McWilliams* Brothers Under the
Skin

John Hunter never knew where he was born, nor when, nor who his parents
were. In all probability his birth occurred in the last decade of the 1700s; as for
the place, Illinois would be as good a guess as any. He assumed that his
parents were pioneer settlers on the western frontier, that they were massacred
by the Indians, and that he was taken captive when he was only an infant. But
he was never sure of it.

His earliest recollections went back to his childhood in a Kickapoo Indian
village, somewhere in the Mississippi Valley. He remembered little of those
early years, except that the Indian children used to tease him because his skin
was white, and they insisted that all white people were squaws. That made
him very angry and led to frequent fights with the other boys in the village. As
a consequence, he became very skillful in all physical activities, and he grew so
adept at hunting that the Indians eventually gave him the name "The Hunter."

About this time traders and missionaries began to visit the village and, finding a white boy there, they invariably tried to persuade him to return with
them. "But," said he, "the accounts of the white people, which the Indians
had been particular in giving me, were in no ways flattering to my color. They
were represented as an inferior order of beings, wicked, treacherous, cowardly,
and only fit to transact the common drudgeries of life. I was assured that my

transportation from them to the Indians was for me a most fortunate occurrence, for now I might hope to become an expert hunter, a brave warrior, a wise counsellor, and possibly a distinguished chief. All this I considered true."

The traders proceeded to correct these errors. They told him that white people were numerous, powerful, brave, generous, and good; that they lived in large houses, some of which even floated on the water; and that they fought with great guns and could kill many at a single shot. Hunter confessed that he partially believed these reports and was filled with wonder and curiosity, but he could not bring himself to accompany the traders on their return to their homes. Occasionally, when he did express a desire to go with them, his Indian friends had little difficulty in dissuading him. They told him that if he did undertake such a journey, he would probably be taken captive and be forced to work in the fields *even after he had grown to the size of a warrior.* That was too much for him, and, said he, "After some reflection the prejudices imbibed in early life returned in their full strength, and I still thought the white people were what they had been represented, and even worse."

Hunter could not, however, permanently resist the impact of white influences any more than could his Indian friends. After a time and as a consequence of some traumatic experiences, he cast his lot with the whites. The transition was not easy. It was with greatest difficulty that he adopted the white world's style of clothing, learned to speak English, and mastered the intricacies of a monetary system. He often had feelings of guilt and regret for what he had done. As Hunter put it, "I looked back with the most painful reflections on what I had been and on the sacrifice I had made." This feeling was especially strong when a white man, taking advantage of his unfamiliarity with monetary matters, swindled him out of a considerable sum. His ancient prejudices returned and he declared that he was convinced again that all he had first been taught about the whites was essentially true: fraud and deceit *were* invariable traits of their character.

One thing, more than any other, prevented him from forsaking the society of whites. John Hunter (he adopted the name John) became, as he said, "literally infatuated with reading, and seldom went anywhere without a book." Books, rather than the various other features of their culture to which the whites pointed with so much pride, convinced him that he would prefer to live out his days in white society. He did just that, as far as we know; although he never ceased to recall the Indian way of life with nostalgia, nor to regard the civilization of the whites with critical, suspicious eyes.[1]

The Nature of Prejudice

Hardly anybody has a good word to say for prejudice now, especially for that variety known as race prejudice. It is commonly denounced as an "enemy of society," as an "insidious disease," or as a "canker undermining the body

politic." H. G. Wells says of it, "There is no more evil thing than race prejudice. It holds more baseness and cruelty than any other error in the world."
It is hard for us to examine objectively something that is so universally hated
— and so widely indulged.

What do we have in mind when we use the word? Literally, of course, it
simply means "a prejudgment." Literal translations of Greek and Latin words,
however, can be misleading. (*Sincere* means literally, "without wax," *salary*
means "salt," and *electricity* means "phenomena associated with amber.") In
the first place, prejudice is hardly a judgment, for a judgment is an operation of
the mind that involves comparison, discernment, examination of facts, logical
processes, and good sense. Prejudice is more emotion, feeling, and bias than it
is judgment.

Nor is prejudice necessarily *pre* anything. To be sure, John Hunter did form
his opinion of white people before he had seen any of them, and many others
have done likewise with respect to other groups. Some scholars, as a matter of
fact, have emphasized this feature in making their definitions of the term.
Powdermaker, for instance, says "Prejudice means jumping to a conclusion
before considering the facts"[2]; and, according to Frazier, "Prejudice is a prejudgment in the sense that it is a judgment concerning objects and persons not
based upon knowledge or experience."[3] These definitions themselves involve
a subtle attack on prejudice, for they imply that if one only knew the facts and
had some firsthand experience with the people who are disliked, the bias would
disappear. There is some truth to this implication, and programs looking
toward the eradication of prejudice have often been built on this assumption.
More often, however, attitudes of hostility arise *after* groups have come into
contact, and presumably know something about each other.

Prejudice, according to Wirth, is "an attitude with an emotional bias."[4]
Every one of us, in the process of socialization, acquires attitudes, not only
toward the racial and ethnic groups with which we come into contact, but
toward all the elements of our environment. We learn to have attitudes toward
dogs, flowers, caviar, democracy, red hair, poetry, communism, television,
Elks, chiropractors, news commentators, modern art, and even toward ourselves. How many of these attitudes have we formed after a careful, scientific
study of the "facts"? These attitudes, moreover, run the whole gamut of feelings from love to hate, from esteem to contempt, from devotion to indifference. John Hunter's prejudices included both an unfavorable attitude toward
whites and a most favorable one toward Indians. Usually, however, when we
speak of *race prejudice*, we are thinking, not of friendly attitudes toward racial
and ethnic groups, but of unfriendly attitudes. Allport is correct in insisting
that "ethnic prejudice is mostly negative."[5] *Antipathy* would really be a more
accurate term than prejudice to describe the phenomenon with which we are
dealing. Antipathy, of course, covers a wide range of attitudes itself, including
hatred, aversion, dislike, enmity, and various other hostile and unfavorable
feelings.

Race prejudice, as the term is commonly used now, includes still other elements, which writers on the subject have emphasized. Many insist that the prejudicial attitude, unlike most of our other attitudes, is essentially "irrational," "rigid," "without sufficient warrant," "immutable." Other attitudes we may change when they conflict with new facts, but prejudices resist change even in the face of knowledge and evidence. Thus Marden defines prejudice as "an attitude unfavorable or disparaging of a whole group . . . based upon some elements of irrationality,"[6] and Simpson and Yinger say that it is "an emotional, rigid attitude toward a group of people."[7] Levin defines it as "interpersonal hostility which is directed against individuals based on their membership in a minority group."[8] The distinction for the simplest definition must go to Howard Ehrlich, who defines prejudice "as an attitude toward any group of people."[9] Others point out that race prejudice implies a disposition to overgeneralize, to categorize too hastily and too readily, to "think of people in bunches, as though they were bananas," to overlook or ignore individual differences, and to assume that every person in a group possesses the objectionable qualities the prejudiced person ascribes to that group. Secord and Backman's definition is more useful than some of the others:

Prejudice is an attitude that predisposes a person to think, perceive, feel, and act in favorable or unfavorable ways toward a group or its individual members.[10]

Prejudice and Discrimination

Prejudice (or attitudes of antipathy) must be distinguished from discrimination. The former refers to subjective feelings, the latter to overt behavior. Discrimination simply means differential treatment accorded individuals who are assumed to belong to a particular category or group. Old people, in many societies, are subject to considerable mistreatment, abuse, and indifference, while in other societies they are accorded privileges and respect. Women, too, have often been denied the rights and privileges enjoyed by the male members of society and have been the objects of discrimination in economic, religious, political, and social affairs. Blacks, Jews, Japanese-Americans, and Chicanos, to mention only a few of our minorities, continually complain of the differential treatment to which they are subjected in this country.

Prejudice and discrimination, however, are not perfectly correlated. Nor can we say that one is cause, the other effect. Our attitudes and our overt behavior are without doubt very closely related, but are neither identical nor coextensive. One may have feelings of antipathy without expressing them overtly or even giving the slightest indication of their presence. For example, we may, without ever revealing the fact by word or deed, feel the greatest antipathy for women's hats, oily hair, pictures hanging aslant, people who "pop" gum or chew food audibly, and innumerable other annoyances. On the other

hand, we may, through our overt behavior, completely conceal the real attitude we hold. We may even flatter a woman for her unbecoming coiffure, or
smile at the destructive antics of our guest's child, or smack our lips over some
detestable delicacy that our host serves us.

This simple fact, namely, that attitudes and overt behavior vary independently, has been succinctly applied by Merton to the problem of racial prejudice and discrimination.[11] There are, he thinks, four types of people, as
follows.

The unprejudiced nondiscriminator or all-weather liberal In this category
belong the confirmed and consistent liberals. They are neither prejudiced
against the members of other racial and ethnic groups nor do they practice discrimination. They believe implicitly in the American creed of justice, freedom, equality of opportunity, and dignity of the individual. Merton recognizes the fact that liberals of this type are the ones who are properly motivated
to diffuse the ideals and values of the creed and to fight against those forms of
discrimination that make a mockery of them. At the same time, the all-
weather liberals have their shortcomings. They "enjoy talking to themselves,"
engaging in "mutual exhortation," thereby giving psychological support to one
another; they succumb easily to the illusion that the consensus that prevails
among them is taking hold in the larger community; they confuse discussion
with action; and since their own "spiritual house is in order," they do not
themselves feel the pangs of guilt, and accordingly shrink from any collective
effort to set things right.

The unprejudiced discriminator or fair-weather liberal This type includes persons who think continually of expediency. Though they are themselves free
from racial prejudice, they will keep the silence when bigots speak out. They
will not condemn acts of discrimination lest they somehow lose status thereby;
they will make concessions to the intolerant and will acquiesce in discriminatory practices for fear that to do otherwise would "hurt business." It is these
who suffer most keenly the pricks of conscience and feel shame for their failure
to harmonize their behavior and their beliefs.

The prejudiced nondiscriminator or fair-weather illiberal This category is for
the timid bigots, who do not accept the tenets of the American creed, but conform to it and give it lip service when the slightest pressure is applied. Here
belong those who hesitate to express their prejudice when in the presence of
those who are more tolerant. Among them are the employers who hate certain
minorities, but hire them rather than run afoul of Affirmative Action Laws,
and the labor leaders who suppress their racial bias when the majority of their
followers demand an end to discrimination.

The prejudiced discriminator or all-weather illiberal These are the bigots, pure
and unashamed. They do not believe in equality, nor do they hesitate to give

free expression to their intolerance both in their speech and in their actions. For them there is no conflict between attitudes and behavior. They practice discrimination, believing that it is not only proper that they do so, but is, in fact, their duty.

Dimensions of Prejudice

Race prejudice is not the simple, unitary attitude some have supposed it to be, but instead is complex and multidimensional. To be sure, there is some evidence to the contrary. The tolerant person seems to have friendly feelings, not only for blacks, but for Mexicans, immigrants, Jews, refugees, and all other minority groups, while the bigot — the person for whom the Ku Klux Klan has an appeal — is contemptuous of blacks, Jews, Catholics, Chicanos, Puerto Ricans, and all foreigners. Allport goes so far as to say, "One of the facts of which we are most certain is that people who reject one out-group will tend to reject other out-groups."

Nevertheless, race prejudice is a phenomenon of many dimensions. Reference has already been made to the dimension of *intensity*. Antipathy toward a minority group may vary from mild aversion or indifference to the most violent animosity; while between these two extremes, one encounters various degrees of unfriendliness, dislike, ill will, and abhorrence. Not only are there discrepancies between how people *feel* toward ethnic groups and how they *act*, but people differ also as to what they *think* about other groups, how they *talk* about them, to what extent they are averse to *contact* with them, and in the *intensity* of their hostility toward them.[12] Nor does one hold a single attitude toward blacks, Jews, and foreigners, but rather varies this opinion with respect to social, political, and economic aspirations. The same individual, too, will hold different degrees of prejudice toward the various minority groups, being bitterly hostile, say, toward blacks, moderately hostile toward Greeks, but having no animosity whatsoever toward French-Canadians.

It is a mistake, too, to regard prejudice as an attitude held only by members of the dominant group for their inferiors. Minorities are not without their prejudices. Blacks have an antipathy for whites; and they share with their native-born, white, Protestant fellow-Americans the usual prejudices toward other ethnic minorities. Jews are frequently hostile toward members of the majority. Often this hostility is a by-product of socialization, in which the culture and lifestyle of the larger society is seen as being inferior to Jewish culture. The following account by Harry Golden shows how this prejudice is learned.

My first impression of Christianity came in the home, of course. My parents brought with them the burden of the Middle Ages from the blood-soaked continent of Europe. They had come from the villages of Eastern Europe where Christians were feared with legitimate reason.

When occasionally a Jewish drunk was seen in our neighborhood, our parents would say, "He's behaving like a Gentile."

For in truth, our parents had often witnessed the Polish, Romanian, Hungarian, and Russian peasants gather around a barrel of whiskey on Saturday night, drink themselves into oblivion, "and beat their wives." Once in a while the rumor would spread through the tenements that a fellow had struck his wife, and on all sides we heard the inevitable, "Just like a Gentile."

Oddly enough, too, our parents had us convinced that the Gentiles were noisy, boisterous, and loud — unlike the Jews. . . .

If we raised our voices, we were told, "Jewish boys don't shout." And this admonition covered every activity in and out of the home: "Jewish boys don't fight." "Jewish boys don't get dirty." "Jewish boys study hard." [13]

Theories of Prejudice

Not long ago reputable scientists and scholars maintained that race prejudice was an inborn, instinctive human characteristic. One can see how they came to such a conclusion. Antipathy for strangers, aliens, and members of the out-group is so widespread, so ancient, and so deep rooted that it is no wonder that it was regarded by students of the subject as inherent in all people.

Somewhat later, when we grew more cautious about attributing human behavior to instinctive tendencies, there were those who still supposed that it was "natural" to look with fear and suspicion on any who were different from us. Thus Professor F. H. Giddings held that race prejudice originated as a sort of secondary or incidental manifestation of what he called "consciousness of kind." Things that are familiar to us, he thought, are congenial and comfortable, while those that are strange provoke in us reactions of hostility and fear. Park and Burgess supposed that race prejudice was based on "fear of the unfamiliar and uncomprehended," [14] and Reuter and Hart attributed it to "the universal fear of things new and strange." [15]

These explanations, however, are subject to grave doubt. It is now apparent that we *acquire* all our attitudes, including our prejudices toward racial and ethnic groups. There are several lines of evidence pointing to the fact that our prejudices are not innate. In the first place, there is the evidence from history. White Europeans, prior to modern times, had no antipathy for mongoloid features or a black skin. The records testify to the frequency of marriages between whites and blacks in Portugal, between whites and Indians in the New World, and even between whites and blacks in Virginia, before slavery became established. In the second place, it is significant that racial prejudice manifests itself unevenly and inconsistently throughout the world. Finally, there are numerous studies of the prejudices of children that indicate clearly how we acquire our attitudes and how they grow and diffuse. [16] It is apparent from numerous studies that, in our society at least, children acquire their prejudices toward racial and ethnic groups at a tender age — usually before they enter the first grade, and often still earlier.   At first these feelings are general and vague, but with the passage of time they become differentiated and increasingly well integrated, for the reasons people give for their prejudices change with age, eventually assuming the form of conventional, acceptable rationalizations. Moreover, it is not uncommon for people to attribute a prejudice to some unique and traumatic experience; but the truth seems to be that we acquire an antipathy, not so much from contact with the particular racial or ethnic group itself, as from other persons who already have the prejudice, especially our parents.

If prejudice, then, is so artificial a phenomenon, how can we account for its wide prevalence?   There has been a paucity of facts but a plethora of theories, many of them purporting to account only for some special manifestation of prejudice, such as anti-Semitism or antiblack feeling.   Among these are the following.

Economic Theories

So decisive are the economic factors in human relations that some scholars have looked to intergroup competition and exploitation for an understanding of race prejudice.   It is natural, according to this theory, for us to develop feelings of antipathy for our rivals, for those who threaten our economic well-being or our social position.   We are reluctant to welcome new competitors in the struggle for the things we want; instead, we seek to exclude, eliminate, or cripple those who would deprive us of our special privileges or force us to share with them our economic goods.

There is much to be said for these economic theories.   Tolerance has often turned to intolerance when the members of an ethnic group have begun to encroach on the business of others.   The Chinese in California were held in high esteem as long as they confined themselves to occupations whites had no desire to follow.   Violent antipathy arose, however, as soon as they presented themselves as competitors; but it subsided again when the Chinese withdrew into their Chinatowns and confined their economic activities to "hand laundries," "curio shops," and "Oriental restaurants."   The same thing occurred in Hawaii with both the Chinese and the Japanese.   Here in the United States the intensity of the feeling toward immigrants has been closely related to economic conditions, and there are reasons for believing that race prejudice is stimulated in periods of depression and economic unrest.

One of the earliest attempts to apply principles of economic competition to race relations occurred in a study by Dollard.[17]   He wanted to find out what occupational advantages whites received from displaying prejudice against blacks. The whites in the Southern town he studied were usually paid more for the same work, were able to get a larger share of the goods and services, and consequently benefited from antiblack prejudice.

Having a large group of individuals around who are discriminated against provides a clear advantage to many members of the majority group.   Those in a position of power who hire the minority can pay them less. Those majority group members who compete with them for jobs will usually have a better chance of getting the job and will probably get paid more.

Prejudice also can be used to get the minority to perform unpleasant and low-paying jobs. Since minorities frequently have difficulty competing with the majority, they are forced to accept whatever jobs are left over. Thus those at the bottom rungs of the majority-group economic ladder are saved from having to perform these undesirable tasks. The experience of many immigrant groups serves as an example. The immigrants usually arrived with little money, few skills, and abundant language problems. It was imperative that they come up with a job immediately and had little choice in wages and working conditions. Consequently, many were exploited and wound up working long hours for low wages. As prejudice against the immigrant groups increased, further justifications and rationalizations for the continued exploitation developed. Taylor has described the working life of these immigrants:

[one] immigrant's standard of living involved working all day in a sweatshop, sharing a room with two others at $8 a month, eating rolls and milk except, once a day, a restaurant meal of soup, stew, bread, pie and beer at thirteen cents — all in order to save for his wife's ticket from Europe. An even less fortunate man might pay fifteen cents for a bed in a lodging-house, or ten cents for a bed without covers, or five cents for the privilege of sleeping on a floor. Others again might be at home, making 3,000 cigars a week, working "from they can see till bed-time."[18]

Economic theories, however, fail to reckon with many phenomena associated with prejudice. They do not account for the fact that antipathies fall so neatly and perfectly within racial and ethnic lines. Why is there greater hostility toward Japanese competitors than Scottish competitors? Why is there prejudice for a group whose numbers are so small as to present no economic threat at all? Antiblack and anti-Semitic feeling runs high in many American communities in which these groups are represented by only a few, if any, members. The intensity of prejudice is not perfectly correlated with the size and strength of the minority group. Nor do economic theories explain the fact that Quakers, Mormons, and other groups have, from time to time, been the objects of hostility when no economic reasons could be offered as an explanation. Furthermore, Myrdal contends that the economic hopes and aspirations of blacks meet with the least opposition from the dominant whites. The fact is that people cherish a great many values, economic and otherwise, and they will undertake to defend them and will develop antipathies for individuals and groups who threaten them or who are suspected of so doing.

Symbolic Theories

There have been many theories, some utterly fantastic, which hold that our prejudices arise from the fact that we see in certain racial and ethnic groups a symbol of that which we hate, fear, or envy. Whites are prejudiced against blacks, according to this theory, because blacks are a symbol of natural, unin-hibited sexual activity; and the whites repressed and inhibited by their Puritani-cal codes, are jealous and envious.[19]

For the most part, however, symbolic theories of prejudice have been offered as explanations of anti-Semitism. Jews according to some, are a symbol of ur-banism, a phenomenon that the predominantly rural Gentiles fear, distrust, and envy. Lewis Browne says, "The hostility between Jew and non-Jew . . . is essentially but an aggravated phase of the universal hostility between the towns-man and the rustic"[20]; and Rose claims that Jews meet with hostility because they serve as a symbol of city life.[21] The impersonality, the pushiness, and the sharpness of the city are the features that arouse the hatred of rustics (whatever their place of residence). At the same time, those who dislike urbanism recog-nize the city as a necessity and even admire and envy its many attractions. Torn thus between admiration and hatred, between fear and fancy, the Gen-tiles solve their dilemma by directing their hostility, not on the city, but on the Jews. For the Jews are indeed an urban people par excellence. Long ago the Jews identified themselves with cities and they have succeeded in making a suc-cessful adjustment to urban conditions. Hence they serve as a perfect and ready symbol for that which disturbs those whose traditions and habits are of a rural character.

Others have attempted to account for anti-Semitism using religious symbol-ism. Maurice Samuel was the first of many to assert that prejudice against the Jews is basically hatred of Christ. Bigots, according to this view, actually hate Jesus and the ideals for which he stood — peace, brotherhood, equality, paci-fism, charity. Many of them, however, are professing Christians, whose mores prevent them from speaking their minds or even admitting to themselves their honest feelings. Instead, they vent their hatred on the Jews, who, because they gave Christ to the world, serve as a symbol for the Christ whom the bigots hate.[22] Other theories of this type have seen in the Jews the symbol of interna-tionalism, therefore, as something to be hated by the chauvinists; or they serve as the symbol of capitalism, communism, or "successful nonconformity" and become, in turn, the enemies of the communists, the capitalists, or those in authority.[23] Needless to say, these theories leave much to be desired and have not met with great acceptance.

Psychological Theories

There have been a number of theories, several of them enjoying wide popular-ity, in which race prejudice is regarded as satisfying some psychic need of the individual or as compensating for some defect in the personality. Prominent among these has been the "scapegoat" theory. Human beings, so it seems, have always been reluctant to blame themselves for their troubles, woes, and shortcomings. Instead, they look elsewhere for some object, some animal, some "force," or some evil spirit on which they gladly lay the blame. Many primitive peoples have made a formal ceremony of thus "passing the buck."[24]

The ancient Hebrews made it an annual event to load all of their sins on a goat, which they promptly chased into the wilderness,[25] and which has come to be known as the "scapegoat," or the goat allowed to escape. The term has come to be applied to any person or group forced to bear the blame for others.

Many minority groups have served as scapegoats. The Romans used to blame the Christians for all the troubles of the Empire, including the burning of their city. Said Tertullian, "If the Tiber rose to the walls of the city, if the inundation of the Nile failed to give the fields enough water, if the heavens did not send rain, if an earthquake occurred, if famine threatened, if pestilence raged, the cry resounded, 'Throw the Christians to the lions!' " Centuries later the English pounced on a colony of French Huguenots living in their midst, and accused them of lowering the standard of living, depriving the English of jobs, and reducing wages. Italians, Norwegians, Irish, Japanese, Jews, and innumerable others have, at one time or another, been forced to play the unwilling role of the scapegoat. So have the Catholics, Protestants, atheists, deists, Quakers, and Baptists.

Racial and ethnic groups have been admirably suited for the role, some much better than others. According to one analysis, a group, to be an acceptable scapegoat, ought to have the following characteristics.[26] First, it should have distinguishing, salient features, and be "highly visible." Physical traits such as skin color or dress best meet this demand, although distinctive names, gestures, language, food habits, or religious customs may serve instead. Second, it should not be too strong, nor be in too good a position to retaliate or to answer back. Preferably, a scapegoat is a safe goat, to use the words of Carey McWilliams. Third, it should be readily accessible, even concentrated in one locality, for a remote scapegoat would hardly serve the purpose. Fourth, it is well for the victim to have been a previous object of blame, against whom a certain latent hostility is directed. And, fifth, the scapegoat should personify some idea that is disliked.

Another psychological theory of prejudice is that of frustration-aggression.[27] According to this theory, hostility for a racial group is a socially approved channel for the expression of the aggressive tendencies people acquire as a consequence of their being frustrated. All of us, simply in the process of growing up in a society, are subject to considerable inhibition and restraint, and these frustrations call for some outlet. There are many things, for instance, that a child wishes, but is not permitted to do, and the resulting frustrations call into action an aggressive tendency. The child seeks some legitimate object toward which aggressiveness and hostility may be directed. Dollard suggests that much of this irrational, latent hostility may be drained off when society presents an object whom one may abuse and detest with a clear conscience. The frustrated individual, in other words, is given social permission to hate the members of a minority group. Thus, the poor whites, kept down by the wealthy landowner or the industrialist, or even by their poor physical environment, find relief from their frustrations through antiblack prejudice. Or the Germans, frustrated by the instability of the government, the failure of their nationalist ambitions, and

a runaway inflation, gave vent to their aggressive feelings in their persecution of the Jews. For that matter, any incompetent, unsuccessful, maladjusted person, whether a member of the dominant or the subordinate group, may find in race prejudice a counterweight to individual failure and futility. This theory, however, fails to explain why one group rather than another is selected as the object of discrimination, and it fails to recognize that frustration need not manifest itself in aggression, and, especially, in aggression toward a minority group. The theory does, however, offer some explanation of the fact that prejudice and discrimination vary greatly in their intensity from one individual to another.

Other investigators, without going so far as to say that prejudice is indicative of either psychosis or neurosis, nevertheless do maintain that it is a function of the personality. The intolerant individual, they say, does have a definite personality structure, and prejudice is a manifestation of, say, fear, and particularly fear for one's status. Research has given support to the theory that race prejudice, far from being an isolated and independent attitude, is in fact a symptom or a function of a basic personality structure. As Allport puts it: "Prejudice is more than an incident in many lives; it is often lockstitched into the very fabric of personality."[28]   The authors of *The Authoritarian Person-ality*[29] report that highly prejudiced persons are characterized by a rigidity of outlook, suggestibility, gullibility, dislike for ambiguity, antiscientific and pseu-doscientific attitudes, and unrealistic ideas as to how to achieve their goals. Allport finds that the following are the "earmarks of a personality in whom prejudice is functionally important":

1. *Ambivalence toward parents*   The prejudiced individuals often insist that they like their parents, but underneath there is jealousy, suspicion, hostility, and vigorous protest.   A relationship of power, rather than of love, prevails.

2. *Moralism*   Prejudiced personalities reflect the anxiety that haunts them by adopting a rigidity with respect to morals.   They tend to place great stress on cleanliness, good manners, and social conventions.   Theirs is not a true mor-alism, which is more relaxed and integral, but instead is tense, compulsive, and projective.

3. *Dichotomization*   Prejudiced persons reject the sentiment expressed in this familiar bit of doggerel:

There is so much good in the worst of us,
And so much bad in the best of us,
That it scarcely behooves any of us
To talk about the rest of us.

On the contrary, they tend to believe that there are two kinds of people, the good and the bad; a right way and a wrong way; the weak and the strong; the pure and the impure.   Things are black or white — not varying shades of gray.

4. *Need for definiteness*   Prejudiced individuals are "intolerant of ambiguity." They cling to old and tried solutions of problems.   They are reluctant to say, "I don't know."   They always have an opinion when asked for one.   They "know all the answers."   They demand a clear-cut structure for the world.

5. *Externalization*   Prejudiced individuals believe that things happen *to* them — that events are not caused *by* them.   They do not feel that they have very much control over their destiny.   It is not one's actions or shortcomings that bring unhappy and undesired consequences, but rather fate, the position of the stars, or some uncontrolled external agency.

6. *Institutionalization*   Prejudiced people are more devoted to institutions than are the unprejudiced.   They are more "patriotic."   They care more than their tolerant friends for their fraternities and sororities.   They manifest greater devotion to their lodges, schools, clubs, churches.   Institutional membership helps them satisfy their need and hunger for safety and security.

7. *Authoritarianism*   Prejudiced individuals have no great fondness for indi-vidualism, freedom, democracy, indefiniteness, disorderliness, and social

change. Instead, they prefer authority, definite power arrangements, discipline, strong leaders, and an orderly society.

Tolerant individuals are just the opposite of all this. In the literature of social psychology dealing with this subject they are described as having come from homes where they were loved and accepted, where punishment was neither harsh nor capricious, where good companionship and wholesome fun were regarded as more important than correct manners and proper behavior. Those who are tolerant do not divide the world into the wholly proper and the wholly improper. Their minds are flexible; they feel secure and self-sufficient; they do not feel that they must always blame others when something goes wrong. They are liberal in their political views and feel a genuine sympathy for the underdog. Tolerant individuals have a high degree of self-insight and are aware of their own capabilities and shortcomings. They have a sense of humor and since they are able to laugh at themselves, they are less likely to feel superior to others.

No doubt these theories are flattering to those who regard themselves as free from prejudice and bias. It is comforting to be told that one is neither psychotic nor neurotic, but that one is, instead, well-balanced, urbane, self-sufficient, altruistic, democratic, sympathetic, intelligent, and high-minded. The evidence on which the theory rests, however, is admittedly scanty. The samples studied have been small, and the individuals tested have themselves been extreme types. Allport recognizes various methodological weaknesses in the research to date, but insists that "we cannot possibly explain away the trends reported." Simpson and Yinger say: "One must be careful not to assume too quickly that a certain tendency — rigidity of mind, for example — that is correlated with prejudice necessarily causes that prejudice. . . . The sequence may be the other way around. . . . It is more likely that both are related to more basic factors."[30] There are those, too, who maintain that race and ethnic prejudice is part and parcel of our American culture pattern. They believe that the rebellious individuals, the nonconformists, tend to be more tolerant, while those who are normal, accepted, and well adjusted tend to conform to, and abide by, the standards and conventions of their society, which include the norms of prejudice and discrimination.

Rationalizations

Whatever be the *real* reasons for racial antipathy and discrimination, they are seldom admitted by the guilty parties even when they, themselves, are aware of these reasons. Instead, plausible and socially acceptable explanations are offered for the prejudices and discriminatory practices that prevail in all biracial and multiracial societies the world over.

Rationalizations of race prejudice and discrimination by dominant groups, wherever encountered and whatever the terms in which they are expressed, invariably fall into four categories: (1) Self-defense. The dominant group maintains that its attitudes and policies are necessary if it is to defend itself, its values, its status, and its way of life. (2) Subordination and superordination are universal, natural, inevitable, and normal phenomena. They have been regarded as sacred and divinely instituted. (3) The fault lies with the minority group itself, for it is either innately and biologically inferior or it is addicted to immoral, filthy, dishonest, and treacherous habits. (4) Prejudice and discrimination, or what appears to be so, are in reality but a manifestation of worthy, unselfish, altruistic motives. Differential treatment is in the best interest of the minority itself.

These rationalizations have been applied in one way or another to all minorities. Jews, blacks, Mexicans, Italians, Greeks, Irish, and others have felt their force. Myrdal has pointed out that, in a society where adult males enjoy a privileged status, these same justifications are offered for the inferior status of women and children.[31]

Not infrequently the very people who voice these rationalizations come to doubt their validity. Usually, however, a dominant group will cast about for newer and better rationalizations when those to which they have adhered begin to give way under attack. Thus when the older theological and Biblical justifications that the Europeans offered for their exploitation of blacks, Indians, and others began to crumble, they eagerly embraced the newer doctrine of evolution, with its emphasis on the universality of struggle, and the "survival of the fit." When this, in turn, lost its force, the results of intelligence tests were offered as justification for discrimination and segregation. Even so, doubts continually arise in the minds of those who seek to justify their exploitation of their fellow human beings. This, as Myrdal maintains, constitutes the white "dilemma," for they believe only halfheartedly in the ground on which they take their stand. Thus the race problem becomes, in the last analysis, a moral problem, a conflict of values, and a burden on the conscience.

The Reduction of Prejudice

Recent years have seen a growing concern, in the United States at least, with problems of race prejudice. Nor is it only the victims of prejudice — Jews, blacks, and Japanese-Americans, for instance — who have spearheaded the movement to reduce, control, and perhaps eliminate it. Many white, native-born Protestants have been no less desirous than their less fortunate fellows to pull its fangs. They have grown acutely aware of the fact that prejudice and discrimination are incompatible with certain values they hold in highest esteem. They have learned, too, that the strength of a nation lies as much in the unity and loyalty of its citizens as it does in armaments. We have realized that our domestic minority policies have worldwide reactions, that lynchings and riots cost heavily in good will, and those we sorely need as friends and allies scrutinize closely our treatment of our minority citizens.

There has arisen, accordingly, a multitude of organizations and movements bent on reducing the racial and ethnic tensions. At the same time, there are skeptics who doubt that racial prejudice can be reduced, at least by any of the techniques currently employed; and there have always been bigots who insist that what we need is not less, but more, race prejudice. These latter have organized, too. The United States has had its full quota of societies for the promotion of intolerance, ethnocentrism, and discrimination — Native American Party, "Know Nothings," American Protective Association, Ku Klux Klan, America First Party, Mason-Dixon Society, Silver Shirts, Black Legion, Society of Forward Men, United Sons of America, Gentile Cooperative Association, Anglo-Saxon Federation, and innumerable others. Seldom have these organizations been regarded as innocuous or ineffective, or have they been accused of working at cross-purposes with one another.

It is not so, however, with the organizations interested in the promotion of tolerance. They differ widely in the goals they seek, the techniques they employ, the philosophy that motivates them, the speed at which they hope to move, the segments of the population toward which their efforts are directed, and the effectiveness of their programs. Some are concerned with education in the schools and others with adult education; some engage in serious research; some promote cultural and recreational activities; some act through the courts to secure legal redress; some are interested chiefly in promoting legislation; and some are engaged in action programs in their local communities. A certain degree of diversity is doubtless necessary and good, yet the most ardent proponents of tolerance deplore overlapping organizations and wasted effort.

Contact and Acquaintance Programs

There are many who believe that people are inclined to be suspicious of, and prejudiced against, that which is strange and unfamiliar to them, that antipathy is increased by isolation and segregation, and that "contact brings friendliness." We find, accordingly, that many efforts are made to bring together the members of different groups, in the belief that tolerance and sympathy will result. Interracial contacts and cooperation have been established in housing projects, in camps and other recreational activities, in various work situations, in interracial churches, in student organizations, and in forums, councils, and committees. In Chicago the device has been employed of bringing together neighbors of various ethnic stocks for the purpose of improving the neighborhood in which they live. It is reported that when they unite thus in a common activity, tolerance and understanding begin to supplant suspicion and antipathy. The proponents of intercultural education in the schools maintain that imparting information is not enough to counteract prejudice, and that the students must make field trips into the neighborhoods where minorities live, must meet and talk with them, and participate with them in festivals and community projects.

The Informational Approach

By and large, however, most organizations concerned with the reduction of prejudice seem to operate on the same assumption that antipathy arises from ignorance, that stereotypes are false, that hostility is unnatural and unrealistic, and that prejudice will disappear if people are only given the facts (skillfully presented, to be sure). The underlying philosophy was expressed by Ambrose Bierce, who said, "Prejudice is a vagrant opinion without visible means of support." The task, then, is to make this point crystal clear, to report the facts about minorities, to correct the misinformation, to destroy the stereotypes, and to expose the rationalizations. No channel of communication has been overlooked: schools, churches, radio, stage, television, motion pictures, the press, billboards, labor unions, and service clubs. Comic strips, sermons, slogans, leaflets, pamphlets, books, lectures, conferences, and workshops are used.

Evaluation

Just how effective these various programs are in reducing prejudice is a moot point. Those who teach in intercultural education and those who engage in the numerous other programs of exhortation, education, and propaganda are no less uncertain than are the critics and cynics. It is suspected that they reach only a limited audience of those who are already convinced. Merton has commented as follows on this fact:

Ethnic liberals are busily engaged in talking to themselves. Repeatedly, the same groups of like-minded liberals seek each other out, hold periodic meetings in which they engage in mutual exhortation and thus lend social and psychological supports to one another. But however much these unwittingly self-selected audiences may reinforce the creed among themselves, they do not thus appreciably diffuse the creed in belief or practice to groups which depart from it.

More, these group soliloquies in which there is typically wholehearted agreement among fellow-liberals tend to promote another fallacy limiting effective action. This is the *fallacy of unanimity*. Continued association with like-minded individuals tends to produce the illusion that a large measure of consensus has been achieved in the community at large.[32]

There are those, moreover, who doubt that prejudices can be changed by facts and logic, however cleverly presented. They insist that the best way to handle the problem of intergroup tensions is to say as little as possible about them. Even members of minority groups themselves often wish that people would stop talking about them as a "problem."

Does contact with members of a minority group make one more tolerant?

There are those who believe that friendly attitudes will emerge merely from bringing together people of different races, nationalities, and religions. However, instances readily come to mind where prejudice and conflict have increased, rather than diminished, when blacks have moved into a white residential neighborhood, when Irish have invaded an Italian community, when public schools have become desegregated, when different racial groups have met at an amusement park or on an excursion ferry. Obviously contact itself does not automatically result in a reduction of prejudice.

On the other hand, there are many instances proving that contact does help to diminish prejudice.[33] Accordingly, we must take into consideration other factors than mere contact. We must consider the frequency and duration of the contacts; whether the persons involved enjoy equality of status or not; whether they meet in a competitive or a cooperative capacity; whether their meeting is voluntary or compulsory; the backgrounds of the persons in association; and whether they meet in a political, religious, occupational, residential, recreational, or casual situation. Trying to make allowances for all these possible variables, Allport comes to the following conclusion regarding the effects of contact:

It would be fair, then, to conclude that contact, as a situational variable, cannot always overcome the personal variable in prejudice. . . . At the same time, given a population of ordinary people, with a normal degree of prejudice, we are safe in making the following general prediction: . . .

Prejudice (unless deeply rooted in the character structure of the individual) may be reduced by equal status contact between majority and minority groups in the pursuit of common goals. The effect is greatly enhanced if this contact is sanctioned by institutional supports (i.e., by law, custom or local atmosphere), and provided it is of a sort that leads to the perception of common interests and common humanity between members of the two groups.[34]

Doubt also prevails as to the effectiveness of formal educational programs in reducing prejudice. Here, again, no small amount of research has been done in an effort to measure the effects of classroom teaching. The results are conflicting. Some evidence indicates that the student's attitudes and prejudices are changed and that there is a positive correlation between knowledge and tolerance; but the results of other studies do not bear this out.[35] Moreover, there are differences of opinion as to the most effective teaching methods. Hardly anyone maintains that merely imparting specific information about minority groups has any effect on prejudice. Pedagogical methods in better repute include the use of movies, dramas, fiction, field trips, area surveys, exhibits, pageants, discussion, sociodrama, and individual conferences. Many insist that it is more effective to approach the subject indirectly through literature, geography, history, and the like, rather than directly. The evidence suggests that knowledge itself does not automatically produce tolerance and understanding,

but there is no evidence that sound factual information makes one more prejudiced. Moreover, in the long run it is probable that scientific facts about race
and about minorities do have important consequences. They gradually penetrate people's attitudes and opinions; they puncture the stereotypes, the rationalizations, and the prejudices; and they furnish the bricks and mortar for other
programs.

There is even more doubt about the effectiveness of the numerous other
devices in common use — sermons, exhortations, comic strips, leaflets, spot
announcements on radio, posters, slogans, "Brotherhood Week," movies, to
mention a few. In fact, certain tentative principles emerge from the studies
that have been made on such devices:

1. Auditory stimuli are more effective than visual.
2. Speakers are more effective than printed matter.
3. Emotional appeals are more effective than logical, though there are exceptions.
4. Oral propaganda is more effective in small groups than in large audiences.
5. The effectiveness of propaganda tends to be greater when linked with prestige symbols.
6. The use of several channels of communication simultaneously is more effective than
the use of only one medium.
7. Pictures and cartoons are more effective in gaining attention than the written word,
and in conveying a message, except in the case of complex and abstract ideas.[36]

The Attack on Discrimination

Many persons believe that the wiser plan is to bypass the problem of prejudice
and attitudes altogether and to set about promptly to minimize and abolish discrimination. MacIver declares, "*Wherever the direct attack is feasible, that is,
the attack on discrimination itself, it is more promising than the indirect attack,
that is, the attack on prejudice as such. It is more effective to challenge conditions than to challenge attitudes or feelings.*"[37] Others believe that attempts to
eliminate discrimination often lead to increases in hostility and conflict.

Some scholars have insisted that antipathy for members of the out-group is
neither an instinctive feeling nor a manifestation of a disturbed personality, but
is, instead, a natural, normal development of group living. In a heterogeneous, multigroup society such as ours, it is inevitable that such prejudices be
numerous and that their intensity cover a wide range.

Attitudes of antipathy for the out-group are widely prevalent and they represent the accepted form of behavior in many societies. It is natural and conventional under such conditions to think of people in terms of their racial or ethnic
background, and on that basis to assign value to them and to differentiate
among them. Young children, of course, begin life without these prejudices,
just as they begin without an understanding of language and without the
various other skills, understandings, and attitudes in their cultural environment. The process by which they acquire prejudices is a subtle and gradual

one. Children are largely unaware of it; and when they reach adulthood and find that they have antipathetic feelings toward blacks, whites, Jews, Gentiles, Irish, Italians, or Mexicans, they can seldom identify the forces and influences which made them the persons that they are. To be sure, individuals in any society vary in the extent to which they adopt the prevailing prejudices, and herein lies something of a mystery. The same thing holds, however, for the other aspects of a culture, which is entirely too broad and complex a phenomenon for anyone to embrace as a whole. Individuals vary, not only in the intensity of their prejudices, but in the extent to which they adopt, understand, and adhere to all the other elements of their culture — language, food habits, laws, patterns of recreation, values, and modes of dress, to mention only a few.

Others have suggested that racial antipathy thrives simply because conflict and antagonism are more exciting than friendliness and good will, just as war is more thrilling than peace, and malicious gossip more eagerly devoured than panegyrics. Still others have seen in race prejudice simply a fascist technique for weakening, and ultimately destroying, a nation.

Obviously, there has been no dearth of theories to account for race prejudice. The fact is, however, that sociologists long ago abandoned their quest for the ultimate *origins* of social phenomena, when they discovered how hopeless and futile that quest proved to be. Moreover, social phenomena have a way of undergoing so drastic a change over the course of time that, even though we could learn how something originated, that information might contribute very little to an understanding of its present form and meaning. Racial and ethnic prejudice would be no exception to such a process. One is forced to conclude that race prejudice is a complex phenomenon, not to be explained by any single factor. Multiple causation is obviously at work. Most, if not all, of the theories previously discussed contain at least an element of truth. Herman Melville once said, "It is vain to popularize profundities, and all truth is profound." Whether or not that observation is generally acceptable, it certainly applies to the problem of race prejudice.

Notes

1. John Hunter, with the assistance of friends, published *Memoirs of a Captivity Among the Indians of North America* in 1823. For a brief summary, see B. Berry, "The Education of John Hunter," *Social Science* 15, no. 3 (July 1940): 258–264. There were many such instances on the frontier of white persons being captured and reared by Indians. See C. C. Rister, *Border Captives: The Traffic in Prisoners by Southern Plains Indians*.

2. H. Powdermaker, *Probing Our Prejudices*, p. 1.

3. E. F. Frazier, *The Negro in the United States*, p. 665.

4. L. Wirth, "Race and Public Policy," *The Scientific Monthly* 58, no. 4 (March 1944): 303.

5. G. W. Allport, *The Nature of Prejudice*, p. 6.

6. C. F. Marden and G. Meyer, *Minorities in American Society*, p. 31.

7. G. E. Simpson and J. M. Yinger, *Racial and Cultural Minorities: An Analysis of Prejudice and Discrimination*, p. 24.

8. J. Levin, *The Functions of Prejudice*, p. 12.

9. H. J. Ehrlich, *The Social Psychology of Prejudice*, p. 8.

10. P. F. Secord and C. W. Backman, *Social Psychology*, 2nd ed., p. 165.

11. R. K. Merton, "Discrimination and the American Creed," in R. M. MacIver, ed., *Discrimination and National Welfare*, pp. 99–126.

12. B. M. Kramer, "Dimensions of Prejudice," *Journal of Psychology* 27 (Second Half, Oct. 1949): 389–451; E. L. Horowitz, "Race Attitudes," in O. Klineberg, ed., *Characteristics of the American Negro*, pp. 143–157.

13. H. Golden, *you're entitle'*, p. 210.

14. R. E. Park and E. W. Burgess, *Introduction to the Science of Sociology*, p. 578.

15. E. B. Reuter and C. W. Hart, *Introduction to Sociology*, p. 263.

16. See Horowitz, "Race Attitudes," pp. 159–184; Allport, *Nature of Prejudice*, p. 297ff.

17. J. Dollard, *Caste and Class in a Southern Town*, pp. 474–480.

18. P. Taylor, *The Distant Magnet*, pp. 189–190.

19. Cf. A. Rose and C. Rose, *America Divided*, pp. 290–291.

20. L. Browne, *How Odd of God*, p. 223.

21. A. Rose, "Anti-Semitism's Roots in City-Hatred," *Commentary* 6, no. 4 (Oct. 1948): 376.

22. M. Samuel, *The Great Hatred*, passim, and especially chap. 11.

23. See Rose and Rose, *America Divided*, p. 286ff.

24. For numerous illustrations, see J. G. Frazier, *The Golden Bough*, vol. 2, p. 182ff; W. G. Sumner and A. G. Keller, *The Science of Society*, vol. 2, p. 1212.

25. Leviticus 16:5–22.

26. G. W. Allport, *ABC's of Scapegoating*, pp. 42–43.

27. See especially Dollard, *Caste and Class*, pp. 474–480, J. Dollard et al., *Frustration and Aggression*, pp. 151–156.

28. Allport, *Nature of Prejudice*, p. 408.

29. T. W. Adorno, E. Frenkel-Brunswik, D. J. Levinson, and R. N. Sanford, *The Authoritarian Personality*.

30. Simpson and Yinger, *Racial and Cultural Minorities*, 3rd ed., p. 91.

31. G. Myrdal, *An American Dilemma: The Negro Problem and Modern Democracy*, vol. 2, Appendix 5, pp. 1073–1078.

32. Merton, "Discrimination and the American Creed," p. 104.

33. Allport, *Nature of Prejudice*, p. 261ff.; R. M. Williams, *The Reduction of Intergroup Tensions*, p. 150ff.

34. Allport, *Nature of Prejudice*, p. 261ff.

35. For the evidence for this statement, see Williams, *Intergroup Tensions*, p. 27ff; Allport, *Nature of Prejudice*, p. 483ff.

36. Williams, *Intergroup Tensions*, p. 31ff. See also A. Rose, *Studies in the Reduction of Prejudice*; Horowitz, "Race Attitudes," pp. 228–243; Allport, *Nature of Prejudice*, pp. 493–495.

37. R. M. MacIver, *The More Perfect Union*, p. 247.

Part Four

RESOLUTIONS
OF INEQUALITY

Chapter Twelve
Assimilation

The melting pot does not always work.

— *Robin M. Williams, Jr., et al.* Strangers
Next Door: Ethnic Relations in American
Communities

Conflict is no doubt the phase of race relations that most easily catches the public's attention. Riots, lynchings, insurrections, and mass expulsions make the headlines and create the impression that racial and ethnic groups are naturally and continually at each other's throats. But race relations also include interactions of a very different sort, which are less conspicuous than conflict, but in the long run are more significant. Annihilation or expulsion of the weaker group by the stronger, which will be discussed later, is not a usual outcome of the contact of races. More common by far is the fusion of the two (assimilation and amalgamation) or the reaching of some modus vivendi (accommodation). We are concerned here with assimilation as one of the consequences of intergroup contact. The following autobiographical sketch written by a young American of Chinese ancestry illustrates most of the processes and problems involved:

My parents came from China in 1900. Father was a herbalist. . . In China herb doctors are very much in demand. . . . When Father settled in Los Angeles, he continued his profession. He was successful almost from the start. He dealt exclusively with "Americans." His knowledge of English was woefully inadequate. "R's" he never could pronounce, and my brothers and I always laughed when we heard him advise his patients to eat "lice."

But my mother doesn't even speak English, although she has been in California now for forty-one years. She lives the protected life of a Chinese lady in China. Except for infrequent Sunday afternoon drives, she seldom leaves the house. . . . Mother has tiny bound feet, wears Chinese gowns always, and drinks nothing but tea, which she has on hand in a thermos bottle, hot, twenty-four hours a day. She loathes milk and cheese, and will refuse anything cooked with butter. . . .

Being China-born, my parents were excluded from American citizenship; and I believe this fact prevented Father, at least, from making a serious effort to adopt American ways. And yet Father was grateful to America too. He named all his sons for American Presidents. . . . He named his first-born Taft . . . the next two William and Howard. . . . Two more became Monroe and Lincoln. . . .

From early childhood, I, with my brothers and sisters, lived a double life. We drooled over ice cream cones at the corner store, we ran wildly over school grounds shouting English insults at our classmates, we played American baseball. . . . We generally spoke English to each other. . . . But to our parents we spoke only Chinese. Father was strict about our learning the language properly. . . . But we'd absent-mindedly divide not only a sentence into Chinese and English words, but the words themselves into Chinese and English syllables. . . .

During all my early youth, and in many respects even now, the American way was more attractive. . . . I use chopsticks, but not to the exclusion of knives and forks; I play mah jongg, but I enjoy contract bridge as well.

Only toward my parents was I uncompromisingly Chinese. Our relationship was formal and reserved. . . . Father was the head of the family, and no one doubted his authority; while Mother had her respected function as matriarch and ruler of the domestic system. . . . To us they were always respectfully "Father" and "Mother," never "my old man" and "my old lady."

Christmas was a big day in our household, which seems odd considering that my parents were not Christians. To this extent Father and Mother became Americanized. They knew how important this day was for children all over America. So they had the tallest and bushiest tree our living room could hold; and all their gifts to us were always labelled in Father's own hesitant scrawl, "From Santa Claus." This holiday was one of the few occasions when the whole family sat down to dinner and ate with knives and forks. Except for such holidays we always used chopsticks. . . .

The Thanksgiving celebration was a more elaborate occasion. The Chinese love any excuse for a feast, and even with their scant knowledge of American history my parents knew that the big idea of Thanksgiving was to have a huge feast. . . . Mother and Father presided, he in his American tailor-made dark suit, and Mother in a beautiful jade and gold lace Chinese gown, wearing her jade earrings and jade pins in her shining black hair.

When we were older, Father let us celebrate New Year's Eve, too. . . . There was dancing for the young crowd and mah jongg and Chinese dominoes for Father's and Mother's friends. . . . Ice cream and cake for us and gai chuk or chicken porridge for the oldsters. . . . But there was no differentiation when it came to ringing in the new year; and it was my Father, it seemed, who always made the loudest toot on his horn come midnight.

Then on every Fourth of July we'd have the biggest demonstration of fireworks on our block. . . . To passersby it must have seemed incongruous that when it came to celebrating the independence of this country, the Chinaman's family always made the biggest noise. . . .

Just before the conclusion of our college years, many of us Chinese-Americans began to face the problem of the future — how to earn a living in a country which was native to us by birth, yet alien in many ways. One girl . . . graduated with high honors, but could not find a job. . . . Another friend who finished an engineering course *magna cum laude* . . . now works as a waiter in a chop suey restaurant. Another . . . today is clerking at a fruit stand.

I decided that my best possibility was to secure a position with some American company doing business in the Orient. . . . That was when I thanked my Father for his insistence on Chinese-language school. . . . Without Chinese it would have been impossible. . . . I wrote letters to three large American companies. . . . I received an offer from two. The company I accepted assigned me to its Hawaiian office. . . . Future work will take me to China. . . . My knowledge of Chinese is not so complete as my knowledge of English, nor do I feel as much Chinese as . . . American. But at least I understand both. [1]

This interesting autobiographical sketch by Lincoln Leung brings out a number of aspects of the assimilation process. Note how eagerly and easily the youngsters in the family adopted American customs, language, and values, and how difficult it was for their parents. The father, to be sure, did accept some of the customs of his adopted home; he tried to learn English, he wore American clothes, and he celebrated the holidays of this strange land, even though he grasped only the external features of those occasions. The mother, on the other hand, clung tenaciously to her Chinese ways, although even she learned to appreciate the advantages of the thermos bottle. Both parents, however, agreed on certain values in their old culture that they were determined to transmit to their children — the Chinese language and the Chinese insistence on respect for elders. No doubt they looked with some misgiving on their children's fondness for ice cream cones, baseball, and dancing, and tried to inculcate in them a taste for mah jongg, gai chuk, and chicken porridge. But their efforts were certainly doomed to failure. They could see their children growing up more American than Chinese; and one does not have to be a prophet to foresee that their grandchildren are likely to have little knowledge about, nor interest in, the language and customs of China. There were many obstacles in their way — their Oriental racial features, their limited contacts with Americans, the fact that the parents could not become citizens — but even these formidable barriers could not long delay the trend toward assimilation.

It is not always this way, however. Chinese have migrated to many parts of the world other than the United States, and the story has been quite different. Long before the Leung family came to America, Chinese were leaving the southeastern provinces of Fukien and Kwangtung and taking up residence in Burma, Thailand, Malaya, the Philippines, and elsewhere in Southeast Asia. With the advent of European colonialism, this migration greatly increased, with the result that today there are some 10 million Overseas Chinese living in that area. The original emigrants certainly had no intention of founding permanent settlements abroad, nor did they have any desire to become citizens of those countries. Their hope was, simply, that by engaging in some kind of legitimate business they might amass a reasonable fortune and eventually return to their homeland. For most of them, however, their plans went awry and they never returned to China. Today, generations later, we find their descendants still living in those areas; and, while they have made an excellent economic adjustment, they are unassimilated, socially distinct, and not identified politically or psychologically with the countries in which they reside.

Maurice Freedman, of the London School of Economics, has made extensive studies of these Overseas Chinese,[2] and he raises the question as to why they have failed to become assimilated. Race is certainly not a factor. In British Malaya, he says, little stands in the way of a Chinese who wishes to become a Malay. Anyone who becomes a Moslem can easily find a place and a spouse in Malay society. It is sometimes said that the failure of the Chinese to assimilate was the direct product of deliberate colonial policies of divide and rule; but Freedman, while recognizing some truth in this assertion, points out that in Thailand, which never fell under European control, there is also an unassimilated Chinese minority. To be sure, there is a certain degree of assimilation. In Malaya there are Chinese who have acquired at least the formal characteristics of the native culture, and they are known as Straits Chinese, or Baba; and in Indonesia one finds the Peranakan, Chinese who speak no Chinese (at least as their native tongue) and have adopted Indonesian habits to a considerable extent. And yet, says Freedman, "It is still the case that every Overseas Chinese community to a greater or lesser degree has the characteristics of a subsociety oriented toward a homeland across the seas."

The Nature of Assimilation

By assimilation we mean *the process whereby groups with different cultures come to have a common culture.* This means, of course, not merely such items of the culture as dress, knives and forks, language, food, sports, and automobiles, which are relatively easy to appreciate and acquire, but also less tangible items such as values, memories, sentiments, ideas, and attitudes. Assimilation refers thus to the fusion of cultural heritages, and must be distinguished from *amalgamation,* which denotes the biological mixture of originally distinct racial strains. It must be distinguished, too, from *naturalization,* a political concept denoting the act or process of admitting an alien to the status and privileges of a citizen. *Americanization,* of course, is simply a special case of assimilation, and refers to the process whereby a person of some foreign heritage acquires the customs, ideals, and loyalties of American society, just as Europeanization, Russianization, and Germanization denote a similar process with respect to those cultures.

These terms are related but are not interchangeable. Assimilation and amalgamation, for example, usually go together. As people acquire the habits and attitudes of another society, they are less reluctant to choose their mates from that society; and, on the other hand, the biological intermingling of different groups usually leads to cultural exchange. It need not be so, however. Full-blooded Indians have acquired the values, loyalties, and skills of our society to such a degree that they made excellent soldiers in our recent wars; while, at the same time, there have been Indian tribes into which considerable white blood has found its way, but little of the white's culture. So with naturalization. Lincoln Leung's father and mother could never hope for naturalization, regardless of how thorough their assimilation might be or how sincere their Americanization, because during their lifetime Chinese were ineligible for citizenship. Nonetheless, many have completed the process of naturalization whose familiarity with American ways was extremely casual and whose loyalty to American society highly dubious. Prior to 1906 the admission of aliens to citizenship was a function of the various states, operating under the general provisions of the federal law. There was, consequently, a great lack of uniformity in the procedure, and in many places naturalization was more or less a farce. Prior to an election immigrants were herded in droves before judges who created new citizens at the rate of hundreds per day, and all who came along would be sworn in. Needless to say, many were naturalized whose assimilation had barely begun.

The Melting Pot

Few people appreciate the difficulty one faces in trying to adjust to a strange civilization. An American, even when visiting England, where the culture is so very similar, will still confront innumerable obstacles. The monetary system is hard to comprehend, the food is different, the utensils with which one is expected to eat are somewhat unfamiliar, and even commonplace objects (elevators, thumbtacks, streetcars, subways, and so on) are called by strange names. Here at home the failure of an alien to conform to our ways is often attributed to backwardness, stubbornness, or stupidity. Assimilation, according to the popular view, is easy, simple, and speedy if one has a mind to discard primitive customs and adopt our own "superior" practices.

Between the late seventeenth century and the Revolution, the most recent immigrants had the most prestige because they were the ones who were most likely to know the latest fashions, speak proper English, have attended the best schools, and know important people. There were some exceptions to this rule. The Puritans felt that the new arrivals were more corrupt than those who came earlier, and most seemed to look down on the Germans and the "wild Irish" immigrants. The colonists knew that the country's prosperity depended on an influx of people from many nations. It was not really until about 1760 that there emerged the concept of such a thing as an "American" or an "American way of life."

At the time of the American Revolution Great Britain had the most lenient rules for naturalization of any country. All Great Britain asked of the immigrant was five years of residence and an oath of allegiance and acceptance of the Protestant establishment.   Most other countries did not allow an immigrant the right to acquire property, vote, or hold office no matter what the length of residence had been.   The interesting thing was that the American colonies were not satisfied with this law and kept trying to pass more lenient laws of naturalization, which England kept overruling.   This caused Thomas Jefferson to declare in his indictment against George III that the king "has endeavored to prevent the population of these states; for that purpose obstructing the Laws of Naturalization of Foreigners" as well as "refusing to pass others to encourage their migration hither."   One of the first acts of the new government after the Revolution was the passage of a naturalization law that required five years of residence and only an affirmation of political loyalty.

Prior to World War I the philosophy that prevailed with respect to the various ethnic elements in the population was symbolized by the phrase "the melting pot."[3]   Blacks, Indians, and Orientals, of course, were not included, but the multitudes who had been crossing the Atlantic were supposed to be undergoing a process of fusion that would eventually produce a great civilization and a race of supermen.   William Jennings Bryan eloquently voiced the faith in these words:

Great has been the Greek, the Latin, the Slav, the Celt, the Teuton, and the Saxon; but greater than any of these is the American, who combines the virtues of them all.[4]

The term "the melting pot" was taken from a play by Israel Zangwill.   In this play a Jewish violinist falls in love with a non-Jewish young woman from Russia.   At one point in the play her father comes to visit the United States and is introduced to the Jewish youth.   The young man faints when he encounters this man.   This individual had been the leader of a pogrom in Russia that had caused the death of the young man's father.   The love affair is threatened, but eventually love prevails.   The story gave Zangwill the opportunity to proclaim that America was the great melting pot in which Old-World hates were boiled out and new individuals emerged.

America is God's Crucible, the great Melting Pot where all the races of Europe are melting and reforming! — Here you stand good folk, think I, when I see you at Ellis Island, here you stand, in your fifty groups, with your fifty languages and histories, and your fifty blood hatreds and rivalries.   But you won't be long like that brothers, for these are the fires of God you come to — these are the fires of God.   A fig for your feuds and your vendettas!   German and Frenchmen, Irishman and English, Jews and Russians, into the Crucible with you all!   God is making the American! . . .   The real American has not yet arrived. . . .   He will be the fusion of all races, perhaps the coming superman. . . .   Ah, what is the glory of Rome and Jerusalem, where all races and nations come to worship and look back, compared with the glory of America, where all nations come to labour and look forward![5]

There is, of course, a large element of truth in this conception.   The error lay in its assumption that the process was easy, rapid, natural, inevitable, and would invariably produce a superior type of person. Assimilation, it was thought, would take care of itself. The melting pot theory represented the doctrine of laissez faire applied to the realm of race and culture contact.

Not everyone, however, accepted the melting pot thesis. Many assumed that a great loss would be incurred by asking the various immigrant groups to give up their previous cultures. Joseph Jacobs, an early twentieth-century historian was one who expressed this view.

The great danger of modern times is the tendency toward what may be termed Chinesism, a fatal and monotonous similarity and mediocrity invading all sections of national life. One of the outward signs of this is a deadly monotony of dress and furniture, which is becoming more and more international. The growth of intercommunication is giving a common set of ideas and ideals to the whole world, and making it more and more difficult for any special culture like the Irish, or the Japanese, or the Jewish, to hold its own. Every such specific culture that disappears would make the final form of humanity, which seems so rapidly approaching, less rich and manifold.[6]

Americanization

The mid-nineteenth to early twentieth century was a time when the United States was experiencing a great wave of immigrants, many of whom were different enough to cause concern. These immigrants tended to concentrate in the large cities and were more conspicuous than the earlier groups. Also a change had taken place in American thinking. During the pre-Civil War years most Americans regarded poverty and immigrant status as temporary situations that could be surmounted without great difficulty or government assistance. By the end of the nineteenth century Americans began to believe that immigrant status condemned the individual to a permanently inferior position in American society. It became apparent that assimilation had not been working as automatically as had been supposed. When the nation began to take stock of itself, the startling fact emerged that there were millions in the country who could neither read, speak, nor write the English language; less than half the foreign-born white males of voting age were citizens; there were thousands of organizations flourishing among the "foreign element," and hundreds of newspapers and periodicals published in foreign languages; immigrants were concentrated in "colonies" in the cities; and foreign governments were in the habit of encouraging their nationals to retain their old allegiance, not without some success.

As a result of these disclosures a new philosophy of assimilation came into being and a program, known as the Americanization Movement, was inaugurated.[7] As one wag put it, "Assimilation means your total absorption into my culture." This was essentially the philosophy that dominated the Americanization Movement. The problem was that of forcing the immigrants to divest themselves of their Old-World civilization, to sever their allegiances, to abandon their loyalties, and to embrace the culture of the United States. It was

Three immigrant children find a peaceful corner, 1889

believed, furthermore, that this American culture that the immigrant was to acquire was a finished product. The melting pot philosophy had implied a give and take. Americanization demanded a casting off of the old culture.

No longer would the assimilation of alien peoples be left to the operation of natural forces. No longer would assimilation be regarded as an inevitable outcome of the meeting of cultures. Deliberate, organized efforts would be made to divest the immigrants of their foreign heritage, to suppress their native language, to teach them English, to make of them naturalized citizens, and to inject in them a loyalty to American institutions. Many agencies participated in the movement — public schools, patriotic societies, chambers of commerce, women's clubs, public libraries, social settlements, and even industrial plants where foreigners were employed.

The movement itself was based on a misconception of the process of assimilation and, as a result, the term "Americanization" (older, of course, than the movement) fell into a certain disrepute from which it has never recovered. It made the mistake of ignoring the values in the cultures of the immigrants and assuming that these must, and could, be discarded as though they were old garments. It involved the tacit implication that American culture was a finished product in an Anglo-Saxon pattern, that it was superior to all others, and that aliens should promptly acquire it. Implicit in the movement was a spirit of coercion, condescension, and suppression, which aroused the resentment of those at whom it was directed and in the end served to defeat its purpose.

An important institution that was entrusted with the task of Americanization was the school. The school transmitted the view to the young that American society was the norm to which all youth must adjust. America was thought to be superior to all other countries and civilizations, and loyalty to the American way of life had to be developed. John Swett, a Yankee from New England who was Superintendent of public instruction in California during this period, described this view of the school best when he said; "Nothing can Americanize these chaotic elements and breathe into them the spirit of our institutions but the public school."[8]

Americanization in the schools was harsher on some groups than on others. Since many Americans were skeptical about the American Indian's potential for assimilation, a rigid policy of Americanization was thought to be imperative for Indian children. The children were treated quite severely and allowed little flexibility in retaining aspects of their culture. In a report by the Commissioner of Indian Affairs in 1881 it was bluntly stated that "the American people now demand that Indians shall become white men within one generation." Among the rules published for Indian schools in 1890 was the provision: "All instruction must be in the English language. Pupils must be compelled to converse with each other in English, and should be properly rebuked or punished for persistent violation of this rule. Every effort should be made to encourage them to abandon their tribal language."[9]

The education of Indian children was actually only a small part of the large effort at Americanization. In the period between 1850 and just before World War II, the main effort at Americanization was directed at the steady stream of immigrants. Between 1870 and 1890 one out of every seven people was foreign born. In some parts of the country almost one-fourth of the people were immigrants.[10]

Schoolteachers often insulted children for their Italian, Irish, or Jewish cultural ways and were not beyond assigning derogatory ethnic names to them. Leonard Covello, who later became a respected educator, recalls: "We soon got the idea that 'Italian' meant something pretty inferior, and a barrier was erected between children of Italian origin and their parents. . . . We were becoming Americans by learning to be ashamed of our parents."[11]

The Americanization process, even when successful for the second generation, produced a tremendous sense of loss for the first-generation immigrants.

The generation gap was often made wider by a cultural gap and a general rejection of the parents' lifestyle. In a story entitled "My Father Sits in the Dark" Jerome Weidman brings across the sense of loss and resignation that often resulted from the Americanization process.

A son speaks, troubled that each night his immigrant father "sits in the dark, alone, smoking, staring straight ahead of him." The father sits in the kitchen, on an uncomfortable chair. "What are you thinking about Pa?" "Nothing." "Is something wrong, Pop?" "Nothing, son, nothing at all." Coming home late one night, the son "can see the deeper darkness of his [father's] hunched shape. He is sitting in the same chair, his elbows on his knees, his cold pipe in his teeth, his unblinking eyes staring straight ahead." There is nothing to be said, neither quarrel nor reconciliation. "What do you think about Pop?" "Nothing," answers the father, "nothing special!" [12]

The pressure toward Americanization sometimes originated from those with similar ethnic backgrounds. Often the second- and third-generation members of the particular ethnic group were fearful that the new immigrants would increase prejudice and discrimination against the whole group and cause a lowering of their own status. The following is from a sixteen-verse poem entitled "What it is to be a Jew" by Minnie D. Louis, which was specifically written to aid in the Americanization of German Jewish immigrants. The poem begins with the image of the ghetto Jew:

To wear the yellow badge, the locks,
The caftan-long, the low bent head,
To pocket unprovoked knocks
And shamble on in servile dread —
Tis not this to be a Jew

and ended with an affirmation of the new image toward which immigrants should aspire while adjusting to the new culture:

Among the ranks of men to stand
Full noble with the noblest there;
To aid the right in every land
With mind, with might, with heart, with prayer —
This is the eternal Jew! [13]

It is not only in the United States that there has been disagreement over what is the best way of dealing with immigrants. Wherever racial and ethnic groups have met, the same problems have arisen. At one extreme is the viewpoint of laissez faire and at the other is coercion. Between these two poles our own policies have fluctuated, not only with respect to the immigrants from Europe, but with respect also to Indians, blacks, Mexicans, and Orientals. The great imperialist countries of Europe have also revealed this same ambivalence and variability, as an examination of their native policies will reveal.

The English always held themselves aloof from the native peoples of British colonies and neither encouraged nor facilitated their acquisition of British culture. The Dutch more or less followed the lead of Britain. The French, on the contrary, tended to display an intolerance and lack of sympathy for the native cultures over which they exercised domain, but approved of their colonials' acquiring the French language and culture and regarding themselves as citizens of France. Spain, Portugal, Belgium, Italy, Russia, and all other nations that have, or have had, colonial empires have been driven to develop policies that fall somewhere between compulsory assimilation, at the one extreme, and opposition or indifference to assimilation at the other.

Principles of Assimilation

The process whereby groups with different cultures come to share a common culture is not too well understood. Much thought and study has been given to the more conspicuous aspects of race relations (conflict, lynchings, riots, discrimination, segregation, and demonstrations), while those phenomena that are quiet and elusive go unnoticed. Even so, one of the first great sociological classics, *The Polish Peasant in Europe and America*, by W. I. Thomas and Florian Znaniecki, dealt with the problems of assimilation, and in the early years of the present century American sociologists did concern themselves with the problems of immigration. A generation ago anthropologists began to turn their attention to preliterate peoples whose cultures had suffered from the impact of European civilization. There are, accordingly, a few principles that are supported by a considerable body of empirical evidence.

It is reasonable to suppose that ethnic groups in contact with each other will, in spite of themselves, take on some of the customs of their neighbors; consequently, a certain degree of assimilation will occur, even though the two groups never merge into one. There is evidence for believing that this is exactly what happens, and there is some basis for the predictions of those sociologists who insist that, given sufficient time, complete assimilation will take place. There are the Fox Indians, described in Chapter 7, who long ago turned their backs on the white civilization and determined to have none of it and who have been very successful in carrying out their resolve. And yet the Fox today are using automobiles and tractors, their tepees are covered with canvas instead of buffalo hides, they consult white physicians when certain diseases strike, they understand money quite well, and in many other ways, where they least suspect it, the effects of their contacts with the whites can be seen. Who would dare predict that the Fox will continue to hold out indefinitely against the forces of assimilation?

So it is with the Tungus and the Cossacks, described in Chapter 6. These two groups have manifested no interest in adopting each other's customs and both regard their respective cultures as being quite satisfactory.   But the Tungus have acquired from the Cossacks a taste for flour, tea, sugar, tobacco, and alcohol; have grown dependent on them for lead, gunpowder, and cotton materials; and have learned from them the value of iron pots and pans, needles, scissors, thread, spoons, and forks. The Cossacks, in turn, have learned to build the Tungus type of conical shelter for use during the harvest, to wear leather garments of the Tungus fashion when they go hunting in winter, and have acquired a taste for bread baked, Tungus style, without an oven.   Centuries hence, if they continue to live in close contact with each other, perhaps their differences will be entirely obliterated.

These, and many similar cases, lend support to the theory that assimilation is an inevitable consequence of the meeting of groups.   There are instances, however, where ethnic groups have been in contact for long periods of time, where the assimilation has been at a bare minimum and where one would have to posit a very long time indeed for the fusion of the cultures.

Handman has reported such a situation on the Transylvanian Plateau in Central Europe.[14] Here, he says, is a population of 4½ million, 55 percent of them Rumanian, 34 percent Magyar, and 9 percent German.   Originally the Magyars and Germans came into the region as conquerors and colonists and they have retained their position of dominance in economic and political affairs.   These three ethnic groups, Handman tells us, have been living in fairly close contact for *nearly 1000 years* and yet have remained culturally distinct. The Magyars are Roman Catholics, Calvinists, and Unitarians; the Germans are Lutherans; and the Rumanians are Greek Catholics and Greek Orientals. Their costumes are different; they have different diets and the food preferences of one group are regarded by another as nasty habits; each group has its own language, to which it is passionately devoted; and each has its own peculiar folkways and traditions pertaining to courtship, marriage, births, funerals, amusements, art, songs, and dances.   Handman recognizes the fact that there has been a certain amount of cultural interchange; the Rumanian language contains a few words of foreign origin, the houses show the German influence, and the architecture of the Magyar peasant betrays Rumanian influence. These are minor considerations, however, in view of a thousand years of contact: and their paucity gives little basis for predicting that the future will see any appreciable assimilation.

From Guatemala comes another suggestion that contact between groups does not invariably lead to their assimilation.[15] The Indians in Guatemala are organized into local groups, known as *municipios*, somewhat comparable to our townships, but actually very important ethnic units. The members of a *municipio* think of themselves as a distinct people, biologically and socially. Each *municipio* has its own typical costume, which distinguishes its wearer from other groups. The various *municipios* differ, also, in their etiquette, types of houses, food and cooking, and in their customs pertaining to birth, baptism, marriage, burial, kinship, and family organization. In short, they are, in reality, distinct ethnic groups. Although they are in constant contact, they have virtually no wish to adopt one another's customs.

Their failure to become assimilated, however, is not due to isolation.   On the contrary, the *municipios* are not far apart and the Indians frequently travel from one to another.   Public markets are a common feature of all the towns, and the Indians gather from near and far to exchange their products on market days.   There are ample opportunities for the Indians of one *municipio* to become acquainted with the customs of another; and, as a matter of fact, they do know a great deal about the cultures of their neighbors.   Neither isolation nor ignorance, therefore, can explain their failure to assimilate.   There does seem to be a minimum of culture borrowing.   New remedies that have proved their worth are likely to be adopted by persons from the other *municipios*, when they learn about them; and so with new crops and new techniques for growing them.   The Indians are not so likely to display conservatism when the new item can be translated readily into dollars and cents.   There are not many items of such a nature, however, and the process of assimilation, accordingly, moves at an incredibly slow pace.

Dr. Tax, who made the study of Guatemala here cited, accounts for the situation on two grounds.   One feature that runs through all the cultures of the various *municipios* is the emphasis placed on the impersonal character of social relations, whether they be economic, religious, or familial.   It is possible, therefore, for one to establish frequent and widespread relations with one's neighbors with a minimum of the kind of intimate contacts that are most conducive to the exchange of cultural items.   Second, and more important, is the fact that cultural variability is regarded by the Indians as a perfectly natural and normal condition, and this makes for great tolerance of differences and no strong wish to imitate each other's practices.   Cultures vary, they think, from place to place just as do flora and fauna, and that is the way it should be. "That is their custom; it is all right for them," is their general attitude.   It is not surprising, then, that one's neighbors in a nearby *municipio* should dress, eat, or worship in a way that is not evaluated as either good or bad, desirable or undesirable.   Such a philosophy, which conceives of culture as so closely tied to geography and biology, would indeed retard the assimilative process.

A third case of ethnic contact that did not result in assimilation has been reported from the continent of Asia.[16]   In the southern part of India, high in the Nilgiri Hills, there live four groups, or tribes: the Todas, a pastoral people; the Badagas, agriculturalists; the Kotas, artisans and musicians; and the Kurumbas, sorcerers, food gatherers, and jungle dwellers.   A century ago the British discovered the plateau on which these peoples live and built roads and developed it as a place of refuge from the summer heat of the plains below.   Prior to that time, however, and for many centuries, these four tribes had the plateau entirely to themselves.

They were in close contact with one another.   Each was highly specialized, and they traded among themselves extensively.   The Todas furnished the dairy products; the Badagas traded their grain and other farm produce; the Kotas specialized in the manufacture of pottery and ironware, and their musicians were called in by the other tribes to perform on important occasions; and the primitive Kurumbas, whose sorcerers were feared and respected, were sought out in times of crisis to practice their magic. Yet in spite of these close and constant contacts, the four cultures had little in common.

Mandelbaum, in his study of the situation, says, "There was some cultural give and take among the tribes; the great wonder is that it amounted to so little." In explaining the failure of these peoples to become assimilated, he points to three facts: (1) the totally different economic base on which each society operated, giving each a focus of interest to which the others could make little contribution; (2) the contacts, although frequent, were narrowly defined, strictly regulated by custom and tradition, and intimacy was stringently tabooed; and (3) the resistance each offered to another's adopting its customs. He cites the occasion when a few Kotas began imitating the Badagas by wearing turbans. The Badagas ambushed and beat up the offenders and thereby prevented the spread of that particular custom.

The arrival of the British, bringing with them Hindus and Moslems, created a new problem for these people. They have not been as successful in resisting the influence of these new civilizations, nor in coping with them, as they had been before. Consequently, rapid and disruptive social changes have been occurring in the Nilgiri Hills during the past century, but the four tribes have reacted differently to this impact, and the effects have been more disastrous for some than for others.

In most instances, when racial and ethnic groups come together, there is considerably more cultural interchange than in the three cases we have cited, and even in these three there is a certain amount of borrowing one from the other. The process of assimilation, then, does seem to operate whenever peoples meet; but there are many situations, in addition to those discussed here, in which the interchange is so restricted and so retarded that one must hesitate before concluding that cultural fusion is an inevitable consequence of intergroup contact. Certainly, there are peoples who have lived in close contact for very long periods without any appreciable degree of cultural fusion having taken place.

A Reciprocal Process

Assimilation involves the *integration* of new elements with the old. The transferring of a culture from one group to another is a highly complex process. It is not a simple matter of addition and subtraction. It often involves the rejection of ancient ideologies, habits, customs, language, and sentiments. It involves, also, the elusive problem of *selection*. Of the many possibilities presented by the other culture, which ones will be adopted? Why did the Indians, for instance, when they were confronted with the white civilization, take avidly to guns, horses, rum, knives, and glass beads, while manifesting no interest in certain other features to which the whites themselves attached the highest value? And, when new items of culture are selected for adoption, the problem of integration is presented, for assimilation means more than the superficial addition of another folkway or the acquisition of another gadget.

In the process of assimilation one society "sets the pattern," for the give-and-take of culture seems never to operate on a "fifty-fifty" basis. Invariably one group receives more than it gives. Various factors interact to make this so. Usually one of the societies enjoys greater prestige than the other, giving it an advantage in the assimilative process; or one is better suited to the environment than the other; or one enjoys greater numerical strength than the other. Thus the pattern for the United States was set by the British colonists, and to that pattern the other ethnic groups have adapted themselves — German, Italian, Greek, black, and Chinese.

This is not to say, however, that assimilation is a one-way process. Most sociologists, anthropologists, and historians who have studied the problem of race relations would disagree and insist that assimilation is reciprocal. The Tungus learn much from the Cossacks, but they also teach them certain things; the Leung family, while it proceeds to acquire a taste for everything American, from thermos bottles to Santa Claus, introduces Americans to a variety of ancient Chinese herb remedies.

The cultural contributions of the various ethnic groups that have migrated to the United States are difficult to trace, but they have been numerous. Most of these contributions have become so thoroughly integrated into our culture that we do not suspect that they are relatively recent additions. Grimm alfalfa was introduced into Minnesota by an immigrant who brought the seed with him from Germany; the Germans did much to develop pure-bred horses, cattle, and hogs; Mennonites, who came from Russia to Kansas, brought with them hard wheat; Russian and Ukrainian farmers brought Kherson oats; Hungarians planted the first Tokay grapes in California; Danes developed the dairy industry; Germans introduced sauerkraut and frankfurters; Italians, spaghetti. Much of our interest in music can doubtless be attributed to the influence of German, Jewish, and Italian immigrants.

It is much easier to determine the extent to which Indians, in the course of their assimilation, have influenced our civilization.[17] Everyone knows, of course, that Indians discovered, utilized, and developed tobacco and maize; but it is not so generally known that we are indebted to the Indians, also, for our knowledge of the potato, the kidney bean, the tomato, the peanut, chocolate, squash, maple sugar, the pineapple, the avocado, and about thirty-five other food plants. Had the Indians not learned to cultivate these plants it is doubtful that the whites ever would have, for they would probably have introduced the crops with which they were already familiar in the Old World. This alone is no small contribution, but it does not begin to exhaust the list. It was from the Indians that the whites learned about the art of woodcraft, various medicinal plants (cascara, witch hazel, cocaine, quinine), canoes, snowshoes, toboggans, moccasins, hammocks, and rubber. Finally, the Indians have had an influence on our art, architecture, and literature; and no less than five hundred words in our language were appropriated from Indian tongues. There can be no doubt that, in the course of our attempts to assimilate the American Indian, the process has been reciprocal.

The assimilative process has been reciprocal for blacks in the United States also. This, however, has not been the accepted theory. Scholarly opinion has long inclined to the view that the blacks, in the course of their enslavement and transportation to the New World, lost every vestige of their African culture. It would have been impossible, the scholars have said, for people to preserve their cultural heritage when they were captured and sold into slavery, when their tribal and family units were broken up and they were widely dispersed in their new environment. Moreover, the slave owners themselves deliberately encouraged the destruction of the African culture, for they realized that the problem of control would be immeasurably greater if their slaves spoke a strange language, retained their old religion, and were permitted to cherish their ancient customs and traditions. Every effort was made, therefore, to destroy the African culture and put in its place a simple version of the white civilization. Frazier has expressed as follows the opinion which has been shared by many another:

Probably never before in history has a people been so nearly completely stripped of its social heritage as the Negroes who were brought to America. Other conquered races have continued to worship their household gods within the intimate circle of their kinsmen. But American slavery destroyed household gods and dissolved the bonds of sympathy and affection between men of the same blood and household. Old men and women might have brooded over memories of their African homeland, but they could not change the world about them. Through force of circumstances, they had to acquire a new language, adopt new habits of labor, and take over, however imperfectly, the folkways of the American environment. Their children, who knew only the American environment, soon forgot the few memories that had been passed on to them and developed motivations and modes of behavior in harmony with the New World. Their children's children have often recalled with skepticism the fragments of stories concerning Africa which have been preserved in their families. But of the habits and customs as well as the hopes and fears that characterized the life of their forbears in Africa, nothing remains.[18]

Herskovits has challenged this widely held theory, which would make assimilation a distinctly one-sided affair as far as the American blacks are concerned.[19] Many suspect that Herskovits, in his zeal to discover a cultural heritage for blacks has overstated the case; but, in the face of the evidence he has presented, no one can insist any longer that the black contribution to American civilization has been negligible. It has long been suspected that African influence may be seen in black music, dancing, and folklore (tales, riddles, proverbs, and jokes) and Herskovits finds considerable support for this view. He maintains, moreover, that Africanisms of many other kinds have survived, such as in methods of planting, codes of polite behavior, conceptions of time, habits of cooperative labor, fondness for lodges and societies, family organization, beliefs and attitudes concerning personal names, customs and superstitions associated with death, and customs and beliefs centering on children. In short, a considerable body of African culture has survived to this day among American blacks and no small part of it has found its way into the thought and behavior patterns of the whites.

The reciprocal character of assimilation is more clearly seen in Brazil, where contacts between white Portuguese and their black slaves were especially close and where the opportunities for the preservation of African culture were greater than they were in the United States. Freyre and Pierson have both reported innumerable items in the Brazilian culture whose origin may be traced back to Africa, including many words in the language, articles of food, methods of cooking, manner of speaking, practices connected with cattle-raising and agriculture, folk tales and folk medicines, gestures, names, costumes, superstitions, music, and dancing.[20]

A Slow Process of Uneven Pace

One fact stands out in bold relief in all the studies of assimilation that have been made, and that is the unhurried pace at which the process moves. Even under the most favorable circumstances, it takes a long time for two cultures to fuse. Individuals who are reared in one society and have acquired its culture could not possibly, in one lifetime, completely divest themselves of all that they have learned and succeed in taking on the customs, language, beliefs, ideals, attitudes, and skills of another society. Even their children are not likely to do so, nor their grandchildren, unless the numerous obstacles to assimilation that are usually present have been removed. No time limit can be given for the assimilative process because it varies so much from place to place, from group to group, and from one item in the culture to another.

The tangible objects of a culture are usually the ones most readily adopted. W. C. Smith records a great number of these.[21] He tells of the Mexican boy who entered a school in Texas and had the harrowing experience of being laughed at by the others because he wore suspenders, following the custom of his people. "After a while," he said, "I got some money and bought me a belt, so I would not have to wear the suspenders." Rumanian immigrants soon realized that their attire was arousing the curiosity, and sometimes the scorn, of people on the streets, and hastened to adopt the dress of Americans. A Puerto Rican in New York grew self-conscious because people looked at him and laughed, until a friend told him that the trouble was with the hat he wore.

Pihlblad, describing the assimilative process as it operated with the Swedes who settled in central Kansas, says:

In matters of making a living and in economic organization adjustment to American conditions was most rapid. The style of farming in Sweden of the sixties was entirely unadapted to Kansas conditions. . . . It would be difficult to find any essential differences in economic organization of these Swedish communities from any pioneer American settlement on the Kansas plains. In clothing and shelter the Swedes were quick to take on the patterns which they found. The early homes were log cabins or dugouts common to all pioneer settlements. . . . In matters of clothing also the prevailing modes of dress were not different from those worn by non-Swedish people. The desire to be like an American in matters of clothing is manifested by the experiences of the writer's grandmother. Her last dollar, on arriving in Kansas City, was spent for the purchase of a hoop skirt in the American style. Pictures from the early period indicate that there was little to distinguish the Swedish immigrant from non-Swedish people.

In general, it may be said that in seeking food, shelter, and clothing the Swedish immigrant immediately adopted the patterns he found in America.[22]

It is a different story, however, when it comes to other items. Pihlblad reports that the Swedes clung to the paternalistic family, looked with disfavor on marriage with non-Swedes, opposed the introduction into their community of movies and pool halls, held to the Lutheran faith, and were slow to replace the Swedish language with English.

Even the adoption of the external, tangible features of the new culture is not without problems. The costume of the Amish has a religious significance and cannot be readily discarded for the prevailing style; and the beard of the orthodox Jew is not shaved off without an inner struggle, even when it is recognized as an economic obstacle. A Greek woman said about American food:

I almost starved before I could learn to eat American food. It seemed to me painfully tasteless. . . . As for the potatoes, I had never seen such quantities in my life. We had them for breakfast, for luncheon and for dinner, in some form or other. Just before we sat down to the table the principal said grace, in which were the words, "Bless that of which we are about to partake." To my untrained ear "partake" and "potatoes" sounded exactly alike, and I wrote home that the Americans not only ate potatoes morning, noon, and night, but they even prayed to the Lord to keep them supplied with potatoes, instead of daily bread.[23]

The assimilation process has run its complete course when the newcomers (or their children, or granchildren) cease to think of themselves as either aliens or hyphenated Americans, but simply as Americans, and are so regarded by the host society.

The various racial and ethnic groups differ widely in the rapidity with which they become assimilated. It is a commonplace observation that British immigrants to the United States are quickly and readily melted and lost, and that others become adjusted more slowly. Occasionally, nations have become impatient over the time it takes immigrant groups to become assimilated and have attempted to speed up the process. This has occurred in the nation of Israel. The pioneers who conceived and established that state were mostly from European countries and it was their desire to transplant Western civilization in the new nation. However, on the very day when the people of Israel declared their independence, they opened their gates to Jewish immigration from the four corners of the earth. Immediately immigrants began to pour into the country, coming from all six continents and from seventy to eighty nations. The entire Jewish communities of Yemen and Bulgaria, and almost all the Jews of Libya,

Tripolitania, Yugoslavia, and Iraq came to Israel. The sheer magnitude of the migration created huge problems of employment, housing, education, and health. An even more startling challenge to the new nation came from the diversity of the cultural backgrounds represented. It was feared by many that Israel might become more Oriental than European in its cultural complexion. Teachers, government officials, social workers, and social scientists began to concern themselves with the problem of assimilating (or "absorbing," to use their word) this flood of non-European Jews. Nor did they think they could afford the luxury of allowing time to take its course. Consequently, a variety of measures was taken and institutions were created to "Westernize" the Oriental Jews who were arriving in such huge numbers. Schools were utilized to the fullest extent, youth organizations undertook tasks of assimilation, methods of foster placement of children were employed, and even the army took on the additional function of introducing immigrants to a new culture.[24]

Problems of assimilation, according to Joseph W. Eaton, have been handled rather wisely by immigrants of a religious sect known as Hutterites, who came to the United States and Canada some ninety years ago and settled in the provinces of Manitoba and Alberta and the states of Montana and South Dakota.[25] The Hutterites consider themselves a people chosen by God to live the only true Christian way of life. They originated in Switzerland in 1528, where they were persecuted by both Protestants and Catholics and were nearly exterminated. In 1770 some of them went to Russia, where they had been promised religious freedom. A century later they fled, because of attempts to enforce Russification on them, and crossed the Atlantic.

The Hutterites are ardent pacifists, and emphasize simplicity in every aspect of living. Their isolated, self-sufficient rural communities are said to be virtually free of crime, divorce, suicide, insanity, lonesomeness, friendlessness, uncertainty, and insecurity. The aged, the ill, and the infirm are generally well protected and cared for. Even quarreling is very rare. They have a communal system of sharing property and products of labor. They have their own schools, and children are indoctrinated systematically so that they grow up to believe and act in accordance with the group's traditions.

They do, however, have some contacts with their American and Canadian neighbors, whom they refer to as "the outside," and there are pressures for change and assimilation. Some of these pressures come from "the outside." Their communities are visited occasionally by salespersons, government officials, teachers, and doctors. They have business contacts with nearby villages. Modern means of transportation place them within an hour or two of Winnipeg, Sioux Falls, or some other city. The women, who in the past seldom left their colonies, now accompany their husbands on trips to town.

There are pressures for change also from the "inside." The younger Hutterites frequently learn to want some of the things they see their neighbors possessing and enjoying. They desire more individual freedom and initiative, and they come to regard as necessities certain items which their elders insist are luxuries.

This situation could very well lead to discord, dissatisfaction, family conflict, cleavage between older and younger generations, and community disorganization. The Hutterites, however, according to Eaton, have developed techniques for bringing about gradual social change and for holding in check the speed of the assimilative process.

"By bending with the wind," says Eaton, "Hutterites have kept themselves from breaking." Believing as they do that people are born to sin, they do not expect perfect and complete compliance with all the rules and traditions of their sect. They do not expel or punish a person for deviating *slightly* from the narrow path of custom. Nor do they possess a body of written rules covering systematically and comprehensively the whole of life. They are governed, rather, by their ancient traditions, which are transmitted to each succeeding generation through example and oral instruction.

They do enact formal rules from time to time. When some innovation or deviation becomes widespread in one or more of their communities, the leaders are likely to decide that a formal and official statement is required. A new rule, accordingly, will be proposed at an intercolony meeting of elected lay preachers. If such a formal rule is adopted by this body, it is read to the governing assemblies of male members in every colony. Adoption or rejection is by majority vote of all baptized males. New rules are not lightly and carelessly proposed. The leaders keep their ears to the ground and never adopt a new rule unless they are convinced that public opinion is solidly behind them. Nor do they repeal a rule that has grown obsolete; they simply refrain from enforcing it. In this manner the Hutterites accept cultural innovations before the demand for them becomes so great as to threaten the group's harmony and cohesiveness.

A few examples will illustrate how this occurs. The Hutterites insist on simple and unostentatious dress for men and women. However, through their contacts with those on "the outside," they become aware of styles and fashions, and some of them succumb to the pressure. Boys and young men began buying grey hats and pith helmets until a rule was adopted stipulating blacks hats only. Tradition demanded that clothes be fastened with hooks and eyes; but a rule was made that buttons "could be retained," indicating that their use had become common. Sweaters began to be worn, until a rule was forthcoming requiring that they be "summarily gotten rid of." Members began wearing shoes that they bought in town, in preference to the homemade ones, and finally the purchase of all types of shoes was authorized, but only in certain approved styles. In similar manner they came to adopt fur linings for winter clothes, mattresses, motor vehicles, refrigerators, and a host of other once-forbidden items. Thus the process of assimilation moves, but is well controlled.

Stages of Assimilation

Gordon[26] believes that the assimilation process involves a series of steps or subprocesses, which he has outlined in Table 12.1. Assimilation can be divided into several parts. First, there is what is known as *behavioral assimilation*, in which the newcomer accepts the cultural norms and behaves outwardly

Table 12.1   The assimilation variables

Subprocess or condition	Type or stage of assimilation	Special term
Change of cultural patterns to those of host society	Cultural or behavioral assimilation	Acculturation
Large-scale entrance into cliques, clubs, and institutions of host society, on primary group level	Structural assimilation	None
Large-scale intermarriage	Marital assimilation	Amalgamation
Development of sense of peoplehood based exclusively on host society	Identificational assimilation	None
Absence of prejudice	Attitude receptional assimilation	None
Absence of discrimination	Behavior receptional assimilation	None
Absence of value and power conflict	Civic assimilation	None

From *Assimilation in American Life: The Role of Race, Religion, and National Origins* by Milton M. Gordon. Copyright © 1964 by Oxford University Press, Inc. Reprinted by permission.

like a native person. Here the individual is trying to act like an inhabitant of the country to which he or she has emigrated.

On the other hand, with *structural assimilation*, the immigrant becomes involved in primary and secondary relationships with the natives. Most immigrants have structural relationships that are of the secondary and impersonal type with storekeepers and others they come in contact with. However, primary types of relationships, in which the immigrant establishes close personal friendships with the native people, seldom develop for the first generation. Intermarriage between an immigrant and a native person usually has to be preceded by primary structural assimilation. Since this is rarely the case with recent immigrants, very few of them marry a native resident of the new country.

Social participation can take place in a number of areas. It begins at the occupational level. The individual who works will have, of necessity, some on-the-job social contact with coworkers. Then the individual's children enter school and interact with the other children. If the individual gets involved with religious activities in the community, contact is made with others of the same religion. A later stage is political participation in which the individual assumes citizenship, votes, and possibly joins political clubs. Finally, social participation on an interpersonal level may occur. It is possible that an individual may be assimilating in all, or only some, of these areas.

This immigrant slept in that cellar for four years, circa 1890

True social participation in a society goes beyond the mere acceptance of norms. It involves an acceptance of and by other people. Complete participation in a society involves not only the acceptance of the norms, but also interaction with members of the society. For example, a person may observe all the norms of a society, but have no interest in participating in social activities with the members of that society. Or a newcomer may observe all the norms and still not be accepted by the native people.

Each society has different levels of roles with which the immigrant must deal. *Universal roles* are patterns of behavior that are demanded of everyone in a society. Many of these are enforced by the law; if the individual does not observe them, he or she will encounter great conflict and will not be tolerated by the society. The next level is *specialized roles*, which are the patterns of behavior that are expected of certain people in society, such as doctors or lawyers. Finally, there are *alternative roles*, which include a wide variety of accepted practices according to individual preferences that are permitted by a society. This area allows a pluralistic society to become a mosaic of varied cultural practices, perhaps inclusive of many Old-World customs.[27]

Every immigrant group, with the exception of the English in the United States, has formed cultural enclaves or homogeneous communities to act as a

Typical immigrant accommodations

buffer between that group and the outside society. To some extent this has made it easier for the group to adjust without an extreme disruption of the previous life its members had known. The first-generation immigrants usually interact with this enclave in a primary fashion and with the rest of society in a secondary manner. The only exception to this rule would be for some professionals and intellectuals who, because of their prestige, move into primary relationships with the native born more quickly than others.

True assimilation usually occurs in the second and third generation, only rarely in the first. The second generation venture out of the enclave and develop primary relationships with the native residents; this step results in inevitable conflict between the members of the first and second generations. The younger generation is often embarrassed by the Old-World customs and behavior of their parents. In the following excerpt, written by Irving Howe about his boyhood, we see an example of this conflict. The interesting thing is that his friends are also second-generation immigrants, yet they are just as embarrassed as he to bring their peers home to meet their parents.

There never seemed any place to go. The thought of bringing my friends home was inconceivable, for I would have been as ashamed to show them to my parents as to show my parents to them. Besides where would people sit in those cramped apartments? The worldly manner affected by some of my friends would have stirred flames of suspicion in the eyes of my father; the sullen immigrant kindliness of my parents would have struck my friends as all too familiar; and my own self-consciousness, which in regard to my parents led me into a maze of superfluous lies and trivial deceptions, made it difficult for me to believe in a life grounded in simple good faith. . . .

So we walked the streets, never needing to tell one another why we chose this neutral setting for our escape at evening.[28]

Both a Conscious and an Unconscious Process

Immigrants who adopt American dress, of course, know precisely what they are doing and why they are doing it. When they study the new language, build a home like their neighbor's, buy a new implement and learn to use it, they are consciously participating in a culture that they hope to make their own. Missionaries, teachers, and foreign representatives of business concerns are deliberately seeking to produce changes in a people's culture and to promote assimilation, whether or not they describe their work in sociological terms. Governments have frequently initiated programs and policies for the stated purpose of promoting homogeneity among their citizens. Many sociologists, however, have been impressed by the relative paucity of these conscious and deliberate changes. Panunzio goes so far as to define assimilation as the process by which "individuals or groups of varying cultures *more or less unconsciously* exchange and fuse culture traits or complexes,"[29] and Park states that "assimilation in any case takes place gradually and by degrees so slight that they are not open to observation or measurement."[30] Changes in one's pronunciation, gestures and mannerisms, attitudes, values, sentiments, loyalties, and tastes do indeed come about by a slow and imperceptible process of which the individual is hardly aware. Jonassen comments on the fact that Norwegians become Americanized without realizing it; and it comes as a shock to them when, returning to the Old Country, they discover that they have lost the mastery of the language (which they had no desire to do) and have grown so far away from the old culture that they no longer feel happy in its presence.[31]

The Rate of Assimilation

Differences in the rate of assimilation, as reflected by various racial and ethnic groups, have received a great deal of attention from sociologists. Certainly there is no single explanation, but rather a number of interacting factors that must be taken into consideration to understand the phenomenon.

Attitudes of the Dominant or Host Group

The attitudes of the dominant group in a society toward the newcomers in its midst are subject to wide variation, but whatever they be, they profoundly affect the process of assimilation. Among many primitive and ancient peoples there was a *general* hostility toward strangers and their presence was not tolerated. This was true of many medieval communities of Europe; and Japan was a thorough-going isolationist nation until 1853, when Commodore Perry opened the country, much against its will. An ancient Japanese proverb had it, "When you see a stranger, count him a robber." In most cases, however, the attitude of hostility is directed toward certain *specific* racial or ethnic groups, while toward others there may be shown sentiments of hospitality, or at least of tolerance.

In the United States certain ethnic groups have consistently been accepted by the host society, while others have had every possible obstacle to social participation and assimilation thrown in their way. The following story of a second-generation American of mixed English and Irish ancestry indicates a process of adjustment that has been relatively painless:

I seldom think of myself as other than American. . . . If, in my youth, I never gave the seemingly spontaneous Americanization of my parents a thought, it probably seemed natural to me that, speaking the same language, my people adjusted themselves naturally and painlessly. It was, therefore, quite a shock to me to hear the statement that the English are the hardest people to Americanize. . . .[32]

The Chinese, on the other hand, are a people whose assimilation has been retarded by the prejudices and discriminations to which they have been subjected. The following story is evidence of that fact:

Lots of people insult me. Once I remember I go barber shop. I sit one hour no ask me what I want. Pretty soon barber say, "What you want?" I tell him I want hair cut, how much? He say $3. That make me mad, but I make him cut my hair just same. I say, "All right, I have my hair cut." He give me good hair cut. When he through I pay him $3.50. He very surprised. He tell me come again. I never go to white bastard again. . . .
   When I in Portland I want to live in residential district, but they make lots of trouble if you try to live outside Chinatown. One friend he buy $6,000 house in select city district. White people make hell lot trouble for him. They take it to court. He fight it. Just the same they kick him out. He can own house but no live there. Those people very uncivilized. Have no regard for humanity. So when my friend have so much trouble I decided to stay in Chinatown. Nobody care there.[33]

Some groups, like the Irish, have seen a great change in attitude manifested toward them. Hansen says that when the Irish first began to pour into New England, they were regarded by the residents as stupid, dirty, diseased, superstitious, and untrustworthy.[34] Farmers would give them jobs only when forced by a labor shortage to do so, and then they complained; and the factories would take them on if no other employees were available, but would give them only the lowest positions. An article in *The Massachusetts Teacher* in 1851 described them as follows:

The Germans who are next in numbers, will give us no trouble. They are more ob-
stinate, more strongly wedded to their own notions and customs than the Irish; but they
have, inherently, the redeeming qualities of industry, frugality, and pride, which will
save them from vice and pauperism, and they may be safely left to take care of themselves. But the poor Irish, the down-trodden, priest-ridden of centuries, come to us in
another shape. So cheaply have they been held at home — so closely have they been
pressed down in the social scale — that for the most part the simple virtues of industry,
temperance, and frugality are unknown to them; and that wholesome pride which will
induce a German, or a native American, to work hard from sun to sun for the smallest
wages, rather than seek or accept charitable aid, has literally been crushed out of them.

The Yankee's attitude toward the Irish has undergone something of a meta-
morphosis, and while Irish ancestry may not yet be an asset, it certainly does
not carry the stigma that it once did, nor does it prevent one's elevation to the
presidency of the United States.

It must be pointed out, however, that a favorable attitude on the part of the
dominant group toward a minority is no assurance of rapid assimilation. The
Useems have shown that the Norwegians in North Dakota have retained much
of their Old World culture even though they have never been persecuted by
their neighbors, or been assigned to an inferior status socially or economically,
or been forced to study and imitate the customs of their neighbors in order to
cater to or compete with them.[35]

Attitudes of the Minority Group

The case of these Norwegians suggests that the rate of assimilation is affected by
the attitudes of the minority as well as by those of the dominant group in the
society. There are, of course, many instances of subordinate groups whose
overwhelming wish is to become completely assimilated, even amalgamated.
American blacks wage a perpetual battle against discrimination and "second-
class citizenship." What they want is integration, or full participation, in
American life. But there are groups that fear assimilation and resist it to the
utmost, while others want it only to a certain degree.

The case is reported from one of the islands of Micronesia, where the chief
of the Kanaka, confronted with all the marvels of white civilization, would
have none of them. When told of the benefits to be derived from an acceptance of Western culture, he replied:

Benefits! Too many benefits! Before the foreigners came we lived in peace. The forest
fed us — simply but sufficiently. We did not work. Is work a virtue when there is
nothing to be gained by it? Neighbors were friendly, children were obedient. Life was
a trade wind without gusts or squalls. But now comes struggle — struggle to make
money. Money for what? We do not need clothing — the sunshine clothes us. We
do not need an iron roof to carry rain water into a cement tank. The water that streams
down the trunk of a tree can be turned into a jar. We do not need farming tools of iron
and steel. We can make our own from the shell of the giant clam. We do not need
alarm clocks and phonographs and electric lights. They spoil the sounds of the forests
and the light of the moon. We do not need the telephone — we can talk to those on

faraway plantations through the shell trumpet. We do not need schools. The father can teach his children all that is necessary for our manner of life. We do not need hospitals. This is a small island — if some did not die there would soon be too many people, too little food. But our young men are upset by the idea that they must do something, even if it is something useless. On the athletic field near the school a track has been made where boys may run around in a circle. That is what civilization is — running around in a circle.[36]

The mere desire on the part of an ethnic group to retain its traditional culture is not, of course, sufficient to ensure it against the forces of assimilation. The Russian Molokans, who migrated to Los Angeles, were determined to perpetuate their way of life, but have found the task too great for them.[37] The Amish and Mennonites, on the other hand, have met with considerable success in their determination to keep their identity.

An interesting case of resistance to assimilation comes from Brazil.[38] At the close of our Civil War several thousand Southerners, convinced that they could not live in a country dominated by blacks and Yankees, emigrated to South America. They went with every intention of perpetuating the culture that they valued. They chose Brazil, in fact, because it was ruled by a rural aristocracy, still had the institution of slavery, and possessed the climate and soil suitable to the cultivation of cotton, tobacco, sugar cane, and watermelons. They had visions of carving out large plantations, building mansions of Southern style, maintaining retinues of slaves, and carrying on as though the war had never been fought.

They made a desperate effort to realize their dream, but the obstacles were greater than they had supposed. The process of assimilation began to operate immediately on their arrival. Most of them had to compromise on their homes, and settle for dwellings more Brazilian than Southern. Indian and black women, whom they engaged as domestics, taught them about the local foods and how to prepare them so that one of them, writing to the editor of the New Orleans *Times* in December, 1867, could say, "We have already learned to love it." Other features of the Brazilian culture were more distasteful to them. The language was an obstacle; the labor force, unaccustomed to continuous work, was exasperating; slavery in Brazil was not the same institution that they had known in the South; roads were nonexistent; they had difficulty in establishing schools and churches; and the operations of the government were disappointing and disheartening. Most difficult of all, however, was the racial situation. Color was not the dominant criterion of status, and the relations between the races were incredibly shocking to them.

Some of them could not take it, and returned to the United States. Others put aside their pride, refused to regard manual labor as degrading, and sought to make the necessary adjustments. Some, failing to make a go of their farms, migrated to the cities, married Brazilians, and their descendants today are doubtless completely assimilated. As far as is known, Vila Americana, in São Paulo, is the only one of their communities remaining. One may see there an occasional American flag, plantation houses of Southern style, and hear English spoken with a Portuguese accent and Portuguese with an English accent;

but the crucial fact is that the grandchildren of the pioneers feel that they are Brazilians, and are so regarded.

Cultural Kinship

The rate of assimilation is greatly affected by the similarity or dissimilarity of the two cultures in contact. Schermerhorn comments on the fact that the Czechs in the United States have become assimilated much more rapidly than their fellow nationals, the Slovaks, and inquires into the reasons.[39] He finds that a differentiation between these two peoples can be traced to their historical backgrounds in the Old World. Their experiences were such that the Czechs became more literate than the Slovaks, they enjoyed a period of political tutelage that fostered democratic tendencies, they acquired a higher standard of living, they became skilled as workmen and professionals, and they developed a familiarity with the highly respected German culture. All these characteristics stood them in good stead when they migrated to the United States and gave them a distinct advantage over the Slovaks, who possessed them all in less degree.

Among the aspects of culture that facilitate assimilation, none is the equal of language. It has been pointed out repeatedly that the rapidity with which the Irish were assimilated into American society can be largely explained by the fact that they already had on arrival a command of English. So important is language, both as the carrier of culture and as the tool for acquiring a culture, that many sociologists regard statistics on the native tongue as the best index of a group's assimilation.

Religion, too, may serve either to retard or to accelerate the assimilation of a people. Huguenots who came to the United States quickly appreciated the fact that their Protestant faith made them more acceptable as citizens; and the widely publicized fact that the Armenians are a Christian people has mitigated the difficulties of their adjustment. On the other hand, those who have brought with them their Buddhist or Moslem faith have simply encountered one more obstacle to their assimilation.

It is so with all the other items and values of the culture. American society places great emphasis on thrift, foresight, and diligence, and accords a readier welcome to those whose social heritage includes these same virtues than it does to those who relegate them to a minor position. In the American hierarchy of values a high place is accorded to literacy, cleanliness, speed, wealth, competition, indulgence of family members, and so on. In other societies entirely different scales of values prevail. The rapidity and the ease with which assimilation occurs depend on the similarity in the rank order of values held by the groups in contact.

Race

The rate of assimilation may be seriously affected by the racial features of the peoples in a contact situation. Societies differ, of course, in the social significance they attach to such characteristics as skin color, hair form, eyes, lips, and width of nose. Among some, no significance whatsoever is attached to these racial traits. The Tungus and Cossacks pay no attention to them at all. In Brazil some weight is attached to them, but not a great deal. In many societies, however, such as those of South Africa and the United States, these biological features are regarded as of prime importance. They profoundly affect the status and role of the individual and largely determine residential patterns, organizational membership, church attendance, and even health and longevity. Needless to say, racial features will play a very important role in the assimilative process in societies of this latter type, determining how long the process will take and even whether or not it will occur at all.

Other Factors

Many other factors affect the rate of assimilation, either favorably or adversely, and have received the attention of sociologists. Among these are: (1) the relative numbers of the groups involved in the contact situation; (2) the rate of entrance of the minority group; (3) the manner of settlement, whether rural or urban, and the extent of its isolation; (4) the age and sex composition of the groups; (5) the influence of certain personalities, either in opposing or encouraging assimilation. Not to be overlooked, too, are the crises which arise, sometimes stimulating the assimilative process and sometimes reversing the trend altogether. The Civil War is a good example that shows that crisis did much to weld together the various ethnic groups in America. Hansen has made much of this fact, assessing its role as follows:

The United States in 1860 was made up not merely of two nations — the North and the South — as is sometimes said, but of many. The North comprised a dozen different peoples who without qualifying their adopted political allegiance lived in the cultural environment of some European nation. What might have been the outcome if the course of development had been uninterrupted no one knows, for the Civil War altered the face of events for both the alien and the native. . . . The poor immigrant of 1857 was the rich farmer of 1865; and his ardent interest in the culture of the country he had left was cooled by the knowledge that the culture of his adopted country now lay within reach. . . .

. . . No longer could the newcomers be taunted about enjoying the benefits of a government which they had no hand in creating, for now they were helping to save it. . . . The past in Europe was overshadowed by the future in America. Four years of anxiety, binding the immigrant family to the fortunes of the struggling nation, created a new attitude toward the society which their sons were fighting to preserve. . . .

The earlier immigrants had desired to perpetuate a social minority in the American environment; the newer comers, whatever their individual inclinations, were obliged to accept the idea that ultimately their distinctive features would disappear. All they could hope for was to add a bit of their own culture to the amalgam formed by the mingling of many peoples.[40]

It is thus a well-established fact that when groups of people who differ culturally come into contact there tends to be some interchange of ideas, customs, beliefs, and material objects. In short, the *process* of assimilation seems to operate invariably when peoples live side by side. Even when one group is most reluctant to adopt the ways of its neighbors and is incredibly adept at erecting barriers against such importations, the forces of assimilation make themselves felt. If assimilation is thought of as a process of cultural give-and-take, there is good reason for regarding it as an inevitable consequence of the meeting of peoples.

If, however, we think of assimilation as a *condition* — as the end result of the process — wherein groups once dissimilar in their beliefs, customs, and attitudes have become similar, then we may well doubt that it is an inevitable consequence of contact. We may insist that eventually the Jews and Indians in the United States will lose their identity and become completely assimilated, but it will be a statement of faith, not of scientific fact. Certainly there are instances where unlike groups have lived together for very long periods without such fusion.

Sociologists have learned a great deal about the process of assimilation, so that many blunders of the past are no longer excusable. The folly of coercion seems well established. A certain Polish priest is credited with the wise remark that "the Germans tried to make Germans of us, and we remained Poles; the Americans do not care; we will soon be Americans." Sociologists have amply demonstrated that assimilation is a long, slow, often painful process.

Much remains to be learned, however, about the process of assimilation. What are the agencies responsible for the transfer of culture from one group to the other? How effective are the various agencies — the public schools, for example? Why are certain items of the strange culture chosen for adoption more readily than others? What elements of the old culture are clung to most tenaciously, and why? What about the time needed for the acceptance and integration of new traits? What happens to old ideas when new ones are introduced? These and a host of other questions remain to be answered before we can say that we fully understand the assimilative process.

Notes

1. L. Leung, "The Twain Meet," *Common Ground* 2, no. 2 (Winter 1942): 100–103.

2. M. Freedman, "The Chinese in Southeast Asia," in A. W. Lind, ed., *Race Relations in World Perspective*, p. 388ff.

3. For a history and analysis of the concept, see M. M. Gordon, *Assimilation in American Life*, chap. 5.

4. Quoted in R. E. Park and E. W. Burgess, *Introduction to the Science of Sociology*, p. 734.

5. I. Zangwill, *The Melting Pot: Drama in Four Acts*, p. 33ff.

6. As cited in L. Wirth, *The Ghetto*, p. 127.

7. Gordon (*Assimilation in American Life*, p. 85) uses the term *Anglo-conformity*, which theory, he says, "demanded the complete renunciation of the immigrant's ancestral culture in favor of the behavior and values of the Anglo-Saxon core group."

8. F. M. Hechinger and G. Hechinger, *Growing Up in America*, p. 56.

9. Ibid., p. 62.

10. Ibid.

11. As cited in Hechinger and Hechinger, *Growing Up in America*, pp. 67–68.

12. As cited in I. Howe, "Immigrant Jewish Families in New York," *New York Magazine*, 13 Oct. 1975, p. 68.

13. Cited in M. Rischen, *The Promised City*, pp. 99–100.

14. M. Handman, "Conflict and Equilibrium in a Border Area," in E. B. Reuter ed., *Race and Culture Contacts*, pp. 86–111.

15. S. Tax, "World View and Social Relations in Guatemala," *American Anthropologist* 43, no. 1 (Jan.–March 1941): 27–42.

16. D. G. Mandelbaum, "Culture Change Among the Nilgiri Tribes," *American Anthropologist* 43, no. 1 (Jan–March 1941): 19–26. See also G. P. Murdock, *Our Primitive Contemporaries*, chap. 5.

17. See H. E. Driver, *Indians of North America*, chap. 26.

18. E. F. Frazier, *The Negro Family in the United States*, pp. 21–22.

19. M. J. Herskovits, *The Myth of the Negro Past*.

20. G. Freyre, *The Masters and the Slaves: A Study in the Development of Brazilian Civilization*, pp. xviii, 78ff., 100ff., 155, 170; and D. Pierson, *Negroes in Brazil*, pp. 94–107, 237–274.

21. W. C. Smith, *Americans in the Making*, p. 126ff.

22. C. T. Pihlblad, "The Kansas Swedes," *The Southwestern Social Science Quarterly* 13, no. 1 (June 1932): 4–5.

23. D. V. Brown, *A Child of the Orient*, pp. 275–276.

24. See S. N. Eisenstadt, *The Absorption of Immigrants*; C. Frankenstein, ed., *Between Past and Future*; R. Patai, *Israel Between East and West*.

25. J. W. Eaton, "Controlled Acculturation: A Survival Technique of the Hutterites," *American Sociological Review* 17, no. 3 (June 1952) pp. 331–340.

26. Gordon, *Assimilation in American Life*.

27. Hechinger and Hechinger, *Growing Up in America*, pp. 58–61.

28. I. Howe, "Immigrant Jewish Families," p. 69.

29. C. M. Panunzio, *Major Social Institutions*, p. 525.

30. R. E. Park, "Assimilation, Social," in *Encyclopedia of the Social Sciences*, vol. 2, pp. 281–283.

31. C. T. Jonassen, *Norwegians in Bay Ridge: A Sociological Study of an Ethnic Group*.

32. H. G. Duncan, *Immigration and Assimilation*, pp. 709–713.

33. Ibid., pp. 811–814.

34. M. L. Hansen, *The Atlantic Migration*, p. 156ff.

35. J. Useem and R. H. Useem, "Minority-Group Pattern in Prairie Society," *American Journal of Sociology* 50, no. 5 (March 1945): 377–385.

36. W. Price, *Japan's Islands of Mystery*, pp. 171–172.

37. P. V. Young, *The Pilgrims of Russian Town*.

38. J. A. Rios, "Assimilation of Emigrants from the Old South in Brazil," *Social Forces* 26, no. 2 (Dec. 1947): 145–152.

39. R. A. Schermerhorn, *These Our People*, p. 316ff.

40. M. L. Hansen, *The Immigrant in American History*, pp. 140–142.

Chapter Thirteen
Pluralism

In the colony he meets with sympathy, understanding and encouragement. There he
finds his fellow countrymen who understand
his habits and standards and share his life —
experience and viewpoint. In the colony he
has a status, plays a role in a group. In the
life of the colony's streets and cafes, in its
church and benevolent societies, he finds response and security. In the colony he finds
that he can live, be somebody, satisfy his
wishes — all of which is impossible in the
strange world outside.

— *Harvey W. Zorbaugh* The Gold Coast and
the Slum

Many people feel uncomfortable when the subject of religious and ethnic
diversity is brought up. They believe that raising the issue is wrong since it
emphasizes the differences rather than the similarities among people. They
will usually allow blacks, American Indians, or Chicanos the option of expressing ethnic consciousness, but feel it is somehow inappropriate for other ethnic
groups to share in this expression. This feeling is prevalent particularly on the
part of those who have recently left their own ethnic heritage behind and feel
that others should do the same.[1]

The Theory of Pluralism

Pluralism, or the development of separate identities within a society, is a philo-
sophical theory that attempts to bring about what is considered to be a desirable
social situation. When people use the term today, frequently they are describing a condition that seems to be developing in contemporary American society.
However, they often ignore the ideological foundation for the existence of the
situation that the term implies. In this chapter we will deal with the theory of

pluralism in order that we may understand how it has come to be an accepted, and even a desirable, condition.

The main person responsible for the development of the theory of cultural pluralism was Horace Kallen. Kallen was born in the area of Germany known as Silesia. He came to Boston at the age of five and was raised in an orthodox Jewish home. However, as he proceeded through the Boston Public Schools, he underwent a common second-generation phenomenon. He started to reject his home environment and religion and developed an uncritical enthusiasm for the United States. As he put it, "It seemed to me that the identity of every human being with every other was the important thing, and that the term 'American' should nullify the meaning of every other term in one's personal make-up. . . ."[2]

Kallen's admiration for the Yankee world eventually led him to become a student at Harvard College. However, once he reached what he thought was the inner sanctum of intellectual America, he experienced a number of shocks. While working in a nearby social settlement, he came in contact with liberal and socialist ideas and observed people expressing numerous ethnic goals and aspirations. This exposure caused him to question his definition of what it meant to be an American.

This quandary was further compounded by his experiences in the American literature class of Professor Barrett Wendell. Kallen saw Wendell as the personification of genteel New England culture. Therefore, when Wendell presented his view of what constituted the American character, the effect on Kallen was profound. Wendell believed that Puritan traits and ideals were at the core of the American value structure. The Puritans, in turn, had modeled themselves after the Old Testament prophets. Wendell even suggested that the early Puritans were largely of Jewish descent. These ideas led Kallen to believe that he could be an unassimilated Jew and still belong to the core of the American value system. It no longer became an either-or type of situation as had been the case under the melting pot thesis. All of his past attempts to throw off his Jewish background were now unnecessary.

After discovering that he could still be totally Jewish and be American, he came to realize that the application could be made to other ethnic groups as well. All ethnic groups, he felt, should preserve their own separate culture without shame or guilt. As he put it, "Democracy involves not the elimination of differences, but the perfection and conservation of differences."[3]

Kallen was rejecting the view that all people are basically alike. Ironically, the racists of that era were doing the same thing. Both Kallen and the racists agreed that fundamental human differences would not disappear in the American melting pot. However, Kallen looked on these differences with a benign gaze, while the racists looked on them as forming the basis for a struggle between unequal adversaries. Kallen believed that the American ensemble of many ethnic groups was working together as an orchestra to play a common tune; the racists believed that harmonious sounds could only come from racial purity.

Professor Wendell also influenced a major spokesperson for cultural pluralism among the black community. W. E. B. DuBois was against the assimilation philosophy. DuBois was opposed to it because he felt that much of it bred contempt on the part of individuals for their origins. Like Kallen, he emphasized the primary importance of one's ethnic or racial community. Whites had always advised blacks to strive as individuals for acceptance by conforming to the values of the larger society. DuBois, however, believed that individuals could not really bring about change; change could only be achieved through collective action.

As DuBois wrote in his essay, "The Conservation of Races,"

For this reason, the advance guard of the Negro people — the 8,000,000 people of Negro blood in the United States of America — must soon come to realize that if they are to take their just place in the van of Pan-Negroism, then their destiny is *not* absorption by the white Americans. That if in America it is to be proven for the first time in the modern world that not only Negroes are capable of evolving individual men like Toussaint, the Saviour, but are a nation stored with wonderful possibilities of culture, then their destiny is not a servile imitation of Anglo-Saxon culture, but a stalwart originality which shall unswervingly follow Negro ideals. . . .

. . . We are the first fruits of this new nation, the harbinger of that black to-morrow which is yet destined to soften the whiteness of the Teutonic to-day. We are that people whose subtle sense of song has given America its only American music, its only American fairy tales, its only touch of pathos and humor amid its mad money-getting plutocracy. As such, it is our duty to conserve our physical powers, our intellectual endowments, our spiritual ideals; as a race we must strive by race organization, by race solidarity, by race unity to the realization of that broader humanity which freely recognizes differences in men, but sternly deprecates inequality in their opportunities of development.[4]

Pluralism Contrasted with Assimilationism

As we can see, pluralism is a reaction against assimilationism and the melting pot idea. It is a philosophy that not only assumes that minorities have rights, but also considers the lifestyle of a minority group to be a legitimate, and even desirable, way of participating in society. The theory of pluralism involves a celebration of the differences among groups of people. The theory also implies a hostility to existing inequalities in the status and treatment of minority groups. Pluralism has provided a means for minorities to resist the pull of assimilation by allowing them to claim that they constitute the very structure of the social order. From the assimilationist point of view, the minority is seen as a subordinate group that should give up its identity as quickly as possible. Pluralism, on the other hand, assumes that the minority is a primary unit of society. The unity of the whole depends on the harmony of the various parts.

The ironic thing about the philosophy of cultural pluralism is that it was most likely to appeal to those people who had already made significant progress toward assimilation. As the historian John Higham noted:

. . . Cultural pluralism would appeal to the people who were already strongly enough positioned to imagine that permanent minority status might be advantageous. It was

Children in Norwegian-American parade

congenial to minority spokesmen confident enough to visualize themselves at the center rather than the periphery of American experience. Accordingly, cultural pluralism proved most attractive to people who were already largely assimilated. It was itself one of the products of the American melting pot.[5]

There are numerous differences between the theory of assimilation and the theory of pluralism. The main difference concerns boundaries. The assimilationist is interested in eliminating ethnic boundaries, while the pluralist is interested in maintaining them. Assimilation is dedicated to the concept of the fellowship of all human beings. Pluralism is involved with local fellowship among the members of a specific small community. Other differences also exist. Assimilation assumes not only rule by the majority, but also the willingness of the entire population to abide by the general will. Basically, pluralism is a theory of minority rights that legitimizes the goals and aspirations of a small segment of society. Adherents to the theory usually resist the rule of the majority and discourage conformity to it. Pluralism sees the democratic society as one in which coalitions between minorities are formed rather than one in which minorities abide by majority rules.

Assimilation strives for an equality of individuals, while pluralism strives for an equality between groups. The assimilationist philosophy assumes that the primary social unit is the individual. Individuals must be free to define themselves as separate from their ancestors and must be allowed to gain recognition apart from their ethnic background. Assimilation demands a breaking of traditional ties. With pluralism, the persistence of the group is of paramount importance; individuals are dependent on the group for determination of their identity.

Since assimilationists and pluralists differ in the importance they assign to the individual and the group, they also differ in their opinion on what binds people together. From the assimilationist viewpoint people are regarded as being held together by a set of principles and ideals such as "The American Way." The pluralist is less interested in what people believe and is more interested in who they are, what their common ancestry is, and what their inherited social bonds are. The pluralist is more likely to stress a distinctive past history rather than a unifying ideology.[6]

From an examination of the basic ideas of the two positions, it becomes evident that both are unrealistic. As Higham states:

Assimilation falsely assumes that ethnic ties dissolve fairly easily in an open society. . . . Many people resist for generation after generation the assault of technology and modern education. . . . No ethnic group, once established in the United States, has ever entirely disappeared; none seems about to do so. People are not as pliant as assimilationists have supposed.

Pluralism makes the opposite mistake. It assumes a rigidity of ethnic boundaries and a fixity of group commitment which American life does not permit. . . .

Pluralism encourages the further illusion that ethnic groups typically have a high degree of internal solidarity. Actually, many of them are unstable federations of local or tribal collectivities, which attain only a temporary and precarious unity in the face of a common enemy. On top of sharp localistic differences, an ethnic group is likely to be split along religious, class, and political lines.[7]

The two views also present other problems. Assimilation assumes failure in adjustment to the new society to be the fate of the individual who remains attached to the old ethnic lifestyles. Consequently, many newcomers whose adjustment is difficult or incomplete are forced into thinking that they were not able to live up to the opportunity American society offered.

While assimilation sacrifices the group for the individual advancement,

The celebration of ethnicity

pluralism presents a different problem in that it sacrifices the individual for the group advancement. Pluralism places limitations on the more autonomous and adventuresome of the group and encourages them to remain as part of a community that may be marked by suspicion, narrow-mindedness, and prejudice. As a result, individual creativity may be hampered.

Much of contemporary American pluralism is not as ideologically rooted as were the earlier forms. The current form is an outgrowth of the alienation of the late 1960s. Assimilation does not seem desirable or attractive if the society is judged to be lacking in some respect. Implicit in the theory of assimilation is a general acceptance of the value system of the host society. Today pluralism is often a rebellion against the status quo. In addition, since the late 1960s there has been an increasing tolerance of diversity of every kind. The establishment and maintenance of boundaries between various groups has been encouraged. Mountain climbers, construction workers, and Italian politicians have all cultivated their own solidarity. Contemporary America seems to have replaced pluralism with a new particularism, which encourages any segment of the population that can define itself as somewhat distinct from the rest of society to maintain solidarity and mutual identification.[8]

Pluralism as a Form of Discrimination

Pluralism, as a method of resolving the conflict between unlike groups inhabiting the same territory, has a special appeal for those who are committed to the ideals of democracy and tolerance. At the same time, the *language* of pluralism is frequently employed by those whose purposes are quite otherwise. For instance, the white Americans who enthusiastically espouse the doctrine of "separate but equal" may be sincere in their belief, but likely as not they are more concerned with the "separate" than with the "equal." For half a century under that doctrine, schools, medical facilities, transportation, and recreation were rigidly separated for whites and blacks, but little or no effort was made to have them equal.[9] So it is in South Africa, where many whites defend their belief in apartheid not on the grounds that it will facilitate their control over blacks, but rather on grounds that suggest a belief in a pluralistic society. This discrepancy between the *theory of apartheid* and *apartheid in practice* has been pointed out by Anthony H. Richmond.[10] In theoretical discussions of race problems in the Republic, he says, the concept of apartheid places emphasis on separation of the races as a means of obtaining social autonomy and minimizing conflict. Its advocates profess a deep interest in preserving the way of life of the natives and of wanting them "to develop along their own lines." A policy of strict separation, according to its advocates, would enable each racial group to preserve its biological purity, to own its own territory, to practice the customs it prefers, to educate its children as it wishes, and ultimately to achieve complete self-sufficiency and sovereignty. Actually, Richmond insists, the practical politicians do not support any such ideal, but rather regard apartheid as an instrument for continued domination of the African, Coloured, and Asian communities by the European.

Pluralism as Public Policy

Pluralism is not merely an ideal, a theory, or a goal toward which its advocates hope that race relations might move; it has been a matter of public policy on numerous occasions. Let us consider some of these.

The Swiss

Switzerland is a small nation of 15,000 square miles — hardly large enough to make a fair-sized American state — and has a population of 4 million. It is a country of great diversity, with high mountains, deep valleys, glaciers, and sunshine. Its people, also, are anything but homogeneous. There is no Swiss language serving to bind these 4 million together as a nation. Instead, a majority of them speak German, or rather a variety of German known as Schwyzerdeutsch, which itself varies from canton to canton. French is spoken by 19 percent of the people; Italian is the language of 10 percent; and slightly less than 1 percent speak an ancient language known as Romansh. These language differences are barely indicative of the deep cultural diversities found in the country. Almost every valley in the high Alps has retained its very distinct characteristics; and there are regional differences in costume, dialect, ways of thought, and ways of acting. Nor does religion serve to bind the people together, for 57 percent are Protestant and 41 percent, Catholic. These religious and linguistic cleavages, which are subject to statistical presentation, are indicative of the conflict between Latinity and Teutonism. This conflict has deep roots and rests on differences of temperament, manners, customs, sense of humor, and other subtle characteristics. In short, Switzerland is composed of very diverse ethnic groups, among whom exist all the potentialities for bitter antagonism.

As a matter of fact, throughout most of its history Switzerland has been a battleground. Far from being isolated and protected by its high mountains, the country is actually astride several highways and has been reckoned with by every conqueror from Caesar and Hannibal to Napoleon and Hitler. The Swiss have had every opportunity to learn about war; and until recently, the word "Switzerland" brought to most people's minds not milkmaids, yodelers, watchmakers, and hotel keepers, but professional soldiers, and ferocious ones at that. The Swiss, in addition to having their own domestic difficulties, participated as mercenaries in most of the wars of other European nations, and the Swiss Guard at the Vatican today is a picturesque survival of an ancient profession.

Despite all this diversity, the Swiss have succeeded in combining these ethnic groups into a national unit. Conceivably, it might have been done on a basis of subordination and superordination, or on a basis of segregation — neither of which, however, would have produced the national loyalty that the Swiss now possess. Instead, an accommodation in the nature of cultural pluralism was reached during the nineteenth century. As to Catholic and Protestant, the principle of complete religious freedom was adopted and liberty of conscience prevails. As for the linguistic differences, German, French, Italian, and Romansh have been designated in the constitution as "national languages," and the first three were declared to be "official languages" — a distinction difficult for an outsider to comprehend. At any rate, all federal documents are translated into the three official languages, all versions being equally authoritative. In the political sphere, cultural pluralism found expression in granting to each of the cantons a large measure of local autonomy and sovereignty, somewhat greater than that enjoyed by the several American states. Other political devices, such as proportional representation, initiative, and referendum, were adopted with the view to safeguard the integrity and the interests of the various ethnic groups. This is not to say that ethnocentrism was suddenly eradicated and a spirit of tolerance instantly engendered. After all, the Swiss are human; and the prejudices of Latin and Teuton, Papist and Calvinist, have deep foundations. Nevertheless, these people have learned to live with their differences and to develop common loyalties. Switzerland does afford an example of diverse ethnic groups dwelling together in harmony and equality and sharing a high degree of national feeling. One writer, attempting to explore the mind of the Swiss, has this to say:

It is difficult to believe that a nation should suddenly reform its habits merely because such action would be to its best advantage. Even if the Swiss were wise enough to mend their errors in the nick of time, it still would be interesting to know why they were so wise, while other nations, hardened in their sins despite their better knowledge, have foundered.
   Yet, does a Swiss really feel Swiss? The question cannot be answered simply. . . .
   A Swiss feels more Swiss on certain days than on others. He feels very Swiss when he stands on a mountain top and looks upon his land; he feels very Swiss when he serves in his army, when he commemorates old battles, when he compares his country with the rest of the world. . . . In his everyday life, he is more likely to feel Argovian, Neuchatelois, or whatever he may be. In his intellectual life he may feel more affinities with the French, the Germans, or the Italians than with those among his fellow Swiss who speak a tongue different from his own. . . .
   Now anyone who unites so many levels of loyalty within his person is unlikely to be swayed overmuch by any particular loyalty. A German Swiss, for instance, will sympathize with Germany — but only culturally, as it were. . . . He will feel strongly for his canton most of the time. But when the question of being Swiss is involved — well, he is a Swiss, and he intends to stay one. What is more, on all levels of loyalty he is equally faithful to his national traditions.[11]

Sociologists, as well as diplomats and political scientists, have tried to determine how the Swiss learned to blend their cultural differences into a national unity. One piece of research has inquired into the demographic basis for this unity.[12] The national languages of Switzerland — German, French, Italian, Romansh — are recognized by the constitution as equal, but they are not actually equal in importance. The German-speaking Swiss greatly outnumber the other three. The explanation lies in differences in fertility, the French-speaking cantons having considerably lower birth rates than most of the German-speaking cantons. These differences in fertility, however, have been offset by internal migrations. The French regions of the country have proved much more attractive to German-speaking migrants than the German regions have to the French-speaking Swiss. Furthermore, the migrants tend to become rapidly assimilated, especially so when they have children who can use only the official language of the region in school. High mountains mark off the boundaries between the Italian-speaking region and the rest of the Switzerland, thus preserving the Italian language intact. Mayer, who made this study of Swiss equilibrium, maintains that no effort whatsoever is made by the German-Swiss, who constitute an overwhelming majority, to impose their language on the nation. This linguistic equilibrium, which represents one of the foremost stabilizing and integrating influences in modern Switzerland, originated at a time before language was made a symbol of national and ethnic identification and the demographic factors have kept it from becoming a focal point. To be sure, this fortunate circumstance has been consciously reinforced by wise political measures designed to prevent language from becoming a focus of division and conflict, as it has elsewhere. Those who embrace the ideal of cultural pluralism would do well to give close attention to the Swiss, for they have been without peers in putting into practice this rare and difficult pattern of accommodation in ethnic group relations.

The Russians

Soviet Russia is another heterogeneous modern nation that has reputedly adopted a policy of cultural pluralism toward the numerous ethnic minorities in the country. That is no easy task for a nation of peoples so diverse as are the citizens of the USSR. The largest group are the Russians, who make up about half of the population; but others, numbering millions each, are the Ukrainians, Jews, Armenians, Georgians, Poles, Tartars, and many more. Altogether there are about 185 distinct ethnic groups, speaking approximately 147 different languages. The cultural differences are incredibly wide. At one extreme are literate, civilized, urbanized, industrialized moderns and, at the other, are preliterate, nomadic primitives. There are Moslems, Jews, and many varieties of Christians, to say nothing of the nonreligious and the antireligious.

The conflicts among these diverse groups were long utilized by the dominant Russians in their efforts to exploit and control the country. Anti-Semitism was fostered and pogroms were launched from time to time to deflect popular discontent from the government. Ethnic groups other than the Jews fared no better. Periodically, they were the objects of a policy of ruthless Russification; steps were taken to cripple their cultures, to restrict the use of their native tongues, and to suppress their religions. Ignorance and illiteracy were condoned. It is estimated that in 1914 only 40 percent of the population nine years of age and older were literate. The utter isolation of masses of the people is suggested by that grim expression, "the deaf villages." The Czars were committed to a policy of "divide and rule." The Armenians were set against the Georgians, and the Germans against the Letts. In promoting such a policy, the government would frequently extend special privileges to one minority group solely for the purpose of creating enmity and jealousy among its neighbors. In short, the czarist program for the numerous minorities had one overall purpose — domination; and, in pursuit of that end, segregation, isolation, forced assimilation, and mass expulsion were employed as the occasion arose.

The revolution saw a complete reversal in this policy. In fact, Stalin himself gave much attention to the problem of minorities, and as early as 1913 wrote:

In the Caucasus there are a number of peoples each possessing a primitive culture, a specific language, but without its own literature; peoples, moreover, which are in a state of transition, partly becoming assimilated and partly continuing to develop. . . .

What is to be done with the Mingrelians, the Abkhasians, the Adjarians, the Svane-
tians, the Lesghians, and so on, who speak different languages, but do not possess a literature of their own? . . .

The national problem in the Caucasus can be solved *only by drawing the backward
nations and peoples into the common stream of a higher culture.* . . .

A minority is discontented not because there is no national union, but because it does
not enjoy liberty of conscience, liberty of movement, etc. Give it these liberties and it
will cease to be discontented. Thus *national equality in all forms (language, schools,
etc.) is an essential element* in the solution of the national problem. A state law based
on complete democracy in the country is required, prohibiting all national privileges
without exception and all kinds of disabilities and restrictions on the rights of national
minorities. [13]

Within one week after the Revolution had broken out in 1917, the new government issued a Declaration of the Rights of Peoples of Russia, which proclaimed, over the signatures of Lenin and Stalin:

1. Equality and sovereignty for the peoples of Russia;
2. The right of the peoples of Russia to self-determination even to the point of separation from the state and creation of a new independent government.
3. Abolition of all religious and nationality group privileges;
4. Free development of national minorities and ethnic groups inhabiting the territories
of Russia.

These principles have been given expression on numerous occasions in the
years since 1917. They have been reiterated in the pronouncements and
speeches of prominent Soviet officials. They were incorporated in the constitution of July 10, 1918, as well as in the constitutions of the Soviet Republics
of the Ukrainians, White Russians, Azerbaijans, Armenians, Georgians, and
others, as they were organized and admitted to the Union. Stalin specified that
each ethnic group should operate its own courts and governmental agencies,
utilize its own language, and be helped to establish its own newspapers,
schools, theaters, clubs, and other institutions. These principles were incorporated in the first Union constitution, adopted in 1924. The next twelve years
witnessed a great revival of ethnic sentiment, even to the point where it
endangered Soviet unity. The largest group, the Great Russians, began to
display considerable ethnocentrism, with the result that Stalin had to denounce
the arrogant attitude of Russians toward the other ethnic groups. However,
these other peoples themselves, under the encouragement shown them by the
government, began to manifest an aggressive nationalistic spirit and to discriminate against minorities within their territories. Thus the Armenians, Ossets,
and Adjarians, dwelling within the Georgian Republic, were the objects of
abuse on the part of the dominant Georgians, and the same thing was occurring
in the other Soviet Republics. Cultural pluralism, as far as the USSR sought
to adopt it as a policy, was not to be easily achieved. When the constitution
was revised in 1936, however, the same principles were again incorporated,
including the following:

Any direct or indirect restriction of the rights, or conversely any establishment of direct or indirect privileges for citizens on account of their race or nationality, as well as any advocacy of racial or national exclusiveness or hatred and contempt is punishable by law.

These Soviet efforts, which were not limited to speechmaking, toward the establishment of equality among the various racial and ethnic groups within their borders won the admiration of liberals all over the world.

At the same time, the Soviet minority policy has come in for a great deal of condemnation, and the motives behind it have been regarded with suspicion. Max Boehm thinks it is only a "sham solution" of national and cultural problems, that there is no sincere concern for the welfare of minorities, and that the whole program serves merely to mobilize the illiterates of these groups against their own upper classes. Others have regarded it as simply a product of expediency, as a technique for maintaining power and extending control.

In spite of their professions of cultural and ethnic toleration and autonomy, in recent years it has become obvious that the Soviets have followed no such policy at all. As an example, anti-Semitism has continued to be severe and virulent. Yiddish journals have been suppressed and publishing houses have been closed "for serious manifestations of Jewish bourgeois nationalism," meaning Zionism; outstanding Yiddish authors have been arrested; Jews have suffered disproportionately in the several purges; Jews have been removed from responsible government posts; anti-Semitism flourishes in the Russian army; and Jews have been squeezed out of the Soviet bureaucracy. Anti-Semitism has also penetrated the urban middle classes, the upper strata of industrial workers, university students, the Communist Youth, and even the Communist Party itself. One rabbi describes the attitude that has arisen among Soviet officialdom as a "creeping, half-heartedly disguised anti-Semitism," bent on relegating Jews to the background of Soviet life.[14]

Russia's professions of pluralism and tolerance for ethnic minorities was challenged by the late Bertrand Russell. Russell was a Western supporter of Russian policy and a friend of Premier Nikita Khrushchev. Russell often mentioned the problem of Russian interference with Jewish life in correspondence with Khrushchev. In one of the letters he wrote the following:

. . . One of the tests of true friendship is the ability to speak frankly without fear of being taken for an enemy or of being misunderstood. I hope, therefore, that you will appreciate the spirit in which I am now writing — one of concern for the Soviet people and not a spirit of condemnation.

The Jews have been subjected to a long and continuous persecution in the history of Europe. The culmination of this cruelty was the wholesale extermination of millions of Jews during our lifetimes, one of the most barbaric crimes in all human history. If ever a people were deserving of understanding and sympathetic treatment after harsh suffering, it is the Jews of Europe.

I should hope, therefore, that the Jews would be permitted full cultural lives, religious freedom and the rights of a national group, in practice as well as in law.

During the last years of Stalin's life, Soviet Jews were totally deprived of their national culture and the means of expressing it. Leading intellectuals were imprisoned or executed by extralegal practices which have since been condemned.

I am a lifelong non-believer in any religion. I have written and campaigned against superstition. Nonetheless, I believe that the freedom to practive religious views should be allowed Jews of the Soviet Union in the same manner that such freedom is granted people of other religious persuasion. I am concerned that the process of restitution of much smaller groups are more plentiful and the closure of synagogues and shortage of religious facilities have impaired Jews in the pursuit of their beliefs. I am troubled that there should be articles in Soviet journals of many Republics expressing hostility of Jewish people as such.[15]

(From *Three Million More?* by Gunther Lawrence. Copyright © 1970 by Gunther Lawrence. Reprinted by permission of Doubleday & Company, Inc.)

As for the other non-Jewish minorities, the prospects are none too bright. Dr. Jacob Robinson, who also has had ample opportunity to know the situation, reports that "Soviet policy is, in some measure, reminiscent of the imperial policy of Czarist Russia," and says:

Soviet theoreticians speak of the Soviet Union as a multinational socialist state. It would be more correct to define it as a multi-lingual state. Even after the shifts which have occurred, Soviet policy does not recognize national traditions, in the full sense, as worthy of perpetuation. While fostering customary folk dances and folk lore, the Soviets impose a deadening uniformity on the national literatures. In principle the cultures of all the nationalities in the Union are supposed to be national in their form only — that is in language — but "socialist in content." . . . A new expression, now being widely used, speaks of the Soviet people, instead of the peoples of the Soviet Union.[16]

Thus it seems doubtful that the Soviets, in spite of all their talk, have ever been committed to a policy of pluralism for their numerous ethnic minorities. Assimilation is their ultimate goal and pluralism, insofar as they have promoted it, is but a temporary and expedient step toward the goal of a monolithic society. As Lenin put it, "We must divide in order to unite"; and Stalin, even before the Revolution, declared:

Regional autonomy in the Caucasus is acceptable because it draws the backward nations into the common cultural development; it helps to cast off the shell of isolation peculiar to small nationalities; it impels them forward and facilitates access to the benefits of a higher culture.[17]

The American Indians

Pluralism might be said to have been the policy of the United States government toward its Indian wards in the period from 1933 to 1950. Historically, the attitudes of the whites toward the Indians in the area now the United States illustrates any and all of the phenomena of race relations. Conflict, for example, has been intermittent; assimilation and amalgamation and mass expulsion have been employed from time to time; segregation and stratification have been practiced; and we find an expression of tolerance and sympathy, even of sentimental idealization, which partakes of cultural pluralism. While all of these policies have prevailed and have even run concurrently, we may recognize particular periods when one or the other has been dominant in Indian-white relations.[18]

From the very beginning the policies of the Spaniards differed from those of the English, Dutch, and others who settled north of the Rio Grande. The Spaniards regarded the Indians as subjects of the crown and the church. To be sure, the Indians were relegated to the inferior status of forced laborers, and were mercilessly exploited, but at the same time, assimilation and amalgamation were deliberately fostered. The Spaniards seldom dealt with the Indian tribes as though they were sovereign powers and did not resort to the purchase of lands and other rights from them; instead, they established missions and set about Christianizing and "civilizing" them.

The Dutch, British, Swedes, and others who settled our Atlantic coast did not deliberately depart from the Spanish precedent; but conditions were so different that a new policy did emerge. For one thing, the Indian population was not nearly so large, and did not pose the danger that the Spaniards faced. More important, however, was the fact that colonization in non-Spanish North America was not a function of the crown, but was a business proposition, undertaken by private enterprise, for the purpose of economic gain. Much to the disappointment of the entrepreneurs who backed them, the colonies never gave much financial promise and never attracted enough capital to warrant military conquest of the native peoples. Accordingly, the policy that was developed was one of dealing with the various tribes as though they were independent, sovereign powers, of recognizing their title to the land and paying them for it, and of negotiating with them by treaties. This policy, of course, led to interminable conflict, for the Indian's conception of land and property was entirely different from that of white society. Moreover, the treaty as an instrumentality assumes a degree of social organization and centralization of authority that certainly did not prevail in Indian society and hardly prevailed in the colonies. All the while there were missionaries and humanitarians who worked for the education and assimilation of the Indians; there were fur traders who preferred to leave them as they were; and there were hard-headed "realists" who advocated their extermination and were assisted in their endeavors by disease, vice, and intertribal wars. The major policy, however, was one of removal or mass expulsion. Thomas Jefferson entertained the idea of moving the Indians across the Mississippi River, and the purchase of Louisiana, he thought, would provide land for them. Presidents Monroe and Adams insisted that the Indians could not be removed without their consent, and often this could not be obtained. Whatever the Indians felt, however, the frontier kept pushing them westward. Treaties depriving them of their land were forced on them by one means or another; worse still, the provisions of many of these treaties have never been satisfied to this day, much to the bitterness and disillusionment of the Indian.

In the middle of the nineteenth century a change in policy developed. The Indian, it was decided, would have to be segregated and isolated. Between 1850 and 1880 most of the reservations, of which there are now more than two hundred, were created. This change from annihilation and expulsion to segregation was a product of gradual development that was interrupted briefly by the Civil War. As a matter of fact, many of the Indian tribes, in ceding their lands to white conquerors, had "reserved" a portion for their own use. By a series of laws and court decisions, the status of the Indians was changed from that of sovereign nations to that of wardship. In 1834 the western portion of the old Louisiana Purchase was set apart as solid Indian territory; but in the same year Indian sovereignty was invaded by the extension of federal criminal law to cover all crimes on Indian territory where a white person was either the victim or the criminal. Just prior to the Civil War many treaties were made extinguishing Indian title to certain lands; and after the war penalties in the form of land cessions were exacted from those tribes that had gone on the warpath and those that had fought on the side of the Confederates. Again, a decision of the Supreme Court held that a treaty with an Indian tribe had no greater force than an act of Congress and that Congress had the right to abrogate the terms of such treaties. Finally, on March 3, 1871, an act was passed that put an end to the use of treaties in dealing with Indians and of recognizing Indian tribes as independent, sovereign nations. Henceforth they would be controlled through segregation on reservations and special legislation by Congress.

Segregation, however, was not successful as a solution to the problem. Nomads did not readily take to a settled life. Hunters would not easily change themselves into farmers. Proud and independent warriors did not appreciate the status of wards and the ministrations of a guardian. To tide them over until the necessary adjustments could be made and to make them contented with their lot, the government issued rations, but this served only to pauperize them. It became evident that the policy of segregation was a failure; and those who had a genuine interest in the Indians' welfare (and some who hoped to do them out of what little they had left) clamored for assimilation and "Americanization."

In the 1880s, accordingly, another shift in policy occurred. The Indian was to be "civilized," assimilated, "Americanized." This meant the destruction of tribal organizations, suppression of pagan religions and ceremonies, cutting the hair of males short and teaching them to dress like whites, making them speak English, emancipating them from their ancient customs, developing in them the ideas and values of white society, making of them rugged, go-getting individualists. As Mr. John Collier, later Commissioner of Indian Affairs, put it, "To smother, to exterminate the entirety of the Indian heritage became the central purpose." The chief instrument of this new policy was the General

Allotment Act, passed by Congress in 1887. This act provided for the destruction of the reservations by giving to each Indian a share of the reservation lands. This share was to be held in trust for a period of twenty-five years, during which time it could not be taxed or sold. After that the Indians would be given a fee patent and be declared competent to manage their own affairs. The sponsors of the bill believed, quite correctly, that destroying the communal ownership of the land would break the backbone of the Indian culture. The Secretary of the Interior of that era remarked, "The enjoyment and pride of the individual ownership of property is one of the most effective civilizing agencies"; and Senator Dawes, whose name is attached to the act, insisted that it would create in the Indian that spirit of selfishness which, in the Senator's opinion, was the main motivation of white civilization.

The breaking up of the reservations was only a part of the program to force and accelerate the Indian's assimilation. Indian children were placed in boarding schools, where they were weaned away from their Indian culture and indoctrinated with the standards of the whites. Indian languages were systematically suppressed; the ancient arts were allowed to wither; and Indian religion, ceremonies, and traditions were discouraged and often forbidden.

No adequate provision was made, however, for the Indian's assumption of the role of citizen. In World War I many noncitizen Indians served in the armed forces; and a law was passed in 1919 conferring citizenship on any honorably discharged soldier who requested it. By 1924 about two-thirds of the Indians had become citizens, in one way or another; and in that year Congress declared that all who were born in the United States were citizens. This, however, did not confer on them the right to vote, which is regulated by the states. In some states Indians were denied this right on the grounds that they were not tax payers and in Arizona they were barred by a law that forbade persons under guardianship from voting. Some years ago the Arizona Supreme Court rendered a decision in favor of the Indian's franchise, and a federal court declared New Mexico's restrictions on them unconstitutional. Now all Indians in the country can vote.

The policy of compulsory and rapid assimilation, which prevailed from the middle of the nineteenth century until the 1920s, proved to be a miserable failure. The boarding school nearly destroyed the Indian's family institution and the concerted attack on Indian culture had a devastating effect. Economically, it ruined the Indians. When the Dawes Act was passed in 1887, Indians owned some 140 million acres of land, an area larger than the state of California. Within forty-five years they had lost all but 48 million acres, and a large part of what remained had never been good land and much of it had become worthless through overgrazing. An investigation made in the 1920s revealed that only 2 percent of the Indians had incomes of over $500 a year, death rates and infant mortality were extremely high, tuberculosis and trachoma were widespread, housing conditions were appalling, sanitary provisions were lacking, diet was poor, and the reservation, far from disappearing, was the only

friendly refuge for children leaving the boarding schools and the center of existence for those who never went to school.[19]   In short, the policy had failed to
assist the Indian in making the transition to the American culture. (See Figure
13.1 for the location of the principal Indian tribes today.)

Another change in policy then had to be made.   All along, it had been
tacitly assumed that the Indians were a "vanishing race," that the particular
policy did not matter very much anyway, and that time would solve the problem.   Instead, the Indians proved very hardy, increasing in spite of conditions
that would have eliminated others; thus the realization dawned that Indians
would be with us for a long time to come.   Under President Herbert Hoover,
accordingly, a new policy of cultural pluralism and gradual assimilation was inaugurated.   In place of "deserving politicians" who had neither knowledge nor
sympathy for their tasks, competent persons were appointed to the Indian
Bureau, who were pledged to a program of reform.   Thus the groundwork was
laid for a new policy, but it remained for the next administration, under President Roosevelt, to put that policy into operation.   John Collier, who became
Commissioner of Indian Affairs, summarized the new principles:

1. Civic and cultural freedom and opportunity for the Indian;
2. Organization of the Indian tribes for managing their own affairs;
3. Economic rehabilitation of the Indian.

This new policy was put into operation on June 18, 1934, with the passage
of the Indian Reorganization Act, which provided for the following:

1. Prohibiting the alienation by sale or foreclosure of land still owned by Indian tribes;
2. Prohibiting individual allotting of lands now in tribal status and lands to be purchased
for Indian tribes;
3. Providing for the purchase of new lands for those tribes in need of land;
4. Providing credit for the use of Indians in financing their farming and other business
enterprises;
5. Permitting consolidation of Indian lands which had become split up through inheritance;
6. Encouraging the organization and incorporation of Indian tribes for the political
and economic management of their resources and affairs;
7. Providing loan funds for Indian students seeking higher education; and
8. Giving preference to Indians for employment in the Indian Service.

The act was to be permissive, not mandatory.   The tribes were asked to vote on
whether they would accept or reject the new law.   Most chose to accept it, but
some preferred to operate otherwise.   The underlying philosophy was stated by
Collier as the "simple principle of treating the Indians as normal human beings
capable of working out a normal adjustment to, and a satisfying life within, the
framework of American civilization, yet maintaining the best of their own culture and racial idiosyncrasies."   The Indians, accordingly, were encouraged to

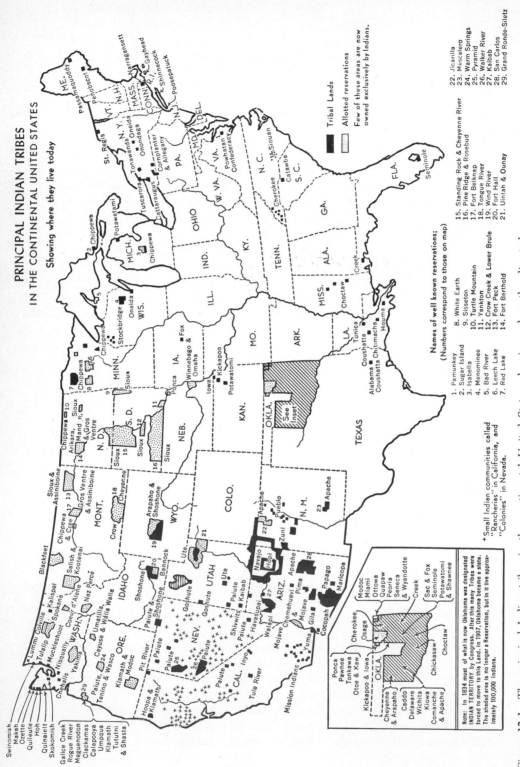

Figure 13.1 The principal Indian tribes in the continental United States, showing where they live today.

revive and develop their ancient arts and crafts, to use their own languages, to worship as they pleased, to practice their ceremonies, and to observe their customs and traditions.

This policy, which we regard as one of pluralism, came under attack from many sources. Critics maintained that it was retrogressive, that it aimed to "re-Indianize the Indian," and that it intended to perpetuate a permanent bureaucracy for controlling Indian Affairs. Others, of unquestionable goodwill toward the Indians, regarded this policy as "mystical and exotic," and insisted that the sooner integration and assimilation could be achieved, the better. One, who certainly had the interests of the Indians at heart, wrote:

I need hardly add how deeply I sympathize with the efforts of the present administration. I must however say, to my regret, that I do not share the implied optimism as to the possibility at this late date of saving the culture and the creativeness of the Indians along the old lines. The material aspects of the situation can certainly be relieved and built up, and the self-respect of the Indian can be restored, but the idea of native cultures existing safely, happily, and creatively in our midst somehow does not fit into my view of the nature and possibilities of our civilization. I hope that I am wrong. . . .[20]

It appears that the official policy of pluralism, with respect to the Indians and their culture, began to shift back to one of assimilation around 1950.[21] This development came about not with a repeal or repudiation of the Indian Reorganization Act, but through a change of the top administrative personnel, bringing with it a different philosophy. One criticism of the trend toward pluralism developed from a view that Indians could only improve their condition by becoming middle-class Americans. Many who were responsible for the shift in policy doubtless believed sincerely that the only hope for the Indian was in becoming completely integrated into the economic, political, social, and cultural life of the United States. They believed that as long as Indians remained isolated on reservations, they would be the victims of poverty, disease, overpopulation, and hopelessness. Those who sincerely believed in assimilation were supported in their efforts by others whose motives were selfish and who were eager to get their hands on the land, timber, and mineral resources the Indians possessed. To them, perpetuating the Indian's culture and social organization was abhorrent.

Another criticism that developed assumed that whatever was distinctive about Indian culture had now vanished and that what remained to be identified as Indian culture was only the "culture of poverty." Here the critics noted the disappearance of native languages, traditional ceremonies, traditional systems of kinship, and past crafts and skills. The assumption was that the Indians, like any lower-class group, needed assistance and encouragement to enter mainstream society. (Table 13.1 shows American Indian population by states.)

Seldom have the Indians themselves been asked what they wanted. However, in June, 1961, a conference held in Chicago was attended by some 450

Table 13.1   American Indian population by states

State	1950	1960	1970	State	1950	1960	1970
Alabama	928	1,276	2,443	Nebraska	3,954	5,545	6,624
Alaska	14,089	14,444	16,276	Nevada	5,025	6,681	7,933
Arizona	65,761	83,387	95,812	New Hampshire	74	135	361
Arkansas	533	580	2,014	New Jersey	621	1,699	4,706
California	19,947	39,014	91,018	New Mexico	41,901	56,255	72,788
Colorado	1,567	4,288	8,836	New York	10,640	16,491	28,355
Connecticut	333	923	2,222	North Carolina	3,742	38,129	44,406
Delaware	0	597	656	North Dakota	10,766	11,736	14,369
District of Columbia	330	587	956	Ohio	1,146	1,910	6,654
Florida	1,011	2,504	6,677	Oklahoma	53,769	64,689	98,468
Georgia	333	749	2,347	Oregon	5,820	8,026	13,510
Hawaii	?	472	1,126	Pennsylvania	1,141	2,122	5,533
Idaho	3,800	5,231	6,687	Rhode Island	385	932	1,390
Illinois	1,443	4,704	11,413	South Carolina	554	1,098	2,241
Indiana	438	948	3,887	South Dakota	23,344	25,794	32,365
Iowa	1,084	1,708	2,992	Tennessee	339	638	2,276
Kansas	2,381	5,069	8,672	Texas	2,736	5,750	17,957
Kentucky	234	391	1,531	Utah	4,201	6,961	11,273
Louisiana	409	3,587	5,294	Vermont	30	57	229
Maine	1,522	1,879	2,195	Virginia	1,056	2,155	4,853
Maryland	314	1,538	4,239	Washington	13,816	21,076	32,386
Massachusetts	1,201	2,118	4,475	West Virginia	160	181	751
Michigan	7,000	9,701	16,854	Wisconsin	12,196	14,297	18,924
Minnesota	12,533	15,496	23,128	Wyoming	3,237	4,020	4,980
Mississippi	2,502	3,119	4,113				
Missouri	547	1,723	5,405	Total	357,499	523,591	792,730
Montana	16,606	21,181	27,130				

SOURCE: Bureau of the Census. *Statistical Abstract of the United States, 1976,* Washington, D.C., Bureau of the Census, p. 131.

representatives of 90 tribal groups.   The conference adopted a "creed" that included:

We believe in the inherent right of all people to retain spiritual and cultural values, and that the free exercise of these values is necessary to the normal development of any people. . . .
   We believe that . . . the Indian has been subjected to duress, undue influence, unwarranted pressures, and policies which have produced uncertainty, frustration, and despair.

They enumerated their demands and aspirations, among which were:

1. Revocation of Joint Resolution 108 of the 83rd Congress, which inaugurated the policy of termination.

2. Economic assistance looking toward the establishment on the reservations of industries and other activities to provide employment for Indians.

3. Participation of Indians in all programs.

4. Revolving loan funds.

5. Better health services and facilities.

6. Improved housing conditions.

7. Provision for retaining, consolidating, and acquiring land.

8. Great expansion in educational facilities, including vocational and on-the-job training, adult education, guidance, and counseling.

   Many of the more radical Indian groups of the 1970s believed that the Indians had to organize as a distinct and unique people.   Even if Indian culture had deteriorated, the Indians could only improve their own ethnic lot by organizing on the basis of their uniqueness.   Consequently, arguments that claimed that Indians should give up trying to perpetuate their past culture since it no longer existed only served the ruling power and did nothing to improve the lot of Indians as a unique ethnic group.   A dissolution of the remnants of Indian culture at this juncture would bring about even greater problems than previously.   Some Indian representatives claimed that if Indian culture were to totally disappear, the Indians would not change into middle-class Americans, but rather into a disorganized and culturally confused lower-class group.[22] The stated goal of these groups was to strengthen the bonds of Indian culture so that they could decide as a strong ethnic group on what basis and to what degree they should interact with American society.
   And so our government's policies toward the Indian swing to and fro.   Our predecessors sought to exterminate them, or at least to drive them into the hinterland.   Later, efforts were made to assimilate them or to segregate them.   For two decades in the recent past we undertook to live with them, to accept them,

and to permit them to be themselves. Through it all the Indians, miraculously, have survived. Those who insist that assimilation is inevitable find little support here. The safest prediction would seem to be that for many years to come we will have with us Indian tribes, Indian communities, and Indian cultures.

Pluralism, as a form of adjustment for the differences of racial and ethnic groups, has a special appeal to those who subscribe to democratic ideals and processes. It is very congenial to those who place high value on fair play, freedom, and the sacredness of human personality. It attracts those who hold that "variety is the spice of life" and who deplore the trend toward uniformity, homogeneity, and standardization. At the same time, it must be admitted that pluralism is a delicate form of accommodation, difficult to achieve, applicable only in rare circumstances, and demanding a high degree of mutual tolerance and sympathy.[23]

Notes

1. A. Greeley, *Why Can't They Be Like Us*, p. 14.

2. As quoted in J. Higham, *Send These to Me*, p. 204.

3. Ibid., pp. 205–207.

4. H. Brotz, ed., *Negro Social and Political Thought, 1850–1920*, pp. 487–489.

5. Higham, *Send These to Me*, p. 211.

6. Ibid., pp. 232–233.

7. Ibid., pp. 233–234.

8. Ibid., pp. 228–229.

9. Cf. L. R. Harlan, *Separate and Unequal*, passim.

10. A. H. Richmond, *The Colour Problem: A Study of Racial Relations*, pp. 81–137.

11. J. C. Herold, *The Swiss without Halos*, p. 135.

12. K. Mayer, "Cultural Pluralism and Linguistic Equilibrium in Switzerland," *American Sociological Review* 16, no. 2 (April 1951): 157–163.

13. Quoted in B. J. Stern, "Soviet Policy on National Minorities," *American Sociological Review* 9, no. 3 (June 1944): 230–231.

14. "The New Anti-Semitism of the Soviet Union," *Commentary* 7, no. 6 (June 1949): 535–545.

15. G. Lawrence, *Three Million More?*, pp. 140–141.

16. J. Robinson, "The Soviet Solution of the Minorities Problem," in R. M. MacIver, ed., *Group Relations and Group Antagonisms*, p. 192.

17. Quoted in Stern, "National Minorities," p. 231.

18. For an account of these various policies, see W. T. Hagan, *American Indians*; D. McNickle, *The Indian Tribes of the United States.*

19. L. Meriam and Associates, *The Problem of Indian Administration.*

20. Goldenweiser, *Anthropology*, p. 439.

21. See J. B. Gittler, ed., *Understanding Minority Groups*, pp. 33–57; D. Van de Mark, "The Raid on the Reservation," *Harper's Magazine* 212, no. 1270 (March 1956): 48–53; J. Collier, "Letter to General Eisenhower," *The Nation* 176, no. 2 (10 Jan. 1953): 29–30; Dorothy Bohn, "Liberating the Indian — Euphemism for a Land Grab," *The Nation* 178, no. 8 (20 Feb. 1954): 150–151; J. Collier, "Back to Dishonor," *The Christian Century* 71, no. 19 (12 May 1954): 578–580; H. E. Fey, "Our National Indian Policy," *The Christian Century* 72, no. 13 (13 March 1955): 395–397.

22. M. L. Wax, *Indian Americans*, pp. 182–183.

23. Some of the problems and difficulties inherent in a pluralistic society are analyzed in M. M. Gordon, *Assimilation in American Life*, chap. 8.

Chapter Fourteen
Amalgamation

The whole history of man has been characterized by the crossing and recrossing of
races.

— *E. V. Stonequist* The Marginal Man

During the closing days of the Vietnam war, many stories circulated about the unhappy plight of mixed-blood babies who were the offspring of American servicemen and Vietnamese women. The May 28, 1973, issue of *Newsweek* reported the following story:

Perhaps the children who suffer the most . . . are the 25,000 mixed blood babies, mostly the offspring of American GI's. (. . . accurate statistics are not available, one American foundation official [said] there could be as many as 100,000 such children.) "These are the forgotten souls of the Vietnam war," says Robert G. Trott, director of CARE in Vietnam. "When the soldiers left, the money that their fathers — or friends of their fathers — had provided left with them.[1]

And another story reports that:

Mixed blood children pose a special problem. The white mixture children are almost pampered as infants, because in Vietnam fair skin is a sign of beauty. When they become gangly and larger than the others in their age bracket, they are rejected. The black mixture babies are rejected from birth. The mountain people, the Montagnards, a very dark, almost Polynesian looking people, have been outcasts in Southeastern Asia for centuries, so the rejection of dark-skinned is traditional. Orphanages have also found that the American mixture children have bigger appetites; thus they become a larger drain on the communal budget.[2]

Stories such as these deal with the most common phenomenon in history. Biological mixing, legal or otherwise, seems invariably to accompany the meeting of racial and ethnic groups. Soldiers are no more guilty than travelers, explorers, settlers, traders, and colonial administrators. Not even missionaries are exceptions. One of the first to carry Christianity to South Africa was the heroic Dutchman Dr. Jacobus Theodorus Vanderkemp, who married a "native" woman to identify himself more completely with the people to whom he devoted his life. His story is doubtless not unique. Gertrude Millin's novel, *God's Stepchildren*, has as its theme the struggle of the children of such a union to achieve the status of white people. In earlier chapters we have seen that when races meet, conflict usually appears and the process of assimilation usually sets in; by combing the literature carefully, we are able to find possible rare exceptions. Not so with amalgamation. According to Reuter, "there seems to be no historical exception to the rule that when peoples come into contact and occupy the same area there is a mixture of blood."[3] Wirth and Goldhamer say, "It is doubtful whether two races have ever lived within the confines of a single society without the process of race mixture setting in."[4] In Fairchild's judgment, amalgamation "is a process that takes place almost automatically when two or more racial groups are brought into juxtaposition,"[5] and Stern says, "Whenever history brought together two or more races in the same territory, unions of persons of different races have occurred."[6]

Apparently it has always been so. Coon finds ample evidence for race mixture in prehistoric times, even describing the "Neanderthaloid hybrids of Palestine"; and when *Homo sapiens* appeared on the European scene, there was no reversal of the process.[7] In fact, the meeting and mixing of racial types is a recurring theme in his book, evidence for which is found throughout the Paleolithic, Mesolithic, Neolithic, Bronze, and Iron Ages. Hooton doubts that Neanderthal man was completely annihilated by the *Homo sapiens* invaders of Europe, for he says, "Whenever men meet they mingle their blood." He suspects, therefore, that the large brow ridges and the retreating foreheads that one sometimes encounters in modern individuals neither prove the survival of Neanderthal man nor represent the results of chance variation, but testify instead to some miscegenation in the distant past.[8] It is this ancient human proclivity to interbreed that makes racial classification so difficult and that casts doubt on the existence of "pure" racial types.

The expansion of Europe gave a great boost to the process of amalgamation. Wherever the Europeans went, they left behind a trail of half-caste and mixed-blood offspring. In his *History of Carolina*, published in London in 1709, John Lawson, who himself traveled among the Indians, had this to say:

The English trader is seldom without an Indian female for his bedfellow, alleging these reasons as sufficient to allow of such familiarity. First, they being remote from any white people, that it preserves their friendship with the heathens, they esteeming a white man's child much above one of their own getting. . . . And lastly, this correspondence makes them learn the Indian tongue much the sooner.

The Portuguese, who were in the vanguard of European expansion, always mixed freely with the people with whom they came in contact. They first reached India in 1498 and established themselves in Goa, on the Malabar coast, from where they proceeded to govern their colonial empire and where they sired a hybrid population, the Goanese. Within twenty years they were on the Chinese coast. These pioneers were truculent people, for the most part, but they finally rented a strip of seacoast at Macao, near Canton, and promptly gave rise to a mixed people known as the Macanese. The process of amalgamation is well nigh complete in the case of the Goanese and the Macanese, and even the assimilation process has virtually run its course. They are reported to be much closer to the native peoples among whom they live than are other Eurasians, although they are devout Christians; today they are found up and down the coast of Asia and as far south as Mombasa, in Africa, where they function as intermediaries between the Oriental and Occidental worlds.[9] And, of course, centuries before the Portuguese reached India, the light-skinned Aryans invaded the country, made war on the dark Dravidians whom they found there, and proceeded to amalgamate with them. The story is much the same wherever we look and whoever be the people whose fortunes we trace. This is not to say that amalgamation occurs with equal facility in all biracial situations. There are ethnic groups that have strong feelings of endogamy, while others are indifferent to, or even favorably disposed to, mating with strangers. Amalgamation, accordingly, displays variations both in the extent to which it is carried and the rate at which it takes place. To some degree, however, it apparently occurs whenever racial and ethnic groups are brought together. Those sociologists, anthropologists, and geneticists who have made generalizations about the universality of race mixing seem to be on solid ground.

Amalgamation and Social Mores

Miscegenation occurs whether or not the mores of the society approve of the practice. The social attitudes, as a matter of fact, cover the widest possible range, from encouragement at one extreme, through tolerance and indifference, to the opposite extreme of grim determination toward prevention. The Jews from about 400 B.C. were strict in their prohibitions against marriage with non-Jews, and yet, says Wirth, "There is a great deal of evidence to support the contention that the Jews, even in the dark ghetto days, frequently intermarried with non-Jews."[10] As a consequence of this interbreeding on a worldwide scale, the Jewish physical type has become so variable that it is manifestly absurd to refer to the Jews as a race at all. The British, when they first moved into India, looked with approval on intermarriage with the native peoples, and an official communication dated April 8, 1687, stated:

The marriage of our soldiers to the native women of Fort St. George formerly recommended by you, is a matter of such consequence to posterity, that we shall be content to encourage it with some expense, and have been thinking for the future to appoint a pagoda to be paid to the mother of any child that shall hereafter be born of any such future marriage, on the day the child is christened, if you think this small encouragement will increase the number of such marriages.[11]

The British policy met with some success, with the result that there are today in India more than 150,000 Anglo-Indians. In the early days of the conquest these mixed bloods enjoyed a certain prestige. They were useful to the English as intermediaries, their services were appreciated, and sometimes they even married into the British nobility. But as the conquerors became firmly established, and as improved means of transportation tied them closer to home, they began to disapprove of miscegenation. The status of the Anglo-Indians began to deteriorate rapidly, until they became a pathetic minority, ostracized alike by English and Indians. They tried despeately to identify themselves with the Europeans, wore British clothes exclusively, and would speak of England as "home" although they had never been there; but all to no avail. They despised their Indian blood and were despised, in turn, by the Indians. As the spirit of nationalism developed in India, their position grew more and more precarious, for the native leaders suspected that their sympathies lay with the British. Their plight was portrayed in these words:

The British disown them as half-breeds and treat them with contempt. They are not admitted to membership in European clubs or other social organizations, save in rare cases. From the Hindu point of view there is no place in the system of caste for persons of mixed blood. . . . Thus the Anglo-Indians are refused admittance into either European or Hindu society, and are caught between the currents of antagonistic cultures. They are a people "without a country."[12]

The anomolous position of the Anglo-Indian has been well portrayed by John Masters in his novel, *Bhowani Junction*. In this story, Victoria Jones, part Scottish and part Indian, fails to identify herself completely with either of the heritages of which she is a product. This uncertainty of status became acute for the Anglo-Indians as India moved toward independence. Many fled to England. Many, whose racial characteristics were sufficiently Caucasoid to make them acceptable there, migrated to Australia. Most of them, however, remained in India, and the indications are that they decided that their best future lay in identifying themselves with India. Mr. Frank Anthony, President of the Anglo-Indian Association, issued the following statement on October 7, 1946: "Our position in India has been made difficult merely because of our past services to the British administration. . . . Our bitterness is steadily increasing. . . . The Anglo-Indian community has now decided that their future lies with the Indian people."[13] Ultimately, their fate may well be their absorption by the native stock.

The British, as they have migrated over the earth, have adhered to a rigid color line, holding themselves aloof from the darker peoples. While it has not been their policy to make use of legislation to prohibit intermarriage, a severe public opinion has usually served as an effective check. Nor do they relax their caste barriers in the case of the mixed bloods, as some nations are in the habit of doing. There are exceptions, to be sure. In the British West Indies the mulattoes occupy a somewhat favored position. Sir Conrad Reeves was a poor mulatto boy who rose to be one of the most famous Chief Justices of Barbados. Even so, the British have frowned on miscegenation, and have discriminated against the offspring of mixed unions. Nevertheless amalgamation, chiefly on an extramarital basis, has proceeded apace, to which the large mixed-blood populations in all those areas where the British have moved — Africa, India, Jamaica, Trinidad, Barbados, and elsewhere — bears witness.[14]

Attitudes of other peoples toward miscegenation have differed from those of the British. The Portuguese, as we have seen, have mixed freely wherever they went; but even they were not without some prejudices in the matter. Those who settled in Brazil did not hesitate to take Indian women as wives and concubines and both church and state placed their stamp of approval on mixed marriages. It was not the same with blacks. Marriages with blacks were frowned on at first and most of the sexual unions were extralegal — a distinction, of course, that has no bearing on the amalgamation process. But whereas marriages of Portuguese men to Indian women were held to be "convenient and noble," one would be condemned as "staining one's self" to marry a black or a Jew.[15] The Spaniards, when they first came to America, forbade marriage with the Indians, but the prohibition was removed in 1514 in the hope that intermarriage would win the friendship of the Indians and at the same time serve as an inducement to permanent settlement on the part of the immigrants. Marriages continued to be rare, however, although concubinage was common. Also, the Spaniards mixed with the blacks they imported as slaves, although marriage was neither favored nor widespread.

The French, too, have always taken a liberal attitude toward miscegenation. As Toynbee says, "In the seventeenth and eighteenth centuries of our era, in North America, when the English settlers were expelling and exterminating the Red Indians, the French settlers were intermarrying with them and assimilating them."[16] In 1685 the French did promulgate their famous Code noir that stipulated a fine of two thousand pounds of sugar as punishment for concubinage between a white man and a black woman that resulted in issue; but if the man married the woman, the fine was remitted, the woman set free, and the children declared legitimate. In 1724 Louis XV decreed that no marriages between whites and blacks in Louisiana should take place, but the prohibition did not apply to Indians. Ideally, the policy of the French has been one of assimilation and amalgamation, but the realities have fallen far short of the ideal.[17]

Here in the United States we have the supreme instance of a society's attempt to halt the process of amalgamation by legislative means. The fact that miscegenation occurred from the time of the earliest intergroup contacts is indicated by the kinds of problems reported in the historical records. When black women who were slaves had children by white men who were either indentured servants or free, could the children be held in slavery? Or when free white women bore children by black men, what would be the status of the children? These and a multitude of other problems arising from miscegenation had to be taken into the courts and legislatures were set to work to deal with them. Virginia soon passed laws providing special penalties for illicit intercourse between blacks and whites, and calling for the banishment of any white person who married a black, mulatto, or Indian. Massachusetts followed with a law punishing fornication between blacks and whites and prohibiting marriage between them; and other colonies were not slow in passing similar legislation. Following the Revolutionary War one state after another either placed on the statute books or wrote into its constitution prohibitions against miscegenation; these measures were disregarded in some states and subsequently repealed in others.

As late as 1966, nineteen states sought to stop miscegenation through legislation. The laws varied considerably and great confusion arose from various court interpretations. One of the main areas of confusion developed from the fact that states did not agree on which racial groups were covered by the prohibitions. All nineteen outlawed marriage between whites and blacks, but in thirteen states whites were not allowed to marry Mongolians and in six states marriage between whites and Indians was forbidden. North Carolina and Louisiana made it impossible for Indians and blacks to marry. Oklahoma went so far as to outlaw any intermarriage between blacks, Indians, or Mongolians. Other states specified such groups as "Malayan and Korean races," mestizos, Kanakas, and "half-breeds." The penalties provided by these laws also varied. Fines ranged up to $2,000 and terms of imprisonment varied from a few months to ten years.

The definitions applied to isolate these so-called races also differed widely, and some were scientifically indefensible. For example, Georgia sought to prevent the marriage between whites and individuals with "any ascertainable trace" of "African, West Indian, Asiatic Indian, Mongolian blood." Quite understandably, the exact provisions of the law were not enforced. Some laws stated the prohibitions in the most general terms (African descent and Negro blood) while others resorted to precise fractions (one-fourth, one-eighth, one-sixteenth).

In 1966 the state of Virginia's Supreme Court of Appeals had to decide on the legality of a marriage that had taken place in Washington, D.C., in 1958 between Richard P. Loving, a white man, and his part-Indian and part-black wife, Mildred Loving. The court unanimously upheld the state's ban on interracial marriages. The couple appealed the case to the United States Supreme Court, which agreed to decide whether state laws prohibiting racial intermarriage were constitutional. Previously, all courts had ruled that the laws were not discriminatory since they applied both to whites and nonwhites. However, on June 12, 1967, the Supreme Court ruled that states could not outlaw racial intermarriage. All other laws that created discriminatory racial classifications had been struck down by this time. The laws against racial intermarriage were the last vestiges of legal racial discrimination.[18]

Even though laws against racial intermarriage were present, the process of amalgamation still continued. The Indian Service estimates that about 60 percent of the Indians in the United States are full bloods, but its definition of full blood allows for a certain degree of admixture. It is doubtful that the statutes have had any effect on the retardation of the Indians' amalgamation. In case of blacks a conservative estimate is that 70 percent of them now have some white or Indian ancestry.[19]

Biological Consequences

Despite the fact that some — notably the protagonists of the melting pot theory — have espoused the mixing of peoples, the opinion has often been expressed that the biological consequences of miscegenation are harmful, even disastrous. The average person has usually defended this thesis and scholars have been fascinated by it. Many who have had first-hand contact with the American Indian have often testified to the treachery of the half-breed, while at the same time extolling the virtues of the full blood. Many a Southerner insisted that the mulattos were the troublemakers, while maintaining that the purebred blacks "knew their place." Stonequist says that in India the Anglo-Indians "have been the subject of much comment concerning the adverse consequences of race mixture; mentally, morally, and physically they have been cited to prove the contention that mixed-bloods inherit the vices of both parent races."[20] Historians have used the mixture of races as the key to understanding the past. Some have attributed the greatness of Egypt, Greece, and Rome to the purity and high quality of the racial stock, while their decline is explained as the consequence of their unwise mixing with peoples of lesser breed. Other scholars, however, have accounted for the very greatness of certain nations — Greece, Rome, England, the United States, and others — by their being the products of diverse strains, and point out that the most backward peoples of the earth are those of purest racial stock — the Southern mountaineers, the Australian aborigines, and the Ainu of Japan, for instance.

There have been several scientific studies of mixed peoples, but much more needs to be done before positive conclusions can be drawn.[21] Some of these support, and some contradict, the contentions of those who take a dim view of

---

The intellectual and personal characteristics of hybrids have also entered into the debate on the consequences of miscegenation. Davenport said that the hybrids of Jamaica did not do so badly on the intelligence tests, but that many of them were "muddled and wuzzle-headed," whatever that means. The Norwegian scientist, Mjen, in his study of Lapp-Norwegian hybrids, professes to have found among them an unusually large number of prostitutes and persons who were "unwilling to work" and who "lacked balance."[29] His explanation of these facts is biological, not social. Much has been written about the personality of the hybrid, even though scientific study of the problem is beset with difficulties. There are many reasons for believing that persons of mixed blood do indeed have unique experiences that leave marks on their personalities, but these changes can better be explained by the social situation than by the blood mixture within them. The intellectual qualities of hybrids, too, have received a great deal of attention, and with contradictory results. Some have shown the mulatto superior to the pure black, or the half-breed superior to the full-blood Indian. Other studies, and usually those more carefully designed, show no relation between color and intelligence.[30]

The truth of the matter seems to be that the biological consequences of miscegenation are in themselves neither good nor bad, but depend on the qualities of the individuals who enter into the mixture. The ill effects of race-crossing, which have been so frequently noted and written about, are social rather than biological in character. Curt Stern, a geneticist, has summarized the present state of our knowledge of the biological consequences of race-crossing in the following words:

Many persons regard hybridization as undesirable. So far as it focuses attention on sociological problems arising from unsolved difficulties in the attitudes of races toward one another, the question of the undesirability of hybridization does not fall within the province of the biologist. Nor is it the geneticist's task to evaluate the historical consequences of a gradual disappearance of the diversity of cultures as a possible result of extensive racial intermingling. Nor are the psychological conflicts which may confront an individual whose parents belong to two racial groups with widely different cultures of primary genetic concern. The opinion is often expressed, however, that there are biological reasons for the undesirability of racial hybridization. The most important arguments for this opinion center on views concerning (1) the breakup of well-adapted racial genotypes; (2) the origin, in the first or later generations, of disharmonious gene combinations; and (3) the superiority of certain races over others. . . .

Differences between human races seem to be dependent, not on a few genes which independently determine striking properties of parts, but rather on polygenic combinations of which each single gene affects to a small degree one or more characters, so that the various allelic combinations of the system are able to direct development toward a reasonably harmonious system. This seems to be the explanation for the fact that no well-substantiated examples of disharmonious constitution resulting from human hybridization have been reported. . . .

Confronted with the lack of decisive evidence on the genetic consequences of hybridization for physical and mental traits, the conservative will still counsel abstention, since the possible ill effects of the breakup of races formed in the course of evolution will not be reversible; whereas the less conservative will regard the chance of such ill effects as

amalgamation. It is said, for example, that *disharmonious combinations* result from the promiscuous crossing of diverse races. An investigation of dubious value of the black-white hybrids of Jamaica is one of the bases for this conclusion.[22] Jennings, relying partly on this study, points to the disadvantages of miscegenation:

In the mixture of races found in the United States . . . some of the stocks differ greatly in physique from others. . . . When such divers [sic] races are crossed, the offspring, receiving genes from both sides, may well develop combinations of parts that lack complete harmony. If a large body is combined with small kidneys, the latter may be insufficient for the needs of the individual. Or a large body might be combined with a small heart . . . [or] large teeth in a small jaw. In consequence the teeth decay. Partly to it, Davenport ascribes the prevalence of defective teeth in the United States. . . . Since inharmonious combinations of physical characteristics that are thus open to precise study are shown to occur as a result of race crossing, it appears probable that similarly inharmonious combinations of a more serious character may likewise occur. Davenport expresses it tersely, "A hybridized people are a badly put-together people."[23]

Meanwhile, other studies have indicated a relatively high degree of homogeneity in hybrid peoples. Williams, who measured a great many Spanish-Maya hybrids in Yucatan, found a low variability[24]; and a similar conclusion has been drawn from the studies of the Polynesian-white inhabitants of Pitcairn Island,[25] and the Boer-Hottentot hybrids of South Africa.[26] Most frequently cited as evidence for the homogeneity of the hybrid is Herskovits's investigation of American mulattos, leading to the conclusion that a definite new physical type, with low variability, is in the making.[27] These investigations, however, have not gone unchallenged either because of the smallness of their samples or because of the physical traits selected for measurement and comparison. Miscegenation, it appears, does not result necessarily in the harmonious blending of racial types, as occurs when colored liquids are poured together, nor does it result in the production of monstrosities. But exactly what does occur has not been definitely and conclusively determined.

It has also been alleged, even by persons of scientific repute, that race-crossing is tantamount to race suicide because it leads to sterility, debility, and demoralization. Sometimes these startling conclusions have been reached by the dubious practice of comparing human beings with mules or with hybrid rabbits, whose reproductive capacity showed some diminution. Fischer, however, found large families among the Boer-Hottentot people; Shapiro saw no evidence of the loss of fecundity among the hybrids of Pitcairn Island; and Boas found half-breed Indian women outstripping their full-blood cousins in the bearing of children. Herskovits disposes of the sterility argument in these words: "As far as has been ascertained, there are no crosses between human groups which carry lethal determinants for the offspring."[28] In fact, some scientists have gone to the opposite extreme in asserting that mixed peoples possess a certain "hybrid vigor." Jennings, who deplores "disharmonious combinations," counts this enhancement of vigor as one of the advantages of race-crossing and he is supported by the reports of Fischer, Shapiro, and others.

small and will not raise his voice against the mingling of races which, from a very long-range point of view, is probably bound to occur anyway. It should not be forgotten, however, that the problem of race is only partly genetic; men and women will have to consider the biological, sociological, and ethical problems when they attempt to plan the future.[31]

(From *Principles of Human Genetics*, Third Edition, by Curt Stern. W. H. Freeman and Company. Copyright © 1973.)

Social Consequences

Nature, it would seem, is quite indifferent to the whole question of miscegenation. Such unions are neither punished with monstrous and inferior offspring, nor blessed with extraordinary specimens of humanity. People, however, have shown great concern over this matter and have produced laws for coping with it. Nature replies to the question of miscegenation with a shrug of the shoulder; people speak out against it and try to stop it.

The social consequences of miscegenation cannot be understood apart from the cultural setting. There are many places where racial and ethnic groups have met and mixed and where there have been no serious social consequences. Pitcairn Island is such a place. In 1789 sixteen of the officers and crew of the British naval vessel, the *Bounty*, mutinied, cast the skipper adrift, and sailed away to a hiding place on the little-known island of Pitcairn in the South Pacific. On the way there, they stopped at Tahiti and persuaded a number of Polynesian men and women to join them. Once this assorted band had landed on Pitcairn, all the phenomena of race relations manifested themselves. Conflict between the whites and the browns was fierce until finally all the Polynesian men, and most of the British, had been killed. Assimilation, in the usual reciprocal manner, occurred, with the result that the present culture of the island is a blend of English and Polynesian, with the former predominating. Amalgamation, too, has been complete, all of the islanders being of mixed blood. Miscegenation in this case has certainly not resulted in any biological disaster; Shapiro, who studied the population, was impressed by the high mental and physical quality of the people.[32] The social consequences of amalgamation have been negligible. The fact that its population is a mixed people plays no part in the social structure of the island and has no perceptible effect on personality. It makes the people feel neither inferior nor superior. Some of them are much darker than others, but this apparently is not used on the island as a basis for discrimination and status. They pay as little attention to skin color as we pay to the color of the eyes or the width of the foot. Isolated as they are from the outside world, the attitudes of others toward the hybrids is of no consequence to them.

The isolation of the Pitcairn Islanders and the fact that all are hybrids do not in themselves account for this indifference to racial features. Another community, equally mixed and isolated, has followed a different course.[33] Tristan da

Cunha consists of three small islands in the South Atlantic. The islands were uninhabited when first discovered by the Portuguese in 1506, but the British took possession of them in 1816 and a small garrison was established there. Their nearest neighbors were on St. Helena, fourteen hundred miles away. The garrison was removed the following year; but three men — a Scot and two Englishmen — requested that they be permitted to remain. The Scot, who had formerly served in Cape Colony, had married a hybrid woman of part-Boer stock and he brought his family to Tristan da Cunha. In the years following others came to the island — mostly shipwrecked sailors of English, Scottish, Dutch, Italian, and Scandinavian nationalities. Some of them remained, but most left as soon as they had the opportunity. In 1827 the Scot's wife was the only woman on the island; but in that year five of the bachelors paid an American whaling captain to bring them women from St. Helena, which he did. These women were all hybrids of uncertain ancestry, but Munch suspects that they were white-black-Malay. He says, further, that in 1938 all the residents had some black and Malay blood with the exception of two, neither of whom were natives. Today most of the islanders look Caucasian, even Nordic, but some are dark, betraying black or Malayan features.

Unlike the Pitcairn islanders, who have attached no social significance to their mixed racial character, those on Tristan da Cunha do show some concern, even though slight. They have a preference for the lighter skin. When it comes to marriage, fair women have an advantage over the darker ones in making a desirable match; and the upper stratum of the society is made up largely of the lighter shades. A dark skin does not doom an individual to low status, but it is a handicap that can be surmounted only by exceptional zeal and industry. Munch thinks that this color prejudice "is due to an indoctrination of European ideas, either as a survival of the social heritage of the settlers or as a more recent indoctrination through European visitors."

Marginality

Usually, however, in those areas where racial and ethnic groups have lived together, miscegenation has not been ignored, as on Pitcairn, or lightly regarded, as on Tristan da Cunha. Instead, it has been looked on as a serious matter and the innocent offspring of such unions have felt the full force of the society's attitude. The mores regarding miscegenation and the hybrid offspring vary both in form and intensity from one society to another. In most parts of the United States one may boast of Indian blood without loss of status, but not of black or Japanese; and a Norwegian grandparent may prove to be an asset, where a Greek grandparent would prove the reverse. Similarly, the problems the hybrid faces are quite different in India, Java, Jamaica, Hawaii, and the United States. Generalization is difficult. Sociologists, however, have been in the habit of discussing the *social* consequences of race-crossing under the concept of the *marginal man*. Marginality, to be sure, need not be a product of diverse racial strains. Stonequist distinguishes the cultural hybrid and the

There are no pure races

racial hybrid, though both are considered as representing types of marginality. Examples of the former are Europeanized Africans, Westernized Orientals, second-generation immigrants, and denationalized Europeans; while examples of the latter are Eurasians, Indo-Europeans, Cape Coloured, and Jamaica "whites." Park, who first used the expression "marginal man," defined him as "one whom fate has condemned to live in two, not merely different but antagonistic cultures"; and Stonequist, who has given the fullest exposition of the concept, says:

The marginal man . . . is one who is poised in psychological uncertainty between two (or more) social worlds; reflecting in his soul the discords and harmonies, repulsions and attractions of these worlds, one of which is often "dominant" over the other; within which membership is implicitly if not explicitly based upon birth or ancestry (race or nationality); and where exclusion removes the individual from a system of group relations.[34]

The concept of the marginal man, despite its wide acceptance by sociologists, has come in for criticism.[35] Certainly, the marginal type of personality is not limited to racial and ethnic hybrids. Many of the symptoms are seen in the hillbilly who migrates to the city or in the Yankee who moves to the South.

Stonequist includes in his analysis such diverse types as the "detribalized native" of Africa and the children of immigrant parents in the United States. Moreover, not all racial and ethnic hybrids display the personality traits of marginality. Some hybrids are simply more sensitive than others, and some, like the Pitcairn islanders, are spared the experiences that call forth the traits. Wirth and Goldhamer question the applicability of the concept to the American mulatto; Goldberg shows that many second- and third-generation Jews regard their mixed culture as normal; and Green contrasts college students of Greek and Polish ancestry, to show that differences in their cultural backgrounds tend to make marginal personalities of the former, but not of the latter.

To apply the concept of marginality more accurately, we must break it down further. There are three different types of marginality. *Cultural marginality* is a situation in which the minority individuals share some of the values and behavior patterns of the dominant group, but also share other values and traits with one or more minority groups. Therefore, the individuals feel somewhat estranged from certain aspects of the dominant society. Hybrid or marginal cultures may arise to insulate these individuals from the psychological strain. *Social marginality* occurs when individuals are not allowed to participate fully in the groups and institutions of the dominant society. They may be rejected or discriminated against and prejudice against them may be widespread in the society. Consequently, they feel their marginality in occupational and interpersonal settings. This rejection is usually supported by informal rather than formal sanctions. Finally, *political marginality* goes further than social marginality in that the prejudice and discrimination are encouraged by laws that prevent the individuals from participating fully in the society. Therefore, there are different degrees of marginality.[36]

Marginality has been a popular theme with novelists, many of whom have portrayed with precision and understanding the emotions of the hybrid who is "neither fish nor fowl." John Masters, in *Bhowani Junction*, mentioned earlier, takes the reader into the mind of the Anglo-Indian and reveals the ambivalence, sensitivity, and frustrations found there. Diana Chang, in her novel *The Frontiers of Love*, does the same thing for the Eurasians of Shanghai, and Lyle Saxon, in *Children of Strangers*, deals realistically with the plight of the black-white hybrids of Louisiana. Playwrights and poets, too, have turned their talents to this universal theme. Langston Hughes gets right to the point in these rapier-like lines:

CROSS

My old man's a white old man
And my old mother's black.
If ever I cursed my white old man,
I take my curses back.

If ever I cursed my old black mother
And wished she were in hell,
I'm sorry for that evil wish
And now I wish her well.

My old man died in a fine big house,
My ma died in a shack.
I wonder where I'm gonna die,
Being neither white nor black?[37]

An Index of Assimilation

Amalgamation and assimilation are related both as cause and as effect. In the biological process of interbreeding, even when illicit, there is at least a minimum of cultural exchange; on the other hand, as people become assimilated and their cultural differences disappear, they are less reluctant to intermarry. Apparently there is no group, *all* of whose members are unwilling to have sex relations with individuals in the out-group — a fact amply proved by the hybrid populations that have arisen wherever contacts have occurred. Inter*marriage*, however, is quite a different matter. Young records a great many comments made by the Russian Molokans of Los Angeles to show the intensity of their feelings with regard to out-marriage. A woman of this group had given a good deal of thought to it:

I had several chances to marry American fellows, but I would not forsake my people. . . . My parents would absolutely disown me. I could never come back to the Colony. Then I figure that not all marriages turn out right. I could never later marry a Russian man. I would be without a husband and without my people too.[38]

One of the insights in Myrdal's study of American blacks is the theory of "rank order of discriminations." He maintains that the primary and essential concern of whites, in their relations with blacks, is to prevent amalgamation and that they are determined to utilize every means to this end. Accordingly, whites insist on segregation and discrimination in nearly all spheres of life; but the closer the relationships come to threatening the antiamalgamation doctrine, the greater are the limitations and restrictions. Myrdal maintains, therefore, that the force of the discriminations the whites place on the blacks takes on a rank order. He has worked out such a division, as follows:

Rank 1. Highest in this order stands the bar against intermarriage and sexual intercourse involving white women.
Rank 2. Next come the several etiquettes and discriminations, which specifically concern behavior in personal relations. These are the barriers against dancing, bathing, eating, drinking together, and social intercourse generally; peculiar rules as to handshaking, hat lifting, use of titles, house entrance to be used, social forms when meeting on streets and in work, and so forth. . . .
Rank 3. Thereafter follow the segregations and discriminations in use of public facilities such as schools, churches, and means of conveyance.
Rank 4. Next comes political disfranchisement.
Rank 5. Thereafter come discriminations in law courts, by the police, and by other public servants.
Rank 6. Finally come discriminations in securing land, credit, jobs, or other means of earning a living, and discriminations in public relief and other social welfare activities.[39]

Myrdal believes, further, that blacks, too, have a rank order that is just about parallel, but inverse, to that of the whites. The greatest concerns of blacks are with economic opportunity and injustice in the courts, while intermarriage with the whites "is of rather distant and doubtful interest."

Sociologists have regarded statistics on intermarriage as a good indicator of a group's assimilation. Drachsler, who studied intermarriage in New York City, stated:

A study of the facts of intermarriage offers a reasonably secure base from which to begin excursions into the elusive problem of assimilation. . . . . Intermarriage, as such, is perhaps the severest test of group cohesion. Individuals who freely pass in marriage from one ethnic circle into another are not under the spell of an intense cultural or racial consciousness.[40]

Opposition to intermarriage, of course, may come from either or both of the groups involved; and some groups have developed much more effective techniques than others for enforcing endogamy. At the same time, the mere *frequency* of out-marriage is not alone proof of assimilation, for there are other factors involved. Anderson, in her study of the city of Burlington, Vermont, found that the Old Yankee stock showed a decided preference for marrying their own kind; the Irish and the Germans, who are well along in the process of assimilation, show a distinct tendency to marry outside their groups; the Italians, although far less assimilated, are forced to marry outsiders, as their numbers are small; and, finally, the French-Canadians are the most endogamous of all.[41] These differences obviously are not perfectly correlated with the groups' assimilability. Similarly, Adams in his investigation of intermarriage in Hawaii reports that the Chinese, when they first came to the islands, took Hawaiian women for wives simply because Chinese women were not available. Recently, however, they have developed an adverse attitude toward out-marriage and have shown a tendency to marry among themselves, now that the ratio of the sexes is more balanced, their own status has become enhanced, and they have developed a greater group consciousness.[42]

Many investigations of intermarriage, however, have clearly shown that assimilation and intermarriage are closely related, that some racial and ethnic groups far surpass others in their tendency toward out-marriage, and that frequency of intermarriage increases with succeeding generations. Pihlblad found that the percentage of Swedish-American children who reported mixed parentage was much greater in the lower grades than in the upper[43]; Hiller discovered a similar trend among the French-Canadians of rural Illinois[44]; and Wessel reported that, in Woonsocket, Rhode Island, the rate of out-marriage for the first generation was 9.6 percent, for the second was 20.9 percent, and for the third was 40.4 percent.[45] Wessel found, also, that the percentage of intermarriage was greater for the British, amounting to 32.4 in the first generation, and that the Irish, French-Canadians, Slavs, Italians, and Jews followed thereafter, in that order.

The Jews are something of a special case, although their record illustrates clearly the close relationship between assimilation and amalgamation. Since they were involved in extensive migration from the earliest periods of their history, they constantly faced the problem of preserving their identity and religious values whenever they experienced prolonged contact with other groups. The Jewish elders clearly feared intermarriage and felt that it endangered the religion. There are many explicit statements in the Bible forbidding the practice. The first of these is expressed in Deuteronomy as follows:

> When the Lord thy God shall bring thee into the land whither thou goest to possess it, and shall cast out many nations before thee . . . thou shall make no covenant with them . . . neither shall thou make marriages with them; thy daughter thou shalt not give unto his son, nor his daughter shalt thou take unto thy son. For he will turn away thy son from following Me that they may serve other gods; so will the anger of the Lord be kindled against thee and He will destroy thee quickly.[46]

Despite the prohibitions, intermarriage between Jews and non-Jews seems to have been quite common during the early history of the Jews. Many of the patriarchs had non-Jewish wives. We are told that Jacob went to his own people for his wife, while his brother Esau chose his from the local non-Jewish population. The practice of out-marriage must have been rather common, for a special ceremony is provided in the regulations of Deuteronomy 21:10–13:

> When thou goest forth to battle against thine enemies, and Jehovah thy God delivereth them into thy hands, and thou carriest them away captive, and seest among the captives a beautiful woman, and thou hast a desire unto her, and wouldest take her to thee to wife; then thou shalt bring her home to thy house; and she shall shave her head and pare her nails; and she shall put the raiment of her captivity from off her, and shall remain in thy house, and shall bewail her father and her mother a full month; after that thou shalt go in unto her, and be her husband, and she shall be thy wife.

Jewish intermarriage in more recent times has been studied by M. L. Barron, who reaches the conclusion that it "does not necessarily adhere to a pattern of increasing incidence. It varies in time and place according to the fluctuations of social conditions."[47] Until late in the nineteenth century, Barron says, European Jews rarely married outsiders, but from the latter part of the nineteenth century until the advent of Hitler, intermarriage increased steadily, even to the point of causing concern among some Jewish scholars for the survival of Judaism itself. In Switzerland the rate of intermarriage per 100 marriages increased from 5.39 in 1888 to 11.66 in 1920; in Hungary intermarriage almost quintupled in the forty years up to 1935; in Sweden the twentieth century saw almost as many intermarriages as in-marriages, until the rabbis protested violently and refused to participate in the ceremonies; in Italy almost all Jewish families had acquired Christian relatives through intermarriage, but Italian legislation in 1938 prohibited marriage between Jews and Christians; in England, Jews of Spanish and Portuguese origin have almost disappeared through intermarriage. In the United States, Barron finds, Jews during the colonial period intermarried at a higher rate than today, with the result that Jewish pioneers in Kentucky, for instance, have disappeared; and in New York, Pennsylvania, Connecticut, and Massachusetts the early Sephardic Jews have virtually become lost through amalgamation.   Elsewhere, and at other times, the rate of intermarriage has been very low, as in Lithuania where, in 1931, it was only 0.39 percent.

Bortnick recently studied interfaith dating among Jewish college students in Florida.   When students in his sample were asked about their willingness to marry non-Jews, only 15 percent were unwilling to do so, 61 percent clearly stated that they were willing to do so, and another 24 percent would do so if the other partner converted to Judaism.   Among those students who were in a serious relationship or were engaged, 61 percent had a Jewish partner, while 39 percent had a non-Jewish partner.   In addition, 21 percent of the students in the sample had a parent or sibling who had married a non-Jew.   However, in nearly half of these cases the non-Jewish partner had converted to Judaism. These findings led Bortnick to reach the conclusion that the stage was set for a rising incidence of intermarriage among Southern Jews.

One important factor in this study that necessitates caution before application of these findings is made to Jews in other parts of the country is the distribution of Jews identifying themselves as Orthodox, Conservative, or Reform in the sample.   The South has a higher concentration of Reform Jews than is generally found in large Jewish communities in other parts of the country. Reform Jews are more likely to intermarry than Conservative Jews, and much more likely to do so than Orthodox Jews.   Bortnick's study reflects this distribution in that 41 percent of the sample polled considered themselves Reform, 45 percent Conservative, and less than 1 percent Orthodox.   Nevertheless, this study may be an indication of a rising intermarriage rate among Southern Jews in the future.[48]

Domestic Difficulties

Sociologists whose special interest is the family institution and persons engaged in marriage counseling have long suspected that unions that cut across racial and ethnic lines are fraught with difficulties.   The literature abounds with cases of family conflict arising from cultural differences between spouses.   Anderson reports the following remarks of a Burlington citizen of German stock:

I don't think we're ready for too much intermarriage yet.   I think we've been too hasty in bringing people together. . . .   I can see the difference in my brother's marriage and mine.   I married a German girl.   He married a Yankee.   We both have difficulties. But whenever a troublesome situation arises, my wife and I can meet it from the same point of view, can measure it in terms of the same values; while he and his wife have to approach it from two different angles, and it is often difficult for them to get together.[49]

Many times the problems are more serious and the outcome of a mixed marriage is tragic, as in the case of the Molokan woman who said:

I was twelve years old when we came to this country. When I went to school for a few years, I thought I was Americanized and married an Irishman. I had a miserable life with him, and was divorced. I realized then what it meant to be away from Russian-Town. A few years later I married a Molokan. . . . Slowly I began to return to *sobranie*. I felt as if I was a newborn person. I craved to hear the women talk, even though it was a sharp rebuke. . . . During our last holiday, on Judgment Day, I was so inspired by the service that I felt I must get up and say something. And say I did. I at once realized that I did the wrong thing, as I heard the people around me comment that a woman of my character should hold her tongue. . . . I was humiliated and broken up over it. . . . I just have to keep on trying until they accept me again.[50]

Marriages that cut across racial lines offer even greater difficulties than those that cross religious and ethnic lines! More interracial marriage has been recorded in recent years than in the past. Some estimates claim that there are 2.5 times as many interracial marriages as in the 1930s. However, we must be cautious before we claim that there has been a major increase in interracial marriage. The increase may be due to a number of other factors such as a mere increase in population, a greater willingness to acknowledge interracial marriage, or more thorough record keeping by the Census Bureau. Even with an increase in the number of racial intermarriages, most estimates claim that no more than approximately 0.1 percent of all marriages are between interracial couples.

Interracial couples have often encountered great difficulty in employment and in obtaining a place to live. They have been subject to social ostracism, not only from the general public, but from friends and relatives as well. In the rearing of children, they often faced problems that were incomprehensible to those who were married within the conventional patterns. For example, one father contemplates the future for his children in the following way:

It'll be all right for the boy. . . . He can choose the black world, whatever that's going to be in 10 or 15 years from now. But the girl she'll be torn. [She's light enough to go into the white world, but] she'll know she's been brought up a Negro. That makes a difference — it's like a secret you dread having. . . . She's a good little girl; I don't think she'll want to turn her back on her daddy and what he is. But what if she falls in love with a white boy and they want to get married and she doesn't tell him — she'll always be worried. . . .[51]

In an early study of interracial marriage Golden found that the couples had many problems. Prior to marriage, they had been forced to conduct a "sub rosa courtship," since most of the white parents and a great number of the black parents disapproved of such relations. The wedding ceremony itself continued the pattern of secrecy, being civil rather than religious. Frequently, the white spouse's family was not notified about the marriage and contacts with the family following the marriage were rare at most. The black family was usually willing to meet the white spouse, but approval of the match was by no means automatic. The black community, Golden found, tends to condemn black-white marriage in general, but is willing to receive the white spouse if personal qualities are acceptable. The families Golden interviewed admitted to having difficulties in finding residential quarters, and usually lived in peripheral areas, on the border between white and black residential districts. There are not many children, and Golden ventures the guess that these families feel so insecure in their married life that they refrain from inviting the additional hazard of children. Other problems, peculiar to these mixed families, include their occupational adjustments, their relations with friends, churches, and the community generally. Even so, Golden concludes that "these marriages have a good chance of survival," despite the obstacles they have had to overcome.

It is not to be denied, however, that mixed couples often feel that there are compensations for their trials, and their marriages are often quite happy.[52] Nor should one jump to the generalization that interracial marriages, regardless of time, place, and race, are unstable. In other countries, where attitudes toward race are different from those in the United States, interracial marriages are doubtless regarded with no more concern than we regard marriages between Methodists and Presbyterians, or between Republicans and Democrats. Even in this country public opinion makes a distinction between the marriage of Jew and Gentile, white and Indian, American and Chinese, Yankee and Mexican.

After World War II thousands of American soldiers married Japanese wives, whom they subsequently brought back to America with them. It was widely predicted that such marriages were doomed to failure and in both the newspapers and the popular magazines there have been stories about the prejudice, discrimination, and the tremendous adjustment problems these couples have faced. The few sociological studies that were made, however, did not bear out these pessimistic reports. Walters studied thirty-five American-Japanese families in Ohio and found that they were making rather successful adjustments.[53] None reported having encountered severe prejudice and discrimination, either on the part of the American families or of the communities. Their children are still too young to have been exposed to prejudicial treatment, but Walters doubts that they will be, for they bear their father's American surname and, in appearance, he found most of them not particularly Oriental.

Strauss has made a study of American-Japanese couples living in the Chicago area, and he concludes that they do not support the assumption that interracial marriages are peculiarly subject to strains and instability.[54] To be sure, there are difficulties and disagreements, but for the most part they are present also in endogamous marriages.

Nevertheless, the preponderance of data that we have suggests that marriages across racial, religious, and ethnic lines are faced with specific obstacles in addition to those that all marriages face. Even though interracial marriages in the United States are relatively few in number, marriages across ethnic and religious lines are increasing. As Bossard said after making a study of intermarriage in New York City, "The melting pot bubbles actively, because there are so many diverse ingredients in it; it fuses somewhat less than one is apt to suppose.[55]

Notes

1. *Newsweek*, 28 May 1973, p. 56.

2. *Mademoiselle*, Dec. 1973, p. 165.

3. E. B. Reuter, ed., *Race and Culture Contacts*, p. 7; "Amalgamation," *Encyclopedia of the Social Sciences*, vol. 2, pp. 16–17.

4. L. Wirth and H. Goldhamer, "The Hybrid and the Problem of Miscegenation," in O. Klineberg, ed., *Characteristics of the American Negro*, p. 263.

5. H. P. Fairchild, *Race and Nationality*, p. 88.

6. C. Stern, *Principles of Human Genetics*, pp. 832, 834, 840.

7. C. S. Coon, *The Races of Europe*.

8. E. A. Hooten, *Up From the Ape*, 1st ed., p. 336.

9. R. E. Park, *Race and Culture*, pp. 122–123.

10. L. Wirth, *The Ghetto*, p. 67.

11. Quoted in Park, *Race and Culture*, p. 130.

12. P. F. Cressey, "The Anglo-Indians: A Disorganized Marginal Group," *Social Forces* 14, no. 2, Dec. 1935, p. 264.

13. Information Cables, Government of Indian Information Services, Washington, D.C., October 8, 1946.

14. E. Williams, *The Negro in the Caribbean*, passim; E. V. Stonequist, *The Marginal Man*, passim.

15. D. Pierson, *Negroes in Brazil*, p. 115ff; G. Freyre, *The Masters and the Slaves: A Study in the Development of Brazilian Civilization*, pp. 84ff., 407ff.

16. A. J. Toynbee, *The Study of History*, vol. 1, p. 225.

17. R. Kennedy, "The Colonial Crisis and the Future," in R. Linton, ed., *The Science of Man in the World Crisis*, pp. 328–330.

18. M. L. Barron, ed., *The Blending American*, p. 84.

19. M. J. Herskovits, *The Anthropometry of the American Negro*, p. 279, and *The American Negro: A Study in Racial Crossing*, p. 10; Wirth and Goldhamer, "Problem of Miscegenation," pp. 268–273; G. Myrdal, *An American Dilemma: The Negro Problem and Modern Democracy*, pp. 132–133.

20. Stonequist, *Marginal Man*, p. 16.

21. For a summary of these studies, see Wirth and Goldhamer, "Problem of Miscegenation," pp. 320–329.

22. C. B. Davenport and M. S. Steggerda, *Race Crossing in Jamaica*. For a criticism of this publication, see Wirth and Goldhamer, "Problem of Miscegenation," p. 328.

23. H. S. Jennings, *The Biological Basis of Human Nature*, pp. 280–282.

24. G. D. Williams, *Maya-Spanish Crosses in Yucatán*, Harvard University, Peabody Museum Papers, vol. 13, no. 1, 1931.

25. H. L. Shapiro, *The Heritage of the Bounty*.

26. E. Fischer, *Die Rehobother Bastards und das Bastardierungsproblem beim Menschen*.

27. Herskovits, *The American Negro*.

28. M. J. Herskovits, "Race Mixture," in the *Encyclopedia of the Social Sciences*, vol. 13, pp. 41–43.

29. Quoted in O. Klineberg, *Race Differences*, pp. 214–215.

30. Klineberg, *Race Differences*, pp. 219–222; Wirth and Goldhamer, "Problem of Miscegenation," p. 330ff.

31. From C. Stern, *Principles of Human Genetics*, pp. 832–840.

32. Shapiro, *Heritage of the Bounty*, pp. 10–11.

33. P. A. Munch, "Cultural Contacts in an Isolated Community — Tristan de Cunha," *American Journal of Sociology* 53, no. 1 (July 1947): 1–8.

34. Stonequist, *Marginal Man*, p. 8.

35. M. M. Goldberg, "A Qualification of the Marginal Man Theory," *American Sociological Review* 6, no. 1 (Feb. 1941): 52–58; A. W. Green, "A Re-examination of the Marginal Man Concept," *Social Forces* 26, no. 2 (Dec. 1947): 167–171; Wirth and Goldhamer, "Problem of Miscegenation," pp. 335–342; A. C. Kerckhoff and T. C. McCormick, "Marginal Status and Marginal Personality," *Social Forces* 34, no. 1 (Oct. 1955): 48–55; M. M. Gordon, *Assimilation in American Life*, pp. 54–59.

36. N. P. Gist and A. G. Dworkin, eds., *The Blending of Races*, pp. 15–17.

37. L. Hughes, *Selected Poems*, p. 158. © 1970. Reprinted by permission of Alfred A. Knopf, Inc.

38. P. V. Young, *The Pilgrims of Russian Town*, p. 78.

39. Myrdal, *American Dilemma*, pp. 60–61.

40. J. Drachsler, *Democracy and Assimilation*, p. 87.

41. E. L. Anderson, *We Americans*, p. 188ff.

42. R. Adams, *Interracial Marriage in Hawaii*, pp. 142–159.

43. C. T. Pihlblad, "The Kansas Swedes," *Southwestern Social Science Quarterly* 13, no. 1 (June 1932): 1–14.

44. E. T. Hiller, et al., "Rural Community Types," *University of Illinois Studies in the Social Sciences* (December 1928).

45. B. B. Wessel, *An Ethnic Survey of Woonsocket, Rhode Island*, chap. 8.

46. Cited in Barron, *Blending American*, p. 68.

47. M. L. Barron, "Jewish Intermarriage in Europe and America," *American Sociological Review* 11, no. 1 (Feb. 1946): 6–13. See also W. J. Cahnman, ed., *Intermarriage and Jewish Life*.

48. D. Bortnick, *Patterns of Interfaith Dating and Religious Observance Among Jewish College Students in Florida*, pp. 45–68.

49. Anderson, *We Americans*, pp. 199–200.

50. Young, *Pilgrims of Russia Town*, p. 79.

51. Barron, *Blending American*, p. 119.

52. See K. Eskelund, *My Chinese Wife*; R. L. Williams, "He Wouldn't Cross the Color Line," *Life* 31, no. 10 (3 Sept. 1951): 81–94.

53. L. K. Walters, *A Study of the Social and Marital Adjustment of Thirty-five American-Japanese Couples*.

54. A. L. Strauss, "Strain and Harmony in American-Japanese War-Bride Marriages," *Marriage and Family Living* 16, no. 2 (May 1954): 99ff.

55. J. H. S. Bossard, "Nationality and Nativity as Factors in Marriage," *American Sociological Review* 4, no. 6 (Dec. 1939): 792–798.

Chapter Fifteen
Segregation

As I walked those streets I thought of the
many personal tragedies that this pattern of
ghetto life had imposed on all of us. A few
miles away, the normal world was moving
along its usual course: the established classes
were living as before, the church bells rang
for litany, and the shops served their customers; business as usual. But in our world
things were different.

— *Eugene Heimer* Children of Auschwitz

Marcus Garvey was one of the first blacks to launch a partially successful Back
to Africa movement. He entered the post-World War I Harlem environment
and exuberantly preached the doctrine of "Africa for the Africans." Garvey
believed that racial integration was impossible and that if blacks persisted in attempting it, there would be an inevitable racial war that blacks would eventually lose because they would be outnumbered by the whites. Consequently,
there was no choice but to leave the United States and set up a nation for
blacks in Africa.

The Negro needs a nation and a country of his own, where he can best show evidence of
his own ability in the art of human progress. Scattered as an unmixed and unrecog-
nized part of alien nations and civilizations is but to demonstrate his imbecility, and
point him out as an unworthy derelict, fit neither for the society of Greek, Jew or
Gentile. . . . Hence, the Universal Negro Improvement Association appeals to each
and every Negro to throw in his lot with those of us who, through organization, are
working for the universal emancipation of our race and the redemption of our common
country, Africa.
   No Negro, let him be American, European, West Indian or African, shall be truly
respected until the race as a whole has emancipated itself, through self-achievement and
progress, from universal prejudice. The Negro will have to build his own government,

industry, art, science, literature and culture, before the world will stop to consider him. Until then, we are but wards of a superior race and civilization, and the outcasts of a standard social system.

The race needs workers at this time, not plagiarists, copyists and mere imitators; but men and women who are able to create, to originate and improve, and thus make an independent racial contribution to the world and civilization.[1]

Segregation means the act, process, or state of being separate or set apart. It is a form of isolation that places limits or restrictions on contact, communication, and social relations. Many people regard segregation as a form of partial ostracism, superimposed on a minority by the dominant group; and it is often treated as though it were synonymous with discrimination. Usually it does indeed involve unequal treatment, and it is commonly a condition forced on one group by another. However, as we can see from the Garvey case, there are many instances where it is voluntary. In fact, segregation need not even be the outcome of either coercion or discrimination. Segregation is essentially a pattern of accommodation, which assumes a wide variety of forms and is the product of many complex motives.

The Nature of Segregation

The practice of resolving conflicts by separating, isolating, or segregating groups of people is as old as the human race itself. The Bible and other early records afford many illustrations, and even preliterate peoples have frequently resorted to this practice. Thus the primitive Ainus, faced with annihilation or absorption when the Japanese invaded their territory, chose to withdraw to the less hospitable islands at the northern end of the archipelago; the pygmy Semang retreated to the jungles to avoid contact with the numerous hordes that for centuries have swept over the Malay Peninsula; and the Bushmen, driven by one people after another, finally found refuge in the Kalahari Desert of Africa. Indian tibes in the Americas, too, have often chosen withdrawal and segregation in preference to annihilation, assimilation, or subordination. Segregation, operating as it has done over so wide a range and under such a variety of circumstances, has assumed a multitude of forms, a few examples of which we now consider.

The Ghetto

Segregation is an old story to the Jewish people, who have experienced it in all its forms — voluntary and involuntary, social and spatial. Even in that distant period, where history and myth can hardly be distinguished, we are told that the Hebrews, during their four-hundred-year sojourn in Egypt, lived apart from the others "in the land of Goshen." From that time to the present day, segregation has been an inseparable feature of their existence.

The word *ghetto* applies strictly to the Jewish quarter of a city, but it is often used nowadays to refer to the Chinatowns, the Black Belts, or the segregated areas occupied by any racial or ethnic minorities. The origin of the term is in dispute. It seems doubtful, as some have supposed, that it is derived from the Hebrew *get*, meaning separation or segregation. Others have suggested that it came from the German *gitter* (bars of a cage), or from the Italian *borghetto* (a small, negligible section), or from the Italian *guetto* or *guitto* (a filthy creature). The probability is, however, that it derives from the Italian *gietto*, the cannon foundry at Venice near which the Jewish settlement was located.[2] The word, whatever its origin, came much later than the practice of Jewish segregation. In medieval Germany there were separate Jewish quarters bearing such designations as *Judenstrasse, Judengasse,* or *Judendorf*; in Portugal it was *Judiaria*; in France, *Juiverie*; in England, *Jewry*; in North Africa, *mella*. These names indicate that in many European cities of the fourteenth century there existed clearly defined areas inhabited by the Jews. No doubt the Jews dwelt together in the cities of the ancient world, long before the fourteenth century, and even before the Christian era, a fact to which the New Testament bears witness.

The first formal recognition of a Jewish area in a city dates from 1084 A.D. In that year Rudiger, Bishop of Speyer, granted the Jews the right to have a separate residential section of their own. He was eager to attract Jews to his city in order, he said, "to add to the honor of our place"; and he was constrained to permit their segregation so that "they might not readily be disturbed by the insolence of the populace." The fact is that segregation, far from being a badge of infamy, was a privilege enjoyed and appreciated by the Jews. Not only did it afford them protection, but, as Wirth points out, it was a convenient administrative device, which facilitated the observance of various religious customs such as the proper preparation of food, attendance at the synagogue, and participation in community affairs.[3] In one city the Jews annually commemorated the establishment of their ghetto with a special ritual, indicating that they recognized the privilege that was theirs; several communities, on losing their ghetto charters, went to the expense of repurchasing them.

In the course of time, however, the ghetto became transformed from a voluntary to a compulsory institution, and from a privilege to a symbol of discrimination and persecution. This transformation did not come about suddenly. Here and there a temporal ruler or a church council would go on record as insisting on the separation of Jews and Christians, or Jews and Moslems. Among the early steps in the direction of compulsory segregation was the following decree issued by an ecclesiastical synod held at Breslau in 1266:

Since the land of Poland is a new acquisition in the body of Christianity, lest perchance the Christian people be, on this account, the more easily infected with the superstition and depraved morale of the Jews dwelling among them . . . we command that the Jews dwelling in this province of Gnesen shall not live among the Christians, but shall have their houses near or next to one another in some sequestered part of the state or town, so that their dwelling place shall be separated from the common dwelling place of the Christians by a hedge, a wall, or a ditch.[4]

In 1311 the provincial council of Ravenna, disturbed by the commingling of Jews and Christians that was apparently the vogue in that section, decreed that "Jews shall not dwell longer than a month anywhere, except in those places in which they have synagogues." The Council of Valencia, in 1388, insisted that Christians dwelling in the Jewish quarter should immediately move out; and the Venetian senate, in 1516, placed compulsory residential restrictions on the Jews. Decrees of this sort were made in country after country in Europe, in Turkey, and in Morocco, between the thirteenth and the sixteenth centuries.

The compulsory ghetto, however, did not become general throughout the Christian world until 1555, when Pope Paul IV called for segregation in a papal bull. It is absurd, the bull declares, for accursed Jews to live openly among Christians, to own real estate, and to employ Christian servants. They should be compelled to live within an enclosure set apart for them and not to appear outside that quarter unless they wear some distinguishing mark, such as a yellow hat for men and a yellow veil for the women. The Roman ghetto, created at that time, was one of the filthiest examples of the institution. It was situated on a low bank of the Tiber and was surrounded by a brick wall; subject to annual floods, it was an incredibly unhealthy and impoverished community. It was not, however, too unlike hundreds of others throughout Europe.

The motives that brought into existence the compulsory ghetto were often stated in the numerous edicts. It was feared that the presence of the Jews would weaken the faith of the Christians, that they would make converts, that they would be a source and a stimulation for heresy. Lestschinsky, however, who looks on the compulsory ghetto as a product of the sixteenth century, thinks these religious arguments were but the rationalization of a more basic conflict.[5] Members of the bourgeoisie, he thinks, were out to eliminate and cripple their competitors. The Jews were playing an important role in trade, commerce, moneylending, and certain handicrafts, and into these fields the bourgeois were edging their way. At the same time, those in the bourgeoisie were endeavoring to obtain greater mutual autonomy from the feudal barons, bishops, kings, and emperors — the very ones who furnished protection to the Jews and who profited so handsomely from them in the form of taxes, loans, and "gifts." Any handicap that could be placed on the Jews, therefore, in the ways of restricting their movement, limiting their economic activities or impoverishing them would return to the bourgeoisie in the form of greater profits and greater freedom from the feudal overlords. The truth probably is that a complex of motives underlay the development.

The compulsory ghetto began to dissolve and to disappear in the eighteenth century. This was a result of forces operating both within the ghetto and without. The movement known as the Enlightenment did not pass the Jews by, but served to liberate them from the provincialism of the ghetto. The German philosopher, Moses Mendelssohn, was the embodiment of this trend; and he, in turn, had no small part in modifying the prejudices of the Christians and in broadening the outlook of fellow Jews. The inhabitants of the ghettos, thus stimulated, began to speak the language of the country in which they lived, to read French and German books, to shave their beards and cut off their ear-locks, and to wear short coats. Wirth mentions, among the other social movements that had profound influence on the dissolution of the ghetto, the growth of socialism, the revival of interest in Hebrew, the birth of Zionism, and the Reform movement that favored cultural assimilation with the general population.[6]

At the same time there were forces stirring on the outside. The people of western and central Europe and their governments began to manifest a change in their attitudes toward the Jews. Up to this time the Jews were virtually aliens in the countries where they lived; they were denied the rights of citizenship, excluded from participation in political affairs, barred from schools and many occupations, denied the privilege of owning land, restricted as to dress and residence, and subject to insult and violence. The first to advocate the mitigation of these handicaps was the Englishman, John Toland, who published a book in London in 1714 under the title *Reasons for Naturalizing the Jews in Great Britain and Ireland, on the Same Foot with All Other Nations.* Forty years later Parliament did discuss a bill to facilitate the naturalization of Jews, but public opposition to it was insurmountable. Other bills were subsequently introduced, several of them passing the House of Commons only to be rejected by the Lords. In 1858 Lionel de Rothschild was permitted to take his seat in Parliament, and in the years following, Jews were admitted to the highest offices in the government and in the universities. The British colonies had even earlier removed restrictions on Jewish citizenship; and the Constitution of the United States and the First Amendment established equality without mentioning Jews. The philosophers of the French Revolution were ardent advocates of Jewish emancipation, and toward the end of the eighteenth century there began a gradual removal of the restrictions under which the Jews in France had been living.

The nineteenth century witnessed the emancipation in one country after another. Belgium emancipated her Jews in 1815; Denmark in 1849; Sweden in 1865. The movement was not steady and continuous because of the periods of reaction that interrupted it. In Germany and Austria the Jews won some rights in the eighteenth century, but these were withdrawn after the fall of Napoleon. Emancipation came in Austria-Hungary in 1869, and in Germany with the formation of the Empire in 1870. In eastern Europe the dates were much later. The rise of Hitler, of course, brought on a catastrophic reversal of this long trend. The fact is, however, that within a century the walls of the compulsory ghetto were leveled and the Jews had everywhere achieved formal and legal equality, except in out-of-the-way places like Yemen and Ethiopia.

There is a difference, however, between formal equality and social equality; and the abolition of the compulsory aspect of the ghetto did not mean the end of segregation. There are still barriers that isolate the Jews and keep them from participating fully in the life of the larger society. Discrimination prevails regarding the holding of public office, in employment, in place of residence, in social intercourse, and in admission to educational institutions. The Jews are still highly concentrated; most of the 6 million Jews in the United States live in Boston, Philadelphia, Los Angeles, Chicago, and New York. As Wirth says:

> There is scarcely a city of any considerable size in Europe or America that does not have a ghetto. Even in towns containing only a score of Jews, there is to be found in all parts of the world some more or less organized Jewish community.
>
> Just as the ghetto arose before formal decrees forced the Jews into segregated areas, so the ghetto persists even after these decrees have been annulled.[7]

Jews are unanimously in favor of their *legal* emancipation. As for *social* emancipation, the attitudes vary. Those who accept the philosophy of assimilation, are, of course, in favor of it; but those who desire the perpetuation of their group and the preservation of their three-thousand-year-old social heritage are faced with the difficult problem of maintaining some sort of balance between the forces that would absorb them and those that would isolate them.

Chinatown

The Chinese were once the objects of bitter prejudice, but are so no longer. Instead, they are regarded with a certain tolerance and indifference by the whites. Many a city considers its Chinatown a commercial asset — an attraction for tourists, a spot where one may go for an exotic meal, for curios, or for a glimpse of a unique people. Though the Chinese live in the very heart of our cities, so great is the gulf that separates them from the rest of society that they are an unknown minority. Those who crossed the Pacific to America have had quite a different experience from those who stopped off at Hawaii.

The records show that only one Chinese was admitted to the United States in 1820 and in 1850 there were only 758 in the country. But they began arriving in great numbers with the discovery of gold in California. About twenty thousand were admitted in 1852 and thirteen thousand in 1854. While they were never welcomed with open arms, there was a place for them in California in those days. The miners, intent on finding gold, did not relish any foreign competitors at all; but there were menial jobs that had to be done, food to be cooked, and clothes to be laundered, and the Chinese were not unwilling to perform these lowly tasks. Their presence, accordingly, was somewhat appreciated; and they were spoken of as "thrifty," "orderly and industrious," "sober and law-abiding." Governor McDougal even recommended that further immigration be encouaraged by land grants, since they were "one of the most worthy of the newly adopted citizens."[8]   The gold fever began to subside by 1856; but after the Civil War the transcontinental railroads were being constructed, and there was a demand for labor that the Chinese were called on to fill.   The Union Pacific, moving from the East, relied largely on the Irish and other European immigrants; but on the Central Pacific, pushing from the West, nine out of ten of the laborers were Chinese.   The final joining of these two roads at Promontory, Utah, on May 10, 1869, marked a historic moment for America, but catastrophe for the Chinese.   It meant that they would have to look for other jobs, and there was a business depression at the time.

The Chinese were willing to do anything. They began as miners, but when the whites resented their competition, they moved into other fields. They worked as domestics and common laborers; they were available for seasonal work; they operated stores and hotels; they engaged in fishing; they became cooks and carpenters; they were employed in the first manufacturing enterprises on the West Coast — cigars, shoes, clothing, soap, and candles. At one time most of the agricultural laborers in California were Chinese.

Conflict appeared whenever the Chinese moved into those occupations in which the whites were engaged.[9]   First, it was mining. The California legislature in 1852 imposed a special tax on all aliens engaged in mining and the tax was increased in succeeding years until it was declared unconstitutional in 1870.   There was agitation against the Chinese cigar makers in 1859; and in 1867 there was a race riot, when whites engaged in the boot and shoe industry blamed a reduction in their wages on Chinese competition.   A smallpox epidemic in 1870 was attributed to the Chinese.   Anticoolie clubs were organized; mass meetings, parades, riots, and destruction of property prevailed; and political parties pledged themselves to rid the state of the "Mongolian menace." The Chinese, once praised for their industry and cleanliness, now found themselves condemned as filthy, deceitful, "moon-eyed lepers."

The Californians made a national issue of their prejudice against the Chinese. They were clever in the way they proceeded, associating the Oriental problem with the black problem whenever possible and pressing the issue especially on the eve of elections, when political parties were eager to please anyone who could cast a vote.   In 1868 the Burlingame Treaty was negotiated, recognizing the right of immigration between the United States and China, but hedging on the matter of naturalization.   This treaty pleased the railroads, which still wanted cheap labor, but incensed white workers.   Finally, after much pressure had been applied, Congress passed the Chinese Exclusion Act in 1882, which suspended all immigration from that source for ten years.   The ten-year extension was renewed in 1892 and was extended indefinitely in 1902.

Many other acts of discrimination against the Chinese were passed; and in 1924 all immigration was suspended for those ineligible for citizenship. As a gesture of friendship to our wartime ally, in 1943 the Chinese were placed under the same quota system as the Europeans, making it possible for 105 to enter the country annually.

How did the Chinese react to this discriminatory legislation and to the incessant vilification and abuse to which they were subjected? First, they fought back in the courts, but to no avail. Second, many of them returned, although some unwillingly, to China. Third, numbers of them moved away from the Pacific Coast to New England, the Middle West, and the South. Fourth, they migrated to the large cities, congregated in tight colonies, and proceed to segregate themselves insofar as possible from the general population. They withdrew socially, politically, and economically, as well as physically. They turned from those occupations that brought them into competition with whites and developed art and curio shops, restaurants specializing in unusual atmosphere and large servings of Chinese food, and hand laundries. They settled their disputes among themselves, deeming it a disgrace to be hauled before the white court. In their Chinatowns they made a concerted effort to preserve their ancient institutions.[10] They established their temples, published newspapers and periodicals, celebrated their Old-World festivals (Ching Ming, Dragon Boat, Moon, Winter Solstice, and so on), and emphasized their clan and family organizations. They developed new institutions, too, to help them adjust to the New-World conditions — tongs, Chinese schools, benevolent societies, and political organizations. In spite of their isolation, however, assimilation did occur. The Chinese learned to observe Christmas, Thanksgiving, Easter, and especially Father's Day and Mother's Day. And they joined the American Legion and the Girl Scouts, attended movie theaters, and acquired American culture.

Not all Chinese crowded into the cities. A Mr. Wong, for instance, migrated to Mississippi in 1875 and settled in the rich farming area known as the Delta. He was followed by others, with the result that in 1940 some nine hundred Chinese were living there.[11] They did not develop the usual Chinese occupational specialties (laundries, chop suey restaurants, and the like), but became independent merchants. During the first fifty years of their residence in the Delta they were not the victims of segregation, as their fellow nationals were in the cities, and their assimilation proceeded rapidly. They joined the white Baptist Church and participated in its services and their children attended the white public schools. Then a trend toward segregation set in. One of their children was expelled from the white school. The case was fought vigorously, but the court ruled for segregation on the ground that its purpose was "to preserve the purity and integrity of the white race, and prevent amalgamation." As a compromise, special schools for Chinese were established in two Mississippi towns.

There are indications that the assimilation of the Chinese proceeds in spite of the obstacles that have been placed in its way. The Chinese, like the Jews, are a people who have a high regard for learning, and they make sacrifices to educate their children. The children, when they acquire an education, are disposed to turn away from the traditional occupations, to enter the professions, and to move out of the Chinese community. Dr. Rose Hum Lee has analyzed the trend with respect to the Chinatowns of America, and her conclusions are:

. . . It is probable that, as the Chinese reside longer in this country and the Chinese-Americans increase in population, another redistribution of their numbers may occur, with settlement in cities under metropolitan status. Where only a few Chinese reside in a community, they are socially well accepted. Acculturation and assimilation are more rapid for "marooned families" and isolated individuals than for concentrated populations. . . .

It appears that the number of Chinatowns in this country will decrease almost to a vanishing point. Only those of historical or commercial importance, as in San Francisco and New York, will remain. . . . As Chinese-Americans become acculturated and strive for higher status . . . this dispersion will be similar to that of any other small minority group already an integral part of American society. With acculturation and settlement among the members of the larger society, amalgamation will increase, and in time assimilation will be attained.[12]

Racial Islands

American blacks, too, have had a long and varied experience with segregation. As far back as 1714 it was proposed that blacks be sent back to Africa. In 1777 Thomas Jefferson headed a committee that explored the possibilities of exporting blacks. Many organizations interested in the problem of slavery included in their program some scheme of resettlement. In 1815 one Paul Cuffe, at his own expense, took thirty-eight blacks to Africa. Thereupon the American Colonization Society was organized, including many prominent names among its members, and soon won widespread support for its plan to establish a colony, choosing Liberia as the location. There were other proposals, too. Haiti, Canada, South America, and even the American West were considered as possibilities. No less a person than Abraham Lincoln at one time entertained the idea that some such plan of segregation offered the best solution for the problem of black-white relations. He once invited a group of free blacks to the White House, urging them as indicated in the following quotation to support his colonization scheme:

Your race suffer greatly, many of them, by living among us, while ours suffer from your presence. In a word, we suffer on each side. If this is admitted, it affords a reason why we should be separated.[13]

These various attempts to solve the race problems by a sort of "black Zionism" have been conspicuous failures. The American Colonization Society, in its palmiest days, succeeded in transporting only some twelve thousand; places other than Liberia have attracted no more than a trickle. Among blacks themselves, some have received these schemes with mild approval, some with bitter opposition, but most have shown utter indifference. Nonetheless, the proposals continue to sprout.

Blacks, however, have often succeeded in withdrawing from the society of whites and establishing segregated communities of their own. There are today no less than fifty all-black communities in the United States, functioning so quietly and so unobtrusively that their presence is hardly suspected by the greater society. Some of these segregated communities were established many years ago. Frazier, who calls them "racial islands," has visited and described a number of them.[14] Among them is the Gouldtown settlement near Bridgeton, New Jersey, concerning the origin of which we have well-authenticated records. It seems that a certain John Fenwick, having been granted a tract of land, came to America in 1675. One of his granddaughters, Elizabeth Adams, became enamored with a black man by the name of Gould, much to the distress of John Fenwick, who threatened to disinherit her

unless the Lord open her eyes to see her abominable transgression against Him, me and her good father, by giving her true repentance and forsaking that Black which hath been the ruin of her and becoming penitent for her sins.

This couple and their children formed the nucleus of the Gouldtown settlement. They were joined by others of mixed black, Indian, and white blood, who together formed a community that maintained itself for more than two centuries, but has recently been dwindling. Some of its members have moved away, intermarried with whites, and lost themselves in the white population, while others have identified themselves with the black race. All of the "islands" that Frazier describes, most of them tracing back to colonial times, were formed by biracial individuals who were reluctant to be classed with blacks and were not acceptable as whites, and who therefore chose this form of segregation as a feasible escape from their dilemma.

Other blacks have turned to the segregated community, not to escape their racial identification, but as preferable to assuming a subordinate position in the white community. Such all-black settlements are found today in Oklahoma, Ohio, Kansas, California, Arkansas, Illinois, Michigan, Pennsylvania, West Virginia, and in all the Atlantic and Gulf states from New Jersey to Texas. Among them is Mound Bayou, Mississippi.[15] This community was established in the late 1880s by the remarkable black man, Isaiah T. Montgomery, who had been a body servant to Jefferson Davis, President of the

Confederacy. Following the Civil War, Davis sold his Mississippi plantation to his former slaves, who managed the estate with outstanding success. Then the falling price of cotton and legal difficulties with the Davis heirs forced the blacks to abandon the plantation. A few years later a railway company acquired a large tract of land that it wanted to develop and, hearing of Montgomery's success as a cotton planter, proposed that he establish a black colony. With the help of his cousin, Ben Green, Montgomery enlisted a band of blacks in the project, and together they purchased 840 acres. The experiment met with success, and other blacks joined them. Fifty years later the community had grown to the size of eight thousand, one thousand of whom lived in the town of Mound Bayou, the others farming the adjoining territory covering thirty thousand acres. Schools, stores, churches, sawmills, and political institutions resemble those of other southern towns, with the exception that they are owned and operated by blacks; and as one of the citizens said, "Here we can hold our faces up." [16]

(Figure 15.1 shows the distribution of black population in the United States.)

Segregation and Restricted Communities

The perception of a threat is the key factor in understanding the events that lead to the voluntary and involuntary segregation of communities whose interactions with the outside society are restricted. On the one hand, this perception can arise within the community itself, in which the outside world is defined as a danger. Then again the perception can arise within the larger society, when an entire group is defined as posing a threat to the larger population. In either case, free access to interaction with others is limited. Table 15.1 will illustrate this point.

Internally Restricted Communities

In Table 15.1 two types of restricted communities are presented. The first is what we will call the *internally restricted community*. This is a community that looks on the outside world as a threat to its existence. This danger is so great that restrictions must be imposed and the normal flow of communication and interaction between the group and the larger society has to be limited. Often this threat is tied to the group's assumption that contact with "undesirables" will produce negative social change that, in turn, will cause the destruction of the group or its value system. To avoid this possibility, the group cuts itself off from the threat. In the internally restricted community, the community decides to restrict its interactions with the larger society to the level at which the basic economic and survival needs will be met. This process can be illustrated

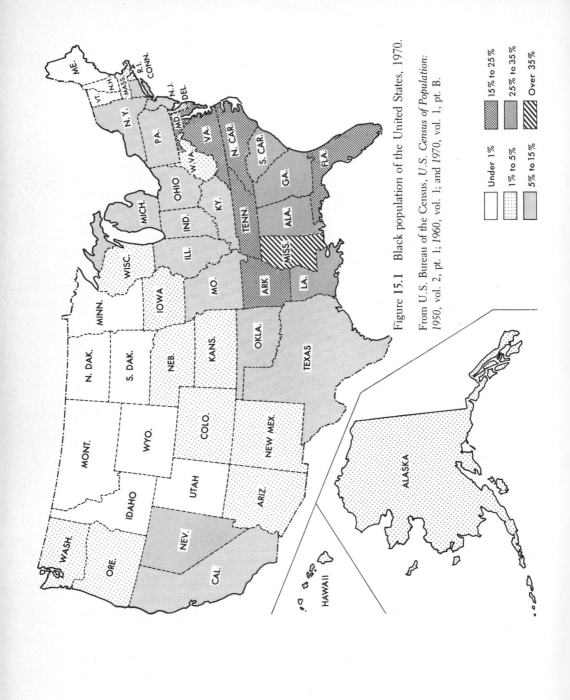

Figure 15.1 Black population of the United States, 1970.

From U.S. Bureau of the Census, *U.S. Census of Population:* *1950*, vol. 2, pt. 1; *1960*, vol. 1; and *1970*, vol. 1, pt. B.

Under 1%

1% to 5%

5% to 15%

15% to 25%

25% to 35%

Over 35%

Table 15.1   Types of communities based on perception of threat

	Group sees society as a threat	Group does not see society as a threat
Society sees group as a threat	Internally or externally restricted community	Externally restricted community
Society does not see group as a threat	Internally restricted community	Interest Interaction Assimilation

by the Mennonites, who have attempted to isolate themselves from the general population to resist the pressures toward assimilation.

The Mennonites began migrating to America from Central Europe in the Colonial period, when William Penn promised them religious tolerance in his colony; and from Pennsylvania they have moved on to a number of other states.   A second wave of Mennonite immigration, this time from Russia to Canada and the United States, began in 1871.   It was prompted by the inauguration of a new Russian policy that threatened to break down the isolation of these people and to foster assimilation.   Accordingly, they fled to the New World, where they proceeded to establish their remote communities, to exclude all outside influences, and thereby to safeguard their social heritage.[17] They have not been as successful as they hoped in rejecting the culture of their neighbors, but they have, to an amazing degree, remained a distinct ethnic group.   Among their many colonies are two in Yamhill County, Oregon, which have been the subject of sociological study.[18]   In these communities many of the old features of Mennonite culture have been retained — the headship of the bishop, the ban against exogamy, the taboo of secret societies and labor unions, the disapproval of commercial insurance, the refusal to participate in elections and to use the courts, the simplicity of dress, the wearing of beards but not mustaches (they shave the upper lip because the mustache was formerly the badge of a soldier).   The Amish, the more conservative of the two communities, even forbid the automobile, the telephone, films, and secondary and college education.   Some do, however, accept electric lights, the daily newspaper, and tractors.   The authors of the study suspect that, in this selection and rejection of new culture traits, there is a disposition to interdict those that facilitate communication with the out-group and that threaten solidarity.   Thus automobiles are forbidden, but not tractors; films are undesirable, but baseball is admitted; the telephone is feared, but not electric lights.   The newspaper is recognized as a danger, but nevertheless they subscribe to be able to "follow news events as they are related to Biblical prophecy."

Externally Restricted Communities

The *externally restricted community* also results from the perception of a threat. Only this time the community does not necessarily want to limit its interactions, but is forced to do so by the larger society. In this instance, the society or those in power define the community as a threatening and dangerous group to be segregated and often controlled. We will be able to see how this type of situation develops by using a case study. Our example involves approximately eighteen thousand German, Austrian, and Polish Jews who settled in Shanghai as a way of escaping from Hitler's campaign of destruction.

Shanghai had become a haven for the oppressed because of a peculiar set of circumstances. After the Japanese invasion of Shanghai, the International Settlement acquired certain rights of administration. However, Shanghai still stood on Chinese soil. Thus the rights of passport control belonged to the government of the Republic of China. However, that government had established its capital at Chungking, Szechuan Province, more than a thousand miles upriver from Shanghai. Consequently, the government offices, including the passport office, had been withdrawn from Shanghai. The government sponsored by the Japanese was not recognized by anyone including the Japanese residents. This tangled legal situation caused there to be no passport control in Shanghai. Anyone could land and after undergoing customs simply walk off the boat.[19]

Most of the refugees ended up in an area known as Hongkew, which became the site of the resulting restricted community. This formerly heavily industrialized area suffered from some of the heaviest Chinese-Japanese fighting. The Chinese scorched-earth policy left stretches of land in complete ruin. It was inhabited by the lower-class Chinese laborers, the poorest of the Russians, and between sixty and seventy thousand Japanese, many of whom came in the wake of the military occupation.[20]

What we need to examine now are the attitudes and reactions of the non-refugees, since they invariably were the ones responsible for the establishment of the restricted community.

The numerous objections to the refugees manifested themselves in various forms, reflecting Shanghai's varied and complex population. Nevertheless, most of the negative reactions can be traced to the overriding fear of economic competition and to the severe housing shortage. By the time the refugees arrived, Shanghai's economy was taking a turn for the worse. There were periodic fluctuations between depressions and booms of varying intensity. There were no flourishing trades or industries that could make use of the refugees' skills to any appreciable degree. In addition, their middle-class mercantile backgrounds and their age (the average was over forty) made their adjustment to the Shanghai economy difficult.

Most of the fears of economic competition did not come from the majority of the Chinese, whose standard of living was far below that of any of the Europeans. Even under such depressed living conditions, the refugees still required a salary four times greater than that of the local Chinese. Therefore, the refugees could not earn a living by competing with the Chinese laborers.[21] Consequently, they tried to compete with the Western-educated Chinese and White Russians (natives of the Byelorussian Soviet Socialist Republic) for white-collar jobs. This competition created additional friction between the newcomers and the local residents.

Most of the twenty to thirty thousand White Russians had not yet found their niche in Shanghai's economy either, and were often out of work or were employed at unskilled low-paying jobs. As a result, they responded sharply to exaggerated rumors of companies firing White Russian workers and replacing them with refugee workers. In some cases refugees would actually work without receiving payment in the hope of eventually ousting one of the White Russian employees.[22]

Nazi followers among the resident German community were also responsible for bringing about antirefugee feelings. These Nazi representatives distributed anti-Semitic propaganda to all sectors of the international community and exploited all possible fears.

Shanghai's wealthy international community, which was not economically affected by the new arrivals, had its own reasons for a generally unsympathetic attitude. The members of this group felt that the white community had suffered a loss of face because of the impoverished refugees. In a society where whites were respected only for their power and/or wealth, the arrival of large numbers of poor whites was looked on as another blow to the already waning influence of the resident community. The decline in status of the white community was all the truer in light of the fact that the new refugees came in the wake of the poor economic adjustment of the previous generation of refugees, the White Russians. In addition *The Shanghai Municipal Court Report* warned the international community that since many of the refugees could not find employment, the wealthy whites might be on the receiving end of a major crime wave.[23]

The Japanese were the ones who eventually made the decision to set up the restricted community. However, they refrained from making any public comment for quite some time. This silence stemmed from the Japanese belief that the Jews were a "secret world power." To the average Japanese individual, the term *Jew* and the structure of the Jewish religion were of little significance. The anti-Semitism of the Western World was basically unknown to most Japanese. The Jews were merely another group of foreigners residing in Shanghai. While the anti-Semites of other countries were trying to eliminate the Jews because of an exaggerated notion of power, the Japanese initially hoped to persuade the Jews to aid Japan in the war effort.[24]

The Japanese, then, were the last to object to the influx of the refugees. However, by May of 1939 the Japanese began to express the view that the refugees were the cause of housing shortages, high rents, and severe economic competition. This shift in attitude became evident with numerous editorials in the Japanese press. On August 9, 1939, the Japanese issued an order that no new arrivals would be admitted after August 21, 1939. In addition, those residing in Hongkew on August 22, 1939, would have to register with the Japanese authorities.

The first stage in the progression toward the restricted community was now completed. Few new refugees arrived after the cut-off date. The actual setting up of the restricted community began with the attack on Pearl Harbor on December 7, 1941. On the next day the Japanese occupied all of China without a struggle.

The original Japanese policy had been to treat the refugees reasonably well in order to persuade foreign investors to establish businesses in the Far East and to avert the aggravation of relations with England and the United States. Once the Japanese were fighting on the side of Germany and Italy, it was no longer necessary to think in these terms. Now it was important to appease the Germans. However, the Japanese policymakers were confronted with certain dilemmas. On the one hand, the Japanese were aware of the German extermination policy, but they were also impressed with Germany's military victories. On the other hand, the Japanese believed that if they emulated Germany's extermination of the Jews, these acts would be used as negative propaganda by England and the United States. Consequently, they compromised by ruling that Jews who formerly held German nationality would be considered stateless and surveillance would be exercised over them.[25]

Once the Japanese started to think in terms of surveillance, it did not take them long to think about establishing a special area for the refugees. In February of 1943 the announcement that was carried over the radio and in the newspapers brought about the realization of the refugees' worst fears. They were given three months to relocate into the designated area. The order also requested that the existing residents move to other areas; Japanese authorities were to offer assistance in this action.

Consequently, from eight to nine thousand refugees, who had managed to overcome the previously mentioned obstacles and to find a means of livelihood and a residence outside the Hongkew area, were forced to leave their homes and relocate into a crowded squalid area of less than one square mile. Once established, the restricted community consisted of forty square blocks of drab housing guarded by Japanese sentries and/or refugee members of the auxiliary police, called the Foreign Pao Chia. The Pao Chia had been organized because of a Japanese plan of self-policing and collective responsibility imposed on the restricted community. All men between the ages of twenty and forty-five served on a rotating basis.

The exits to and from the restricted community were guarded and one needed a properly stamped pass to leave. Those refugees who received passes were easily identifiable by the red or blue badges they had to wear on their lapels on which was printed in Chinese letters, "May Pass." [26]

As can be seen from the preceding discussion, the refugee population in Shanghai proved to be a threat to several groups in many ways. Clearly there was no place for the refugees in the Shanghai economy. Objectively, we must wonder that the results were not worse than the establishment of a restricted community, given the circumstances and the climate of the times. With the German pressure, a small and powerless resident Jewish population, and the resentments of the resident European population, it seems fortunate that a deportation to German death camps or an extermination policy did not emerge. As it was, the restrictions merely ended once the war was concluded. The threats can be summarized as follows:

1. Economic competition with White Russians;

2. Housing shortages;

3. Threat to status quo and lifestyle of Europeans vis-à-vis the Orientals;

4. Fear of a crime wave due to refugee poverty;

5. Anti-Semitism spread by resident German population;

6. Strong German pressure on Japanese to pursue an anti-Semitic policy;

7. Fear of sabotage.

Consequently, we have all the factors necessary to bring about the establishment of a restricted community: a relatively small and powerless population, weak support or protection from outside the group, value differences, many real or imagined threats to the larger society, and a pivotal event (war with the United States).

It appears, then, that in all parts of the world and for untold centuries racial and ethnic groups have sought to resolve their conflicts by some form of segregation, by restricting their contacts and relations with one another. There are few who would deny to any group the right to withdraw itself, if it chooses to do so. Most of us would doubtless grant the Jews the right to establish a homeland of their own, or the Amish to live by themselves in isolated communities, or the people of Canada and the United States to restrict the numbers of immigrants whom they will admit as citizens. It is a different matter, however, when a strong group forces segregation on a weaker group that does not wish it, especially when such segregation involves discrimination and exploitation, as it invariably does. The wisdom of segregation and isolation is also debatable, but the judgment depends on one's scale of values. From the practical standpoint, however, segregation as a pattern of intergroup accommodation grows increasingly difficult. With the increase in mobility, the growth of interdependence, improvements in communication and transportation, the spread of democratic ideals, and the diffusion of education and literacy, the possibility of a group's living by itself, whether or not it chooses to do so, becomes less and less feasible.

Notes

1. A. Jacques-Garvey, ed., *Philosophy and Opinions of Marcus Garvey*, cited in H. Brotz, *Negro Social and Political Thought: 1850–1920*, p. 564.

2. "Ghetto," *The Jewish Encyclopedia*, vol. 5, pp. 652–655; L. Wirth, *The Ghetto*, pp. 1–2; J. Lestschinsky, "Ghetto," *Encyclopedia of the Social Sciences*, vol. 6, pp. 646–650.

3. Wirth, *Ghetto*, p. 18ff.

4. Quoted in Wirth, *Ghetto*, p. 30.

5. Lestschinsky, "Ghetto," vol. 6, p. 648.

6. Wirth, *Ghetto*, pp. 97–110. See also, S. Baron, "Jewish Emancipation," and S. Dubnow, "Jewish Autonomy," *Encyclopedia of the Social Sciences*, vol. 8, pp. 391–399.

7. Wirth, pp. 117–123. For a description of these communities, see T. Shafter, "The Fleshpots of Maine," *Commentary* 7, no. 1 (Jan. 1949): 60–67; I Graebner and S. H. Britt, eds., *Jews in the Gentile World* (Chapters by L. Bloom on "The Jews of Buna," and S. Koenig on "The Socio-Economic Structure of an American Jewish Community"); A. I. Gordon, *Jews in Transition*; J. R. Kramer and S. Leventman, *Children of the Gilded Ghetto: Conflict Resolution of Three Generations of American Jews*.

8. M. R. Coolidge, *Chinese Immigration*, pp. 21–22.

9. For accounts of this conflict, see B. Shrieke, *Alien Americans*, p. 8ff.; C. McWilliams, *Brothers under the Skin*, chap. 2; L. G. Brown, *Immigration*, chap. 14; D. Y. Yuan, "Voluntary Segregation: A Study of New York Chinatown," *Phylon* (Fourth Quarter, 1963): 255ff.

10. R. H. Lee, "Social Institutions of a Rocky Mountain Chinatown," *Social Forces* 27, no. 1 (Oct. 1948): 1–11.

11. See R. W. O'Brien, "Status of Chinese in the Mississippi Delta," *Social Forces* 9, no. 3 (March 1941): 386–390.

12. R. H. Lee, "The Decline of Chinatowns in the United States," *American Journal of Sociology* 54, no. 5 (March 1949) p. 432.

13. Quoted in J. H. Franklin, *From Slavery to Freedom*, p. 277.

14. E. F. Frazier, *The Negro Family in the United States*, chap. 11.

15. W. Waldron, "All Black: A Unique Negro Community," *Survey Graphic* (Jan. 1938): 34ff.

16. For accounts of similar communities, see M. C. Hill, "A Comparative Analysis of the Social Organization of the All-Negro Society in Oklahoma," *Social Forces* 25, no. 1 (Oct. 1946): 70–77; C. L. Spellman, *Elm City: A Negro Community in Action*.

17. E. K. Francis, "The Russian Mennonites: From Religious to Ethnic Group," *American Journal of Sociology* 54, no. 2 (Sept. 1948): 101–107.

18. W. C. Smith, V. Fugua, and P. Louie, "The Mennonites of Yamhill County, Oregon," *Research Studies*, State College of Washington, vol. 7, 1940, pp. 33–38.

19. A. Jovishoff, "A City of Refugees," *The Menorah Journal* 27 (Spring 1939): 213.

20. M. Rosenfeld, "History of the Jews in Shanghai, III," p. 4, YIVO Institute Shanghai File #1.

21. E. M. Hinder, *Life and Labour in Shanghai*, p. 77.

22. Ibid.

23. F. Gruenberger, "The Jewish Refugees in Shanghai," *Jewish Social Studies*, vol. XII, 1950, pp. 331–332.

24. M. Dicker, *Wanderers and Settlers in the Far East*, p. 75.

25. Ibid., pp. 113–114.

26. H. Burkhard, *Tanz Mal Jude: Von Dachau Bis Shanghai*, p. 165.

Chapter Sixteen
Annihilation and Expulsion

That's your grave, over there. Haven't you
realized it yet? You dumb bastards, don't
you understand anything? You're going to be
burned. Frizzled away. Turned into ashes.

— *Elie Wiesel* Night

Among the several ways in which a conflict between races may be resolved is
for one group to exterminate the other. Annihilation, to be sure, is not always,
or even usually, a consequence of the meeting of peoples. Contact with
strangers has often had a stimulating effect on a society, both numerically and
culturally. One student of the problem has reached the conclusion that, except in those cases where native peoples are destroyed by the initial and early
contacts, "the population growth of native peoples is an inevitable resultant of
European cultural incursion." In support of this thesis, the population statistics from Japan, India, China, Ceylon, Java, Egypt, Formosa, Algeria, and the
Philippines are presented.[1] Here in the United States the Navajo Indians are a
notable case. Today they number more than eighty thousand, whereas they
were but a small and insignificant band at the time of the arrival of whites in
this hemisphere.

Hoormann has looked into this phenomenon and has come up with the
theory that societies that experience downward trends after contact with whites
are those that are based on a subsistent, self-sufficient, nontrading type of
economy, such as food gatherers and shifting agriculturalists. Those that experience upward trends, on the other hand, are the so-called peasant peoples.[2]
He believes, moreover, that these differences arise not from any "racial" susceptibility or immunity to disease, nor some innate breeding propensity, nor

exploitation and abuse, nor ill-advised programs for the inhabitants such as insistence on wearing clothes, but rather from the precontact situation of the groups involved, specifically, the way of life and the demographic equilibrium attained before contact. For example, isolated folk peoples have few or no endemic diseases because the organisms causing such diseases need large human populations to remain viable. In the larger, relatively dense populations of the peasant societies disease-inducing organisms remain virulent by virtue of the fact that they can keep moving; that is, they are endemic, and periodically become epidemic. Moreover, isolated folk peoples "see" their population problem as one of keeping their numbers within those absolute numerical limits that their experience tells them will mean extinction or survival for the group, while peasants see their problem as one of increasing or guaranteeing the food supply available to them. The former seek to control population; the latter, food supply. Hoormann investigates still other aspects of folk and peasant societies that might account for the fact that the former usually decline and disappear under the impact of Europeans, while the latter seem to thrive. The extinction of native peoples following contact with European civilization is a phenomenon that has been widely noted and discussed, but Hoormann insists that the phenomenon is "not quite as universal as is frequently assumed."

Nevertheless, the number of societies that have disappeared altogether remains a tragic fact. Many tribes of American Indians became extinct soon after the arrival of the Europeans, often within a few years. Such was the fate of the Missouri.[3] This proud and numerous people first came to the attention of the whites in 1673. Within a century smallpox had reduced them to a helpless little band however, who were forced to seek the protection of their kinsfolk, the Otoes, farther west. In 1907 the last full-blooded Missouri died in Oklahoma. Today the Indian has virtually disappeared from the eastern United States, eastern Brazil, Uruguay, most of Argentina, and the West Indies. Tribes once numerous and flourishing have left no trace of their former presence, other than a name for some river, lake, state, or mountain.

Disease and Disorganization as Decimators

As we have implied already, annihilation need not be deliberate and malicious. Accounts of the contacts between whites and other races abound in testimonials to the ravages of disease. It is a familiar story how tuberculosis and measles decimated the Polynesians, destroying whole villages, and how smallpox wiped out tribes of American Indians. Stefansson has reported on the destruction that was wrought in the Arctic area by a disease common to the white race:

. . . it is true in the Mackenzie district, as it is among the Arctic Eskimo, that measles is the deadliest of all diseases. There have been several epidemics, so that it might be supposed that the most susceptible had been weeded out, and yet the last epidemic (1903) killed about one-fifth of the entire population of Mackenzie Valley.[4]

He tells, also, about the tragedy that befell the Canadian Indians when they were exposed to tuberculosis and when they learned to desire "civilized-looking dwellings," two developments for which they have only whites to blame:

No dwelling could be more sanitary and more likely to forestall tuberculosis than the tipi of the Indians. . . . It is not only always filled with fresh air, but it never becomes filthy, because it is moved from place to place before it has time to become so; but when a house is built, it cannot be moved. The housekeeping methods which are satisfactory in a lodge that is destined to stand in one place only two or three weeks at a time, are entirely unsuited for the log cabin. . . . Eventually the germs of tuberculosis get into the house. . . . The members of the same family catch the disease, one from the other, and when the family has been nearly or quite exterminated by the scourge, another family moves in, for the building of a house is hard work and it is a convenient thing to find one ready for your occupancy; and so it is not only the family that built the house that suffers but there is also through the house a procession of other families moving from the wigwam to the graveyard.[5]

The great destroyer, then, has been those diseases against which no immunity had been built up and with which the afflicted peoples had neither the knowledge nor the skills to cope. George Catlin, the distinguished artist and ethnologist, has given us a picture of how the Indians were overwhelmed when smallpox struck:

Terror and dismay are carried with it [the disease]; and awful despair, in the midst of which they plunge into the river when in the highest state of fever, and die in a moment; or dash themselves from precipices; or plunge their knives into their hearts, to rid themselves from the pangs of slow and disgusting death.[6]

Only slightly less important as exterminators of peoples have been heavy drinking, prostitution, and other vices that followed contact with Europeans. Disease would reduce the population to a fraction of its former size and vice served to demoralize those who managed to survive. In many parts of the world even the primitive peoples have long had an acquaintance with alcohol, but American Indians had only slight knowledge of it and they fell prey easily to its inducements.[7] Some of them did possess fermented beverages and it is possible that a few even had acquired the skill of distilling liquor. For most, however, alcohol provided a new experience, one for which their culture provided no folkways of control. White settlers soon realized that liquor was a dangerous article in the hands of the Indians and even the traders, morally lax as they were, knew that too much rum made a poor customer. Consequently, although there were even fewer prohibitionists in colonial times than there are today, laws regulating the sale of liquor to Indians were promulgated as early as 1670. The first explorers, however, unlike settlers and traders, felt no responsibility for the behavior of the Indians, and they took delight in getting them drunk. A story has it that Henry Hudson invited several Indians aboard the *Half Moon*, gave one of them a potent drink that sent him reeling; when he recovered, he recounted to his companions his experiences in the spirit world.

One myth has it that the very name Manhattan means "the place of the first big drunk."[8] Be that as it may, the Indians soon acquired a taste for drink and it played havoc with them.

Indian leaders recognized the evil and sought to eliminate it. The pitiful plea of the Delaware to the white colonists in 1698 is typical of many that were made, but to no avail:

We know it to be hurtful to us to drink it. We know it, but if people will sell it to us, we so love it that we cannot refuse it. But when we drink it, it makes us mad; we do not know what we are doing; we abuse one another; we throw one another in fire. Through drinking, seven score of our people have been killed.[9]

Even in the journals of hardheaded fur traders we find reports on the devastating effects of alcohol on the Indians, of the noisy fighting, the injuries and deaths, children neglected and abused by drunken mothers, the debauchery and theft to which the victims resorted to procure liquor.

What has been said here about the ravages of disease and vice among the American Indians is not unique, and similar stories could be told of primitive peoples in many parts of the world who had the misfortune to be "discovered" by civilized Europeans.

Even where extermination has *not* been a conscious and deliberate policy, the surviving group or race has often regarded these natural processes of destruction with favor. The Pilgrims, for instance, felt this way about the plagues that struck the Indians. When they arrived at Plymouth in 1620, they found the deserted Indian village of Pautuxet, with its corn fields cleared and fertile, and one lone survivor to tell them the tragic story. They learned that a plague, presumably smallpox, had swept through the New England tribes in 1616. The disease had been introduced either from the French settlements to the north or from the English fishing and lumber ships that had been plying the New England coast for a decade or more prior to the arrival of the Pilgrims. The toll in lives had been ghastly. The English trader Morton, who traveled through the hinterlands in 1622, saw the ghost villages and the quantities of bones and skulls and said that the place "seemed to me like a new Golgotha." The Massachusetts tribe was reduced from ten thousand to one thousand souls. *The Pilgrims were delighted with all of this* and regarded it as a justification for their taking the Indians' lands without payment. One of their early historians expressed the viewpoint in these words:

There befell a great mortality among them; the greatest that ever the memory of father or son took notice of; desolating chiefly those places where the English afterward planted; sweeping away whole families, but chiefly young men and children, the very seeds of increase. . . . Their wigwams lie full of dead corpses. . . . By this means, Christ, whose great and glorious works throughout the earth are all for the benefit of his churches and chosen, not only made room for his people to plant, but also tamed the hearts of these barbarous Indians.[10]

Genocide

But not all have had such faith that Providence would exterminate the competitive racial group; or, alternatively, they have become impatient with the slow pace at which the divine plan moved and have, accordingly, taken the matter into their own hands in many instances. A new word, *genocide*, has rather recently been introduced into the language to designate this practice of deliberately exterminating a whole race or ethnic group. The term was coined by Raphael Lemkin to describe the crimes committed by the Nazis during World War II. Genocide refers to the denial of the right to live of an entire group of people in the same way that homicide is the denial of the right to live of an individual person.

It was without doubt the deliberate policy of the Nazis to exterminate the Jewish people in their midst, and they came very near to succeeding. When the high-ranking Nazi government officials, generals, and admirals were being tried at Nuremberg, Mr. Justice Jackson, in making his charges against the defendants, delivered the following accusation:

What we charge against these defendants is not those arrogances and pretensions which frequently accompany the intermingling of difficult peoples and which are likely, despite the honest efforts of government, to produce regrettable crimes and convulsions. It is my purpose to show a plan and design, to which all Nazis were committed, to annihilate all Jewish people. . . . The persecution of the Jews was a continuous and deliberate policy. . . . The plan to exterminate the Jewish people was so methodically and thoroughly pursued that despite the German defeat, this Nazi aim largely succeeded. Only the remnants of the European Jewish population remain in Germany, in the countries which Germany occupied, and in those which were her satellites. Of the 9,600,000 Jews who lived in Nazi-dominated Europe, 60 per cent are authoritatively estimated to have perished.

While the term *genocide* may be of recent origin, the practice itself is an ancient one. The Bible records many instances of a stronger group exterminating its rival. The Hebrews, fighting centuries ago for a foothold in Palestine, came into conflict with various peoples. We are told with complete candor in the third chapter of Deuteronomy:

Og the king of Bashan came against us, he and all his people . . . and we smote him until none was left to him remaining. And we took all his cities at that time . . . and we utterly destroyed them . . . with the women and the little ones. But all the cattle, and the spoil of the cities, we took for a prey unto ourselves.

And also, in II Kings 15:16:

Menahem smote Tiphsah, and all that were therein, and the borders thereof, from Tirzah: because they opened not to him, therefore he smote it; and all the women therein that were with child he ripped up.

It must not be supposed that the Hebrews were abnormally brutal; they were simply following the practices of their time. The Assyrians and Babylonians were every bit as ruthless, and used to delight in a certain amount of torture as well; and Egyptian monuments show their monarch butchering his defeated enemies with his own hands. In fact, the Hebrews usually killed only the males, taking the women and children as captives.[11]

We have no right to console ourselves with the thought that genocide is a practice limited to ancient peoples, like the Hebrews, or to latter-day fanatics like the Nazis. The fact is that the prospect of solving a *race* problem by extermination has appealed to many modern minds. Arnold J. Toynbee maintains that it has characterized "the English method of overseas settlement."[12] A clear case in support of Toynbee's thesis comes from the island of Tasmania, where the British succeeded in wiping out the native population in the brief span of seventy-three years. The gruesome tale has been summarized as follows:

The colonists regarded the aborigines as a degenerate race, not so much human beings as wild beasts to be ruthlessly exterminated. Even more barbarous in their treatment of the natives were the bushrangers, convicts who had escaped into the bush where they lived a life of brigandage. These outlaws hunted the blacks for sport. They stole their women, chaining them up, outraging them, and in the end killing them. One . . . used regularly to hunt natives in order to provide his dogs with meat.

The aborigines, though naturally disposed toward peace and friendship with the whites, were roused to fury by these outrages, and retaliated in kind. But spears and waddies were no match for firearms. The blacks were driven steadily back as the settlements advanced, and their numbers were decimated. . . .

Finally Governor Arthur, realizing that the depredations of the natives were acts of vengeance for the injuries they had received, resolved to put an end to the prevailing anarchy. To discourage killing the natives, he offered a reward of £5 for every adult captured alive and £2 for every child. This plan had unanticipated consequences. It sanctioned and encouraged the formation of capture parties. . . . Arthur then turned to another plan. Nearly five thousand soldiers, police and civilians, armed with guns and handcuffs, were formed into a cordon stretching across the island. In October, 1830, this line started to move southward to drive all the natives into the Tasman Peninsula and pen them there. But when this human dragnet had closed in, it had caught only one native man and a boy. The others had all slipped through the line "like a sunbeam through a butterfly net."

What this great drive had failed to do was accomplished singlehanded by a Methodist bricklayer, George Robinson, who had a warm sympathy for the natives and was one of the few white men they trusted. Unarmed and accompanied by only a few friendly natives, he went into the bush to reason with the aborigines and to explain that, however the settlers and bushrangers might treat them, the government desired to protect them. At the imminent risk of his life he tramped hundreds of miles from one secret retreat to another. Through his unaided efforts all the surviving blacks — now only 203 in number — were gathered together in 1835 on Flinders Island in Bass Strait. Thus the "Black War" came to an end.

Though kindly treated from then on, the natives could not withstand the changed conditions of life. Unsuitable food, catarrhal disorders, and pneumonia, close confinement and the wearing of clothes and the restrictions of captivity, caused them to pine and sicken and die. Twelve years later, in 1847, when their numbers had been reduced to forty, they were transferred to a reservation near Hobart. But they were already doomed to extinction. The last aboriginal male died in 1869, and in 1876, with the death of the woman Truganina, . . . the Tasmanian race became finally extinct. This in brief is one chapter in the history of the triumph of "civilization" over "savagery." [13]

Instances of this sort could be recited indefinitely, and no race or nationality can show itself innocent of the charge. The Dutch who first settled on the Cape of Good Hope, and especially those who pushed as pioneers into the interior, were bent on exterminating the native blacks. Dr. I. D. MacCrone, who has written an account of these racial contacts, states that in the eyes of the European stock farmer in South Africa the natives were held in utter contempt, and were regarded as an inferior race with no rights of their own to speak of. [14] Bushmen and wild animals were bracketed together as dangerous vermin to be shot at sight whenever the opportunity presented itself. It seems never to have occurred to any of the whites that the Bushmen might be the injured party, being deprived of their means of existence by the encroachments of the Europeans; and that in preying on the frontier settlers, stealing and crippling their cattle, the native residents were simply reacting to an invasion of their territory as would any other people the world over. Such a suggestion, says Dr. Mac-Crone, would have been quite incredible to the Dutch stock farmer, who insisted that "the only good Bushman is a dead Bushman" — an expression, incidentally, not unlike one familiar to American ears.

Genocide is not always practiced with the blatancy of the Nazis, or the ruthlessness of the British in Tasmania and the Dutch in South Africa. It can be done with a certain finesse. Pierson tells us that the Portuguese in Brazil were intent on exterminating those Indians who offered any resistance to their settlement, and one of the popular means for achieving that goal was to plant in the Indian villages clothing taken from recent victims of the smallpox. The Indians, strangers to this malady, quickly succumbed. [15] Bacteriological warfare is an old story to the student of race relations and is encountered in many other situations than the Portuguese. Again a convenient and inexpensive device is to take advantage of the cleavages within the enemy's camp, to pit faction against faction and tribe against tribe, and encourage them to kill each other. This policy was deliberately advocated and pursued in the United States. As early as 1717 a prominent citizen of the colony of South Carolina was insisting: "We must assist them in cutting one another's throats. . . . This is the game we intend to play if possible . . . for if we cannot destroy one nation of Indians by another, our country must be lost." [16] Governments have often seen advantages in encouraging their citizens to take the initiative in annihilating the troublesome minority. All our colonies followed the practice of paying bounties for Indian scalps. Shrieke says that the policy was first adopted in 1641 by the Dutch in New Amsterdam, following the lead of their compatriots in the East Indies who had earlier learned that it is cheaper to encourage individuals to destroy the enemy on a commission basis than to maintain an army for the purpose. [17] The other colonies soon adopted the ingenious policy of the Dutch, paying scalp bounties as an "encouragement to the enterprise and bravery of our fellow citizens." This is not to say that scalping was a Dutch invention. As a matter of fact, a good many Indian tribes had followed the practice before the arrival of the whites; but the introduction of the rifle, and of iron and steel knives, greatly facilitated the process, and the paying of bounties raised it to a major interest with both Indians and whites. The Puritans, as early as 1637, had made a practice of giving rewards for Indian heads, since the more convenient practice of merely removing the scalp lock had not occurred to either the Puritans or the Indians.

The Genocide Convention[18]

Genocide, then, is a new word which refers to a very ancient practice. Long before the rise of modern science and the development of our present-day weapons of destruction, people had discovered that extermination was one way of solving so-called race problems.

As we have already mentioned, the largest and most appalling record of genocide occurred when the Nazis attempted to exterminate the Jews. The sheer magnitude and horror of this action provoked outrage and attempts by the nations of the world to prevent such circumstances from arising again. The initial impetus for international legislation against genocide came on November 2, 1946, when the delegations from Cuba, India, and Panama asked the Secretary General of the United Nations to put the item "the prevention and punishment of the crime of genocide" on the agenda of the General Assembly. The Assembly referred the item to its legal committee for study.

On December 11, 1946, the General Assembly passed by unanimous vote a resolution affirming that genocide was a crime under international law that the civilized world condemned and for the commission of which both principals and accomplices alike would be held accountable and would be punished. Thereupon the Assembly called for the preparation of a Convention on Genocide that would define the offense more precisely and provide enforcement procedures for its repression and punishment.

After two years of study and debate the draft of the Convention on Genocide was presented to the General Assembly, where it was adopted. President Truman then submitted the resolution to the Senate on June 16, 1949, to receive advice and consent for ratification. Hearings were held by a Subcommittee of the Committee on Foreign Relations. However, the Senate never did act on the measure and the United States did not sign the document.

The Convention came into force January 12, 1951, ninety days after it had been ratified by the requisite twenty nations. Subsequently, more than fifty-five other nations accepted the Convention.

Article II of the Convention defines genocide as follows:

Genocide means any of the following acts committed with intent to destroy, in whole or in part, a national, ethnical, racial or religious group as such:

(a) Killing members of the group;
(b) Causing serious bodily or mental harm to members of the group;
(c) Deliberately inflicting on the group conditions of life calculated to bring about its physical destruction in whole or in part;
(d) Imposing measures intended to prevent births within the group;
(e) Forcibly transferring children of the group to another group.

The Convention furthermore provided that any of the contracting parties could call on the United Nations to take action under its Charter for the "prevention and suppression" of acts of genocide. In addition, any of the contracting parties could bring charges before the International Court of Justice.

According to Article III, the following acts are punishable under the Genocide Convention:

(a) Genocide;
(b) Conspiracy to commit genocide;
(c) Direct and public incitement to commit genocide;
(d) Attempt to commit genocide;
(e) Complicity in genocide.

In 1970 President Nixon again requested the Senate to hold hearings on the Convention so that it could be signed. Many countries have criticized the United States for not signing the document and have attempted to exploit this lack of support as providing proof of the imperialistic intentions of the United States. However, the reasons for not signing the Convention in 1949 and the objections raised again in the 1970s are quite interesting and reflect an attempt to prevent the limitation of the Constitutional rights of United States citizens, rather than an endorsement of genocide. The last attempt to have the Convention passed by the Senate occurred in February of 1974, at which time it was again defeated because of a filibuster.

The United States has not signed the Genocide Convention primarily because of legal objections raised by American lawyers and the American Bar Association. Some of the objections have centered around the following questions.

What constitutes a group?   Most of the objections noted that the various articles were too vague. To begin with, in Article II(a) a question was raised about what actually constitutes "a national, ethnical, racial or religious group as such." It was pointed out that there are all kinds of groups, such as groups that get together for bargaining on a labor contract, protest groups, groups that go on trips together, and rock groups. Could actions against these groups be considered as genocide? The Nazis in their mania went so far as to institute a genocidal policy against prisoners whose appearance was unappealing. A conference was held on this "problem" in which the individuals were referred to as "outwardly asocial prisoners." A summary of the conference reads:

During various visits to the penitentiaries, prisoners have always been observed who — because of their bodily characteristics — hardly deserve the designation human; they look like miscarriages of hell. Such prisoners should be photographed. It is planned that they shall be eliminated. Crime and sentence are irrelevant.[19]

Do the prisoners constitute a group and would this action be considered as genocide under the rules of the Convention?

In addition, questions were raised about how many people are needed to make up a group. Is a group made up of two, or three, or millions? A police officer who wantonly shot two Black Muslims or two Italians would be charged with homicide in a State Court. However, if it could be claimed that the individuals were shot because they were members of a particular group, the crime would no longer be homicide alone, but genocide as well, and the accused could be brought before a federal court or an international tribunal.

What constitutes mental harm? Article II(b) states that genocide involves "causing serious mental harm to members of the group." Here again the wording was considered to be too vague. Mental harm was assumed to mean permanent injury or impairment to the mental faculties. However, some could claim that segregation of schoolchildren could constitute genocide since the Supreme Court in the *Brown* v. *Board of Education of Topeka Kansas* case of 1954, ruled that segregating black schoolchildren from whites caused feelings of inferiority, and damaged the personalities and learning capabilities of the blacks in ways that could not be undone. For example, a quotation from the decision reads, "segregation with the sanction of the law therefore has the tendency to retard the educational and mental development of Negro children."

What constitutes physical destruction? Another objection was raised about Article II(c), which states that genocide also includes "inflicting on the group conditions of life calculated to bring about its physical destruction in whole or in part." It was argued that this could be interpreted to mean that a city could be charged with genocide for causing its black or minority populations to live within a ghetto or slum.

What constitutes the prevention of births? In Article II(d) genocide is meant to include "imposing measures intended to prevent births within the group." Here questions were raised about whether compulsory sterilization of mental defectives or encouragement of the use of contraceptives among the poor could be construed as genocide. The opponents pointed to numerous instances where birth-control clinics and individuals dispensing birth-control information to blacks, Puerto Ricans, and other minority groups had been accused of genocide.

What constitutes forcible transfer of children? The last item in Article II reads that genocide also includes "forcibly transferring children of the group to another group." The opponents asked whether the compulsory busing of black children to white schools and vice versa could be construed as genocide.

The senators were also concerned about the fact that certain actions that would be protected under the free speech amendment would be outlawed under the genocide convention.   For example, racial slurs or stronger statements such as "kill Whitey" or "Off the Pigs" could be considered as "incitement to commit genocide" under Article II of the Convention.

Questions were also raised about how genocide differs from modern warfare in which hundreds of thousands of people could be killed with one bomb. The following exchange between Senator Frank Church, chairman of the Subcommittee on the Genocide Convention, and Bruno V. Bitker, an attorney, has a bizarre and frightening quality to it, which shows the level to which the potential for human destruction has progressed.

Senator Church: In your judgment, what distinguishes between genocide and the kind of mass killing that typifies the modern wars in which we have engaged? . . . These wars are characterized by unlimited bombings of open cities as well as unrestricted efforts to destroy as many of the inhabitants of the opposing country as we can reach with our weapons.

Mr. Bitker: Mr. Chairman, I think that it is — unless it is done with the intent to wipe out the people, then it is not genocide within the meaning —

Senator Church: In other words, if it is done as a means for bringing about the surrender of an opposing government, it is not genocide.

Mr. Bitker: That is something different; that is right.

Senator Church: If it is done however, with the intent to kill people for the purpose of killing people —

Mr. Bitker: Just because they are —

Senator Church: (continued) Then it is genocide.

Mr. Bitker: Just because they are nationals of a certain nation, then it is genocide.[20]

The fine line that is being drawn in this interchange certainly would not be acceptable to many people, who would label both of the actions described as genocide.

Many other objections to the Convention also have been raised on technical matters such as extradition treaties and due process under the law.

Now that the Genocide Convention has been in existence for some time, it is becoming clear that it serves more of a symbolic purpose, by asking nations to go on record that they are opposed to genocide, and does not really represent an effective means of dealing with actual instances of genocide. There have been numerous instances where nations have engaged in actions that clearly could be considered as genocide by the definition of the Convention. Actions in Biafra where millions of Ibo were killed by the Nigerians, the case in which the Soviet Union transferred thousands of Greek children after World War II, and the circumstances in Brazil where thousands of Indians have been killed should all be punishable under the agreement. However, no charges have been brought against these countries, and to date there are no instances in which the tribunal powers have been instituted.

It appears that it is too much to hope that the United Nations will be able to eliminate genocide. However, the world's attention has been focused on the issue and public opinion can be aroused against the nations suspected of the crime. Still, the horror of the crime seems to have in no way eliminated the possibility of genocide recurring.

Mass Expulsion

Racial and ethnic conflicts are often resolved when one group expels another from the territory in which it resides. For the victors the end result is comparable to that attained by annihilation, but the process is somewhat more humane. We say "somewhat" more, because mass expulsion is often carried out in an atmosphere of massacres, riots, and other forms of violence. However, there are instances where the dominant group has manifested a degree of consideration for those who were being expelled, permitting them to convert their properties into movable wealth and affording them protection from mob attack. Mass expulsion, moreover, has often been resorted to when other methods have failed. There are instances where a minority group has been driven from a country only after a policy of extermination has failed, for one reason or another. On the other hand, mass expulsion has been adopted after concerted efforts to assimilate a minority have proved fruitless. Thus at the dawn of the modern era, when Spanish rulers were determined to promote homogeneity in their realm, they tried to convert the Jews to Christianity; when that failed, they expelled them.

So it was with the Moors. Those who embraced Christianity came to be known as Moriscos (that is, "little Moors") and stayed on in Spain. They were subjected to strict supervision, and from time to time efforts were made to change their foreign habits. Landlords liked them, for they were docile and industrious tenants; but their competition weighed heavily on the Spaniards and excited their envy. In 1568 the government of Philip II ordered them to renounce all their Moorish ways of life and to give up their children to be educated by Christian priests. One result of this policy was a rebellion in the city of Granada that was put down only with great difficulty. The Moriscos were expelled from the city and scattered throughout Spain. In 1608 it was decided to expel the whole body of them from the country, when it became evident that their forcible conversion had produced only superficial conformity. The edict of expulsion was published on September 22, 1609, and was carried out with the greatest cruelty. The number driven from Spain is variously estimated from one hundred and twenty thousand to 3 million. The loss to Spain was irreparable, for it deprived the country of a substantial portion of its labor force. It was worse, however, for the Moriscos because their return to Morocco was bitterly resented by their kinsfolk there from whom they had been estranged so long and from whom they had grown far apart. It is estimated, moreover, that less than one-fourth of those who were so cruelly expelled succeeded in surviving the ordeal.[21]

There are innumerable instances in history of the mass expulsion of minority racial and ethnic groups. The empires of the ancient world and the traditions of preliterate peoples afford many examples of this practice. The Jews have been subjected to this kind of treatment on countless occasions. Henry VIII drove the Gypsies from England. The Acadians, who lived in what is now Nova Scotia and who have been immortalized in Longfellow's *Evangeline*, were expelled by the British because they refused to take up arms against the French and were scattered among the colonies on the Gulf of Mexico and the Atlantic Coast. The Huguenots were driven from France, and Mennonites and Dukhobors have suffered a similar fate from time to time.

For instances of mass expulsion of racial, religious, ethnic, and national minorities, however, one does not have to look at the past. The twentieth century more than any other has witnessed this phenomenon on a scale hitherto unequalled, especially if we include along with those deported or expelled the millions of refugees and displaced persons who have fled their native lands because of fear, threats, or persecution.[22]

The Trail of Tears

A classic example of mass expulsion, taken from our own history, is that of the forced removal of the Cherokees from their homeland in the East. The magnitude of the injustice and the toll of lives have caused the Indians to call this incident "The Trail of Tears."[23]

The Cherokees were a powerful people who lived in that region where Georgia meets Tennessee and North Carolina. Their first contact with the whites came in 1540, when DeSoto marched through their country; but there was nothing in the conduct of the Spaniards to make the Indians regard them as superior and they hoped they would see no more of such people. A century and a half later the whites came again, this time the British. The initial contacts were friendly, for the Indians were far removed from the settlements and the white visitors were bent on establishing cordial relations for reasons of trade and security. But as the frontier advanced, the Cherokees began to feel the encroachment of the land-hungry Europeans. There was friction; the Indians lost some of their territory; but in the meantime they had learned many things from the whites that had made them a stronger, more prosperous, even a civilized people.

By 1825 there were more than thirteen thousand Cherokees living in their Eastern home, while approximately seven thousand others had been induced to migrate across the Mississippi. Contact with the whites, then, had greatly stimulated the growth of their population. They had willingly received into their group many white men and women who had taken Cherokee spouses. They still owned 7 million acres of land. Schools and churches had been established, their farms were prosperous, they managed their political affairs well, the nation was out of debt, they were at peace, and they owned more than one thousand black slaves. One of their number, Sequoya, among the truly great men of American history, had invented a Cherokee alphabet and he was on his way to turning them into a literate people.

The tide was turned when gold was discovered in the Georgia hills, for the whites were determined to get possession of it. On December 19, 1829, the legislature of Georgia passed an act appropriating a large area of the Cherokee lands. It provided, also, that the laws of the Cherokees would henceforth be null and void in that area, and all persons living therein would be subject to the laws of the state of Georgia. Finally, the act provided that "no Indian or descendant of an Indian . . . shall be deemed a competent witness in any court of this state to which a white person may be a party." The Governor warned the Indians that they would be liable to punishment if they mined the gold on the lands the state had appropriated. A lottery system was set up to distribute the Indian lands among the whites.

The Cherokees appealed to President Andrew Jackson; but he was no friend of theirs, old Indian fighter that he was. In fact, it was he who had been responsible for having Congress enact the Indian Removal Act, which placed on his shoulders the task of driving all Indians to lands beyond the Mississippi. The Cherokees then appealed to the Supreme Court, but the Court declared that it was not its function to meddle in such affairs. The various branches of the government, far from seeing justice done to the Indians, actually connived in the theft. The President's commissioners, in fact, illegally persuaded a handful of the tribe's members to sell all of its 7 million acres to the government and the Senate quickly ratified this "treaty." The Cherokees, however, denounced the treaty and remained on the land.

General Winfield Scott moved in with seven thousand troops and an unruly rabble of civilians. Indian men, women, and children were rounded up; homes and barns were burned; cattle and household goods were seized by the mob. Even graves were opened, and the silver and other valuables, which by Indian custom were buried with the dead, were taken with the loot. The captives were herded into stockades, conducted under guard down the Tennessee, Ohio, and Mississippi Rivers and up the White, and shoved into the territory that is now Oklahoma. The cost of all of this was charged to the Indians.

The details of this mass expulsion and of the westward trek are revolting. The suffering was intense, and the toll of life staggering. More than ten thousand Cherokees were driven west, and of that number it is estimated that four thousand perished along the way. One who is interested in reading the wretched story will find it in Grant Foreman's *Indian Removal*.

President Van Buren, in his address to Congress on December 3, 1838, was able to report: "The measures for Cherokee removal authorized by Congress at its last session have had the happiest effects. . . . The Cherokees have emigrated without any apparent reluctance."

The West Coast Japanese

A more recent case of mass expulsion occurred during World War II, when some 110,000 persons of Japanese ancestry were forcibly evacuated from the area bordering the Pacific Ocean and including parts of Washington, Oregon, California, and Arizona. Ostensibly this was nothing more than a wartime measure undertaken in the interest of national security. But actually, as we gain the perspective of time, it appears to be simply one more chapter in the long conflict between whites and Japanese. Let us review that conflict.

The Japanese are among the most recent immigrants to enter the United States. For a long time Japan was opposed to its citizens leaving their own country. Prior to 1854 emigration was a crime punishable by death and the construction of ocean-going vessels was forbidden by imperial decree. Then an occasional shipwrecked sailor or a stowaway came to these shores. Their numbers were negligible, however, for there were only 55 Japanese here in 1870 and 148 in 1880. But in 1884 the Hawaiian Sugar Planters' Association prevailed on the Japanese authorities to reverse their traditional opposition to emigration and immediately the numbers of Japanese in other countries began to swell. They went to Hawaii in droves, and many came to Canada, the United States, and South America. There were 2,039 here in 1890; and in the first decade of the present century some 55,000 arrived from Japan, and another 37,000 from Hawaii.

They were never warmly received in the United States, even though their labor was needed in the West where they settled. At the time they began to arrive in large numbers, Japan was emerging as a world power; and many Californians regarded the Japanese immigration as the spearhead of invasion. An anti-Japanese meeting was held in San Francisco on May 7, 1900; and in 1905 the Hearst newspapers launched a major attack on them. Various repressive and discriminatory measures were adopted. In 1907 President Roosevelt, by executive order, stopped Japanese immigration from Hawaii, Canada, and Mexico; and he negotiated the famous "gentleman's agreement" with the Japanese government, putting an end to immigration from that source, except for the so-called picture brides. These measures, however, did little to halt the tide of anti-Japanese prejudice. Hostile bills and resolutions were introduced in a number of state legislatures, California placed restrictions upon ownership of land by Japanese, and several other states followed her example. The culmination of the struggle came in 1924, when Congress passed a law barring the immigration of persons "ineligible for citizenship," which was intended, and interpreted, as a blow to the Japanese.

The Japanese have never been one of our large minorities, being greatly outnumbered by blacks, Jews, Mexicans, and even Indians. On the eve of World

War II there were only 126,947 in the continental United States, two-thirds of whom, by virtue of their having been born on American soil, were citizens. They were concentrated, however, and this was a factor contributing to the misfortune they later suffered. At the outbreak of the war, 43 percent of those gainfully employed were in agriculture, more particularly in the production of vegetables and fruits for the local urban markets; 23 percent were engaged in the wholesale and retail trade, chiefly the distribution of Japanese-grown products; 17 percent were employed in service industries — domestic service, cleaning and dyeing, and the operation of hotels, barber shops, and restaurants; and others owned stores or were engaged in the professions. In these latter areas, as a result of discrimnation and boycotts, the patrons and clients were chiefly Japanese.

The attack on Pearl Harbor gave the anti-Japanese forces their great opportunity. They began to clamor for expulsion. The Hearst newspapers took up the cry. Rumors of espionage and sabotage began to circulate, entirely without foundation in fact, for Japanese-Americans, both in Hawaii and in the United States, have a clear record on that score. Lobbyists went to work, and West Coast representatives in Congress recommended to the President "the immediate evacuation of all persons of Japanese lineage." Accordingly, the War Department was authorized in an executive order to set up military areas and to exclude from such areas any persons regarded as dangerous. Mr. Stimson, Secretary of War, delegated this authority to General J. L. DeWitt, who was commanding officer of the Western Defense Command.

The naive racial beliefs and prejudices of General DeWitt are clearly manifested in his various public utterances, reports, and his testimony before Congressional committees. Said he, "The Japanese race is an enemy race and while many second and third generation Japanese born on United States soil, possessed of United States citizenship, have become 'Americanized,' the racial strains are undiluted." And he declared before the House Naval Affairs Subcommittee that Japanese-Americans "are a dangerous element, whether loyal or not. There is no way to determine their loyalty. . . . It makes no difference whether he is an American; theoretically he is still a Japanese, and you can't change him. . . . You can't change him by giving him a piece of paper."

In a series of orders General DeWitt called for the evacuation of all persons of Japanese ancestry from the area of the West Coast. President Roosevelt, realizing that some agency other than the Army would be needed to perform the task of removal, created the War Relocation Authority. At the outset, evacuation was on a voluntary basis and some ten thousand did depart. But it took money to leave, which many of them did not have; and those who did move suffered many unpleasant experiences. Many of them had substantial investments and businesses and they could not bring themselves to believe that their rights as American citizens would be so lightly dismissed. The policy of voluntary evacuation, therefore, gave no promise of succeeding and a shift to compulsory evacuation was made.

On the date fixed by the Army all persons of Japanese lineage reported to control stations, from which they were escorted to improvised assembly centers — race tracks, fair grounds, parks, and pavilions.   Within about four months more than one hundred thousand persons had been transferred to these centers and placed under guard.   Next they were moved to the relocation camps, of which there were ten, situated in Utah, Arizona, California, Idaho, Wyoming, Colorado, and Arkansas.   Here, housed in barracks and surrounded by barbed wire, the inmates carried on as best they could.   Attempts were made to estimate the loyalty of the Japanese, and those found disloyal were shipped away to the camp at Tule Lake in California.   As a matter of fact, the overwhelming majority of them gave every evidence of loyalty, and even most of those who, on the basis of tests, were classified as disloyal hardly deserved that stigma.[24]

Originally it was intended that these camps would become actual relocation centers, but the Japanese did not remain there long.   Employers needed workers to meet the labor shortage and the evacuees were issued work permits and were assisted in finding jobs in various parts of the country outside the prohibited zone.   Students were granted leave to attend college and high schools.   Though the evacuees had been declared "ineligible for military service," this decision was rescinded in 1943 and thousands entered the Army, where they distinguished themselves for their valor and where their knowledge of the Japanese language enabled them to play an indispensable role in the war as interpreters and intelligence officers.   In 1944 the ban on their returning to the Pacific coast was lifted; and in March, 1946, the last relocation center was closed.   Many of the Japanese have returned to their former homes, but large numbers of them have chosen to settle in other states and start new lives.[25]

This mass expulsion of the Japanese from the West Coast has been called "our worst wartime mistake."   In the first place, the necessity for their removal for reasons of national security had no basis in fact.   There were enemy aliens of German and Italian extraction in the country at the time who were not subjected to such treatment.   While there were dangerous and disloyal persons among the Japanese, these were well known to the authorities, who had been checking on them for years, and they were promptly arrested at the beginning of the war.   Other suspicious ones were under constant surveillance.   General DeWitt's defense of his action, which he based on "military necessity," "the threat of sabotage," "the necessity of protecting the Japanese from the violence of mobs," is supported neither by reason, fact, nor subsequent developments.

In the second place, the injustice inflicted on these hundred thousand persons was colossal.   Neither the Army nor the WRA was in a position to act as custodian for the property of the Japanese, who had to move with haste and who suffered great losses in the process.   Radios and refrigerators were sold for a pittance, and cars were disposed of for a fraction of their value.[26]   No estimate can be placed on the intangible losses that the Japanese suffered — the businesses and professions, products of years of effort, that were wiped out and the humiliation and shock that expulsion gave to their pride and status.

Finally, this treatment of persons holding American citizenship presents a threat to certain basic principles of our society. It involved a sweeping deprivation of the civil rights of citizens and it was done on a racial basis. It dealt a blow to the sacred principle that individuals are presumed innocent until they are proved guilty, that all citizens stand on an equal footing before the law regardless of race, color, or previous condition of servitude; and it came dangerously near upsetting the traditional principle of the subordination of the military to the civil authority. Eugene V. Rostow, Professor of Law at Yale University, gives the following estimate of the gravity of the affair:

The original program of relocation was an injustice, in no way required or justified by the circumstances of the war. But the Supreme Court, in three extraordinary decisions, has upheld its main features as constitutional. This fact converts a piece of wartime folly into national policy — a permanent part of the law — a doctrine enlarging the power of the military in relation to civil authority. . . . As Mr. Justice Jackson has said, the principle of these decisions "lies about like a loaded weapon ready for the hand of any authority that can bring forward a plausible claim of an urgent need." All in all, the case of the Japanese-Americans is the worst blow our liberties have sustained in many years. Unless repudiated, it may support devastating and unforeseen social and political conflicts. [27]

One way to be sure of solving the problems of race relations is for the stronger group to annihilate the weaker, or, if that be too reprehensible a device, to drive it out of the country. Instances of both these practices are commoner than we like to think.

Notes

1. E. N. Palmer, "Culture Contacts and Population Growth," *American Journal of Sociology* 53, no. 4 (Jan. 1948): 258–262.

2. B. L. Hoormann, "Rigidity and Fluidity in Race Relations," in A. W. Lind, ed., *Race Relations in World Perspective*, p. 25ff.

3. B. Berry, "The Missouri Indians," *Southwestern Social Science Quarterly* 17, no. 2 (Sept. 1936): 1–12.

4. V. Stefansson, *My Life with the Eskimo*, p. 26.

5. Ibid., p. 23.

6. G. Catlin, *The North American Indians*, vol. 2, p. 28.

7. For a discussion of the Indians' knowledge and use of alcohol prior to the arrival of Columbus, see J. H. Steward, ed., *Handbook of South American Indians*, vol. 5, pp. 539–546; and H. E. Driver, *Indians of North America*, pp. 93–97.

8. An amusing translation, but highly dubious. The probability is that Manhattan means "island of hills." See F. W. Hodge, ed., *Handbook of American Indians North of Mexico*.

9. Quoted in C. Wissler, *Indians of the United States*, pp. 267–268.

10. W. C. MacLeod, *The American Indian Frontier*, p. 50.

11. H. N. Brailsford, "Massacre," *Encyclopedia of the Social Sciences*, vol. 10, pp. 191–194; "War," in J. Hastings, ed., *The Dictionary of the Bible*, pp. 964–965.

12. A. J. Toynbee, *A Study of History*, vol. 1, p. 465.

13. Reprinted with the permission of Macmillan Publishing Co., Inc. from *Our Primitive Contemporaries* by George Peter Murdock, pp. 16–18. © 1934 by Macmillan Publishing Co., Inc., renewed 1962 by George Peter Murdock.

14. I. D. MacCrone, *Race Attitudes in South Africa*. See especially pp. 89–136.

15. D. Pierson, *Negroes in Brazil*, p. 6.

16. Quoted in D. D. Wallace, *History of South Carolina*, vol. 1, p. 213.

17. B. Shrieke, *Alien Americans*, p. 5. On the subject of scalping, see also A. Locke and B. J. Stern, *When Peoples Meet: A Study in Race and Culture Contacts*, pp. 165–170; Wissler, *Indians of the United States*, pp. 302–303.

18. The word *convention* has many meanings. In common practice it means only an assemblage of people or some kind of social custom. In international law the term refers to an agreement between sovereign nations. It is more than a resolution or an expression of opinion. It is a legal compact that pledges the several signatory countries to accept certain obligations. Broadly speaking, it is a treaty between a number of nations.

19. R. Hilberg, *The Destruction of the European Jews*, p. 643.

20. Hearings before a Subcommittee of the Committee on Foreign Relations, United States Senate, 1970, p. 92.

21. H. C. Lea, *The Moriscos of Spain: Their Conversion and Expulsion*.

22. J. J. Senturia, "Mass Expulsion," *Encyclopedia of the Social Sciences*, vol. 10, pp. 185–189.

23. G. Foreman, *Indian Removal*, pp. 229–314; M. L. Starkey, *The Cherokee Nation*, pp. 282–301; Wissler, *Indians of the United States*, pp. 126–131; J. Collier, *The Indians of the Americas*, pp. 117–125.

24. G. Eleanor Kimble, "The 'Disloyal' at Tule Lake," *Common Ground* 6, no. 2 (1946): 74–81.

25. The social and economic losses suffered by the Japanese-Americans are documented convincingly in L. Bloom and R. Riemer, *Removal and Return*.

26. B. Smith, "The Great American Swindle," *Common Ground* 7, no. 2 (1947): 34–38; "Legalized Blackmail," *Common Ground* 8, no. 2 (1948): 34–36.

27. E. V. Rostow, "Our Worst Wartime Mistake," *Harper's Magazine* 191, no. 1144, (Sept. 1945): 194.

Chapter Seventeen
Reactions to Minority Status

And thy life shall hang in doubt before thee;
and thou shalt fear night and day, and shalt
have no assurance of thy life.

— *Deuteronomy 28:66–67*

How do the members of minority groups react to their subordinate status? How do they feel about discrimination, disfranchisement, segregation, and second-class citizenship? What are their attitudes toward the dominant group, which looks down on them as inferiors and which jealously guards its prestige and its privileges?

The members of dominant groups like to feel that subordinate peoples regard them with admiration, respect, and even gratitude for the favors they have received. Colonial powers insist that their subjects, except for disgruntled agitators, deeply appreciate the blessings that have been brought to them by their conquerors — peace and order, relief from tyrants, sanitation and medical care, commerce and industry, education, Christianity, and a higher standard of living. Dominant peoples everywhere, it seems, comfort themselves with stereotypes of contented, unambitious, humble subordinates, blissfully ignorant of the cares and burdens of superiority.

Disorganization

Anthropologists have long said that contacts between racial and ethnic groups frequently result in disorganization and demoralization. This was put very well by an inhabitant of the Solomon Islands, who said:

You white men give us orders; we no longer give orders to ourselves. . . . The white man has come and tells us we must behave like *his* father. Our own fathers, we must forget them. . . . In the olden days we did this thing, we did that thing. We did not stop and say to ourselves first, "This thing I want to do, is it right?" We always knew. Now we have to say, "This thing I want to do, will the white man tell me it is wrong and punish me?"[1]

The literature of ethnology abounds in reports of primitive tribes in all parts of the world that have been well-nigh shattered by the impact of European civilization. These are not the dismal travelogues of biased or myopic whites, but the careful descriptions of competent, sympathetic observers. They tell of one-time vigorous peoples who are now "dying of boredom," or who are "losing their zest for life," or who are "lazy, indolent parasites, devoid of all stamina and ambition." The story is much the same, whether the victims be the nonliterate peoples of Asia, the American Indians, Melanesians, Polynesians, Eskimos, African blacks, or the Australian aborigines. To cite one instance:

The ancient warriors are tired. Despite such injustices as the tribe claims to have suffered at the hands of the whites, they remember that these *suyapi* pacified the land. One can trade, though warily, even with the Blackfoot. Battle, murder, and sudden death stalked the land in the old days. . . . The women particularly appreciate the fact that they can go to sleep at night and wake up free instead of as despised captives. Sometimes the old warriors will admit as much.

Intelligent informants do claim that the old days were busier and therefore healthier and happier. They deprecate the modern custom of living in houses, blaming this practice as bitterly as the smallpox for the decimation of their people. In those old days men hunted. Everybody fished. Women, children, and old men gathered berries and roots. The hunter carried the quarry to his lodge and dropped it. His work was finished. Women worked hides continually, pounded pemmican of deer, and, in season, of bison. Bones were boiled for succulent broth. Women packed in firewood. The industrious were respected and loafers despised. True, the men had the easier and more interesting work, but their constant danger was appreciated by their wives and mothers. The modern protected men still expect spoiling and hence cause bitterness among the women and scorn among the uncomprehending whites. But formerly a wife who had any affection for her husband at all was anxious to pamper her husband. The Blackfoot were indomitable.[2]

Another account tells the tragic story of the Sioux Indians.[3] Two and a half centuries ago these Indians moved from the Eastern woodlands out onto the plains and adapted themselves to the hunting of the buffalo. A century ago whites began to encroach on their territory, destroying their food supply and disrupting their way of life. The result was a series of struggles, which have found a prominent place in the folklore and history of America and which ended in 1869 when the Sioux were removed to reservations. Thus for nearly a hundred years these Indians have been reluctantly traveling the rough road leading to the white civilization. The victors were on hand to help, for it was their policy "to civilize" and "to humanize" them. Children were virtually kidnapped and placed in the government schools. Their hair was cut. Their Indian clothes were thrown away. They were forbidden to speak their own language. Punishment was meted out to those who ran away, or who persisted in clinging to their old ways. Even when the older policy of rapid and compulsory assimilation was abandoned, the hope remained that the Indian might be made over according to the social and economic ideals of white Americans.

It has indeed been a rough road, marked by one defeat after another, and ending finally with the loss of their cattle and their grazing lands. Even more tragic, however, has been the loss of their ancient virtues of honor, bravery, generosity, and moral integrity, all of which were prominent among them. Many have now lost the skill of leadership and the sense of responsibility.

The children, exposed, on the one hand, to the residue of the old Indian culture and, on the other, to the confusion of an alien white culture, present a distressing picture. They are described by MacGregor as "immature, resigned, and apathetic." The total effect of such an environment on them is the creation of personalities that are insecure, passive, without purpose, and without hope. MacGregor insists that it is not too late to salvage this once-stalwart people; but a program, to be successful, must be focused not only on goals of material rehabilitation, but also on the restoration of pride, responsibility, and self-confidence.

Even missionaries, for all their good intentions, have often had a demoralizing effect on the very people they desired to help. This is not to deny that their accomplishments have frequently, perhaps predominantly, been beneficial. Cultural diffusion is as old as human history. Long before missionaries appeared on the scene, culture was being carried from place to place by soldiers, traders, captives, thieves, bootleggers, and nomads. Diffusion has a disconcerting effect, regardless of who the bearers of the new item are. Missionaries are no exception. They are, by their own admission, bent on changing the lives of the people among whom they labor; but the changes are not always the ones they anticipate. Ako Adjei, himself a member of the Ga tribe of the Gold Coast, has this to say:

The theory which supported the action of the early Christian missionaries in Africa was that everything African or indigenous was bad and contrary to the Will of God but that everything European or foreign was good and acceptable to the Will of God. The effect of this theory on African social institutions was great. Application of the theory brought about a great disruption of African social life. Nobody was baptized into the Christian Church until he . . . had agreed to abandon the African and follow the European way of life. For example, the missionaries changed even the traditional names of individual Africans — names which have deep meanings and spiritual significance in African culture. . . .

The activities of Christian missionaries have brought about a great confusion and suspicion in the minds of many Africans. They have also brought about a conflict between the basic values that are dominant in African culture and the incipient European social ideals. One of the major effects of Western civilization upon African life is that many Africans have lost their respect for the traditional institutions of African society.[4]

Sociologists, too, have noted the bewilderment and disorganization that have so frequently characterized the initial reaction of immigrants in the United States. This fact is continually encountered in the autobiographies of immigrants, in letters, and in the records of legal aid societies, criminal courts, juvenile courts, and various welfare agencies. One immigrant to America wrote as follows:

How can one find happiness in this Hell where people rush as though mad, over the ground and under the ground and even, God forgive them, through the air; where everything is entirely different from what one is accustomed to at home; where it is impossible to distinguish to what social class a man belongs; where it is impossible to understand a single word of what they say; where baptized Christians are run after by street boys even as a non-Christian, a Turk, would be run after at home?[5]

It was this problem of disorganization, as a matter of fact, that was a theme of one of the early sociological classics, *The Polish Peasant in Europe and America.*[6] The authors of this study attempt to explain the demoralization so common among Polish immigrants and their children. The Polish immigrants, they say, were born and reared in a permanent, coherent primary group in an agricultural community that was settled for many hundreds of years in the same locality, changing so slowly that each generation was able to adapt to the changes with little effort. Their conduct was regulated by habit and custom and by the immediate and direct suggestions and reactions of their associates. It was all quite different, however, when they crossed the Atlantic and settled in an American city. Here they were isolated and practically unknown, economically poor and insecure, surrounded by people who were indifferent, contemptuous, and often hostile, whose language they did not speak and whose ways they did not understand. This well-nigh insurmountable problem of adjustment, however, does not always lead to active demoralization and antisocial behavior. Many of these people, to be sure, made the transition with apparent ease, though Thomas and Znaniecki insist that "a certain lowering of moral level is inevitable," and that there is a "partial or general weakening of social interests, a growing narrowness or shallowness of the individual's social life." Many an immigrant family, however, found the adjustment to be more than it could manage, and the authors point to the wide prevalence of crime, economic dependency, divorce, desertion, delinquency, and prostitution as evidence of widespread disorganization.

W. C. Smith has made a good analysis of the process of disorganization through which so many immigrants have passed, with varying degrees of anguish.[7] Immigrants, he says, often misperceive the life about them. They see the new culture not through intimate and personal contacts with the older residents, but through such secondary media as newspapers, moving pictures, politics, and business activities, where keen competition, graft, and misrepresentation are common practices. They find themselves in a totally different situation, where their old standards do not apply. They rub shoulders with other groups, who have different customs and values, and they cannot easily and immediately organize a workable scheme from this tangled maze. Many of them suffer a loss of status, being forced to stoop to the lowest form of common labor and being ridiculed for being "queer."[8] As one of them said:

When I first came I thought I could not stand it here, so many people would refer to the southern European class and refer to the peasant class of people with great disdain. They seemed to look down upon Europeans from our land. I know that many have a serious misconception of class. Our peasant is a landholder, more nearly compared to the American farmer, and is far from the bottom of the social scale. We have classes of peasants, the half peasant, the quarter and even the eighth peasant with smaller holdings of land. Below them are still lower classes of laborers, cottiers, and other workers. As in America the standing is measured by the stock he holds. Our peasant is a link in a long line of family inheritance and tradition which oftentimes runs back many centuries with a name, a reputation to sustain and a posterity. So my blood would boil when many an uneducated person would look down upon me and speak in a condescending way. For a long time these sarcastic remarks hurt me, and worried me.[9]

The immigrants become torn by inner conflicts when they discover that their moral codes and behavior are not applicable and are even ridiculed. If these sacred elements in their life are false, then what is dependable? Moreover, their language, dress, customs, and mannerisms are objects of sneers and disdain. With the breakdown of the old patterns of behavior there is an ever-increasing development of individualization. Group consciousness gives way to egoistic attitudes. They think only of themselves, and tend to gratify their own wishes even at the expense of their fellows.

More Permanent Adjustments

Disorganization and demoralization, however, are not permanent conditions. Occasionally, as we saw in Chapter 16, the subordinate racial or ethnic group is annihilated, but more often some form of accommodation is reached. One of the groups achieves a dominant status, enjoying prestige, power, and privilege, while the other is relegated to a position of subordinate status. Let us consider now the various adjustments the members of the minority groups are obliged to make to the discrimination, segregation, and indignity to which they are subjected by the dominant group. The problem has been treated by many social scientists in a variety of ways.

The "Sambo" Personality

Minority status can also produce major adjustments in personality and behavior. The historian Stanley Elkins has written about slavery; and while his comments are primarily relevant to an extreme type of oppressive situation, they do provide us with an example of the pervasiveness of the effects of minority status.[10] Elkins examined the "Sambo" stereotype of the black plantation slave in North America. According to the stereotype often cited in the literature of the times, the Sambo slave was "docile but irresponsible, loyal but lazy, humble but given to lying and stealing; his behavior was full of infantile silliness and his talk inflated with childish exaggeration." Most Southerners, and many Northerners, assumed that this behavior was due to certain innate qualities that made blacks markedly different from whites.

In his discussion Elkins showed that the Sambo behavior was a form of adjustment that allowed the slaves to survive. He pointed out that the Sambo personality was not innate, but was forced on the slaves. We must realize that slavery was a closed system that often included instances of extreme cruelty. Consequently, it is not unreasonable to assume that behavioral adjustments had to be made to deal with such adversity.

Elkins noted that the Sambo personality traits did not exist in Africa. African society was not in a savage state, as was commonly assumed, and did not encourage the Sambo qualities. There was tremendous diversity among the tribes making it impossible to generalize about the Africans who were transported to the United States. There was a wide variety of religious customs among the slaves and slave ships buzzed with many different languages. In fact, the inability of the slaves to communicate with each other, caused by the great diversity of languages, was counted on to minimize insurrections. One eighteenth-century slave trader advised that:

the safest way is to trade with the different Nations, on either side of the River, and having some of every Sort on board, there will be no more likelihood of their succeeding in a Plot, than of finishing the tower of Babel.

In spite of the differences mentioned, the tribes did have in common certain cultural characteristics, a fact that counteracted the theory that the Sambo personality was innate. The agricultural life of the tribes demanded hard work and self-discipline to produce enough food. As Elkins noted, "The typical West African tribesman was a distinctly warlike individual; he had a profound sense of family and family authority; he took hard work for granted; and he was accustomed to live by a highly formalized set of rules which he himself often helped to administer."

A form of slavery existed in Africa prior to its introduction to the New World; however, it was markedly different from the type that existed in the United States. The West African slaves were recognized members of the household who had certain rights. They were allowed to marry, to own property, and even to own slaves of their own. Here again, Elkins noted that the Sambo personality was not present.

Elkins explained the existence of Sambo tendencies on the total dependence of the North American slaves on their masters. The slaves were a part of a closed system over which the masters had virtually complete power. Survival meant finding some way of adjusting to this adverse situation. In framing his argument, Elkins drew on concentration camp literature and noted similarities in the adjustment of the concentration camp victims and the plantation slaves. The survivors of the concentration camps experienced depersonalization, or what has been known as a subject-object split. They felt as if they were separated from their bodies and were watching things happening to themselves. In the camps they lost their past identities, acquired a childlike dependence, and also took on the values and interests of children. This type of behavior made for greater survival in the camps since any form of rebellion was immediately punished by death.

In many ways the experience of the plantation slave was similar to that of the concentration camp victim, only less severe. Certainly the first generation of slaves, who were captured in Africa, marched to the coast to the waiting slave ships, endured a horrendous three-month trip from Africa to the New World, and then were sold into slavery, had experiences similar to those of the concentration camp victims.

The two main disagreements over Elkins's argument have centered on whether or not these stereotypes actually ever existed and, if they did, whether the behavior was, in fact, assumed or was actually a permanent part of the slave personality. However, the point that concerns us here is that it is possible for the dominant group to force the minority to act in a certain fashion. Later this behavior can be used as an excuse for continued subjugation. For example, claims that blacks were better off under slavery since they could not care for themselves were common among those who believed that Sambo traits were innate. Clearly, the behavior described here had an adjustment value for the slaves since if they acted like children and were assumed to be harmless, fewer restrictions would be placed on them. In addition, the masters in their more benevolent moments would feel an obligation to help the slaves.

Jews in Ancient Palestine

It is a far cry from the slave community of the South to the Jewish community of Palestine two millennia ago. Yet though widely separated in space and in time, these two communities have one thing in common — an oppressed minority faced with the necessity of adjusting to a dominant group. In the case of the Jews, the dominant group was first the Greeks and later the Romans.[11]

The Jews were not of one mind as to the proper adjustment, any more than blacks were during slavery. They, too, had their Uncle Toms, their compromisers, assimilationists, fighters, and isolatonists. The labels they attached to these social types were unique and different, but the viewpoints have a familiar ring. The Jews, two thousand years ago, had their Sadducees, their Pharisees, their Essenes, and their Zealots.

The Sadducees were an aristocratic group who wished to see the Jews a nation among nations. Religion to them was a matter of some indifference. They were sympathetic with the culture of the Greeks and Romans, and were disposed to assimilate it and to have a part in its diffusion. The Pharisees, on the contrary, were strictly religious. Foreign domination they regarded as God's punishment for the sins of the people. Their desire was to make of Judea an isolated religious commonwealth, removed as far as possible from contamination with the life and culture of the heathen. In the meantime they would withdraw from everything that might defile them. They were scrupulous in the observance of religious customs, traditions, and rules. To achieve their goal of an isolated Jewish commonwealth, they were forced by circumstances to participate in the religious struggles rife in Palestine at the time. Growing sick at heart when their efforts to found a political kingdom met with no success, they began to look more eagerly to the coming of a divine Messiah who would drive out the Romans and bring in the Kingdom of God.

The Essenes went far beyond the Pharisees in their determination to separate themselves from contamination with the world. Whereas the Pharisees, driven by circumstances, were forced to participate in political affairs, the Essenes withdrew farther and farther into the loneliness of the wilderness and the region of the Dead Sea. They were ardent pacifists and were among the first to condemn slavery as a violation of the ideal of the brotherhood of man. They turned their backs on wealth and scholarship and devoted themselves to meditation, prayer, and religious ceremonies. They supported themselves by agriculture and handicrafts, but would have nothing to do with trade, for fear that it would develop covetousness within them.

The Zealots, finally, were militant in their protest. In many respects they were akin to the Pharisees, and looked forward to complete political independence from Rome. They came to despair of the coming of a divine deliverer, grew tired of exercising faith and patience, and eventually resorted to arms and revolution. Their rebellion precipitated the catastrophic massacre of the Jewish people at the hands of the Romans in 70 A.D., and the dispersion of the remnant to the corners of the earth.

Sadducees, Pharisees, Essenes, and Zealots have long since passed out of existence, but their spiritual successors may still be found among the Jewish people in their varied reactions to the persecution and discrimination that have continually been their lot.

Japanese-Americans

An excellent opportunity to observe the reactions of a minority group to discrimination and domination was afforded when more than a hundred thousand Japanese-Americans were forcibly expelled from the Pacific Coast states soon after the United States entered World War II. These people were sent to ten relocation centers in the West and Middle West. Most were American citizens by virtue of having been born in the country and there were no charges of subversive activity laid on them. Even though the authorities undertook to treat them with consideration, it is generally recognized now that the whole procedure was a momentous blunder and that tens of thousands of innocent, loyal

American citizens were subjected to deprivations, discomforts, and indignities that they did not deserve. They had every reason to feel resentful of such discrimination. "They can't do this to me!" many of them kept saying. But "they" did, nevertheless.

An excellent report is available on the relocation center at Poston, Arizona, where some seventeen thousand of these evacuees were stationed.[12] A. H. Leighton, the author of the report, discusses, among many other things, the reactions of the Japanese to the injustices they suffered. He classifies these reactions as (1) cooperation, (2) withdrawal, and (3) aggressiveness; moreover, he believes that these represent *"three universal kinds of behavior with which individuals react to authority when subject to forces of stress that are disturbing to the emotions and thoughts of the individual. . . .* These reactions have been seen in every kind of human group that has ever been carefully studied. They are particularly evident in minorities where it is often possible to divide a community roughly into three parts in terms of those who show predominantly cooperation, withdrawal, or aggression in relation to the majority group. This pattern has been noted in many American Indians, among blacks, in Jewish communities, among Italian-Americans and among Spanish-Americans, and it was, of course, true of the Japanese in America long before the war."[13]

There were many at Poston who chose the path of cooperation. They carefully obeyed the regulations, worked enthusiastically in building the center, assisted in the maintenance of law and order, and offered their services as administrative aides. Especially in the early days of the center, there was much overcrowding and there was a lack of equipment and material necessary for comfort and privacy. Even so, there were those cooperative souls who submitted quietly to these discomforts. Some would insist that the food was satisfactory, even when it was inadequate by any normal standards.

Withdrawal, Leighton thinks, was perhaps the most widespread of all the reactions of the Japanese and took many different forms. At one extreme was the individual who persisted in living alone out in the mesquite, coming in occasionally for a supply of rice to supplement the fish caught in the nearby river. At the other extreme were patients who were brought to the hospital for "mental trouble," and who were apparently escaping from the stresses of life in the center by flight into fantasy worlds of their own. Between these two extremes were the many who stoically bore their tribulations, withdrew from painful contacts, refrained from "sticking their necks out," and followed a policy of "lying low." There were those, too, who found an escape from hard reality in magic, prophecy, and religious cults.

Finally, aggressive attitudes were present among the evacuees. There were those who heaped abuse on the Administration, made inflammatory speeches, registered interminable complaints, and issued threats. They would disregard the regulations, refuse to work, and steal government property. They were continually clamoring for more living space, better food, more hospital facilities. They circulated petitions. They would make a flourish of Japanese nationalism. They would attack other evacuees suspected of being informers, whom they called "dogs." The culmination of their aggressive activities was a major strike, which virtually brought the operation of the center to a standstill.

Patterns of Reaction

The three cases we have cited may seem to have little in common. The minority groups themselves are about as different as human groups can be; the problems they faced were quite dissimilar; and their reactions and adjustments appear to be quite distinct. Basically, however, there is much similarity. After all, there is a limit to the ways in which an oppressed minority *can* react, and it is not surprising to find that subordinate peoples everywhere respond to dominance in somewhat the same manner. They will, of course, be influenced by the culture in which they live. If they choose to resist, for instance, they will invariably employ the weapons at their disposal — spears and tomahawks, bows and arrows, or guns and bombs. They will be influenced, too, by the intangible elements in their cultural environment — the beliefs, folkways, attitudes, and philosophies. Passive resistance comes readily to the Hindu mind, whereas it would be incomprehensible to a Zulu or a Sioux.

Glick's Social Types [14]

Clarence E. Glick, as we saw earlier (pp. 153–154), believes that race relations move through a series of stages, and that each stage produces typical personal reactions, or social types. It will be recalled that, according to Glick's theory, the phases through which race relations progress are (1) a precontact phase, (2) a contact and predomination phase, (3) a domination phase, and (4) a post-domination phase. Social types characteristic of race relations situations do not make their appearance in the first phase, nor in the early parts of the second phase. At first, contacts occur between persons from indigenous societies and "foreigners" (mostly Europeans, but also Chinese, Indians, Arabs, and so on). Roles and statuses have not had time to take form, and conduct tends to reflect the ways in which immediate situations are sized up by those involved in them. Under such circumstances a person's latent disposition manifests itself in ways that, in a more stable situation, would be subjected to social restraints. Traders, for instance, who had learned their roles in their own society might develop patterns of behavior that differ greatly from those that would be tolerated at home, and native chiefs might develop self-concepts quite different from those that they would hold if contact did not occur. Similarly, new types of native leaders might arise, including some who under normal circumstances would never rise to positions of leadership.

The domination phase produces a variety of social types. Some will become the "apathetic government wards," listless and lazy. There emerge the "cooperative natives," enjoying certain privileges by virtue of their attitudes toward their masters rather than from the support of their own group. There are also the "professional natives" — singers and dancers, hunting and fishing guides, tour assistants, ethnological "experts," and the like — who flourish on the tourist frontier. As the foreign power becomes more firmly planted and schools are established, there appears the "educated native," who is envied by some and disparaged by others. Under the plantation system we find the familiar types of "the missus," the overseer, "the mammy," the field hand, the fugitive, the pensioner, the "toady," and many others.

Social types also make their appearance in the dominant group. There is the "empire builder," the *sahib* and the *mem-sahib*, the *tuan besar* and the *baas*. Early in the present century there emerged in Hong Kong and Shanghai the *tai-pan* (great manager), the *griffin* (somewhat wild junior executive), and the "old China hand."

Finally, we come to the postdomination phase, when the erstwhile masters begin to lose their power, and when the long-suffering native population begins to make its demands either in the form of nationalistic movements or in movements for integration. Social types in the dominant group that formerly symbolized respected roles ("old master," *baas, mem-sahib,* and so on) are held up to ridicule by the nationalist leaders. The cooperative native is also the object of disparagement and contempt. Among the social types conspicuous in this phase of race relations are the "cracker," the "peckerwood," the "scared liberal," the "right guy," the "dyed-in-the-wool liberal," the "straight-shooter," the "status quo conservative," the "racial demagogue," the "gradualist," the "radical reformer," the "left-wing revolutionary," the "color blind," and others.

Generalizations

Attempts have been made from time to time to generalize about the reactions of the members of minority groups to the discrimination, prejudice, and inferiority that are their lot. Stonequist, for instance, maintains that there are three patterns of adjustment available to the racial or cultural hybrid: (1) the intermediary role, (2) the nationalist role, and (3) assimilation and passing.[15] Davie, discussing the reaction of blacks to their status, recognizes seven types of responses: (1) acceptance, (2) resentment, (3) avoidance, (4) overcompensation, (5) race pride, (6) hostility and aggression, and (7) protest.[16] Johnson, also thinking of American blacks, makes a fourfold classification: (1) acceptance, (2) avoidance, (3) direct hostility and aggression, and (4) indirect or deflected hostility.[17]

Professor George E. Simpson, who has made intensive studies of race problems in Jamaica and elsewhere in the Caribbean, maintains that members of minority groups make six types of adjustment to their disprivileged social position; and these adjustments, which are to be thought of as constituting a continuum rather than as a set of absolute categories, are:

Type I. Acceptance.   Some members of subordinate groups embrace their disprivileged position and accept the dominant group's definition of their status and role.

Type II. Withdrawal through the invention of a symbolic Utopia.   Certain persons solve the problems of their minority status by adopting a fundamentalist religious orientation which stresses preparation for the next world.

Type III. Political withdrawal combined with verbal aggression.   This category includes those who hold the values of the dominant group but are convinced they cannot achieve them under existing institutions and conditions.   Simpson feels that the members of the Ras Tafari cult of Jamaica fall into this type.   This cult is a semireligious, semipolitical movement.   Its adherents are violently antiwhite, regard Haile Selassie, Emperor of Abyssinia, as the living god, and see no hope for the black man in the British West Indies.   They withdraw from such activities as voting and attending political meetings, and they expect no real achievements from labor unions.   They look forward to their early "return" to their homeland in Ethiopia, and in the meantime they keep up their verbal attack on the white man.

Type IV. A type of adjustment between Ras Tafarianism and active participation in protest organizations in the United States.   In this category belong those who are more optimistic and realistic than the members of Ras Tafari, but less sophisticated than are the members of politically active organizations such as the N.A.A.C.P. in the United States.   These are the somewhat less aggressive members of a racial or cultural minority.   Simpson believes that, in the United States, the average small-town northern Negro, if not the average northern Negro, represents this type of adjustment.

Type V. Full acculturation to the values of the dominant society.   This includes those who drop the withdrawal (supernatural, political or geographical) theme completely and work for full assimilation.   Active participants in the N.A.A.C.P. exemplify this type of adjustment.

Type VI. Political withdrawal combined with physical aggression.   In this category are those who renounce the values of the dominant group altogether and attempt to free themselves from its control.   Here are the rebels and insurrectionists.   The Mau Mau movement in Kenya included persons of this type.[18]

   Simpson, Davie, Johnson, and Stonequist are fundamentally in agreement. For our purposes we will borrow from all of them and distinguish *four patterns of reaction to dominance,* which seem characteristic of subordinate peoples everywhere: (1) *acceptance,* (2) *avoidance,* (3) *assimilation,* (4) *aggression.*

   As a rule, one will find all these reactions manifested continually in a minority group.   Every oppressed people seems to have its Sambos and its Nat Turners, its Pharisees and its Sadducees, its Scarlett O'Haras and its Melanie Hamiltons, its assimilationists and its survivalists.   There are times and places, of course, where one or another of these responses is the prevalent and popular one.   The Amish, for instance, have consistently followed a policy of avoidance, while the Cape Coloured and the Anglo-Indians, despite the barriers erected against them, have never wavered in their desire for assimilation. There are other instances where the dominant group has effectively suppressed certain patterns of reaction, or has been able to enforce the pattern it approved. Even so, one invariably finds rebellious individuals who choose to react otherwise.

How Do Minorities React?

Acceptance

It is an amazing fact, but one amply affirmed, that some human beings have an infinite capacity to endure injustice without retaliation and apparently without resentment against their oppressors. Instances of this phenomenon are numerous and they come from every part of the world where one group dominates another. Militant leaders of protest movements have been driven to despair by the apathy they have encountered among those they would lead to freedom; and members of dominant groups have often commented on the cheerfulness and loyalty they observe among those who would seem to have no reason for such sentiments.

Tulto, an Indian from the pueblo of Taos, has suffered much at the hands of the whites, but apparently he bears no grudge against them.[19] As a boy he lived the normal life of his pueblo, riding his pony, driving the cattle, and playing shinny, mumblety peg, and leapfrog. He hunted rabbits and deer, prayed to the Sun Father, and was thrilled by the religious dances on the plaza. His story has a charm all its own:

When I was about thirteen years old I went down to Santa Fe to St. Michael's Catholic School. Other boys were joining the societies and spending their time in the kivas being purified, and learning the secrets. But I wanted to learn the white man's secrets. I thought he had better magic than the Indian. . . . My father was sad but he was not angry. He wanted me to be a good Indian like all other boys, but he was willing for me to go to school. He thought I would stop soon. There was plenty of time to go into the kiva.

While I was there a white man — what you call an Indian Agent — came and took all of us who were in that school far off on a train to a new kind of village called Carlisle Indian School, and I stayed there seven years. . . . Seven years I was there. I set little letters together in the printing shop and we printed papers. For the rest we had lessons. I learned to talk English and to read. There was much arithmetic. It was lessons: how to add and take away, and much strange business like you have crossword puzzles only with numbers. The teachers were very solemn and made a great fuss if we did not get the puzzles right. There was something called Greatest Common Denominator. I remember the name but I never knew it — what it meant. When the teachers asked me I would guess, but I always guessed wrong. We studied little things — fractions. I remember that word too. It is like one half of an apple. And there were immoral fractions.

They told us that Indian ways were bad. They said we must get civilized. I remember that word too. It means "be like the white man." I am willing to be like the white man, but I did not believe Indian ways were wrong. But they kept teaching us for

seven years. And the books told how bad the Indians had been to the white men —
burning their towns and killing their women and children. But I had seen white men
do that to Indians.

We all wore whiteman's clothes, and ate whiteman's food, and went to the whiteman's church, and spoke whiteman's talk. And so after a while we also began to say
Indians were bad. We laughed at our own people and their blankets and cooking pots
and sacred societies and dances. I tried to learn the lessons — and after seven years I
came home. . . .

It was a warm summer evening when I got off the train at Taos station. . . . Here
came my father and my mother and many brothers and cousins. They all began hugging me, and we all cried and were very happy. . . . Every time a new cousin would
come we would all cry again. It was a happy night. . . .

But the chiefs did not want me in the pueblo. Next morning the governor of the
pueblo and the two war chiefs and many of the priest chiefs came into my father's
house. They did not talk to me; they did not even look at me.

The chiefs said to my father, "Your son who calls himself Rafael has lived with the
white men. He has been far away from the pueblo. He has not lived in the kiva, nor
learned the things that Indian boys should learn. He has no hair. He has no blankets.
He cannot even speak our language and he has a strange smell. He is not one of us."

The chiefs got up and walked out. My father was very sad. I wanted him to be
angry, but he was only sad.

And I walked out of my father's house and out of the pueblo. . . . I walked until I
came to the whiteman's town. I found work setting type in a printing shop there. Later
I went to Wyoming and Colorado, printing and making a good living. . . . I worked
in some blacksmith shops and on farms. . . . All this time I was a white man . . . but
I was not very happy . . . and after many years I came back to Taos.

My father gave me some land from the pueblo fields. . . . I took my money and
bought some cattle. I built a house just outside the pueblo.

My father brought me a girl to marry. . . . She was a good girl and she came to live
with me in my new house outside the pueblo. . . . When we were married I became
an Indian again. I let my hair grow. . . . I put on blankets, and I cut the seat out of
my pants. . . . I grew my farm like the other Indians, and my woman cooked Indian
food. I wanted to be among my people. But I wanted to live in the kind of house I had
learned to like.

When I settled with my woman in this new house, the chiefs came over from the
pueblo, and they said I must burn my chairs and bed and break the glass out of my windows. And they thought my house was too large. But I said to them, "I have built outside the pueblo. You rule inside and let me alone here."

I want to live at peace.

It seems that minority peoples everywhere, either because they "want to live
in peace" or for some other reason, learn to accept a social system that discriminates against them and bestows prestige on some other group. Indeed, it
would be difficult, in fact impossible, for one people to dominate and exploit
another if a substantial number of the minority did not more or less accept it.

Acceptance, however, as a type of response to domination, is capable of wide
variation. On the one hand, there are those who are completely accommo-
dated, such as a black man in Nashville who said, "I know how white folks is

and I understand their ways. I always stand fair with my white folks. They always been fair to me, and I been good to them."[20] Another said, "They've always been friends to me; they are nicer than colored sometimes. I am sick of colored people." Others accept the situation, but with resentment, such as the man who said, "I don't like it, but the best thing I can do is keep from worrying about it."

The foregoing rationalizations were given by members of the lower classes. There are also upper-class blacks who assume the role of acceptance, and they too seek to justify their actions. Some even profess not to be aware of discrimination and deny its existence. Johnson records a number of such accounts. A black professional in Houston said:

I haven't seen anything special that a Negro is expected to do. If he is, I must have been wrong a number of times, because I don't even know what it is. . . . We do not belong to the same organizations as the whites, *but they co-operate with us* in anything that we attempt in our little organizations.

More often, however, those of the upper classes whose reaction to dominance is basically one of acceptance, comply under duress and with bitter hearts.

To some degree, conformity to the prevailing etiquette of race relations is an unconscious matter, to which one becomes conditioned in the process of socialization. Much of it, however, is the conscious, rational acceptance of a role, which one may dislike, but accepts as being necessary for survival. In short, it is not uncommon for one to conform externally while rejecting the system mentally and emotionally.

Avoidance

Minority groups, from the beginning of time, have sought to solve their problem by running away from it. The Hebrews, under the leadership of Moses, fled from Egypt, where they were slaves, and endured the hardships of the Red Sea, the wilderness, and implacable enemies. American Indians living on the Atlantic seaboard, overwhelmed by the influx of Europeans, sought refuge beyond the Appalachian Mountains; and when the inescapable whites followed there, they pressed on across the Mississippi River. Following the Civil War thousands of southern whites fled to Mexico and Brazil rather than submit to the domination of blacks, Yankees, and "carpetbaggers." American blacks, unwilling to accept domination, forbidden to assimilate, and sensing the futility of resistance, have often cherished the dream that they might flee from it all. Various schemes have been proposed, beginning in the 1700s.[21] Some have looked to Africa as a possible refuge and considerable numbers have gone there. Others have cast hopeful eyes on Central America or Western Canada. Still others have proposed the establishment of a separate state for blacks only, as do the Black Muslims today. A generation ago Marcus Garvey won a tremendous, but temporary, following by offering Africa to blacks as an avenue of escape. And there are in the United States today not less than fifty all-black communities.

The modern Zionist movement is essentially an avoidance reaction. Many who are attracted by the prospect of a homeland in Israel are motivated by a desire to flee from annihilation and persecution. Still others are fleeing from the equally-unwanted prospect of assimilation. Said Theodor Herzl, the great pioneer of Zionism:

I referred previously to our "assimilation": I do not for a moment wish to imply that I desire such an end. Our national character is too historically famous, and, in spite of every degradation, too fine to make its annihilation desirable. We might perhaps be able to merge ourselves entirely into surrounding races, if these were to leave us in peace for two generations. But they will not leave us in peace. . . . Thus, whether we like it or not, we are now, and shall henceforth remain, a historic group with unmistakable characteristics common to us all.[22]

There are many devices for avoiding one's oppressors, however, other than fleeing to Africa, Israel, South America, or to a self-contained ethnic community. Burrows correctly infers that "many and devious are the ways of withdrawing from an intolerable situation"; and he discusses some of those techniques that he observed among the minority peoples of Hawaii in their reactions to *haole* prestige.[23] He suspects, and with some reason, that insanity is one mechanism of escape, alcoholic intoxication another, and opium still another for those of Oriental ancestry. The Hawaiians, he thinks, take flight into the romantic past, much of it synthetic; and many of them have participated in a revival of the culture of their ancestors, on which they had formerly been disposed to turn their backs. He quotes Romanzo Adams, an authority on Hawaiian affairs:

It is easy for one who has been in contact with Hawaii's young people for a long time to note the beginning of a change in attitude toward the culture of their ancestors. Fifteen or twenty years ago one was impressed by the tendency of Hawaiian born and educated young people to deprecate the customs and ideas of their parents. As American citizens they were trying to win an economic status superior to what their parents possessed, and they felt that the persistence of old country traditions was burdensome and that it was an obstacle to achievement.

But in the more recent years young people of the same age — the younger brothers and sisters or, perhaps, the nephews and nieces — are undergoing a change of attitude. . . . They evaluate old country customs more discriminatingly. They find some things that seem to be permanently good and there is beginning to be a tendency to idealize the traditional ways followed by their ancestors.

American blacks are, however, without peers when it comes to improvising techniques for avoiding those they dislike. Avoidance is indeed of major importance as a pattern of black response to white dominance. Investigators have recorded many such comments as the following:

I found that the best way to get along with white folks is just to be pretty careful and come in contact with them as little as possible.

I stay as far away from 'em as I can.

The farther they is from me, the better I like it.

Avoidance is no easy task for blacks, bound as closely as they are, economically and politically, to the white population. They have, nevertheless, made that choice and Johnson describes many of the subtle devices whereby they keep their contacts with whites to the barest minimum.[24] Some have found in farm ownership an effective means to maintain their independence. Those of the middle and upper classes will pay their bills by mail to avoid the necessity of contacts with white "collectors." They will do as much of their routine shopping as possible by telephone, since, as one cultivated woman said, her voice and diction get more consideration than her face. They absent themselves from public gatherings where they suspect they will be subjected to insults and indignities. They patronize places of business where they are known and their trade is appreciated, and avoid stores where they are rudely treated.

Nor is it only the gross forms of discrimination that they wish to avoid; they also want to escape the necessity of having to conform to the patterns of behavior prescribed by the caste system. And they want to preserve their dignity, to "save face." There are sly and subtle ways of doing this, too. Richard Wright tells how he did it on one occasion:

There are many times when I had to exercise a great deal of ingenuity to keep out of trouble. It is a southern custom that all men must take off their hats when they enter an elevator. And especially did this apply to us blacks with rigid force. One day I stepped into an elevator with my arms full of packages. I was forced to ride with my hat on. Two white men stared at me coldly. Then one of them very kindly lifted my hat and placed it upon my armful of packages. Now the most accepted response for a Negro to make under such circumstances is to look at the white man out of the corner of his eye and grin. To have said: "Thank you!" would have made the white man *think* that you *thought* you were receiving from him a personal service. For such an act I have seen Negroes take a blow in the mouth. Finding the first alternative distasteful, and the second dangerous, I hit upon an acceptable course of action which fell safely between these two poles. I immediately — no sooner than my hat was lifted — pretended that my packages were about to spill, and appeared deeply distressed with keeping them in my arms. In this fashion I evaded having to acknowledge his service, and, in spite of adverse circumstances, salvaged a slender shred of personal pride.[25]

Assimilation

One may well insist that the happiest response for the members of minorities to make is that of merging themselves with the dominant group. "When in Rome do as the Romans do." "If you can't lick 'em, jine 'em." Economically, mentally, and emotionally, there are advantages in being with the majority. According to the assimilationist philosophy, immigrants in a new land should transfer their loyalty to the country of their adoption. They should become citizens as quickly as possible, learning the language, discarding their quaint costumes for the conventional dress, acquiring the food habits, acquainting themselves with the nation's ideals, learning to like its sports and pastimes, conforming to its laws, abiding by its institutions, and, above all, rearing their children in accord with the standards of the new culture. This conformity is what the members of the dominant group like, generally speaking. They are ethnocentric, as nearly all people are, and are flattered to think that strangers recognize the superiority of their ways. Besides, it is a nuisance to have people around who do not understand the language, who are "queer," whose habits are "outlandish," and whose morals and ideals are "questionable."

Assimilation, however, is not a painless process. It is not easy to learn a new language and to speak it without an accent. One does not immediately feel comfortable in strange garments, or acquire a taste for new foods, or enjoy baseball on the first exposure to it, or learn to handle new systems of weights, measures, and money. These skills and tastes take many years to acquire and they are but a small part of any strange new culture. How much longer, then, does it take a person to absorb the intangibles — traditions, ideals, values, beliefs, attitudes, and loyalties? Sociologists have learned that it takes several generations, even under the most favorable circumstances.

The circumstances, moreover, are not always favorable. Members of minority groups are seldom prepared to discard their culture *in toto*, as one would trade in an old car for the latest model. They are strongly attached to it. They believe that most of it is good and they want their children to have it. Assimilation, therefore, does not appear to them as the solution of their problem of adjustment. They may agree that assimilation is desirable, up to a point; but beyond that point they will resist it. The dominant group, on the other hand, may insist on assimilation, may prate about "Americanization," may do its utmost to indoctrinate the alien, and may even try to accelerate the process at a dangerous speed; however, at the same time it erects obstacles to the very thing it urges.

Passing   Members of certain minorities, if they choose to identify themselves with the dominant group, will be commended for their wisdom. If a German immigrant family, for instance, decides to Anglicize its name, it may do so openly and will not be suspected of sinister motives. If members decide to transfer their church membership from the Lutheran, which is not represented in their community, to the Methodist, they will be welcomed with open arms. If they become naturalized citizens and boast of their preference for the progressive, democratic American society, they will be praised for good sense. But suppose a Jewish family changes its name and joins the Christian Science Church; will it not be under suspicion? And what of a black person of light color who decides to join the whites? Or an Indian who, to make life easier, claims to be an American of swarthy European ancestry?

Passing is a phenomenon reported from many parts of the world, and is a type of reaction to dominance that is known to most minority groups. It has received considerable attention, however, in the United States, and especially in relation to blacks. Passing has been a popular theme with novelists and playwrights.[26]

The amount of passing that takes place among American blacks is obviously a most difficult phenomenon to measure. Some of the difficulty arises from the fact that passing itself is not easy to define. Much of it is deliberate and intentional. On the other hand, it is quite common for members of minorities, including very light-skinned blacks, to find themselves, through no fault of their own, mistaken for members of the dominant group. Students of race problems, accordingly, have made a distinction between *conscious* and *unconscious* passing, although one may question the advisability of including "mistaken identity" as a form of passing. There is a difference, however, between *temporary* and *permanent* passing. Quite often blacks will pass as white in the workaday world to gain the obvious economic advantages, while preferring to remain as blacks except when on the job. Many will pass temporarily to be admitted to a restaurant, to attend a theater, or to obtain service in hotels or on trains. Passing, moreover, is usually an individual matter, although there are instances of whole communities striving collectively to win acceptance as whites or Indians. Typical examples of the latter are the Croatans of North Carolina, the Brass Ankles of South Carolina, and similar peoples in many other eastern sections of the United States.[27]

Despite the difficulties of measuring so elusive a phenomenon, many estimates have been suggested and some effort has been made to determine the extent of it. Ottley maintains that between 40,000 and 50,000 blacks "pass" into the white community yearly, and that "between 5,000,000 and 8,000,000 persons in the United States, supposed to be white, possess a determinable part of Negro blood."[28] Asbury has guessed that the yearly number who pass is 30,000.[29] Few would accept so high a figure, however. A generation ago, Hart concluded from a study of census data that approximately 25,000 annually change their racial identification from black to white.[30] More recently Hart's interpretation of the data has been criticized by both Burma and Eckard, who conclude that 2000 or 2500 would be a more accurate figure.[31] Day, using an entirely different approach to the problem and making a case study of 346 families of mixed blood, also suggests this lower figure.[32] If this conservative estimate is correct, the prospect of black amalgamation through the passing process is remote indeed. Robert Stuckert maintains, however, that more than 20 percent of the white population of the United States "are descendants of persons of African origin."[33]

Why, then, do not more members of minority groups solve the problem of discrimination by passing? It does seem that passing generates no wide appeal even to those persons who would have little difficulty in doing so. The fear of exposure is doubtless effective in some cases; but loyalty to family and friends and a normal pride in one's group are usually sufficient to make passing a distasteful adjustment. It is also true that the individual who passes suffers a loss in status. Finally, minority groups themselves seldom look with favor on the passing technique, although there is a certain ambivalence in their attitude. Says Myrdal:

Most Negroes, particularly in the upper strata, know of many other Negroes, sometimes half a hundred or more, who pass as whites. As they usually do not expose them, this shows a significant degree between the two castes in the attitude toward passing. Many Negroes obviously take a sort of vicarious satisfaction out of the deception of whites. It is a big joke to them. Some show envy. This is particularly apparent among darker Negroes who cannot think of passing. Negroes realize, of course, that as a mass they cannot find an escape from the lower caste by passing. Further, they are increasingly brought to the compensatory feeling of race pride. [34]

All in all, passing is a dubious way of adjusting to dominance and discrimination. It is fraught with feelings of uncertainty, insecurity, guilt, and disloyalty. Even so, there are many who choose it, and who see passing as a solution to the problems created by discrimination.

Aggression

The members of minority groups have a fourth alternative — aggression. Not for long will people calmly accept subordinate status. Avoidance of contact with the dominant groups is less and less feasible in the modern world. Assimilation is distasteful to some, unobtainable for others, and difficult for most. From time immemorial, however, the members of oppressed minorities have taken the offensive, have asserted themselves, have resisted, opposed, attacked, and rebelled against their superiors. They have given vent to their resentment and hostility in innumerable ways. By the term *aggression* we mean any behavior whose goal is the destruction, injury, frustration, embarrassment, discomfiture, or annoyance of another person or group. Let us consider some of the variegated forms that aggression has assumed.

Tecumseh   The form of aggression that is most obvious and familiar to us is that manifested by most American Indians when they saw whites moving into their territories, taking their land from them, destroying their game, disrupting their way of life, and challenging their power and sovereignty. The Indian, very understandably, struck back, and our histories abound with tales of that conflict. The leaders of the Indians' counterattack are legendary figures, not altogether forgotten nowadays, and among them one of the greatest was Tecumseh.

In the fall of 1811, five thousand Indians of the Muskogee tribes gathered on the banks of the Tallapoosa River in Alabama for their annual Grand Council. This was to be a special occasion, however, for the distinguished Shawnee warrior, Tecumseh, had sent runners ahead to announce that he would pay them a visit. Tecumseh, as almost everyone on the continent knew, was bent on forming a confederation of Indian tribes to stem the advance of whites. An American frontier settler, Sam Dale, was present at the time and has given us an account of the whole affair.[35]

On the second day of the council Tecumseh marched into the great square at the head of his band of twenty-four chosen Shawnee warriors. "They were the most athletic body of men I ever saw . . . austere . . . and . . . imperial," said Dale. Their faces were painted red and black, indicating that they had not yet made a choice between peace and war. They were approached in dead silence by Big Warrior, the colossal chief of the Creeks, who offered his pipe to Tecumseh and then pointed to the lodge that had been prepared for them.

Several days passed, in which Tecumseh spoke not a word. He was apparently waiting for the Government Agent, Colonel Hawkins, to leave the grounds, which he eventually did. Whereupon, at high noon, Tecumseh and his retinue emerged from their guest cabin, their bodies painted black, and entirely naked except for loin cloths and war clubs. They marched in single file to the center of the square, where they sprinkled tobacco and powdered sumac leaves on the ground, saluted Big Warrior with a "diabolical yell," and proffered the Shawnees' pipe. Then for the first time since his arrival, Tecumseh spoke. Dale said, "I have heard many great orators, but never one with the vocal powers of Tecumseh, or the same command of the muscles of his face. Had I been deaf, the play of his countenance would have told me what he said. . . . Stern warriors shook with emotion. . . . Tomahawks were brandished in the air. Even Big Warrior, who had been true to the whites . . . was visibly affected. . . . More than once I saw his huge hand clutch, spasmodically, the handle of his knife." These were Tecumseh's words:

In defiance of the white warriors of Ohio and Kentucky, I have traveled through their settlements, once our favorite hunting grounds. No war whoop was sounded, but there is blood on our knives. The palefaces felt the blow, but knew not whence it came.

Accursed be the race that has seized our country, and made women of our warriors! Our fathers, from their tombs, reproach us as slaves and cowards. I hear them now in the wailing winds.

You Muskogees were once a mighty people. The Georgians trembled at your war whoops. Now your very blood is white; your tomahawks have no edge; your bows and arrows are buried with your fathers. Oh, Muskogees, brush from your eyelids the sleep of slavery! Once more strike for vengeance. . . . Let the white race perish. They seize your land; they corrupt your women; they trample on the ashes of your dead. They must be driven back — back whence they came — on a trail of blood. Back, aye, into the great water. . .   Burn their dwellings! Destroy their stock! Slay their wives and children! The red people own the country. . . . War now! War forever! War upon the living! War upon the dead! Dig their very corpses from the graves; our country must give no rest to a white man's bones!

The Indians, to be sure, had their quislings and collaborators; there were assimilationists among them who urged the adoption of white ways; there were cautious souls who, when pressed on the frontier, advised withdrawal deeper into the wilderness. Tecumseh, however, was one of a long line — which included King Philip, Pontiac, Black Hawk, Sitting Bull, and others — who chose to resist the white advance by a show of arms. Apparently there were few, if any, who rose to positions of leadership, who were so naive as to suppose that red and white could live together in peace, harmony, and equality. One elementary fact of race relations was obvious to them all: when races meet, a well-nigh universal consequence is the domination of one and the subordination of the other. Most Indians, and especially the Shawnees, were proud people, who valued highly their independence and their status. To Tecumseh, certainly, death was preferable to subjection and submission. After the disastrous battle at Tippecanoe,[36] he allied himself with the British — not that he respected or trusted them, but he hated the Americans more — and he lost his life in the War of 1812. The Kentuckians who slew him scalped and flayed his corpse and distributed his skin among them for razor strops.

Aggressive behavior, as manifested by Tecumseh, failed to resolve the problem with which the Indians were faced. It is not always so, however. For an example, with a very different outcome, let us turn to the island of Haiti.

Toussaint L'Ouverture The island of Haiti was the first country in the New World to sweep away the institution of slavery, and this was largely the result of the efforts of an incredible individual by the name of François Dominique Toussaint L'Ouverture.[37] The date of his birth is not known, but it was presumably about 1744. Toussaint was one of more than a thousand slaves on the great Breda plantation. The owner of the plantation was Count de Noe, a benevolent man, who lived in France. He instructed the manager of his plantation to show consideration to his slaves, and his instructions were obeyed, for the Breda slaves were reputedly treated with comparative humanity.

It is difficult for us to realize today the enormous importance to Europe of the islands of the West Indies two centuries ago. Haiti (or Saint Domingue as it was then called) was by far the wealthiest of the French colonies, and it is small wonder that the French government, and later Napoleon, showed constant interest and anxiety over the affairs of that distant island. The products of the island were at first cocoa, indigo, and tobacco; but in the middle of the seventeenth century sugar cane was introduced, bringing about a great economic revolution. Large plantations supplanted the small farms, which had until then prevailed, and these plantations, with their own mills, became manufacturing as well as agricultural establishments. The manufacture of sugar called for great outlays of capital. It called also for an abundant supply of labor, which could not be satisfied with indentured servants. Blacks, accordingly, were imported in great numbers from Africa.

By 1789 nearly a million blacks had been transported to the colony. In that year some 30,000 whites sat in authority over 452,000 slaves. There were, in addition, 24,000 free blacks and mulattos living on the island.

The slaves were considered to be scarcely human. In theory, the owner's power over slaves was limited. The law permitted the master to inflict corporal punishment only for laxness in a slave's work, and then only to a reasonable degree. All other offenses were to be punished by the authorities, who, it must be admitted, had no reputation for leniency. The law, however, was scarcely observed, for the plantations were far removed from the communities in which the authorities resided. Hilliard d'Auberteuil, who sought to reform the institution of slavery without abolishing it, said:

Negroes die daily in chains and under the lash. . . . Every act of cruelty against them remains unpunished. In St. Domingo any white man can ill-treat a Negro with impunity. The situation is such that the Negroes may be said to be the slaves not only of their masters, but also of the general public.[38]

It was commonly believed among the managers of the plantations that it was preferable to buy and import slaves than to breed them, and that it was profitable to amortize a slave in seven years. During that period slaves should be driven to the limits of their endurance. If, after that time, any slaves became useless or died, it did not matter — new slaves could be bought to take their place. There were those, however, who insisted that great efficiency could be employed in the management of plantations if slaves were exhausted in four years. It need hardly be added that the death rate among slaves in Haiti exceeded the birth rate.

Many black slaves did not meekly accept this situation. Some of them fled to the mountains in the interior. There were occasional slave rebellions, but these were quickly and effectively suppressed. They did, however, continually resort to aggressive behavior. Many would hang themselves or cut their throats with the object of inflicting injury and loss on their masters. They formed suicide pacts and a dozen or more on a plantation would kill themselves simultaneously. Death was regarded by many of them as a form of migration back to Africa. Their most effective weapon for aggressive behavior, however, was poison. Arsenic was readily available on the plantations since large quantities of it were used in combating the dreaded sugar ant. The slaves also used ground glass, dogwood root, and black-eye. With these they frequently dispatched cattle, mules, other slaves, and the masters themselves. The whites lived in perpetual fear of such a fate; and it is said that many planters who had nothing more than a stomachache imagined themselves poisoned and tortured a slave to force a confession.

News of the French Revolution in 1789 caused great concern to the whites in Haiti; and its watchwords — liberty, equality, fraternity — fell on fertile soil among the slaves. Oddly enough, it was the whites themselves who were the principal disseminators of these ideas. Visitors to the island were astonished at the recklessness with which the whites discussed the revolution in the presence of their slaves. Says Korngold.

Imagine a formal dinner party at a plantation house, with a slave in attendance behind every chair. Letters and newspapers have arrived from France, and the host describes with dramatic emphasis how his uncle or cousin has had to flee with his family because his scoundrelly peasants have burned down his castle, have looted his stores and will no longer recognize him as their lord. . . . Others tell of similar misfortunes that have befallen their relatives. One asks if those present have read the shameful proclamation of the Rights of Man, which asserts that all men are created free and equal. Another remarks that if the *Amis des Noirs* had their way, this would even apply to Negro slaves!

The household slaves listen. . . . Their expression does not change, but something in them has been kindled. Many have relatives among the field hands and mill slaves. . . . They sit with them around the fire and tell the exciting news they have heard. . . . The idea germinates in the minds of several that the black slaves of St. Domingo ought to follow the example of the white slaves of France.[39]

The revolt of the slaves began on August 22, 1791, at about ten o'clock in the evening. Men, women, and children on one of the plantations poured from their cabins, the men grasping their machetes with an air of resolution. The white overseers came running, whips in hand; but when they found that the slaves would no longer bare their backs meekly to receive the lash, they retreated to the plantation house and barricaded themselves. They were not molested. The slaves, lighting their way with torches, moved from plantation to plantation, swelling their numbers as they marched. The revolution was orderly at first; buildings were not burned nor were the whites massacred. Trouble soon began, however, when on one of the plantations the mob killed the manager, swarmed into the house, and set about helping themselves to whatever struck their fancy. Presently, someone touched a torch to the house, releasing a spirit of destruction. Building after building burst into flame and other rebels ran with torches into the fields and set fire to the dry sugar cane.

The movement spread rapidly. Within two months a hundred thousand slaves were in revolt and more than a thousand plantations had ceased to exist. Atrocities were committed by both sides. The slaves, drunk with rum and thirsty for revenge, indulged in an orgy of violence. Thousands of whites were slain, and many more blacks.

The slaves had a number of shrewd leaders — Boukmann, Dessalines, Christophe, Chavannes, Rigaud, and Oge — but the greatest of all was Toussaint L'Ouverture. He was an able soldier, and certainly more humane than his followers. For six years he was the dominant figure on the island. He waged relentless war against the soldiers from France and emerged victorious. Napoleon regarded Toussaint as an obstacle to his dream of creating a French empire in the New World, and sent an army of twenty-five thousand men under General LeClerc to subdue the island. Even this large and experienced force was unequal to the task of conquering the blacks, ably assisted as they were by yellow fever, malaria, and the rains. But LeClerc by a ruse captured the intrepid Toussaint, who was shipped to France, where he died in prison on April 6, 1803.

The exploits of Toussaint and his successors had reverberations throughout the world. Americans were terrified at the news of what was happening in Haiti, and measures were taken in a number of states to discourage the further

ix feet long.
bows, gam-
formed was

tic trances.
would see
nd joining
conscious-
visions.
it took on
l and Red
e dance so
h Dakota,
ian war.
ommand-
the chief
nds. Fi-
d of hos-
ed Knee
ir arms,
al firing
n men,
ty-three
a bliz-
attle of
ked the
it had

d from

prop-
arned
ncies
hina-
ality.
eting
lave
our-
ks.
za-
n

ery movement was intensified and defined.
groups took advantage of the situation to
lavery legislation. Historians even suspect
gain control of Haiti was a decisive factor in
t territory of Louisiana to the United States.

Aggressive behavior of an entirely different
host Dance, which swept through the Ameri-
de of the nineteenth century. The Indians by
ths of despair, poverty, and discontent. The
es seemed destined to destroy what little of their
e religion of the Ghost Dance was one way in
whites, whom they blamed for most of their

was Wovoka, a Paiute, who was known to the
as born in Nevada, and was probably the son of
a dreamer. Like most of his tribe, Wovoka had
satisfactory adjustment to the white settlers. He
hite man, David Wilson, from whom he received
ing a good living, had acquired some knowledge of
about Christianity. Until he was thirty he lived
an isolated valley in Nevada, surrounded by ice-

88 Wovoka went into a trance and had a spiritual ex-
evolved his new teaching. It was not entirely new; in-
ather, it was obviously a composite of various beliefs
by the Indians, plus a dash of Christian theology.
had a message for the Indians that he had received
estors. He urged them to do right, love one another and
with the world, and pray and hope for a day of reunion
happiness for all Indians, living and dead. A Messiah
he taught, and with him would come their ancestors in
would arise a great whirlwind, and the whites would
and other game would be restored, and the Indians would
he pristine conditions of the "golden age."
at this day of deliverance was close at hand, but the In-
its advent by dancing the Ghost Dance and by performing
They should cast aside the white ways and garments, and
of the Indian again. Above all, they should dance, dance,

t from tribe to tribe preaching this new religion and teaching
dance itself would begin in the middle of the afternoon, or
al instruments were used, except those held by individual
of them would wear a "ghost shirt," almost always made of
ored in the Indian fashion. No metal was to be worn. The

leader carried red feathers, red cloth, and a "ghost stick" about s
Other articles used in the dance included arrows with bone heads,
ing wheels, and sticks. The ground on which the dance was pe
consecrated.

The participants would shake with emotion and fall into hypnd
They professed to see Indians in the beyond dancing too. They
them playing games, gathering for war dances and the hunt, a
together in their ancient societies and brotherhoods. On regaining
ness, they would relate to the others all that they had seen in their

The Ghost Dance began to spread throughout the plains area, and
a hostile expression among the dissatisfied Sioux, where Sitting Bul
Cloud had long been the irreconcilable enemies of the whites. The
excited the Sioux that R. F. Roger, Indian Agent at Pine Ridge, Sout
wired for troops. Many settlers left their homes in fear of a major Ind

Troops arrived on October 19, 1890. General Nelson A. Miles, c
ing officer in that area, ordered the apprehension of Sitting Bull, but
was killed while resisting arrest. Skirmishing followed in the Badla
nally, on December 28, American troops discovered the principal ban
tile Indians, under the leadership of Big Foot, camped on Wound
Creek, South Dakota. The Indians were ordered to lay down the
which most of them promptly did. A few resisted, however, and gene
began, resulting in the slaughter of more than two hundred India
women, and children. White losses were twenty-nine and thi
wounded. Many wounded Indians, left on the field, froze to death in
zard the following night. History refers to this incident as the B
Wounded Knee, but it was actually a massacre. At any rate, it mar
climax of the Ghost Dance and the tragic attempt at resistance, that
called into being.

Nativistic movements similar to the Ghost Dance have been reporte
many parts of the world.

Organized Protest

Aggressive behavior is most likely to achieve its goal when it is organized,
erly directed, and expertly led. Minority groups again and again have le
the value of organization, with the result that we find innumerable age
operating in the area of race relations and having as their purpose the elir
tion of prejudice and discrimination and the assurance of justice and equ
American blacks, during slavery, were deprived of the opportunity of mee
together and organizing their aggressive desires. There were, of course, s
revolts that called for a degree of organization, but which failed in their
pose. In the North there was some concerted action on the part of bl
They formed their separate church bodies, they protested against the cold
tion of free blacks in Africa, and they took an active part in the abd
movement.

Organized black protest in the United States, however, assumed sign

March Against Racism, Boston, 1976

proportions early in the present century when certain of the black intelligentsia began to challenge the Booker T. Washington doctrine of industrial education, conciliation, and compromise. A group of men, under the leadership of W. E. B. DuBois, met at Niagara Falls, Canada, in 1905, and drew up a platform of aggressive action. Thus was launched the Niagara Movement, and a number of subsequent meetings were held at Harpers Ferry, West Virginia, Boston, and Oberlin, Ohio.

At the same time another organization was being formed by liberal whites, which eventually absorbed the Niagara Movement. In 1908 there occurred in Springfield, Illinois, a race riot that served to dramatize the insecurity of blacks. The riot provoked considerable discussion in the press, including an article entitled "Race War in the North," by William E. Walling, which was published in *The Independent*, September 3, 1908. The author forcefully argued that the only alternative to race war was the treatment of blacks "on a plane of absolute political and social equality." This article made an especial appeal to Miss Mary White Ovington, a New York social worker who had long been interested in the problems of blacks. She, in consultation with others, decided to call a conference for Lincoln's Birthday in 1909 to accept the challenge announced in Walling's article. The young radicals of the Niagara Movement were invited to the conference, and most of them accepted. A program was adopted, which included the following objectives:

Abolition of all forced segregation.

Equal educational advantages for black and white.

Enfranchisement of blacks.

Enforcement of the Fourteenth and Fifteenth Amendments.

From this conference there eventually emerged a permanent organization known as the National Association for the Advancement of Colored People.

The Association became a most effective organization in this country fighting for the rights of blacks. It set about immediately to open up industrial opportunities for blacks, to ensure them greater police protection, to abolish lynching, and to combat lawlessness. It has established an impressive record of successful court battles against discrimination in social, educational, legal, and political relations.[40] So effective has it been that the proponents of White Supremacy regarded the NAACP as their principal *bête noire*, and sought by one means or another to outlaw it or to destroy it.

American blacks have formed other organizations to give direction to their protest. The National Urban League, while chiefly concerned with meeting the social and economic problems arising from the mass migration of blacks to northern cities, has also functioned as an agency for the elimination of prejudice and discrimination. Its methods have generally been more pacific than those of the NAACP and its program has tended to be only slightly more liberal than the prevailing attitudes in the communities in which it operates. Among the many other organizations formed for the purpose of expressing black protest are the Congress of Racial Equality, the Southern Christian Leadership Council, the Student Nonviolent Coordinating Committee, the Black Muslims, and others.

Not only blacks, however, but other minorities as well, along with their sympathizers, have found that aggressive action can best be expressed through organization. To mention only a few, the Jews have their American Council for Judaism, the American Jewish Committee, the American Jewish Congress, the Jewish Defense League, and the Anti-Defamation League of B'nai B'rith. Working for the Indians are the Association on American Indian Affairs, the American Indian Movement, the Indian Rights Association, and the National Congress of American Indians. The Japanese in the United States have their Japanese-American Citizens League; and the Mexican immigrants have their Mexican-American Movement.

Minority Communities

Throughout the centuries, one common reaction to minority status has been to form segregated communities that are partially insulated from the onslaughts of the larger society. While we have commonly thought of the ethnic and racial ghettos of the cities as areas that arise primarily because the inhabitants cannot find suitable housing in other areas, we should recognize that such enclaves do not represent totally disagreeable circumstances that lead only to suffering and degradation for their inhabitants. Since many problems are created by being a part of a minority group, these areas often serve an important psychological function for the inhabitants in that they provide an opportunity for the resolution of many tensions created by minority status. In this section we will concentrate on the adjustment value of the minority community. It should be understood that we are in no way trying to make life in the poverty pockets of the city seem desirable, nor provide ammunition for those who are more fortunate to say that life in the ghetto is not as bad as it has been portrayed. The point that we wish to emphasize is that the minority community allows people to deal with the larger society as a unit, instead of as individuals.

The community created by territorial segregation allows the members to come to terms with the social deprivation and psychological degradation that is imposed by the larger society. The community gives its members the opportunity to cope with the inherent frustrations of minority status. For example, the inhabitants of the original medieval ghettos of Europe realized that there were many advantages to living in confined areas. As noted in a history of the ghetto:

. . . at times the communal life of the ghetto was better organized than that of the Christian towns in which it was situated. There were even Jews who did not ignore the positive aspects of the ghetto. In Verona and Mantua it was customary to commemorate the anniversary of its establishment by a special prayer in the synagogue.[41]

Louis Wirth in his discussion of the ghetto noted that "life in the ghetto was probably always more active and teeming than was life outside."[42] Let us examine these positive characteristics in more detail.

The concept of community encompasses a total way of life. It involves all the institutions established as a collective basis for the solution of life problems. Territorial segregation facilitates the development of community, since it leads to a consciousness of kind. With the recognition of differences between themselves and outsiders, the community members create social bonds that lead to a sense of solidarity. As Nisbet notes, community "achieves its fulfillment in a submergence of individual will that is not possible in unions of mere convenience or rational assent. Community is a fusion of feeling and thought, of tradition and commitment, of membership and volition."[43]

The fact that most of the members of minority communities have endured similar difficulties allows them to develop mutual understandings that might otherwise be lacking. These bonds alleviate the feelings of exclusion and alienation that might arise in the individual representative of a minority adrift in the larger society. This sense of belonging may be a function of nothing more than a common exclusion by others in the outside society. However, it still leads to a feeling of a shared social fate. As Goffman notes:

Knowing from their own experience what it is like to have this peculiar stigma, some of them can provide the individual with instruction in the tricks of the trade and with a circle of lament to which he can withdraw for moral support and for the comfort of feeling at home, at ease, accepted as a person who is really like any other person.[44]

We would be safe in saying that it is psychologically easier for an individual to live in a segregated community than to have free access to a society in which he is treated with discrimination as a representative of a minority. Kurt Lewin noted this:

In the ghetto period a Jew may have been exposed to especially high pressure when acting outside his group, but on the other hand there was for him some region in which he felt "at home," in which he could act freely as a member of his own group, and did not need to stand by himself against pressure from without. In other words, even when the pressure was high, there were regions in which this pressure had not the character of a differential pressure acting on the Jew as an individual person.[45]

The minority community reflects a continuing adaptation to the socially disadvantaged position of its members. Many of the structures serve to protect the members from the definitions that are imposed on them by the larger society. The formation of the community is the result of the low status of its members within the larger society. It is not formed because of its own exclusiveness necessarily, but because of exclusion by others. The community is therefore sensitive to the label of social inferiority that is applied by others. On the outside, the common and ascribed status of the group as a whole takes precedence over the achieved status of the individual members. The community serves its greatest psychological function in allowing its members once again to form definitions of self through achieved channels.

The new activities within the minority community counteract the feelings of social inferiority by allowing the members to see themselves as individuals. The dominant society may define them as socially inferior, but their peers can appreciate their individual achievements. These peers, then, and not the members of the dominant society, are the significant others whose responses are valued. Shibutani and Kwan note that:

Within the segregated community a man lives a life in which he is his own master in a world in which men are equal. . . . A person's prestige within the minority group is more or less independent of his rank in the outside world.[46]

Clearly, the individual's status is not entirely independent of the evaluations of the dominant group, but it is independent enough to allow the protection of self-esteem.

The members of the community have in common a restricted lifestyle. Since they share common perceptions and values, they become socialized to common patterns of response to adversities. Understandings develop from these shared responses that may be unintelligible to outsiders. The shared definitions permit individual acceptance or rejection by one's peers, instead of the categorical rejection by the outside society. Fear and anxiety are reduced by the individual triumphs achieved in interaction with the other members. A sense of normalcy prevails.

Within the minority community, the individual is allowed to live and interact almost as if dominant exclusion did not exist. By partially freeing the members from the negative consequences of their minority position, the community provides a sense of autonomy and allows for individual aspirations and achievements. The community provides for the individual a feeling that at least certain aspects of one's life are under control. However, the community is more than just a buffer between its members and the hostile society. It is a social reality in itself. Events taking place outside the community have very little bearing on the day-to-day activities inside the community. Shibutani and Kwan note that one of the characteristics of minority peoples is their extreme preoccupation with the affairs of their own world. They have a detailed knowledge of what goes on within their own group, but have only a vague notion of the events on the outside.[47]

A community that is cut off from contacts with the outside, whether voluntarily or involuntarily, has little potential for social change based on experiences occurring in the rest of society. As Wirth noted, the "ghetto is a closed community, perpetuating itself and renewing itself with a minimum of infusion of influences from without, biologically and culturally."[48] With exclusion there is little knowledge of what is occurring in society and an absence of alternative responses to problems. Hence the rational choice of alternatives is made more difficult since there is little knowledge of the connection between events in the larger society and the consequences for the members of the community. Therefore, a false feeling of security is more likely to occur in this type of closed situation than when minority members are free to interact with the larger society.

The secure feeling produced by being a member of a tightly knit Jewish community may have been exactly what contributed to the pervasiveness of the destruction under the Nazi extermination policy. It is difficult for an individual to believe that destruction is imminent and that the only potential for escape is through individual, rather than group, action, when an internally strong Jewish community, which has grown out of and survived thousands of years of attack, provides security and a feeling that "this too shall pass." Had the internal structures of the Jewish community not been so comforting and had the resulting isolation not been so great, many Jews might have been able to save themselves. This point is made evident in the following statement of a high-ranking SS official named Von dem Bach, who was involved in the killing of Jews from 1941 until the end of the war. He notes:

The mass of Jewish people were taken completely by surprise. They did not know at all what to do; they had not directives or slogans as to how they should act. That is the greatest lie of anti-Semitism because it gives the lie to the old slogan that the Jews are conspiring to dominate the world and that they are so highly organized. In reality they had no organization of their own at all, not even an information service. If they had had some sort of organization, these people could have been saved by the millions: but instead they were taken completely by surprise. Never before has a people gone as unsuspectingly to its disaster. Nothing was prepared. Absolutely nothing.[49]

There is only sparse research to substantiate the assumption, but many who escaped the destruction may have been the most iconoclastic or least well-integrated members of the Jewish community. They were the ones who were most likely to receive accurate information and were the most likely to respond to it in a self-interested fashion. For example, the following quote is from a woman who was well integrated into the Jewish community. While enduring the hardships of the Warsaw ghetto, she nonetheless responded to the proposal to live outside the ghetto with false Polish identity papers, by stating that it:

seems to me like treason against my own people. Here, in the worst, most awful moments, I am after all among my own. Never have I felt myself so strongly a Jew, never was I so strongly united with my brothers as now. Intellectually I admit that hiding out among 'Aryans' is perhaps the best, perhaps the only solution. Emotionally I consider it desertion.[50]

Someone who was less well-integrated within the Jewish community might have been more willing to try purely individualistic and self-serving escape routes. It is probably no accident that so many of those who perished were the deeply religious Jews living in the Jewish cultural centers of eastern Europe. They were the ones most likely to gain security from the rich religious and cultural life of the community.

Within the minority community there is a sense of superiority and communal chauvinism that defines the rest of society as inadequate. The members take particular pleasure in outwitting the representatives of the dominant group, because it overcomes the humiliation of subordination. The members of the minority community also develop strong prejudices against the dominant group and engage in stereotyping as well. The following excerpt from a poem by Israel Zangwill provides an example.

Go not outside the Ghetto.
Should your footsteps be forced to their haunts,
Walk warily, never forgetting
They are Goyim,
Foes of the faith,
Beings of darkness,
Drunkards and bullies,
Swift with the fist or the bludgeon . . .[51]

Feelings of security also arise from the common link with the past that the members of the minority community have. Since they live together and associate with each other, the feeling of solidarity is enhanced and they come to feel a sense of responsibility for one another.

Simmel has noted that, "Even in the most oppressive and cruel cases of subordination, there is a considerable measure of personal freedom."[52]   This freedom is what allows the members of minority enclaves to maintain some sense of dignity in the face of persecution and discrimination; if it did not exist, it is hard to imagine how they would survive.

What is the "best" solution for the problems of intergroup relationships? Certainly there is no simple answer, nor even a single one. Nor is there a permanent one. Too much depends on the temperament of the individual and on the values to which one is attached. Those who prize homogeneity will give one answer, while those who prize heterogeneity will give another. There are patient individuals who take a long view, and there are restless ones to whom time is the very essence of the problem. Those who exalt the unity of the state will differ from those whose concern is for human personality and individuality. Those who long for assimilation and integration will disagree with those who are interested in the preservation of traditions and values they hold dear. There are those to whom peace is priceless and others who find conflict exhilarating, or at least preferable to discrimination. We have tried to present the information in this book in such a way that the reader can gain as much of an understanding of the dynamics of intergroup relations as possible. In the end, each individual will respond to other people based on his or her particular knowledge and experience. We hope that the knowledge gained from this book will lead to some reflection on how each of us can personally improve our contacts with our fellow human beings.

Notes

1. H. I. Hogbin, *Experiments in Civilization*, pp. 153–154.

2. H. H. Turney-High, *The Flathead Indians of Montana*, Memoirs of the American Anthropological Association, no. 48, 1937, p. 149.

3. G. MacGregor, *Warriors Without Weapons*.

4. Ako Adjei, "Imperialism and Spiritual Freedom: An African View," *American Journal of Sociology* 50, no. 3 (Nov. 1944): 194. See also, in the same issue, R. E. Park, "Missions in the Modern World"; H. Stunz, "Christian Missions and Social Cohesion"; G. G. Brown, "Missions and Cultural Diffusion."

5. V. Korolenko, *In a Strange Land*, p. 52.

6. W. I. Thomas and F. Znaniecki, *The Polish Peasant in Europe and America*, especially vol. 5, p. 165ff.

7. W. C. Smith, *Americans in the Making*, p. 61ff.

8. This loss of status was an especially acute problem with the refugees of the 1930s, as pointed out by M. R. Davie in *Refugees in America*, p. 395. See also J. Kosa, *Land of Choice: The Hungarians in Canada*, passim.

9. Smith, *Americans in the Making*, pp. 67–68.

10. S. Elkins, *Slavery: A Problem in American Institutional and Intellectual Life*, pp. 81–133.

11. See S. Mathews, *A History of New Testament Times in Palestine*.

12. A. H. Leighton, *The Governing of Men.*

13. Leighton, *The Governing of Men,* p. 263.

14. C. E. Glick, "Social Roles and Types in Race Relations," in A. W. Lind, ed., *Race Relations in World Perspective,* p. 239ff.

15. E. V. Stonequist, *The Marginal Man,* pp. 159–200.

16. M. R. Davie, *Negroes in American Society,* pp. 434–455.

17. C. S. Johnson, *Patterns of Negro Segregation,* pp. 244–315.

18. G. E. Simpson, "The Ras Tafari Movement in Jamaica: A Study of Race and Class Conflict," *Social Forces* 34, no. 2 (Dec. 1955): 167ff.

19. His story, summarized here, is recounted by E. R. Embree in *Indians of the Americas,* pp. 223–233.

20. This and the following comments from blacks are taken from C. S. Johnson, *Negro Segregation,* pp. 244–266, and H. Powdermaker, *After Freedom,* pp. 325–353.

21. J. H. Franklin, *From Slavery to Freedom,* pp. 234–238, 481–483.

22. T. Herzl, *The Jewish State,* pp. 38–39.

23. E. G. Burrows, *Hawaiian Americans,* p. 139ff.

24. Johnson, *Negro Segregation,* pp. 267–293.

25. R. Wright, *Uncle Tom's Children,* pp. 21–22.

26. Among the films are "Pinky" and "Lost Boundaries." Novels and plays include J. W. Johnson, *Autobiography of an Ex-Colored Man;* D. Heyward, *Brass Ankle;* F. Hurst, *Imitation of Life;* L. Saxon, *Children of Strangers;* G. M. Shelby and S. G. Stoney, *Po' Buckra,* C. R. Sumner, *Quality;* C. Van Vechten, *Nigger Heaven.*

27. B. Berry, *Almost White.*

28. R. Ottley, "5 Million U.S. White Negroes," *Ebony* 3, no. 5 (Mar. 1948) p. 32ff.

29. H. Asbury, "Who Is a Negro?" *Colliers,* 3 Aug. 1946.

30. H. Hart, *Selective Migration as a Factor in Child Welfare in the United States, with Special Reference to Iowa,* pp. 28–29.

31. J. H. Burma, "The Measurement of Negro Passing," *American Journal of Sociology* 52, no. 1 (July 1946): 18ff; E. W. Eckard, "How Many Negroes Pass?" *American Journal of Sociology* 52, no. 6 (May 1947): 498ff.

32. C. B. Day, *A Study of Some Negro-White Families in the United States,* Harvard African Studies, vol. 10, 1932.

33. R. Stuckert, "African Ancestry of the White American Population," *Ohio Journal of Science* 58, no. 3 (May 1958): 155ff.

34. G. Myrdal, *An American Dilemma: The Negro Problem and Modern Democracy,* p. 687.

35. J. M. Oskison, *Tecumseh and His Times,* chap. 11. Also C. Wissler, *Indians of the United States,* pp. 79–83; A. Britt, *Great Indian Chiefs,* pp. 126–155.

36. Tippecanoe was a noted Indian village site on the west bank of the Wabash just below the mouth of the Tippecanoe River in Indiana. It was occupied successively by Miami, Shawnee, and Potawatomi. Tecumseh and his brother, The Prophet, made it their headquarters in 1808. In 1811 when the Indian revolt had grown to threatening proportions, General William Henry Harrison marched with nine hundred troops against the town. Tecumseh was absent in the South at the time. Near the town, at daybreak on November 7, the whites were attacked by the Indians under the leadership of The Prophet. A desperate engagement ensued, resulting in the complete defeat and dispersion of the Indians.

37. Among the many biographies of him, two are especially recommended: B. Korngold, *Citizen Toussaint;* and S. Alexis, *Black Liberator: The Life of Toussaint L'Ouverture.*

38. Quoted in Korngold, *Citizen Toussaint*, p. 30.

39. Korngold, *Citizen Toussaint*, pp. 63–64.

40. For information on the NAACP, see M. W. Ovington, *The Walls Came Tumbling Down*; E. F. Frazier, *The Negro in the United States*, p. 523ff.; J. H. Franklin, *From Slavery to Freedom*, p. 437ff.; Myrdal, *American Dilemma*, pp. 819–938; Davie, *Negroes in American Society*, p. 449ff.

41. Keter Publishers, *Anti-Semitism*, p. 113.

42. L. Wirth, *The Ghetto*, p. 36.

43. R. A. Nisbet, *The Sociological Tradition*, pp. 47–48.

44. E. Goffman, *Stigma: Notes on the Management of Spoiled Identity*, p. 20.

45. K. Lewin, *Resolving Social Conflicts*, p. 155.

46. T. Shibutani and K. Kwan, *Ethnic Stratification*, p. 290.

47. Ibid., p. 288.

48. Wirth, *The Ghetto*, p. 226.

49. R. Hilberg, *The Destruction of the European Jews*, pp. 662–663.

50. L. Dawidowicz, *The War Against the Jews, 1933–1945*, p. 222.

51. I. Zangwill, "The Goyim" cited in Wirth, *The Ghetto*, p. 119.

52. K. H. Wolff, ed and trans., *The Sociology of Georg Simmel*, p. 182.

Bibliography

Abrahams, Roger D. *Positively Black*. Englewood Cliffs, N.J.: Prentice-Hall, 1970.

Adams, Romanzo. *Interracial Marriage in Hawaii*. New York: Macmillan Co., 1937.

Adorno, T. W., et al. *The Authoritarian Personality*. New York: Harper & Row, 1950.

Alexis, Stephen. *Black Liberator: The Life of Toussaint L'Ouverture*. New York: Macmillan Co., 1949.

Allport, Gordon W. *ABC's of Scapegoating*. New York: Anti-Defamation League, 1959.

———. *The Nature of Prejudice*. Cambridge, Mass.: Addison-Wesley Publishing Co., 1954.

Anderson, E. L. *We Americans: A Study of Cleavage in an American City*. Cambridge, Mass.: Harvard University Press, 1937.

Aptheker, Herbert. *Negro Slave Revolts in the United States, 1526–1860*. New York: International Publishers, 1939.

Baldwin, James. *Nobody Knows My Name*. New York: Dell Publishing Co., 1962.

Barron, Milton L., ed. *The Blending American*. Chicago: Quadrangle Books, 1972.

Barth, Fredrik. *Ethnic Groups and Boundaries*. Boston: Little, Brown & Co., 1969.

Berger, Peter L. *Invitation to Sociology*. Garden City, N.Y.: Doubleday & Co., 1963.

Berry, Brewton. *Almost White*. New York: Macmillan Co., 1963.

———. *The Education of the American Indians*. Washington, D.C.: U.S. Dept. of Health, Education and Welfare, 1968.

Berson, Lenora E. *The Negroes and the Jews*. New York: Random House, 1971.

Beveridge, A. J. *Abraham Lincoln, 1809–1858*. Boston: Houghton Mifflin Co., 1928.

Biddiss, Michael D. *Father of Racist Ideology: The Social and Political Thought of Count Gobineau*. New York: Weybright and Talley, 1970.

Bierstedt, Robert. *The Social Order*. New York: McGraw-Hill Book Co., 1963.

Blaustein, Albert P., and Zangrando, R. L., eds. *Civil Rights and the Black American*. New York: Simon & Schuster, 1968.

Bloom, Leonard, and Riemer, R. *Removal and Return: The Socio-Economic Effects of the War on Japanese Americans*. Berkeley and Los Angeles: University of California Press, 1949.

Bortnick, David. *Patterns of Interfaith Dating and Religious Observance among Jewish College Students in Florida*. Unpublished doctoral dissertation, Florida State University, 1975.

Brigham, Carl C. *A Study of American Intelligence*. Princeton: Princeton University Press, 1923.

Britt, Albert. *Great Indian Chiefs*. New York: McGraw-Hill Book Co., 1938.

Brotz, Howard, ed. *Negro Social and Political Thought, 1850–1920*. New York: Basic Books, Inc., 1966.

Brown, Demetra V. *A Child of the Orient*. Boston: Houghton Mifflin Co., 1914.

Brown, L. G. *Immigration: Cultural Conflicts and Social Adjustments*. New York: Arno Press, 1969.

Browne, Lewis. *How Odd of God*. New York: Macmillan Co., 1934.

Brunner, E. de S. *Immigrant Farmers and Their Children*. New York: Doubleday, Doran and Company, 1929.

Burkhard, Hugo. *Tanz Mal Jude: Von Dachau Bis Shanghai*. Nurnberg: Richard Reichenbach KG, 1967.

Burrows, E. G. *Hawaiian Americans*. New Haven: Yale University Press, 1947.

Cahnman, Werner J., ed. *Intermarriage and Jewish Life*. New York: Herzl Press, 1963.

Carlson, Lewis H., and Colburn, G. A. *In Their Place: White America Defines Her Minorities, 1850–1950*. New York: John Wiley & Sons, 1972.

Carroll, Joseph C. *Slave Insurrections in the United States, 1800–1860*. Boston: Chapman and Grimes, 1938.

Catlin, George. *The North American Indians*. London: Chatto & Windus, 1880.

Cleaver, Eldridge. *Soul on Ice*. New York: Dell Publishing Co., 1968.

Collier, John. *The Indians of the Americas*. New York: W. W. Norton, 1947.

Cooley, Charles H. *Social Organization: A Study of the Larger Mind*. New York: Charles Scribner's Sons, 1909.

———. *Social Process*. Carbondale, Ill.: Southern Illinois University Press, 1966.

Coolidge, Mary Roberts. *Chinese Immigration*. New York: Henry Holt & Co., 1909.

Coon, C. S. *The Origin of Races*. New York: Alfred A. Knopf, 1962.

———. *The Races of Europe*. New York: Macmillan Co., 1939.

Cutler, James E. *Lynch Law: An Investigation into the History of Lynching in the United States*. New York: Longmans, Green & Co., 1905.

Davie, M. R. *Negroes in American Society*. New York: McGraw-Hill Book Co., 1949.

———. *Refugees in America*. New York: Harper & Row, 1947.

Davis, A., Gardner, B. B., and Gardner, M. *Deep South: A Social Anthropological Study of Caste and Class*. Chicago: University of Chicago Press, 1941.

Dawidowicz, Lucy S. *The War Against the Jews, 1933–1945*. New York: Holt, Rinehart, and Winston, 1975.

Dicker, Marvin. *Wanderers and Settlers in the Far East*. New York: Twayne Publishers, 1965.

Dollard, John. *Caste and Class in a Southern Town*. New York: Harper & Row, 1949.

Dollard, John, et al. *Frustration and Aggression*. New Haven: Yale University Press, 1939.

Drachsler, Julius. *Democracy and Assimilation*. New York: Macmillan Co., 1920.

Drake, St. Clair, and Cayton, H. R. *Black Metropolis*. New York: Harcourt, Brace and World, 1945.

Driver, Harold E. *Indians of North America*. Chicago: University of Chicago Press, 1961.

DuBois, W. E. B. *Dusk of Dawn*. New York: Harcourt, Brace and World, 1940.

Duncan, H. G. *Immigration and Assimilation*. Boston: D. C. Heath & Co., 1933.

Ehrlich, Howard J. *The Social Psychology of Prejudice*. New York: John Wiley & Sons, 1973.

Eisenstadt, S. N. *The Absorption of Immigrants: A Comparative Study Based Mainly on the Jewish Community in Palestine and the State of Israel*. New York: Free Press of Glencoe, 1955.

Elkins, Stanley. *Slavery: A Problem in American Institutional and Intellectual Life*. Chicago: University of Chicago Press, 1959.

Embree, E. R. *Indians of the Americas*. Boston: Houghton Mifflin Co., 1939.

Eskelund, Karl. *My Chinese Wife*. Garden City, N.Y.: Doubleday & Co., 1945.

Eysenck, Hans J. *The IQ Argument*. New York: Library Press, 1971.

Fairchild, H. P. *Race and Nationality*. New York: Ronald Press, 1947.

Fischer, Eugen. *Die Rehobother Bastards und das Bastardierungsproblem beim Menschen*. Jena: G. Fischer, 1913.

Foreman, Grant. *Indian Removal*. Norman Okla.: Oklahoma University Press, 1932.

Frankenstein, Carl, ed. *Between Past and Future*. Jerusalem: Henrietts Szold Foundation for Child and Youth Welfare, 1953.

Franklin, J. Hope. *From Slavery to Freedom*. New York: Alfred A. Knopf, 1956.

Frazier, E. Franklin. *Black Bourgeoisie*. New York: Free Press of Glencoe, 1957.

———. *The Negro Family in the United States*. Chicago: University of Chicago Press, 1939.

———. *The Negro in the United States*. New York: Macmillan Co., 1949.

Frazier, J. G. *The Golden Bough: A Study in Magic and Religion*. 12 vols. London: Macmillan & Co., Ltd., 1913–1915.

Fredrickson, George M. *The Black Image in the White Mind*. New York: Harper & Row, 1971.

Freyre, Gilberto. *The Masters and the Slaves: A Study in the Development of Brazilian Civilization*. New York: Alfred A. Knopf, 1946.

Garrett, Henry E. *IQ and Racial Differences.* Cape Canaveral, Fla.: Howard Allen Enterprises, 1973.

Gelfand, Donald E., and Lee, Russell D., eds. *Ethnic Conflicts and Power: A Cross National Perspective.* New York: John Wiley & Sons, 1973.

Gist, Noel P., and Dworkin, A. G., eds. *The Blending of Races.* New York: John Wiley & Sons, 1972.

Gittler, Joseph B., ed. *Understanding Minority Groups.* New York: John Wiley & Sons, 1956.

Glazer, Nathan, and Moynihan, D. P. *Beyond the Melting Pot.* Cambridge, Mass.: M.I.T. Press and Harvard University Press, 1963.

Gobineau, Joseph Arthur. *Essai sur l'inégalité des races humaines par le comte de Gobineau.* Paris: Firmin-Didot et Cie, 1940.

Goffman, Erving. *Stigma: Notes on the Management of Spoiled Identity.* Englewood Cliffs, N.J.: Prentice-Hall, 1963.

Golden, Harry. *you're entitle'.* New York: Crest, 1962.

Goldenweiser, Alexander. *Anthropology.* New York: F. S. Crofts & Co., 1937.

Goldschmid, Marcel L. *Black Americans and White Racism.* New York: Holt, Rinehart, and Winston, 1970.

Gordon, Albert I. *Jews in Transition.* Minneapolis: University of Minnesota Press, 1950.

Gordon, Milton M. *Assimilation in American Life.* New York: Oxford University Press, 1964.

Gossett, Thomas F. *Race: The History of an Idea in America.* Dallas: Southern Methodist University Press, 1963.

Graebner, Isacque, and Britt, S. H., eds. *Jews in the Gentile World.* New York: Macmillan Co., 1942.

Greeley, Andrew M. *Ethnicity in the United States.* New York: John Wiley & Sons, 1974.

———. *Why Can't They Be Like Us?* New York: E. P. Dutton, 1971.

Griesman, B. Eugene. *Minorities.* Hinsdale, Ill.: The Dryden Press, 1975.

Hagan, William T. *American Indians.* Chicago: University of Chicago Press, 1961.

Hansen, Marcus L. *The Atlantic Migration.* Cambridge, Mass.: Harvard University Press, 1942.

———. *The Immigrant in American History.* Cambridge, Mass.: Harvard University Press, 1942.

Harlan, Louis R. *Separate and Unequal.* Chapel Hill, N.C.: University of North Carolina Press, 1958.

Hart, Hornell N. *Selective Migration as a Factor in Child Welfare in the United States, with Special Reference to Iowa.* Iowa City: University of Iowa Press, 1921.

Hastings, J., ed. *The Dictionary of the Bible.* New York: Charles Scribner's Sons, 1898–1904.

Hechinger, Fred M., and Hechinger, G. *Growing Up in America.* New York: McGraw-Hill Book Co., 1975.

Herold, J. Christopher. *The Swiss without Halos*. New York: Columbia University Press, 1948.

Herskovits, M. J. *The American Negro: A Study in Racial Crossing*. New York: Alfred A. Knopf, 1928.

————. *The Anthropometry of the American Negro*. New York: Columbia University Press, 1930.

————. *The Myth of the Negro Past*. New York: Harper & Row, 1941.

Herzl, Theodor. *The Jewish State*. New York: Zionist Organization of America, 1941.

Higham, John. *Send These to Me*. New York: Atheneum, 1975.

Hilberg, Raul. *The Destruction of the European Jews*. Chicago: Quadrangle Books, 1961.

Hinder, Eleanor M. *Life and Labour in Shanghai*. New York: Institute of Pacific Relations, 1944.

Hodge, F. W., ed. *Handbook of American Indians North of Mexico*. Washington, D.C.: Government Printing Office, 1912.

Hogbin, H. Ian. *Experiments in Civilization*. London: George Routledge and Sons, 1939.

Hooten, E. A. *Up From the Ape*. New York: Macmillan Co., 1946.

Howe, Irving. *World of Our Fathers*. New York: Harcourt Brace Jovanovich, 1976.

Hughes, Henry. *Treatise on Sociology, Theoretical and Practical*. Philadelphia: Published by the author, 1854.

Hughes, Langston. *Selected Poems*. New York: Alfred A. Knopf, 1970.

Hunt, Chester L., and Walker, L. *Ethnic Dynamics: Patterns of Intergroup Relations in Various Societies*. Homewood, Ill.: Dryden Press, 1974.

Hunter, John D. *Memoirs of a Captivity among the Indians of North America*. London: Longman, Hurst, Rees, Orme, and Brown, 1823.

Jennings, H. S. *The Biological Basis of Human Nature*. New York: W. W. Norton & Co., 1930.

Jenson, Arthur R. *Educational Differences*. London: Methuen, 1973.

Johnson, Charles S. *Patterns of Negro Segregation*. New York: Harper & Row, 1943.

Jonassen, C. T. *Norwegians in Bay Ridge: A Sociological Study of an Ethnic Group*. Ann Arbor, Mich.: University Microfilms, Inc., 1948.

Keter Publishers. *Anti-Semitism*. Jerusalem: Keter Publishing House Jerusalem Ltd., 1974.

Killian, Lewis, and Grigg, C. *Racial Crisis in America*. Englewood Cliffs, N.J.: Prentice-Hall, 1964.

Kinloch, Graham C. *The Dynamics of Race Relations*. New York: McGraw-Hill Book Co., 1974.

Kippis, Andrew. *Narrative of the Voyages Round the World Performed by Captain James Cook*. London: Bickers & Sons, 1878.

Kitson, Arthur. *Captain James Cook, The Circumnavigator*. New York: E. P. Dutton and Co., 1907.

Klineberg, Otto, ed. *Characteristics of the American Negro.* New York: Harper & Row, 1944

Klineberg, Otto. *Race Differences.* New York: Harper & Row, 1935.

Korngold, Ralph. *Citizen Toussaint.* Boston: Little, Brown & Co., 1945.

Korolenko, Vladimir G. *In a Strange Land.* New York: Bernard G. Richards Co., 1925.

Kosa, John. *Land of Choice: The Hungarians in Canada.* Toronto: Toronto University Press, 1957.

Kramer, Judith R., and Leventman, S. *Children of the Gilded Ghetto: Conflict Resolution of Three Generations of American Jews.* New Haven: Yale University Press, 1961.

Kriesberg, Louis. *The Sociology of Social Conflicts.* Englewood Cliffs, N.J.: Prentice-Hall, 1973.

Kroeber, Alfred L., and Waterman, T. T. *Source Book in Anthropology.* New York: Harcourt, Brace and Co., 1931.

La Piere, Richard T. *Sociology.* New York: McGraw-Hill Book Co., 1946.

Lapsley, Arthur B., ed. *The Writings of Abraham Lincoln.* New York: G. P. Putnam's Sons, 1905–06.

Lawrence, Gunther. *Three Million More?* Garden City, N.Y.: Doubleday & Co., 1970.

Lea, H. C. *The Moriscos of Spain: Their Conversion and Expulsion.* Philadelphia: Lea Brothers & Co., 1901.

Lee, A. M., and Humphrey, N. D. *Race Riot.* New York: Dryden Press, 1943.

Leighton, Alexander H. *The Governing of Men.* Princeton: Princeton University Press, 1945.

Lenski, Gerhard E. *Power and Privilege: A Theory of Social Stratification.* New York: McGraw-Hill Book Co., 1966.

Levin, Jack. *The Function of Prejudice.* New York: Harper & Row, 1975.

Lewin, Kurt. *Resolving Social Conflicts.* New York: Harper & Row, 1948.

Lind, Andrew W. ed. *Race Relations in World Perspective.* Honolulu: University of Hawaii Press, 1955.

Lindquist, Gustavus E. E. *The Indians in American Life.* New York: Friendship Press, 1944.

Linton, Ralph. *The Study of Man.* New York: D. Appleton-Century Co., 1936.

Linton, Ralph, ed. *Acculturation in Seven American Indian Tribes.* New York: D. Appleton-Century Co., 1940.

———. *The Science of Man in the World Crisis.* New York: Columbia University Press, 1945.

Locke, Alain, and Stern, B. J. *When Peoples Meet.* New York: Progressive Education Association, 1942.

London, Herbert I. *Non-White Immigration and the "White Australia" Policy.* New York: New York University Press, 1970.

Lyman, Stanford M. *Chinese Americans.* New York: Random House, 1974.

MacCrone, I. D. *Race Attitudes in South Africa.* London: Oxford University Press, 1937.

MacGregor, Gordon. *Warriors without Weapons.* Chicago: University of Chicago Press, 1946.

MacIver, Robert M. *The More Perfect Union.* New York: Macmillan Co., 1948.

MacIver, Robert M., ed. *Discrimination and National Welfare.* New York: Harper & Row, 1949.

————. *Group Relations and Group Antagonisms.* New York: P. Smith, 1951.

Mack, Raymond W., ed. *Prejudice and Race Relations.* Chicago: Quadrangle Books, 1970.

MacLeod, William C. *The American Indian Frontier.* New York: Alfred A. Knopf, 1928.

Mangum, Charles S. *The Legal Status of the Negro.* Chapel Hill, N.C.: University of North Carolina Press, 1940.

Marden, Charles F., and Myer, G. *Minorities in American Society.* New York: American Book Co., 1962.

Marx, Gary T., ed. *Racial Conflict.* Boston: Little, Brown & Co., 1971.

Mathews, Shailer. *A History of New Testament Times in Palestine.* New York: Macmillan Co., 1921.

McNickle, D'Arcy. *The Indian Tribes of the United States.* New York: Oxford University Press, 1962.

McWilliams, Carey. *Brothers under the Skin.* Boston: Little, Brown & Co., 1943.

Meriam, Lewis, and Associates. *The Problem of Indian Administration.* Baltimore: Johns Hopkins Press, 1928.

Merton, Thomas. *The Seven Storey Mountain.* New York: Harcourt, Brace and World, 1948.

Mill, John Stuart. *Principles of Political Economy.* 2 vols. New York: Colonial Press, 1899.

Mindel, Charles H., and Habenstein, R. W. *Ethnic Families in America.* New York: Elsevier, 1976.

Montagu, Ashley. *Man's Most Dangerous Myth: The Fallacy of Race.* New York: Oxford University Press, 1974.

————. *Race and IQ.* New York: Oxford University Press, 1975.

Murdock, G. P. *Our Primitive Contemporaries.* New York: Macmillan Co., 1934.

Myrdal, Gunner, with the assistance of Richard Sterner and Arnold Rose. *An American Dilemma: The Negro Problem and Modern Democracy.* New York: Harper & Row, 1944.

Nam, Charles B. *Population and Society.* Boston: Houghton Mifflin Co., 1968.

Newman, Jeremiah. *Race: Migration and Integration.* London: Burns & Oates, 1968.

Nisbet, Robert A. *The Sociological Tradition.* New York: Basic Books, 1966.

Osborne, Richard H. *The Biological and Social Meaning of Race.* San Francisco: W. H. Freeman and Co., 1971.

Oskison, John M. *Tecumseh and His Times*. New York: G. P. Putnam's Sons, 1938.

Ovington, Mary W. *The Walls Came Tumbling Down*. New York: Harcourt, Brace and Co., 1947.

Panunzio, Constantine M. *Major Social Institutions*. New York: Macmillan Co., 1939.

Park, Robert E. *Race and Culture*. New York: Free Press of Glencoe, 1949.

Park, Robert E., and Burgess, E. W. *Introduction to the Science of Sociology*. Chicago: University of Chicago Press, 1924.

Parkes, James W. *The Jewish Problem in the Modern World*. New York: Oxford University Press, 1946.

Patai, Raphael. *Israel Between East and West*. Westport, Conn.: Greenwood Publishing Co., 1970.

Pierson, Donald. *Negroes in Brazil*. Chicago: University of Chicago Press, 1942.

Plotnicov, L., and Tuden, A., eds. *Essays in Comparative Social Stratification*. Pittsburgh: University of Pittsburgh Press, 1970.

Porter, Jack N., and Dreier, P., eds. *Jewish Radicalism*. New York: Grove Press, 1973.

Porteus, Stanley D. *Calabashes and Kings: An Introduction to Hawaii*. Palo Alto, Calif.: Pacific Books, 1945.

Powdermaker, Hortense. *After Freedom*. New York: Viking Press, 1939.

————. *Probing Our Prejudices*. New York: Harper & Row, 1941.

Price, Willard. *Japan's Islands of Mystery*. New York: John Day Co., 1944.

Reuter, E. B., ed. *Race and Culture Contacts*. New York: McGraw-Hill Book Co., 1934.

Reuter, E. B., and Hart, C. W. *Introduction to Sociology*.

Richmond, Anthony H. *The Colour Problem: A Study of Racial Relations*. Baltimore: Penguin Books, 1955.

Rischen, Moses. *The Promised City*. New York: Harper & Row, 1970.

Rister, Carl C. *Border Captives: The Traffic in Prisoners by Southern Plains Indians*. Norman, Okla.: Oklahoma University Press, 1940.

Rose, Arnold. *Studies in the Reduction of Prejudice*. Chicago: American Council on Race Relations, 1947.

Rose, Arnold, and Rose, C. *America Divided*. New York: Alfred A. Knopf, 1948.

Rose, Peter I. *They and We*. New York: Random House, 1974.

Rose, Peter I., ed. *Nation of Nations: The Ethnic Experience and the Racial Crisis*. New York: Random House, 1972.

Ross, Edward A. *Social Psychology*. New York: Macmillan Co., 1908.

Samuel, Maurice. *The Great Hatred*. New York: Alfred A. Knopf, 1941.

Schermerhorn, R. A. *These Our People*. Boston: D. C. Heath & Co., 1949.

Secord, Paul F., and Backman, C. W. *Social Psychology*. New York: McGraw-Hill Book Co., 1974.

Shapiro, Harry L. *The Heritage of the Bounty*. New York: Simon and Schuster, 1936.

Shay, Frank. *Judge Lynch: His First Hundred Years*. New York: Ives Washburn, Inc., 1938.

Shibutani, Tamotsu, and Kwan, K. *Ethnic Stratification: A Comparative Approach*. New York: Macmillan Co., 1965.

Schrieke, B. *Alien Americans*. New York: Viking Press, 1936.

Simpson, George E., and Yinger, J. Milton. *Racial and Cultural Minorities: An Analysis of Prejudice and Discrimination*. New York: Harper & Row, 1972.

Sklare, Marshall. *America's Jews*. New York: Random House, 1971.

Smith, W. C. *Americans in the Making*. New York: D. Appleton-Century Co., 1939.

Sowell, Thomas. *Race and Economics*. New York: David McKay Co., 1975.

Spellman, C. L. *Elm City: A Negro Community in Action*. Tallahassee, Fla.: Florida A. and M. College, 1947.

Starkey, Marion L. *The Cherokee Nation*. New York: Alfred A. Knopf, 1946.

Stefansson, Vilhjalmur. *My Life With the Eskimo*. New York: Macmillan Co., 1926.

Stern, Curt. *Principles of Human Genetics*. 3rd ed. San Francisco: W. H. Freeman & Co., 1973.

Stern, Selma. *The Court Jew*. Philadelphia: Jewish Publication Society of America, 1950.

Steward, Julian H., ed. *Handbook of South American Indians*. Smithsonian Institution, Bureau of American Ethnology Bulletin 143. 5 vols. Washington, D.C.: Government Printing Office, 1946–1949.

Stonequist, E. V. *The Marginal Man*. New York: Charles Scribner's Sons, 1937.

Stroeber, Gerald S. *American Jews: Community in Crisis*. Garden City, N.Y.: Doubleday & Co., 1974.

Strong, E. K. *The Second-Generation Japanese Problem*. Palo Alto, Calif.: Stanford University Press, 1934.

Sumner, William G. *Folkways*. Boston: Ginn & Co., 1940.

Sumner, William G., and Keller, Albert G. *The Science of Society*. New Haven: Yale University Press, 1927.

Taylor, Philip. *The Distant Magnet*. New York: Harper & Row, 1971.

Thomas, W. I., and Znaniecki, F. *The Polish Peasant in Europe and America*. 5 vols. Boston: R. G. Badger, 1918–1920.

Thompson, Edgar T., ed. *Race Relations and the Race Problem*. Durham, N.C.: Duke University Press, 1939.

Tischler, Henry L. *Free Societies of Captives: Towards the Development of a Theory of Restricted Communities*. Unpublished doctoral dissertation, Northeastern University, 1976.

Toynbee, A. J. *A Study of History*. 6 vols. London: Oxford University Press, 1934.

Turney-High, H. H. *The Flathead Indians of Montana*. Memoirs of the American Anthropological Association, no. 48, 1937.

Walker, Deward E., Jr., ed. *The Emergent Native Americans*. Boston: Little, Brown & Co., 1972.

Wallace, D. D. *History of South Carolina*. 4 vols. New York: American Historical Society, 1934.

Walters, L. K. *A Study of the Social and Marital Adjustment of Thirty-Five American-Japanese Couples*. Unpublished M.A. thesis, Ohio State University, 1953.

Watson, John B. *Behaviorism*. New York: W. W. Norton, 1926.

Wax, Murray L. *Indian Americans*. Englewood Cliffs, N.J.: Prentice-Hall, 1971.

Weinreich, Max. *Hitler's Professors: The Part of Scholarship in Germany's Crimes Against the Jewish People*. New York: Yiddish Scientific Institute-YIVO, 1946.

Weisbord, Robert G., and Stein, A. *Bittersweet Encounter: The Afro-American and the American Jew*. Westport, Conn.: Negro Universities Press, 1970.

Wessel, B. B. *An Ethnic Survey of Woonsocket, Rhode Island*. Chicago: University of Chicago Press, 1931.

Wiesel, Elie. *Night*. New York: Avon Books, 1969.

Wilcox, Roger. *The Psychological Consequences of Being a Black American*. New York: John Wiley & Sons, 1971.

Williams, Eric. *The Negro in the Caribbean*. Washington: Associates in Negro Folk Education, 1942.

Williams, Robin M., Jr. *The Reduction of Intergroup Tensions*. Washington, D.C.: Social Science Research Council, 1947.

Williams, Robin M., Jr., et al. *Strangers Next Door: Ethnic Relations in American Communities*. Englewood Cliffs, N.J.: Prentice-Hall, 1964.

Wirth, Louis. *The Ghetto*. Chicago: University of Chicago Press, 1928.

Wissler, Clark. *Indians of the United States*. New York: Doubleday, Doran & Co., 1940.

Wolff, Kurt H., ed. and trans. *The Sociology of Georg Simmel*. New York: Free Press, 1950.

Wright, Richard. *Uncle Tom's Children*. Cleveland: World Publishing Co., 1943.

Young, Donald. *American Minority Peoples*. New York: Harper & Row, 1932.

Young, Pauline V. *The Pilgrims of Russian Town*. Chicago: University of Chicago Press, 1932.

Zangwill, Israel. *The Melting Pot: Drama in Four Acts*. New York: Macmillan Co., 1921.

Zorbaugh, Harvey W. *The Gold Coast and the Slum*. Chicago: University of Chicago Press, 1929.

Index